Asian Perspectives on Financial Sector Reforms and Regulation

Asian Perspectives on Financial Sector Reforms and Regulation

MASAHIRO KAWAI
ESWAR S. PRASAD
editors

ASIAN DEVELOPMENT BANK INSTITUTE
Tokyo

BROOKINGS INSTITUTION PRESS
Washington, D.C.

ASIAN DEVELOPMENT BANK INSTITUTE
Kasumigaseki Building 8F, 3-2-5 Kasumigaseki, Chiyoda-ku
Tokyo 100-6008 Japan
www.adbi.org

THE BROOKINGS INSTITUTION
1775 Massachusetts Avenue, N.W., Washington, DC 20036
www.brookings.edu

Library of Congress Cataloging-in-Publication data
Asian perspectives on financial sector reforms and regulation / Masahiro Kawai and Eswar S. Prasad, editors.
p. cm.
Includes bibliographical references and index.
Summary: "Examines Asia's emerging markets, which survived the financial debacle of 2008-09 with only modest declines in growth; discusses activities that could dampen continuing development in these markets including inflation, surging capital inflows, asset and credit bubbles, and rapid currency appreciation; and offers strategies to promote financial stability"—Provided by publisher.
ISBN 978-0-8157-2210-6 (pbk. : alk. paper)
1. Finance—Asia. 2. Financial institutions—Government policy—Asia. 3. Capital market—Asia. 4. Financial crises—Asia. I. Kawai, Masahiro, 1947– II. Prasad, Eswar. III. Title.
HG187.A2A874 2011
332.1095—dc23 2011032249

9 8 7 6 5 4 3 2 1

Printed on acid-free paper

Typeset in Adobe Garamond

Composition by Circle Graphics
Columbia, Maryland

Printed by R. R. Donnelley
Harrisonburg, Virginia

Contents

Preface

The financial systems of most Asian emerging markets proved relatively resilient to the global financial crisis. Still, as they attempt to maintain high and stable growth, these economies face substantial challenges in terms of developing their financial markets and strengthening regulatory frameworks. New paradigms for financial development and regulation will have to be suitably reframed for Asian emerging markets, many of which have institutional and capacity constraints.

This book presents selected papers from the proceedings of three conferences held in Asia during 2010 to discuss these issues. Each of these conferences brought together leading academics as well as senior policymakers and practitioners. Those papers, now chapters in this volume, set the basis for the discussions, which were frank and wide-ranging. They attempt to link together various aspects of financial market development, including broadening financial access and improving regulatory frameworks to enhance financial stability. This volume also highlights the tensions among some of these objectives and provides theoretical and practical approaches for resolving them.

This is a joint project of the Asian Development Bank Institute, the Brookings Institution, and Cornell University. We thank the organizations that generously hosted the conferences in the several venues: the British High Commission (Mumbai, February 2010), the China Banking Regulatory Commission (Beijing, May 2010), and Bank Negara Malaysia (Kuala Lumpur, August 2010). We are also grateful for funding provided by the Institute for Financial and Management Research Trust (India), the International Center for Financial Regulation (United Kingdom), the International Growth Center (United Kingdom), and the International Monetary Fund (Washington).

Introduction

ESWAR S. PRASAD

The global financial crisis that ravaged financial systems in the advanced economies and many emerging markets as well has necessitated the reconsideration of even the basic principles of financial regulation. Remarkably, emerging market financial systems in Asia have in general proved to be more robust and less affected by the global turmoil than their advanced economy counterparts. In light of that, it is important to carefully filter out the right lessons from this outcome. Moreover, the imperative of financial development remains as strong as ever in Asian emerging markets, although the focus is more on basic elements, such as strengthening the banking systems and widening the scope of the formal financial system, rather than on sophisticated instruments and innovations.

The crisis highlights the need for strengthening financial systems to make them more resilient to shocks. Asian emerging markets face particular challenges in stabilizing their nascent financial systems in the face of shocks, both domestic and external, and financial reforms are critical to these economies as they pursue sustainable high-growth paths.

Policymakers in Asian emerging markets are grappling with a distinct set of issues, including the lessons the crisis can offer for the establishment of efficient and flexible regulatory structures, the avenues that should be pursued to enable

This book adopts the Asian Development Bank naming convention of referring to its member economies. The Brookings Institution takes no position on the legal status of Taipei,China.

effective regulation of financial institutions with large operations in multiple countries, and the ways to achieve greater financial inclusion. A broad reconsideration of the optimal structure and appropriate regulatory and supervisory frameworks of financial institutions is needed for these economies.

The chapters in this volume provide different perspectives on designing effective strategies for maintaining the momentum of financial development and inclusion in Asian emerging markets, while strengthening macroeconomic and regulatory frameworks to promote financial stability.

Macroeconomic Frameworks for Financial Stability

Because of the financial crisis, attention has been drawn to the intricate interplay between macroeconomic and financial policies, both national and global. The absence of stable macroeconomic policies can hinder financial development. In addition, weakly supervised and inefficient financial systems can hamper the effectiveness of policy transmission mechanisms and make it harder to manage stable policies. Capital accounts that are becoming more open in both de jure and de facto terms add a further layer of complications in determining the right structure of macroeconomic frameworks.

In the aftermath of the financial crisis, policymakers in emerging markets are again being confronted by conditions that are creating risks to monetary and financial stability. In chapter 1, "Monetary Policy Challenges for Emerging Markets in a Globalized Environment," Sukudhew Singh explores three of these policy issues. One of them is easy monetary policies in the advanced economies, specifically unconventional monetary policies. The chapter argues that these policies are fostering volatility and distortions in the financial markets and creating risks for emerging markets. The second policy issue is management of asset price bubbles. Asian central banks will have to adopt a proactive approach and overcome the current intellectual paralysis regarding the role of central banks in managing asset price bubbles. The third policy issue is that, in a period of low global interest rates and ample liquidity, commodity prices are again on the rise, which could have dire consequences for emerging markets. Central bank vigilance to guard against spillovers into broader inflationary consequences is essential.

In mid-September 2008, following the bankruptcy of Lehman, international interbank markets froze, and interbank lending beyond very short maturities virtually evaporated. Despite massive central bank support and purchases of key assets, many financial markets remained impaired. Why was this funding crisis so much worse than other past major bank failures, and why has it proved so hard to cure? In chapter 2, "The Great Liquidity Freeze: What Does It Mean for International Banking?" Dietrich Domanski and Philip Turner suggest that much of the answer lies in the balance sheet between banks and their customers. It outlines the basic building blocks of liquidity management for a bank that operates in many currencies; it then discusses how the massive development of the foreign exchange market (forex) and interest rate derivatives markets transformed banks' strategies in this area. It explains how the pervasive interconnectedness between major banks and markets magnified contagion effects. Finally, it provides some recommendations for how strategic borrowing choices by international banks could make them more stable and how regulators could assist in this process.

Chapter 3, "Macroeconomic Policy and the International Financial Crisis through an Indian Prism," by Alok Sheel, provides a specific set of perspectives from one of the key Asian emerging markets. This chapter includes a critical analysis of the literature and traces the recent evolution of thinking about the macroeconomic policy response to the international financial crisis through both global and Indian perspectives. The chapter analyzes both monetary and fiscal policy responses to the crisis and discusses the relationship between them, particularly about how they worked in tandem and were often indistinguishable from each other. The chapter argues that, in the recent financial crisis, monetary policy proved impotent beyond a point and that effective fiscal policy was essential to counteract the crisis. In terms of monetary policy, the chapter argues that central banks should have a dual objective—targeting liquidity through short-term rates and targeting financial stability through legislation.

Macroprudential Regulation

Combining the bottom-up regulation of individual financial institutions with a top-down systemic perspective on financial regulation is one of the key challenges facing regulatory authorities around the world. While this sounds like a sensible and desirable approach to financial stability, there is no clear framework for integrating these two strands of regulation into a coherent and unified approach. Consequently, a patchwork of pragmatic approaches has been adopted by regulatory authorities in each country. The chapters in this section deal with some of these conceptual challenges and also describe how some countries have dealt with them.

New lessons, challenges, and debates have emerged from the recent subprime crisis. While the macroeconomic orientation of regulatory policies is in fact not new, and has always been among the classic tool kits of central banks in ensuring financial stability, the current explicit articulation and specification of such tools as a global standard is new. Chapter 4, "Macroprudential Approaches to Banking Regulation: Perspectives of Selected Asian Central Banks," by Reza Siregar, presents a broad review and analysis of the measures adopted by the central banks and monetary authorities of selected Asian countries to strengthen their prudential regulations, particularly the macroprudential component.

Chapter 5, "The Role of Macroprudential Policy for Financial Stability in Asia's Emerging Economies," by Yung Chul Park, provides an additional set of perspectives from Asia. This chapter analyzes the role and scope of macroprudential policy in preventing financial instability in the context of East Asian economies. It looks at the behavior of the housing market in a dynamic setting to identify some of the factors responsible for the volatility of housing markets and their susceptibility to boom-bust cycles, which it identifies as a key source of financial imbalances in these economies. It then discusses the causal nexus between price and financial stability and the roles and complementary nature of macroprudential and monetary policies in addressing aggregate risk in the financial system. The chapter identifies currency and maturity mismatches, which contributed to the 1997–98 Asian financial crisis, as ongoing concerns in these economies—although the high levels of reserves in the region now act as a buffer.

The next two chapters provide the views of two front-line practitioners who have dealt with these challenges in their own economies. Chapter 6, "Macroprudential Approach to Regulation: Scope and Issues," by Shyamala Gopinath, provides an overview of the Reserve Bank of India's approach to macroprudential regulation and systemic risk management and reviews lessons drawn from the Indian experience. The chapter emphasizes the need for the harmonization of monetary policy and prudential objectives, which may not be possible if banking supervision is separated from central banks. It also notes that supervisors need to have the necessary independence and flexibility to act in a timely manner on the basis of available information. Macroprudential regulation is an inexact science with limitations, and it needs to be used in conjunction with other policies to be effective.

In chapter 7, "Macroprudential Lessons from the Financial Crises: A Practitioner's View," Kiyohiko Nishimura provides a stylized account of the financial imbalance buildup in the late 1980s in Japan from a macroprudential perspective. It draws lessons in comparing the similarity of the recent U.S. experience to that of Japan in the 1980s. First, when excessive optimism prevails in the market, macroprudential measures alone may be insufficient; monetary policy may be needed in addition to macroprudential measures to rein in excessive optimism. Second, when excessive optimism prevails in financial markets, the central bank should be careful to avoid nourishing an expectation of prolonged low interest rates relative to their long-run, sustainable levels. The chapter argues that it is desirable to develop and operationalize early-warning indicators to detect signs of financial imbalance buildups and to rein them in early, before it becomes quite costly to do so.

Financial Development

Financial market development remains a key priority for Asian emerging markets. The global financial crisis has shifted the emphasis of the financial development agenda toward the basics of strengthening banking systems, developing basic derivative markets such as currency and commodity derivatives, and increasing the depth and liquidity of corporate and government debt markets. The chapters in this section review progress in these efforts and then hone in on a particular case—that of India—to evaluate the role of regulatory, institutional, and other barriers to financial development.

In chapter 8, "Financial Deepening and Financial Integration in Asia: What Have We Learned?" Raymond Atje reviews lessons learned from the Asian financial crisis and seeks to explain why the more recent financial turmoil had a milder impact on financial systems in East Asia. According to Atje, in the aftermath of the 1997–98 East Asian financial crisis, countries in the region attempted to promote regional financial integration as a way to address the mismatches (maturity and currency) in debtor balance sheets. Regional governments, with assistance from the Asian Development Bank, have been trying to foster the development of local currency debt markets. While the exact nature of the link between financial development and growth remains unclear, what is clear is that a sound and sophisticated financial system promotes the efficiency of investment and, hence, economic growth and that a poorly functioning financial system can inhibit economic growth and increase vulnerability to crises.

In chapter 9, "The Development of Local Debt Markets in Asia: An Assessment," Mangal Goswami and Sunil Sharma provide an assessment of the progress made in developing local debt markets in emerging Asia. The development of these markets has been limited by hurdles confronting players and institutions that are or could be the borrowers and lenders, by issues faced by current and potential liquidity providers, and by the absence of supportive government policies and regulations. The key challenge in Asia is to generate financial assets, in line with its economic growth, that can provide the underlying collateral for expanding fixed-income markets and hence domestic investment opportunities. Emerging Asia also needs to foster a credit culture to further deepen its local debt markets. The issue of critical size could be addressed through an integrated regional market for local currency bonds that provides greater scale, efficiency, and access.

The next two chapters discuss in depth the challenges of financial market development and regulation in India. Chapter 10, "Indian Financial Market Development and Regulation: What Worked and Why?" by Jayanth Varma, examines the regulation and development of financial markets in India over the last two decades and attempts to identify the strategies and approaches that have worked and contrast them with approaches that have not worked. The author argues that technology, competition, and regulatory reform have been the key drivers of market development in India, as many success stories are characterized by regulatory reform that unleashed competition and actively pushed rapid adoption of new technology. The chapter makes the case that the growing power of domestic and institutional investors, rather than direct state intervention, brought about a number of changes. The chapter also examines some of the regulatory challenges that lie ahead for the Indian financial markets and discusses lessons for Indian policymakers from the global financial crisis.

In chapter 11, "Financial Development in India: Status and Challenges," Rajesh Chakrabarti presents an overview of financial development patterns in the country. The chapter argues that financial markets in India have come a long way in the past decade and a half in terms of economic reforms, making India a leader in Asia in terms of financial deepening. However, challenges remain, especially in the areas of institutional and business environments, elements outside the direct control of financial policymakers. In light of the financial crisis, increasing attention is being paid to systemic risks and to the interconnectedness of markets. These issues have led to new regulatory priorities, like a more extensive overview of large financial conglomerates and the creation of a macroprudential regulator. Coordination, if not unification, of regulators appears essential to enable such macroprudential monitoring of the system. The chapter makes the case for a shift to principles-based regulation in India but notes that such an approach has its own challenges in terms of regulatory sophistication and capacity.

PART I

Macroeconomic Frameworks for Financial Stability

1

Monetary Policy Challenges for Emerging Markets in a Globalized Environment

SUKUDHEW SINGH

In the period before the financial crisis, the prolonged period of low real interest rates in advanced economies led to financial imbalances in these economies. The outcome was a search for yield that resulted in carry trades and the increased financialization of commodity markets, which led to volatility in capital flows and exchange rates as well as to escalating commodity prices. These developments had a bigger impact on emerging market economies (EMEs) than they did on advanced economies. However, low interest rates and the search for yield, combined with dubious financial innovations, also led to an excessive and substantially misdirected expansion of credit and asset price bubbles in a number of advanced economies.

In response to the crisis, unconventional policies adopted by the advanced economies have again pushed interest rates to very low levels, even lower than before the crisis. No doubt these interest rates were appropriate when the economies were looking into the abyss of depression, but the longer they are maintained in the current circumstances the greater the potential that they will once again lead to imbalances similar to those seen before the crisis. Only this time they are likely to affect the EMEs more than the advanced economies.

In particular, this chapter discusses how the search for yield combined with optimism about the growth prospects of Asian EMEs could lead to increased capital inflows into these economies. The outcome is likely to be an appreciation of regional exchange rates, increasing asset prices, and rising commodity prices. If sustained, such trends could lead to imbalances that could undermine growth in some of these economies at a time when the world is looking at EMEs to lead the global economy out of the recession. This chapter looks at the issues from the perspective of EME policymakers. It discusses the policy measures already undertaken by policymakers in Asia as well as those that could potentially be undertaken.

Introduction

Following the bursting of the Internet bubble in 2000, real policy rates trended downward globally (figure 1-1). What is even more striking, though, is that the real policy rate in the United States was below 1 percent from about the second quarter of 2001 right through to the second quarter of 2006, or a period of five years. It was in fact persistently negative for four of those years—that is, from about the fourth quarter of 2002 to the fourth quarter of 2005. Real interest rates in other industrial countries, while never turning negative, were also very low, falling below 1 percent around the end of 2002 and remaining below that level until the third quarter of 2006. In contrast, policy rates in Asian EMEs were considerably higher, being at the level of those in advanced economies only briefly in 2004. In Latin America real policy rates were even higher than those for other economies for almost the entire period. Therefore, there was a sustained period of very low interest rates in the advanced economies during the last decade and also a significant divergence in interest rates between the advanced economies and the EMEs.

While these interest rates were possibly appropriate for these countries given the monetary policy frameworks adopted by them, the sustained period of low real interest rates in the advanced economies and the divergence in interest rates relative to those in EMEs set off a chain reaction of developments that culminated in the current crisis. As we emerge from the current crisis, EME policymakers are

Figure 1-1. *Real Policy Rates, by Country or Region, 2000–08*

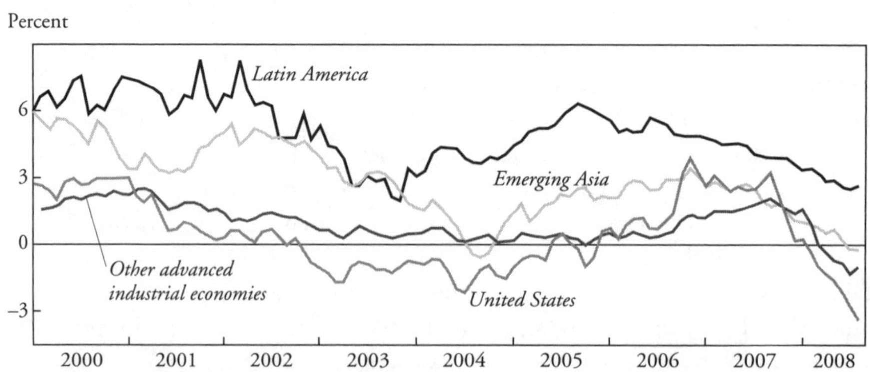

Source: Cecchetti, Mohanty, and Zampolli (2010).

again confronted by conditions that are creating risks to monetary and financial stability in their economies. In this chapter I explore three of these policy issues.

The first has to do with the implications for EMEs of the easy monetary policy conditions in advanced economies, specifically the unconventional monetary policies adopted. The volatility and distortions in the financial markets are creating risks for EMEs in a number of areas. Most important, the potentially large capital flows into EMEs can lead to volatility of exchange rates, which could create difficulties for open, trade-dependent, economies. They can also lead to significant volatility in bond and equity markets, as large volumes of foreign funds move in and out of these markets.

The second policy issue is the potential impact of capital flows driven by carry trades and the search for yield on the valuation of EME assets. Asset price bubbles have affected a number of the economies at the epicenter of the current crisis. In the period since the crisis, asset prices are likely to be again stoked; only this time there is a high risk that those bubbles will be in the EMEs. Large capital inflows will amplify such distortions. In managing these bubbles, central banks will have to overcome the current intellectual stalemate regarding the role of central banks in managing asset price bubbles. Asian central banks may need to adopt a proactive approach, even if many central banks in the developed countries have preferred not to play an active role.

The third and final policy issue has to do with the growing role of commodities as an asset class for investors. In a period of low global interest rates and ample liquidity, commodity prices are again on the rise, and this could potentially have more dire consequences for the EMEs than for the more advanced economies.

Effect on Emerging Market Economies of Unconventional Monetary Policies in Advanced Economies

The rapid growth in capital flows between advanced and EMEs has been significantly influenced by the monetary policies of the advanced economies. Research by the Institute of International Finance notes that since the 1970s there have been three major upswings in net private capital flows to EMEs.[1] As a percent of GDP, each peak in the up cycle has been higher than the previous one. It also notes that, based on the resumption of flows in 2009, the fourth upswing could be just beginning. There are compelling reasons to believe that EMEs could once again see a surge of capital inflows.

There is the expectation that economic and financial conditions in EMEs would be better than in the advanced economies. It has also been noted that, following the crisis, many EMEs are in better fiscal positions than a number of large advanced economies and are, therefore, better able to support growth. Further-

1. Institute of International Finance (2010).

Figure 1-2. *Expected Returns from Interest Rates and Exchange Rates, Select Economies, End January 2010*[a]

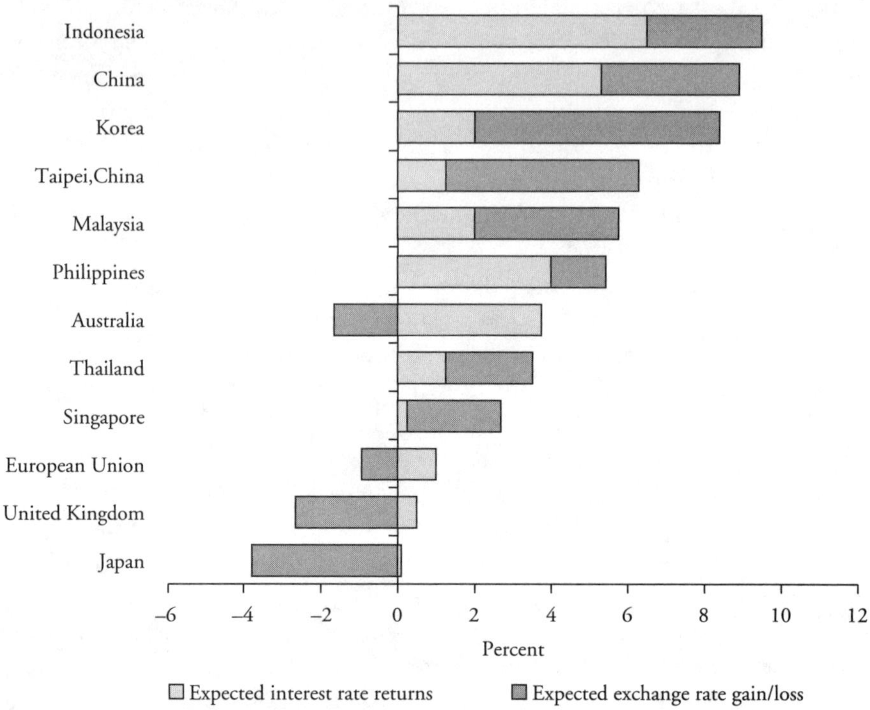

Source: Author's calculations based on Bloomberg.

a. Interest rate returns are the annualized three-month interbank rates of each country; returns on exchange rates are the expected appreciation of each currency against the U.S. dollar by end-2011 based on estimates of market analysts.

more, it is generally agreed that policy interest rates in the advanced economies would have been close to zero for most of 2010 and possibly into 2011. While there has been talk of policy exit in the countries that have undertaken quantitative easing, this is within the context of the unwinding of the vast liquidity support facilities and not in terms of increasing interest rates off the floor.[2] EMEs in Asia also dropped their interest rates in 2008–09 in response to concerns about the deflationary impact of developments among their advanced trading partners.

However, unlike in advanced economies, financial systems in Asia have remained largely functional, and banks have continued to provide financing. This means that the monetary transmission mechanism in the Asian economies continues to work and that the central banks in the region have not had to adopt the quantitative easing adopted by their peers in the advanced economies (figure 1-2). Interest rates, although still higher than those prevailing in the advanced economies,

2. Ben Bernanke, chair, Federal Reserve, testimony before Congress, *Financial Times,* February 25, 2010.

Figure 1-3. *Net Equity Flows, Five Asian Countries, 2008–10*

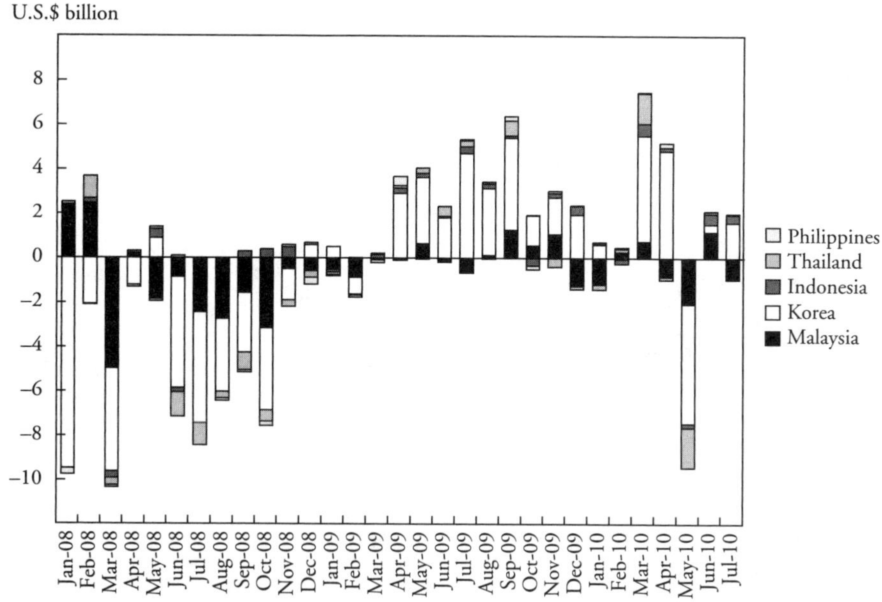

Source: Bloomberg.

were nevertheless at historic lows. This creates the risk that the low interest rate environment, if sustained for too long, could lead to a rapid growth in credit and the disintermediation of deposits (see appendix to chapter). Therefore, there is a need to normalize interest rates among Asia's EMEs. However, if they do, this would lead to widening interest rate differentials between Asia and the advanced economies. This is likely to raise expectations of the appreciation of Asian currencies, which could further increase the attractiveness of Asian assets.

In fact, the signs started emerging in the second half of 2009. Carry trades and the search for yields are back in fashion. Investors are once again funding out of cheap currencies and investing in high-yielding ones. Only this time, instead of the yen being the favorite funding currency, it is the U.S. dollar. These funds are being invested in higher yielding assets globally, but given the higher growth prospects for Asian EMEs, it is conceivable that a substantial portion of these funds will end up in the region (figure 1-3).

The return of capital flows to Asian economies puts an upward pressure on a whole range of Asian assets (figures 1-4 and 1-5). Asian equities have risen to levels that are almost close to the peaks of early 2008. Hong Kong, China and Singapore have had to implement a number of measures to control rapidly rising prices in their property sectors. Renewed flows into EME bonds have also resulted in a sustained increase in bond prices. As a result, Asian currencies have been on an appreciating trend since early 2009 (figure 1-6).

Figure 1-4. *Equity Indexes, Selected Asian Economies, January 2, 2008, to September 14, 2010*

Source: Bloomberg.

Figure 1-5. *Asian Property Price, Four Asian Countries, and Emerging Market Bond Prices*

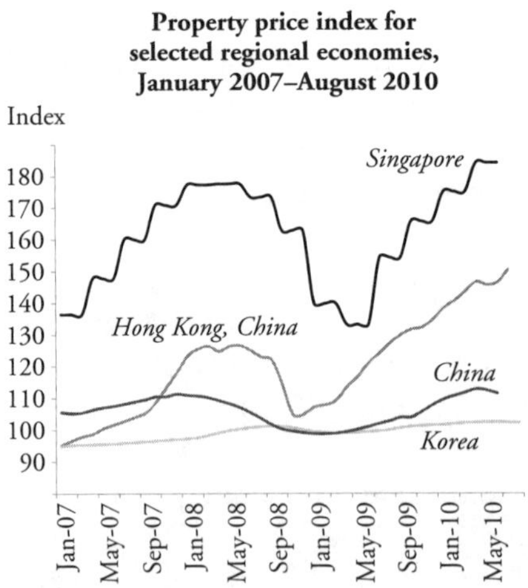

Source: Bloomberg. Korea (housing price index), Hong Kong, China (price index for domestic premises), China (price index for buildings), Singapore (price index for private residential properties). Quarterly data for Singapore and China; monthly data for Hong Kong, China and Korea (national sources).

Figure 1-6. *Emerging Market Currencies as Measured against the U.S. Dollar, 2008–2010*

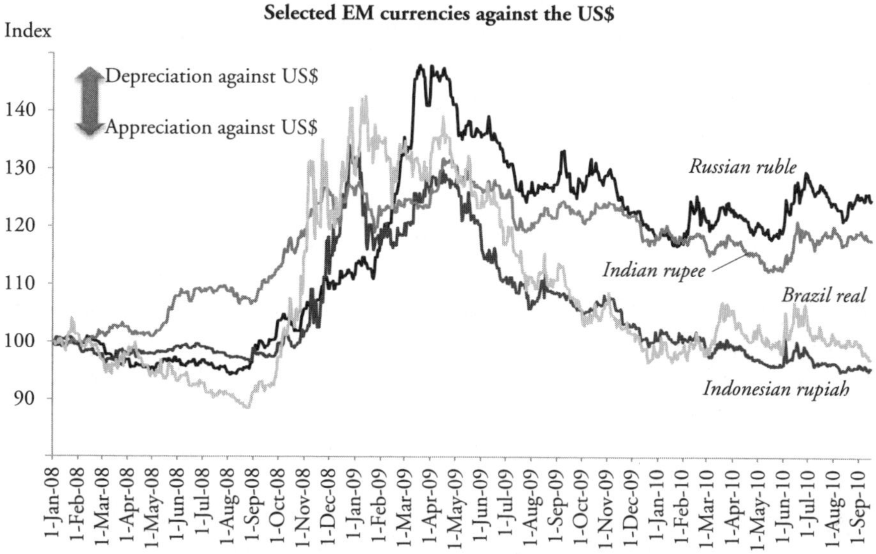

Source: Bloomberg.

Shifting investor expectations are likely to create volatility in capital flows to EMEs, with consequential volatility in asset prices in these economies. Based on the experience before and during the crisis, we can anticipate that risks will be created as inflows lead to rising asset prices, followed by painful declines in prices as the flows reverse—possibly in response to a rise in interest rates in the United States or in response to the EMEs failing to live up to expectations.

This then raises the question of how EMEs should deal with these volatile capital flows, to avoid significant disruptions of domestic monetary and economic conditions. It remains to be seen whether the regulatory reforms being considered in the advanced economies are helpful in reducing the volume of these flows. From recent experience, we know that quite a significant proportion of the short-term flows into EMEs were backed by high levels of leverage. If the regulatory reforms that are now being contemplated act to limit the leverage that investors can pile up, then this may to some degree help limit the size of these flows.

Based on the experience before and during the financial crisis, having a good buffer of reserves would help. In previous episodes, many EMEs intervened to absorb these inflows, which—although not entirely insulating domestic asset prices—greatly mitigated the potential impact on the exchange rate (figure 1-7). When the flows reversed, they were again offset by central bank intervention, with the consequence that, although reserves fell, a sharp depreciation of exchange rates was avoided. The capacity of a country to use its reserves in this manner would depend in an important way on the overall size of its reserves relative to short-term flows and the composition of those reserves. The reserves level should be sufficient to meet the outflows and high enough to maintain confidence in the country's international liquidity. This implies that there must be an underlying foundation of more permanent reserves built from longer term flows, such as current account surpluses and inflows of foreign direct investment. It also means that reserves picked up off short-term inflows should not be used to fund increased imports, or the country could find itself vulnerable when the inflows reverse.

However, under prevailing conditions, it has become more difficult for EME central banks to use reserves in this manner. This is because the operating environment has changed in an important way. Interest rates in the countries or regions that issue traditional reserve currencies are likely to remain very low, which makes the cost of intervention and sterilization more expensive. Therefore, building up reserves, while minimizing the impact of the inflows on monetary and financial conditions, is now more expensive—not impossible, but certainly more difficult and expensive.

Some would argue that having deeper financial markets would allow EMEs to better absorb these capital inflows. This may or may not be the case. It is not easy for EMEs to develop such deep markets, and even if they do, deeper financial markets are a double-edged sword. While the availability of more instruments and participants may mitigate the extreme volatility seen in shallow markets, it may also

Figure 1-7. *International Reserves Measured against U.S. Dollar, Four Asian Countries, 2000–10*

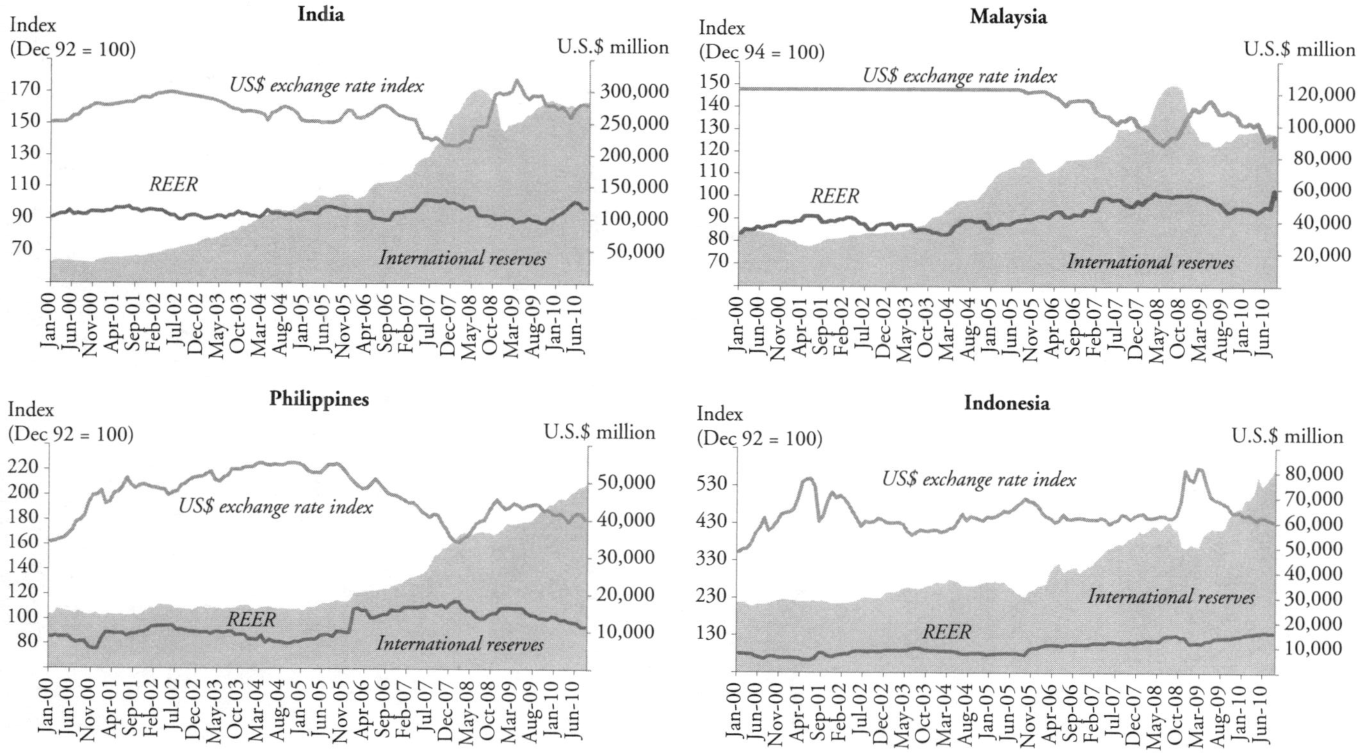

Source: Bloomberg (Forex reserves and exchange rate of national currency against the U.S. dollar); BIS (Real effective exchange rate).

Figure 1-8. *Strategies to Manage Capital Flows*

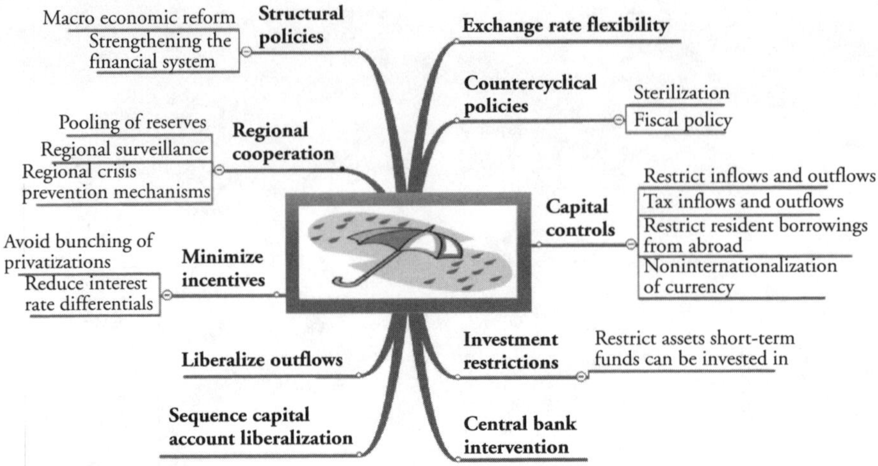

be the case that the availability of deep and liquid markets may end up attracting more capital inflows. In that sense, the job of the central bank may be no easier. In fact, with the larger flows, it may be that the central bank would have to hold a higher volume of reserves in order to mitigate the impact of these flows on the domestic financial system.

So what else can countries do? There are a number of options in the literature for dealing with capital flows; these are summarized in figure 1-8. If the policy measures just discussed prove to be ineffective, then countries may have no choice but to take more interventionist measures to restrict the inflows of short-term capital. First among these would be restrictions on the type of assets that foreign investors can hold and the requirements of a minimum holding period. As noted in box 1-1, countries like Indonesia and Taipei,China have already taken such measures. Alternatives would be to increase the cost for foreign investors to invest in the country or to erode some of their potential gains. Measures such as the tax on foreign portfolio inflows implemented by Brazil in 2009 fall in this category. These tools can be effective in reducing the returns that foreign investors hope to derive from investing in local financial assets and thereby help to reduce inflows of short-term funds. However, the magnitude and pervasiveness of such controls may need to be adjusted depending on how intense and sustained the capital inflows are. As countries increasingly liberalize their capital accounts, measures of this nature may be needed to prevent large capital inflows and outflows from undermining macroeconomic and financial stability and to maintain a degree of policy independence.

The instrument of last resort is to place a restriction on inflows and outflows. However, to carry this off successfully requires an efficient mechanism to ensure effective implementation, to minimize inconvenience, and to ensure that it does

Box 1-1. *Measures Adopted to Manage Capital Flows, Four Asian Countries*

Korea

—Requires banks to raise the ratio of long-term foreign currency funding to long-term foreign currency lending to 90 percent.

—Reduced the ceiling on foreign exchange derivative contracts of domestic and foreign banks to, respectively, 50 percent and 250 percent of their capital.

—Restricts companies' currency derivative trades to 100 percent of the value of their physical foreign trade transactions.

—Tightened regulations on the use of foreign currency bank loans. New loans are only for use overseas.

—Set up a center for monitoring capital flows, taking over the surveillance role from other agencies, including the central bank.

—Initiated the Seoul G-20 summit to build global safety nets through international cooperation.

People's Republic of China

—Tightened rules on individuals transferring yuan and foreign exchange between bank accounts.

—Restricts individuals from buying more than 20,000 yuan a day.

Indonesia

—Requires a minimum one-month holding period for central bank (SBI) debt.

—Introduced longer tenure SBI and a nonsecurities monetary instrument in the form of term deposits with the central bank.

Taipei,China

—Bans foreign investors from investing in local currency time deposits.

—Requires that foreign investors invest a maximum of 30 percent of remitted funds into short-term financial assets; the remaining 70 percent must be invested in long-term assets.

not hinder real economic activity. In particular, it is necessary to distinguish between foreign direct investment and foreign portfolio investment and to allow normal flows for current account transactions. The authority's ability to do this would depend on the available information systems, the extent to which forex transactions are conducted through the banking system, and the effectiveness of the enforcement mechanism. These controls are best maintained only for short periods and then eased gradually as conditions stabilize. Such controls will be ineffective if used for anything other than managing short-term flows—as for example when controls on outflows are used as a substitute for real policy reform relating to large fiscal deficits, high inflation, current account deficits, or a loss of confidence in the banking system.

Within Southeast Asia, regional cooperation is another alternative, although its efficacy to date remains largely untested. The recent expansion and formalization of the Chiang Mai Initiative among the ASEAN+3 countries is a step in that direction. The next step would be to set up a surveillance mechanism to support the initiative and to develop a regional crisis management framework. There are already ongoing consultations among regional policymakers at the various forums. The addition of a rigorous regional surveillance mechanism could enhance the capacity of these countries to react to potential threats preemptively. There could also be opportunities for regional central banks to cooperate in the formulation and timing of their exit strategies. As an example of this, three Asian central banks—Bank Negara Malaysia, the Hong Kong Monetary Authority, and the Monetary Authority of Singapore—established a tripartite working group in July 2009 to map out a coordinated strategy to exit blanket deposit guarantees in their respective jurisdictions; they successfully completed the exit at the end of 2010.

Asset Price Bubbles in Emerging Markets

The potential impact of the capital flows driven by carry trades and the search for yield on the valuation of EME assets is the second issue investigated here. Asian policymakers in particular, seeing the surge in capital inflows, have been alarmed by the possible volatility in asset prices.[3] The low interest rate environment in high-savings Asian countries, combined with their functional banking systems, already creates risks of asset prices rising excessively (see appendix to chapter). The inflow of foreign capital into these markets would be adding fuel to the fire.

Given these risks, recent experience should provide some perspective to the debate on the appropriate role of policymakers, especially central banks, in preventing and managing asset price bubbles. This is not a new issue; the "lean or clean" debate has been going on for some time. However, the extent and severity of the impact of the bursting of the recent bubbles provides some perspective on the issue, especially in terms of how expensive the clean option could be. This has led to renewed interest in preventing such a buildup in asset prices. Nevertheless, the role of central banks in preventing such a bubble continues to be the subject of debate. I believe that most central banks do care about asset price bubbles, given their implications for monetary and financial stability, and central banks would like to prevent such imbalances from building up. The key problem behind the

3. "Since the fourth quarter of 2008, the amount of inflow of funds [into Hong Kong, China] has exceeded HK$640 billion, increasing the potential risk of creating asset-price bubbles. We are also concerned that if capital flows were to reverse or interest rates rebound, asset prices would become more volatile. This in turn may affect the stability of our financial system and the recovery of the real economy." John Tsang, financial secretary of Hong Kong, China, speech, February 24, 2010 (www.budget.gov.hk/2010/eng/speech.html).

apparent lack of resolve is the difficulty in reconciling this additional responsibility with the adopted monetary policy frameworks.

Asset bubbles tend to replicate previous asset bubbles. As shown in figure 1-9, at the initial stages, asset price increases are driven by such fundamental factors as prospects of sustainable growth in an environment of low and stable inflation. Empirical studies show that expectations of rising asset prices can be self-fulfilling. Hans-Joachim Voth, in his review of five asset price bubbles across the world, notes that a bubble is more likely to develop when inflation is low and economic growth is strong.[4] If he were to review the recent episodes of asset price bubbles across several major economies, he is very likely to have come to the same conclusion. Stephen King argues that "the achievement of low inflation in itself has encouraged excessive risk taking, which in turn has contributed to the emergence of financial and economic bubbles."[5]

As observed by Alexander Hamilton, the expectation of continued low inflation and low interest rates has led to an illusion of high affordability of servicing debts to purchase real property.[6] This is also noted by Peter Brain, who argues that people do not rationally plan financially for the long term and usually assume that today's economic environment will last forever.[7] The expectation of continued benign macroeconomic conditions feeds into expectations of a continued increase in asset prices, which essentially involves extrapolating past trends into the future.

Financial system incentives are very much biased toward the short term, and the recent financial turmoil is the outcome of exactly that type of skewed incentives that discourages consideration of longer term consequences. Central bank communications thus have an important role to play in countering these exaggerated assessments and in providing warnings when unsustainable trends are developing in the financial markets. However, central banks have largely been reluctant to tread into this territory. As a consequence, the bubbles have grown unchecked and have resulted in a high cost to the economy when they burst. I believe that central banks do know that asset prices need to be managed but are constrained by at least four concerns.

The first concern is related to the risk of talking down the economy. There has certainly been a dramatic shift in the level and intensity of central bank communications about their assessments of the economy and the rationale for their policy actions. Nevertheless, given the tendency of financial markets to have a very near-term focus and herd-like reactions to news, central banks may at times be reluctant to deliver bad news. This is particularly so for providing assessments of asset valuations. How to balance between the need to provide the right information

4. Voth (2000).
5. King (2002).
6. Hamilton (2005).
7. Brain (2002).

Figure 1-9. *Formation of Asset Price Bubbles and Policymakers' Concerns*

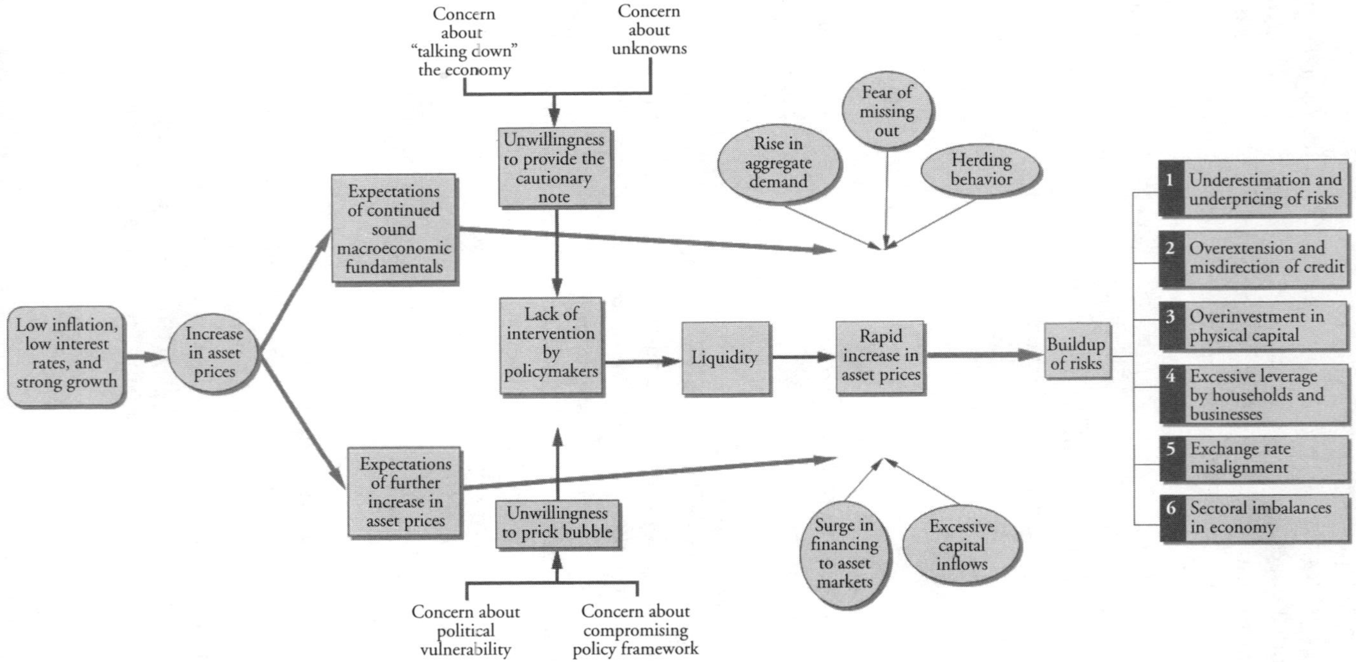

and the need to maintain confidence and prevent overreaction by markets is the fundamental dilemma.

The second concern is that central bankers, and monetary policymakers in particular, are very aware of the information gaps they are working with: the many known unknowns of current states and future outcomes. Central banks are also aware that, given the dynamic nature of the economy, there could also be unknown unknowns. This is particularly true of asset valuations. Economists and their models are prisoners of historical data, and while such models are widely used for assessing current developments and making projections, there is recognition that these models do not capture structural changes in the economy, nor do they flag emerging risks.

The reservations of central bankers with respect to asset prices are captured in the following quote from Alan Greenspan: "But how do we know when irrational exuberance has unduly escalated asset values, which then become subject to unexpected and prolonged contractions, as they have in Japan over the past decade?"[8] Recent experience also highlights another source of vulnerability in the central banks' assessment of asset prices, and that is excessive reliance on the assessments of financial market participants. How this came about is not clear to me. It could be due to the belief in the efficiency of markets. Whatever the source, excessive reliance by central banks on the assessments of participants in financial markets opens them to being influenced by the rationalizations of players who are either justifying or trying to sustain existing trends.

A recent example of this influence was the worldwide increase in commodity prices beginning in 2007. In talking about the sources for the increase, the consistent refrain from financial markets was that it was demand from EMEs, especially the People's Republic of China (henceforth referred to as China) and India, that was causing prices to escalate—this even as many financial institutions were acting as conduits for billions of dollars of noncommercial investments in commodities. I have more to say on this later. The point I want to make here is that policymakers should treat the assessments and rationalizations of participants in buoyant markets with great caution, for they could lead to misleading assessments of the forces and trends affecting asset markets.

The third concern arises in scenarios in which central banks "take away the punch bowl just when the party starts getting interesting."[9] They are usually talking about consumer price inflation and not asset price inflation. Most central banks are fearful of taking away the punch bowl during asset price inflation, even though asset markets have as much, if not more, potential to become inebriated on heady expectations as do consumer goods markets. One reason for this

8. Alan Greenspan, speech, "The Challenge of Central Banking in a Democratic Society," American Enterprise Institute, December 5, 1996.

9. William McChesney Martin, Federal Reserve Board Chairman, 1951–70.

dichotomy could be that it is politically tougher to deal with asset price inflation. In the case of consumer price inflation, the benefits to some are offset by some very clear costs to a major part of society, and therefore it is easier for central banks to justify the painful measures necessary to manage inflationary expectations. By contrast, when asset markets are in a bubbly state, everyone appears to be benefiting, and powerful vested interests could put up barriers to ensure that the central bank does not spoil the party. A second reason is that, in the case of consumer price inflation, central banks have a mandate to keep inflation within a broadly agreed-upon acceptable range. When inflation breaches this range, the central bank has a mandate for action. No such acceptable ranges exist for asset prices, and therefore the central bank is more vulnerable in making a judgment call.

The fourth concern involves monetary policymakers' unresponsiveness to asset prices, as this is not consistent with their adopted monetary policy frameworks. In most cases, monetary policy frameworks require stabilizing consumer price inflation. This requirement gives rise to two possibilities. First, even when central bank policymakers recognize the need to respond to asset price bubbles, they are constrained because of their monetary policy framework, whether implicit or explicit. Second, it is possible that some central banks do actually respond to asset price inflation, but in their policy statements and other communications with the public, such policy actions are rationalized as responses to the output gap. In other words, to remain consistent with the prevailing policy framework, even when they are in fact responding to asset price inflation, policymakers rationalize their monetary policy decisions within the output gap context (that is, growth and inflation) and not asset price inflation.

After the massive loss of welfare caused by the recent financial crisis and bursting bubbles, central banks need to think about overcoming these concerns and developing strategies to address them. Remaining a bystander is irresponsible, but jumping in without the appropriate mandates and tools would be foolish. The key challenge in moving forward remains one of developing a consensus around what needs to be done and how it is to be done. As the inflationary episodes in the 1970s and 1980s were crucial in creating a consensus around managing inflation, it may be that the current crisis has created a similar opportunity to develop a consensus around managing asset prices. However, for that to happen, a consensus must first develop within the central banking community itself. In addition, central banks must design mechanisms to identify and address developing asset price bubbles, because we now know that the price of inaction can be high.

While central banks want to encourage growth, such growth must be good quality growth, and it must be sustainable growth. If easy monetary policy leads to excessive lending for activities that may provide a temporary boost to economic growth but could extract from growth over the longer term, then such a monetary policy cannot be optimal for promoting sustainable growth. A lesson from this crisis is that even if monetary policy is appropriate from the perspective of macroeconomic stability over the monetary policy horizon, it could still lead to imbalances that may result in financial instability and reduced economic growth well beyond that horizon.

Before the current crisis, it is my observation that, with some notable exceptions, those who favored a proactive approach by central banks generally recommended the use of interest rates as a tool for managing asset prices. The debate following the crisis has been varied, but there is a strain that questions whether interest rates are the right tool to deal with asset prices, and there seems to be a growing acceptance of the use of macroprudential measures.[10] While an easier monetary policy stance is appropriate to support growth, it needs to be supplemented with macroprudential measures to ensure that excessive credit does not get diverted into activities that can lead to financial distortions and asset price bubbles. Central banks and regulators in Asia have generally been ahead of those in the advanced economies in using various macroprudential tools to manage asset prices and excessive growth in credit. A number of Asian central banks and regulators introduced such measures to manage potential bubbles in their property markets (box 1-2).

In the case of emerging markets, a number of factors favor the use of macroprudential measures. Malaysia faced similar pressures on stock and equity prices during the period 1994–96. While interest rates had already been raised during the period, raising them further was unlikely to discourage participants in the asset markets given the strength of the speculative pressures in the markets and the exuberant expectations of high prices and returns. Interest rates would have to be raised significantly before they dampened the asset markets. However, raising interest rates to these levels would be counterproductive, as they could cause significant damage to the real economy. Furthermore, in an open economy like Malaysia's, raising domestic interest rates too far above international levels could lead to significant short-term capital inflows, which would not only fuel asset price increases but would also put upward pressure on the exchange rate. Therefore, in such circumstances, macroprudential measures, rather than interest rates, were considered the optimal policy choice.

However, when real interest rates are very low, I do believe that there is a much higher likelihood that households and firms will overborrow and that bank deposits will be disintermediated into the asset markets. Having an excessively easy monetary policy can fuel credit binges and lead to excessive investment in assets. Therefore, having appropriate interest rates should still be a starting point in managing asset price bubbles. Then if credit continues to grow rapidly and asset prices are rising too fast, macroprudential measures should be applied.

10. The *Financial Times* (January 28, 2010) reports Lord Turner of Britain's FSA as saying that regulators needed new macroprudential tools to control credit and prevent asset price bubbles.

Box 1-2. *Measures Adopted to Address Rising Property Prices, Five Asian Countries*

Korea

—Imposed controls on mortgage lending in Seoul and other urban areas by reducing loan-to-value ratios from 60 percent to 50 percent.

—Requires banks to scrutinize borrowers' income when granting loans.

China

—Increased supply and clamped down on hoarding of land.

—Introduced minimum down payments for purchases of land and second homes.

—Requires banks to set mortgage rate for purchase of second homes at no less than 1.1 times the benchmark rate.

—Reinstated a sales tax on homes sold within five years of purchase.

—Adopted measures to curb involvement of property developers in speculative escalation of property prices.

—Instructed seventy-eight state-owned enterprises without a core business in property to pull out of the property market.

Hong Kong, China

—Adopted the following measures to reduce transactions involving luxury property: a down payment of 30–40 percent; an increased government levy on transactions; tighter regulations on mortgage lending, including loan-to-value ratio reduction from 70 percent to 60 percent.

—Adopted measures to mitigate speculative "churning" of properties.

—Plans to release additional land plots for sale to property developers in 2011.

Singapore

—Withdrew the interest absorption scheme and interest-only loans, making it harder for home buyers to defer payments.

—Reduced loan-to-value ratio to 80 percent and subsequently to 70 percent.

—Shifted from flat property taxes to progressive property taxes.

—Imposes a seller's stamp duty on all residential properties and land sold within a year (later three years) of purchase.

—Released more land for development.

Taipei,China

—Requires that loan-to-value ratio for purchase of second home not exceed 70 percent; borrowers are to repay both interest and capital.

—Urges banks to tighten lending procedures.

—Raised rates on mortgages from two state-owned lenders; cut the amount of their loans to buyers of luxury homes and to property investors.

The implication of this is that central banks will have to start looking beyond risks that affect inflation to risks in the financial and asset markets and take these into consideration in setting monetary policy. This is necessary to avoid a repeat of the experience of the previous decade, where real policy rates in the advanced economies were negative or close to zero for many years. An additional tool is to overcome the first concern, noted earlier, and to use central bank communication avenues to highlight risks and raise concerns about incipient asset price bubbles, to provide an alternative view to the euphoric predictions of market participants. Certainly, the risk of market overreaction cannot be discounted, but it needs to be managed, and that risk should be weighed against the cost of inaction.

To increase the accuracy of their analysis of asset price bubbles, central banks and regulators will have to enhance their surveillance mechanisms. More effort would need to be put into developing indicators and surveillance frameworks for asset prices, as has already been done for consumer prices. For instance, the analysis of monetary and credit aggregates has generally fallen out of favor among many central banks. Given the experience of the recent crisis, I believe that credit aggregates do have value in setting monetary policy, as a detailed analysis of credit flows can be helpful in identifying risks to macroeconomic and financial stability. In emerging markets, improving the quality of data and indicators is important. Structural changes in the patterns of financing arising from changes in the structure of the economy and financial system need to be understood so that anomalies can be better identified and understood.

Aside from macroprudential tools, equipping financial institutions with better information systems that support their risk assessments could play an important role in preventing overleveraging by individuals and firms. One example I can share from our own experience at Bank Negara Malaysia is our Central Credit Reference Information System (CCRIS), which we introduced after the Asian financial crisis.[11] It is a centralized repository of borrower information, provided by all participating financial institutions, and is managed by the central bank. It has proved to be an invaluable tool in enhancing the banks' risk management and credit evaluation. Not only has it made it easier for financial institutions to make informed and responsible lending decisions in a timely manner, the existence of the system has also sensitized individual and corporate borrowers on the importance of maintaining a sound credit history. Aside from such systems, regular engagements by regulators and supervisors are another useful source of information for banks because feedback on the outcome of assessments carried out on the lending practices of individual banks can provide the inducement for more prudent lending practices.

In considering the macroprudential approach, an obstacle is the fragmentation of regulatory authority over the financial system in some countries. Ideally, central

11. For more information, see http://creditbureau.bnm.gov.my.

banks should have responsibility for regulating and supervising the parts of the financial system that have access to their lender-of-last-resort facility. This ensures that, in dealing with asset price bubbles, central banks have the full spectrum of information to diagnose the problem and also the policy tools to manage the problem preemptively. Where regulatory and supervisory control lies outside of central banks, this would obviously not be possible. What would be needed then would be for the central bank and the regulatory agency to establish a good working relationship, with good exchange of information and a coordinated response when problems are detected. Otherwise, as highlighted by the crisis, there is a high risk of policy blind spots and of things falling between the cracks. Finally, if central banks are given the mandate to act against the development of asset price bubbles, they can only effectively do so if the tools available to them include more than just control over short-term interest rates.

Commodities as an Asset Class and Implications for Emerging Economies

The evidence shows that financial flows into commodities increase prices for a broad range of commodities. Figure 1-10 shows that, after a brief pause following the last run-up, commodity prices are again on a broad upward trend. As with the previous episode of rising commodity prices, there are many factors behind this trend. These include factors related to both supply and demand. However, as in the previous episode, financial factors are also playing a leading role.

In my observation, the financialization of commodities probably started at around the beginning of the 2000s and increased substantially during the period of easy global liquidity. Initially, the move reflected diversification motives as well as investors' desire to hedge against inflation and the risks of adverse developments in the foreign exchange, bond, and equity markets. However, as more money poured into these markets, prices started becoming delinked from fundamentals, and market participants started generating stories about all types of fundamentals to justify the escalating prices. In reality, there was a huge element of a speculative bubble. "Aluminum used to be something that made airplanes and drink cans. Now it is a financial instrument."[12] Derivative trading in commodities has outpaced physical trading in recent years. Between 2003 and 2007 the global physical exports of commodities increased by 17 percent, whereas commodity derivative trading on exchanges rose by 200 percent. The ratio of exchange-traded derivatives to production of precious metals was thirty times in 2005 and is likely to have increased further since. The notional value of outstanding over-the-counter commodity derivatives rose by 500 percent, to $9 trillion in 2007.[13] Dietrich

12. "Speculation Heats up Aluminum Trade," *Financial Times*, February 17, 2010.

13. International Financial Services London (2008).

Figure 1-10. *Prices, Five Commodities, 2000–10*

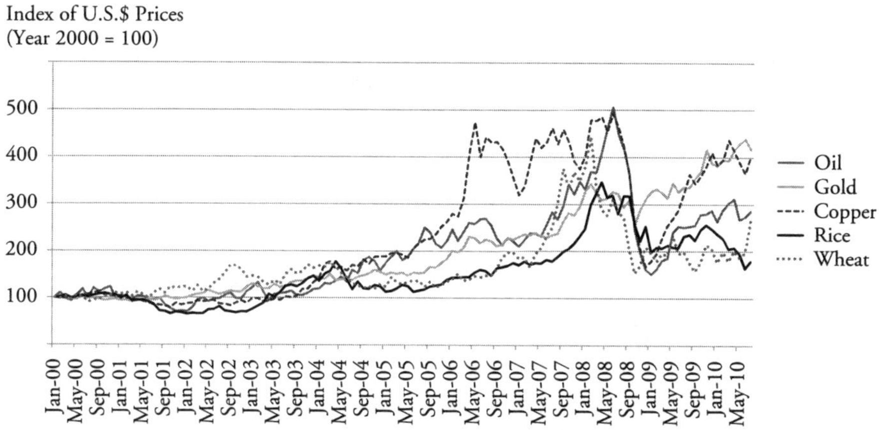

Source: IMF Primary Commodities database.

Domanski and Alexandra Heath, in a study published in the *BIS Quarterly Review,* conclude that "while physical characteristics, such as inventory levels and the marginal cost of production, remain important, commodity markets have become more like financial markets in terms of the motivations and strategies of participants."[14]

Low interest rates and high amounts of liquidity are once again pushing large amounts of funding into commodities and contributing to the increase in prices. For instance, about 75–90 percent of the world's physical aluminum stocks are reported to be tied up in financial arbitrage deals.[15] What is the likely impact on EMEs? The previous episode of high commodity prices provides some guidance and lessons. Higher commodity prices are likely to affect a significant number of countries and will raise a wide range of macroeconomic and welfare issues. These will include issues such as the negative effect on the economic welfare of the poor and vulnerable, higher prices for consumer goods and services, deteriorating balance-of-payment positions for commodity-importing nations, and worsening fiscal positions due to higher subsidy expenses and lower tax collections.

The previous episode also exposed the monetary policy dilemma that regional central banks faced following the supply-related price shocks. While there were valid calls for higher interest rates to manage the inflationary consequences, the rise in a broad range of prices also undermined economic growth by eroding consumer spending capacity. While a stronger currency may reduce the inflationary pass-through to domestic inflation, it could also reinforce higher interest rates by

14. Domanski and Heath (2007).
15. "Speculation Heats up Aluminum Trade."

Figure 1-11. *Food Prices as Portion of Consumer Price Index, Thirteen Countries*

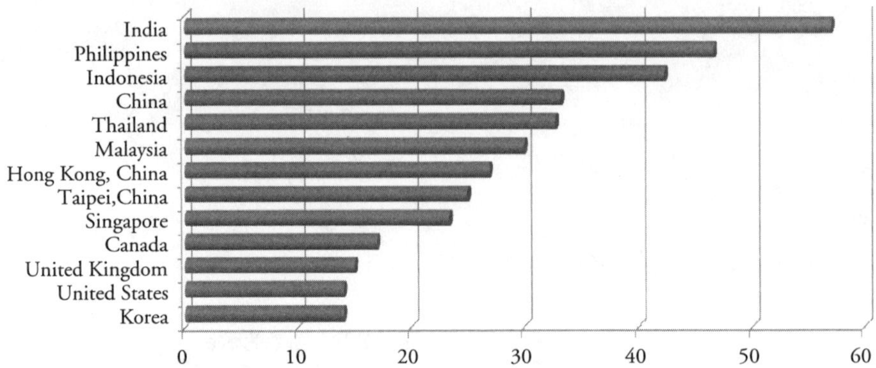

Source: National statistics departments. Weight of food in CPI index is as of September 2010.

attracting new capital inflows. At the same time, higher interest rates and exchange rates result in slower economic growth. These effects could make monetary policy a less useful tool for managing the consequences of the increase in commodity prices, and alternative policies will be needed.

Commodity-exporting countries would certainly benefit from the better terms of trade, and their appreciating currencies may help mitigate some of the impact on domestic inflation. Stronger reserves from export receipts and healthier fiscal positions as a result of increased tax revenues are likely to support economic fundamentals. For commodity-importing EMEs, the situation would be more difficult, as deterioration in the terms of trade and depreciation of exchange rates feed into domestic inflation.

While a commodities-based surge in inflation is likely to pose difficult choices for policymakers globally as they face weak economic conditions, the choices are likely to be particularly difficult for policymakers in EMEs. Higher food and fuel prices would be particularly corrosive to living standards in the EMEs, because these basics of human existence account for a much larger share of the incomes of EME populations than of the incomes of consumers in advanced economies. The food component is especially high for EME populations (figure 1-11). This fact makes higher food prices a social and political issue in EMEs. The last episode saw rioting and demonstrations on the streets of a number of EME capitals, as angry consumers vented their frustration at the escalating prices of essentials. In my recollection, no such demonstrations were observed in the capitals of the advanced economies.

Consequently, if the current trend of rising food and fuel prices is sustained, it is again likely to put pressure on governments to enact policies and programs to protect vulnerable segments of society. Box 1-3 provides a list of the measures to

Box 1-3. *Administrative and Fiscal Measures to Address Inflation, Six Asian Countries, 2007–08*

Cambodia

Trade-based policy measures
—Increased supply, using reserves
—Buildup of reserves and stockpiles
—Increased import and tax restrictions
—Export restrictions
—Price controls and consumer subsidies

Producer-oriented measures
—Actions against profiteers, appeals to profiteers

China

Trade-based policy measures
—Reduced import duties
—Increased supply, using reserves
—Higher export duties
—Export restrictions
—Price controls and consumer subsidies

Producer-oriented measures
—Minimum price supports
—Assistance and subsidies to farmers
—Self-sufficiency promotion
—Actions against profiteers, appeals to profiteers

Safety net programs
—Cash transfers

Indonesia

Trade-based policy measures
—Reduced import duties
—Increased supply, using reserves
—Increased import and tax restrictions
—Higher export duties
—Price controls and consumer subsidies

Safety net programs
—Food rationing, food stamps

Korea

Trade-based measures
—Reduced import duties
—Increased supply, using reserves
—Price controls and consumer subsidies

(continued)

Box 1-3. *Administrative and Fiscal Measures to Address Inflation, Six Asian Countries, 2007–08 (continued)*

Producer-oriented measures
—Self-sufficiency promotion

Malaysia
Trade-based policy measures
—Increased import and tax restrictions
—Higher export duties
—Price controls and consumer subsidies

Producer-oriented measures
—Assistance and subsidies to farmers

Philippines
Trade-based policy measures
—Reduced import duties
—Buildup of reserves and stockpiles
—Increased import and tax restrictions
—Price controls and consumer subsidies

Producer-oriented measures
—Minimum price supports
—Assistance and subsidies to farmers
—Self-sufficiency promotion
—Actions against profiteers, appeals to profiteers

Safety net programs
—Food rationing, food stamps

address inflation in commodity prices that were adopted by various Asian countries in the earlier crisis. While there may be a need for more such policies, the conditions this time may be less favorable, particularly government finances. After the strong fiscal stimuli implemented to ward off the deflationary impact of the financial crisis, some governments may not be in a position to underwrite a significant increase in subsidies, even if these are for the poor and vulnerable. When the earlier commodity price boom occurred, the balance sheets of households and the government were healthier. Having weathered the financial crisis, that is no longer the case. Now, a significant surge in commodity prices could undermine growth in emerging countries, just when the world is hoping that demand in EMEs will support global growth.

Conclusion

The view put forward at the early stage of the crisis that the EMEs could decouple from the advanced economies has now been proven to be not true. It took a while for the crisis to reach the shores of the Asian EMEs, but in the end, there was no question that trade and financial linkages made the fates of the two regions inextricably linked. Similarly, the policy response of the advanced economies to the crisis has also shown that, in such a globally linked world, the EMEs are not insulated from the fiscal and monetary policies of the advanced economies. At this stage, it is difficult to say precisely when the low interest rates in the advanced economies will normalize to higher levels. However, the message from policymakers in the advanced economies continues to be that low interest rates are likely to prevail for a sustained period.

It is my view that, now that the depth of the crisis is behind us, monetary policy in the advanced economies needs to normalize and that, given the still weak growth of these economies, fiscal policy needs to continue to aggressively support demand. However, my fear is that what we are actually likely to see is the reverse: there will be widespread retrenchment of fiscal stimulus, but monetary policy will remain too easy for too long. Given the weakened positions of both financial institutions and households in the advanced economies, it is conceivable that financial distortions may not emerge in the advanced economies. However, EMEs can take no such comfort. The large amounts of liquidity created in response to the crisis will have to find a home, and as long as interest rates and economic growth in the advanced economies remain low, global private capital flows will likely continue to be attracted toward EME assets and commodities.

If the trends highlighted in this chapter are borne out, there will be a very challenging policy environment for EME policymakers. Although they could adopt a national approach to deal with these challenges, one lesson from the Asian financial crisis is that this is not a very effective way to deal with regional challenges. A more collaborative approach may be best. It could be about policy coordination, but it could also be about developing greater cohesion in regional policymakers' views of developments affecting the region and of adopting a common stand on these issues and, possibly, common policy responses.

Appendix

Appendix: The Dilemma of High-Savings Societies in a Low-Interest-Rate Environment

Rising inflation has differential effects on savers and borrowers. By implication, rising inflationary expectations could also have a different effect on high-savings societies than on low-savings societies. The impact of low real interest rates could

Figure 1A-1. *Gross National Savings as Portion of GDP, Thirteen Countries, 2007*

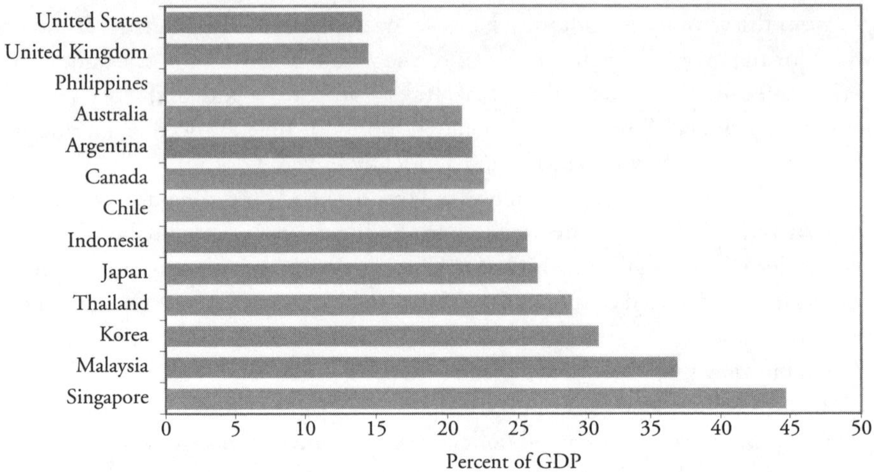

Source: IMF International Financial Statistics, 2007.

also be different between these two types of society. (Figure A-1 shows gross national savings as a portion of GDP in both advanced and emerging economies.)

In highly indebted societies, and in societies in which the bulk of savings are in investments or physical assets, rising inflationary expectations could be associated with expectations of rising economic welfare due to the expected erosion in the value of debt obligations and the appreciation of asset prices. The situation would perhaps most reflect the conditions prevailing in the advanced economies, where, as I show earlier, real interest rates have fallen to very low levels. At the same time, technological innovations and the emergence of new financial instruments have also greatly reduced the liquidity constraint faced by households—to the extent that they could rely more on borrowed funds to sustain their expenditure. The outcome is that, while household savings in these economies have fallen sharply, households have also been able to accumulate a high level of debt to finance the acquisition of houses, equities, and other assets. The capital gains from rising asset prices and financial innovation that enable net equity withdrawals appear to support higher consumption and allow households to live with a lower level of savings. Consequently, in such societies, low interest rates would largely be supportive of increased household welfare.

Conversely, in high-savings societies like those in Asia—especially those where the bulk of savings still reside as deposits in the banking system—higher inflationary expectations not accompanied by expectations of higher interest rates would lead to expectations of a diminution in the value of savings and a loss of economic welfare. In many developing Asian economies, financial markets are not well developed, and financial innovation has been less prevalent; consequently, the bulk of household savings are in the form of bank deposits. Given that much of these savings are for long-term objectives, or reflect precautionary responses to the lack of social safety nets and welfare benefits, high inflation or low real interest rates may actually result in higher savings, as savers attempt to offset lower interest income by raising the volume of savings. This is certainly not quite the response expected by policymakers when they lower interest rates to stimulate consumption and investment.

Low returns can encourage a search for yields among savers, which can lead to the disintermediation of deposits and increased investments in land, houses, and equity. Low interest rates could also make depositors vulnerable to financial scams and lead to disintermediation of savings into the informal sector of the economy. It could also lead to the rapid accumulation of leverage by households and businesses. Often such cheap credit is used to place speculative bets. The main point here is that sustained low interest rates create risks anywhere but could potentially be more dangerous in high-savings societies.

Therefore, dropping interest rates to very low levels, or having negative real interest rates, may clearly be positive in societies with highly indebted households but may not be so helpful in high-savings societies.

References

Brain, Peter. 2002. "Trend in Household Debt and Its Consequence." Paper prepared for the ITSA Bankruptcy Congress 2002, National Economics (NIEIR).

Domanski, Dietrich, and Alexandra Heath. 2007. "Financial Investors in Commodity Markets." *BIS Quarterly Review* (March).

Hamilton, Alexander. 2005. "Asset Price Bubble and Manias: How Much Was the Property Boom Driven by Collective Psychology and Herding Behaviour?" Master's dissertation, City University London.

Institute of International Finance. 2010. "Capital Flows to Emerging Market Economies" (January 26).

International Financial Services London Research. 2008. "International Commodities Report" (June 30).

King, Stephen. 2002. "Why Price Stability Is Not Enough." *Central Banking Journal* 12, no. 3.

Voth, Hans-Joachim. 2000. "A Tale of Five Bubbles: Asset Price Inflation and Central Bank Policy in Historical Perspective." Paper 416. Centre for Economic Policy Research.

2

The Great Liquidity Freeze: What Does It Mean for International Banking?

DIETRICH DOMANSKI AND PHILIP TURNER

In mid-September 2008, following the bankruptcy of Lehman, the financial crisis became global. International interbank markets froze (box 2-1 lays out the main events). Interbank lending beyond very short maturities virtually evaporated. Three-month Libor (London interbank offered rate), the key benchmark for a wide range of financial contracts in money markets, rose sharply. Interest rate and forex swap markets became dysfunctional (figure 2-1). The financial markets in the emerging economies, which had risen for several months after the onset of the crisis in August 2007, fell sharply.

Tensions began to ease only after the announcement, in mid-October, that the U.S. Federal Reserve would provide to other central banks in the major industrial countries unlimited funds in U.S. dollars. Central banks in the emerging markets were also forced to act to support their currencies or their local interbank markets. Massive central bank support operations—unprecedented in scale, in form, in counterparty, and in duration—eventually contributed to a gradual normalization of pricing conditions in the largest wholesale markets during 2009.[1] Despite substantial central bank purchases of illiquid assets, however, many financial

A particular debt is owed to Bill Allen for many illuminating insights into these issues. We are also grateful for helpful comments from Stephen Cecchetti, Guy Debelle, Mario Mesquita, Richhild Moessner, Yung Chul Park, and Eswar Prasad. We have drawn heavily on recent CGFS reports, which are cited in the text. Thanks to Clare Batts, Pablo García-Luna, Patrick McGuire, and Karsten von Kleist for assistance in preparing this note.

1. On central bank operations over this period, see Allen and Moessner (2010); Turner (2010).

Box 2-1. *Chronology of the 2008 Liquidity Freeze, September 7 to October 29*

September 7

Fannie Mae and Freddie Mac are taken into government conservatorship.

September 15

Lehman files for bankruptcy.

September 16

A large U.S. money market fund "breaks the buck," triggering large volumes of fund redemptions. AIG supported by U.S. government.

September 18

Central banks address the squeeze in U.S. dollar funding with $160 billion in new or expanded swap lines.

September 19

The U.S. Treasury announces a temporary guarantee of money market funds. It proposes to remove troubled assets from bank balance sheets (the Troubled Asset Relief Program, or TARP).

September 25

The authorities take control of Washington Mutual, the largest U.S. thrift institution, with some $300 billion in assets. This is followed by the effective nationalization of several European financial institutions.

September 29

TARP is rejected by the U.S. House of Representatives.

September 30

The Irish government announces a guarantee of all deposits, covered bonds, and senior and subordinated debt of six Irish banks; other governments take similar initiatives over the following weeks.

October 3

The U.S. Congress approves the revised TARP plan.

October 8

Major central banks undertake a coordinated round of policy rate cuts.

October 13

Major central banks jointly announce the provision of unlimited amounts of U.S. dollar funds to ease tensions in money markets.

October 29

To counter the protracted global squeeze in U.S. dollar funding, the U.S. Federal Reserve agrees on swap lines with the monetary authorities of Brazil, Republic of Korea, Mexico, and Singapore.

Source: Bank for International Settlements (2009).

Figure 2-1. *Three-Month Spreads in Basis Points, Three Measures, 2007–09*[a]

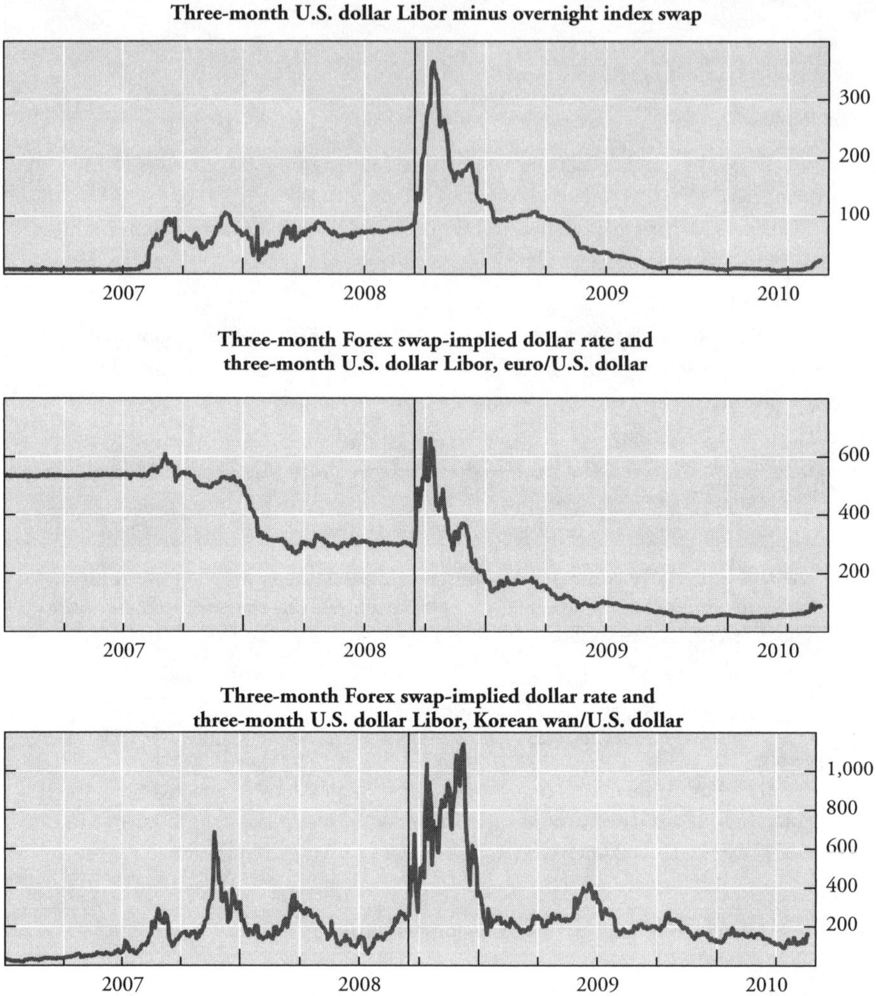

Source: Bloomberg; Datastream; BIS calculations.
a. The vertical line marks September 15, 2008, date of Lehman Brothers bankruptcy.

markets remained impaired. A further round of turbulence triggered by the Greek fiscal crisis led to the renewal of funding pressures on major banks in May 2010, once again leading to the reinstatement of central bank support operations (notably intercentral bank swap operations that had been phased out).

Tensions in interbank markets following the failure of a major bank are not new. For instance, the loss of confidence in, and subsequent failure of, Continental Illinois in 1984 led to similar tensions, as the money center banks found it more costly to borrow in wholesale markets. But the Federal Reserve was able to stabilize this run of deposits from a single bank essentially by reshuffling dollars from other U.S. banks. Hence, it managed to do this without significantly increasing the total reserves supplied to the banking system. This crisis went deeper and lasted longer because:

—There was a simultaneous loss of confidence in large banks in the United States and Europe.

—Corporations worldwide (and in some countries, households) had denominated their bank loans (and derivative exposures) in dollars on a substantial scale.[2]

—A large expansion by non-U.S. banks in dollar lending and holdings of dollar-denominated securities either had been financed by short-term dollar (or foreign currency) deposits or had relied on the ready availability of wholesale hedging markets to roll over currency or maturity mismatches.

—The wholesale funding operations of banks remained vulnerable for some time.

Why was this funding crisis so much worse and why has it proved so hard to cure? Much of any answer to these questions lies in the balance sheets of banks and of their customers. Balance sheets tend to change slowly, and the balance sheet structure of major banks at the outset of the crisis took many years to develop. These structures made banks much more vulnerable to currency, maturity, and refinancing risks than they had been at the start of the 2000s. But the development of more and more complete hedging markets masked the threats posed by such vulnerabilities. Banks are now in the process of reappraising their international business strategies, and bank regulators are examining liquidity issues more closely.

Building Blocks of Liquidity Management in Many Currencies

What does liquidity management in many currencies mean? This is not an easy question to answer, because liquidity is a notion that covers many distinct elements. It is therefore useful to begin by breaking down complex strategies into two simple components: liquidity management in one currency and currency mismatches.

Liquidity Management in One Currency

Even for a bank that operates locally in its own currency, liquidity management is very complex. The ultimate aim (to be sure of being able to meet claims as they arise) is easy to state but not so easy to make operational. It must consider several elements: maturity mismatches between assets and liabilities, refunding risk, what central banks will accept as collateral, and local liquidity rules.

2. Or in another major international currency such as euros. For simplicity, in this chapter the dollar is used as a shorthand for all international currencies.

MATURITY MISMATCHES BETWEEN ASSETS AND LIABILITIES. Banks make money from maturity transformation—by borrowing short and lending long. By doing this, banks traditionally perform the valuable function of financing fixed and illiquid investment in real assets by creating liabilities that are liquid for the individuals who hold them. Banks must therefore manage the resultant maturity mismatches that arise from this transformation. This has at least three elements:

Asset liquidity. This covers how readily an asset can be sold. The usual measures of market liquidity in normal times are microeconomic.[3] But such measures may be quite misleading guides to liquidity in times of stress. Jean Tirole argues that a better measure is what he calls the macroeconomic dimension of liquidity: an asset is liquid when it keeps its value in those circumstances when its holder wants to liquidate it for cash.[4] Government short-term bills are usually seen as the benchmark asset that is safe even in times of stress. There are additional risks to long-term government paper that depend on the nature of the shock (inflationary or deflationary) and on the country's fiscal position. The European debt crisis underlines such risks. What the central bank accepts as collateral will also influence asset quality.

Duration gap between assets and liabilities. The greater this gap, the more vulnerable the bank is to movements in the yield curve. The underlying duration of assets may be longer than apparent on the surface. For instance, a construction company engaged in long-term projects may finance itself by regularly renewing short-term loans (that is, with a notional duration that is short) but may be unable to repay at short notice. In such circumstances, the bank may be forced to roll over these loans in order to avoid losses, which means that the underlying duration is longer than in the contract.

Duration of wholesale liabilities. A severe economic or financial market shock may lead to the effective closure of some of the markets used by banks to refinance their liabilities. A bank therefore needs to have cash or near-cash to be able to meet liabilities falling due the following day (or week or month) without new borrowing in these markets.

In deciding on these elements, a bank will have to weigh the profits earned from its exposures against the risks created by its mismatch exposures. There is no simple, one-size-fits-all, optimum for any of these elements. Any element could in theory be traded off with another element. In addition, the credit risk of assets is important. The market's assessment of a bank's ability to meet its short-term obligations—and hence the bank's ability to borrow—will be influenced by the market's judgment about the quality or marketability of its assets.

3. These microeconomic elements are usually defined and measured as follows: depth is the market's ability to absorb large transaction volumes with small changes in price (measured by average turnover), tightness is cost efficiency (measured by low bid-ask spreads), and resilience is ability to absorb random shocks (day-to-day price volatility).

4. Tirole (2008).

A bank with low credit risk exposures may therefore be able to run larger maturity mismatches.

REFUNDING RISK. Retail deposits in the local currency have traditionally been regarded as a more stable or reliable source of funding than borrowing in wholesale markets. But depositors are likely to flee weak banks in a crisis, unless the deposit protection schemes in force convince them that their money is safe. Hence it would be more accurate to say that retail deposits guaranteed by the government could be regarded as stable in a crisis.

CENTRAL BANKS AND COLLATERAL. In Bagehot's day, the Bank of England would accept only short-term exchange bills and thus avoided the capital value risks of long-term paper. Such bills were self-liquidating (usually financing trade) and had the guarantee of acceptance house endorsement. This also had the advantage of creating a large diversified pool of liquid assets, which meant less market contagion than would have arisen if all the banks had to liquidate identical assets in a crisis. This preference for commercial bills—and not government-issued Treasury bills—lasted well into the 1920s. Indeed, it was by monitoring the quality of commercial bills in money markets that the Bank of England kept some oversight of the stability of the banking system.[5]

Since that period, and given the massive rise in government debt, the Bank of England came to accept long-term government paper in its discount operations with commercial banks. Indeed, the near-universal convention nowadays is that central banks accept bonds issued by "their" government as their most preferred collateral. Such paper is not risk free. When debt ratios are high, there is a risk of sovereign default, particularly if monetary arrangements rule out an inflationary "solution." There is also interest rate risk (which can be accentuated by inflation risks). The fact that the central bank will accept long-term bonds as collateral for a short-term loan to a commercial bank makes such bonds more liquid, even if they might not be very liquid in the absence of such acceptance.

Central bank lending practices could in theory seek in addition to discriminate among banks. They could, for instance, seek to reduce moral hazard risks by "rewarding" banks that had maintained more liquid balance sheets in normal times by giving them greater or cheaper access to central bank liquidity in a crisis. In practice, few (if any) do so. But many observers suggest rules to make access to central bank liquidity conditional on past behavior.[6]

LOCAL LIQUIDITY RULES. Bank regulators may take account of the elements listed above to impose liquidity rules. Practices on the use of liquidity ratios vary widely across countries. In some countries (particularly developing countries), bank reserve ratios—a specific example of a liquidity ratio—are still important for

5. See Goodhart and Tsomocos (2007). As Sayers (1976, p. 277) notes, "The rule against 'all but commercial bills' . . . implied a frown on Treasury bills as well as private finance bills."

6. Turner (2010) summarizes a number of proposals.

the implementation of monetary policy. In most industrial countries, however, bank reserve ratios no longer play a central monetary policy role.

Before the 1980s a central focus of bank regulators was on various liquidity ratios. Banks had to provide regular reports on the maturity profiles of their assets and liabilities. Regulators paid particular attention to asset liquidity, and banks were often required to invest a certain percentage of their total assets in government bills or bonds or in high-quality paper issued by the private sector. During the 1980s, however, this emphasis on liquidity ratios waned. There were two reasons for this.

One was that monetary policy implementation became more centered on short-term interest rates and less on liquid asset ratios. In the United Kingdom, for instance, the reserve asset ratio required of banks was a central instrument of monetary control in the 1970s: its aim was to contain credit growth, not to protect bank depositors. Nevertheless, the Bank of England at the time recognized that its abolition in 1981 (as new arrangements for monetary control were introduced) left something of a prudential gap:

> The reserve asset ratio is not a prudential ratio . . . but as its constituents are liquid assets, it has had some relevance to the maintenance by banks of adequate levels of liquidity . . . The Bank would expect any changes [in banks' management of their liquidity] on the abolition of the reserve asset ratio to be made only gradually and after full consultation . . . the Bank will seek to develop a single comprehensive measurement of the overall liquidity of banks.[7]

This "single comprehensive measurement," however, proved to be elusive. The desire for such an indicator remained in the background for decades and has been reignited only by the recent crisis.

Another reason why the emphasis on liquidity ratios waned was the developing consensus on the central importance of international banks having adequate capital. Because any well-capitalized bank would always be able to access deep wholesale money markets with only miniscule spreads, so the argument went, the liquidity of assets became unimportant. What mattered was access to markets to fund positions (funding liquidity).

Until the Basel III standards, there were no international rules about how quantitative liquidity rules should be formulated. Differences in the depth and breadth of wholesale money markets and in central bank discount practices have always made it difficult to formulate rules to apply worldwide. And because rules on the assets that commercial banks must hold on their balance sheets will influence what they pledge to the central bank as collateral, central banks may resist any attempt by regulators to have the first claim on a bank's "best" collateral.

7. See Bank of England (1981).

Currency Mismatches and Liquidity Risks from Operations in Foreign Currency

Lending and borrowing by banks in foreign currency adds further complications. In the late 1970s and the early 1980s, such foreign currency operations were dominated by the lending in dollars by European and Japanese banks. Their customers were (usually) large international companies, foreign governments, and banks in developing countries. Further globalization in succeeding decades brought the banks of many more countries into international interbank markets.

DIRECT CURRENCY MISMATCHES. Commercial banks do not generally take large unhedged positions in foreign currency. Regulators usually impose capital charges on such positions, including, in some countries, ceilings on aggregate exposures.

There are, however, several ways that unanticipated direct currency mismatches could arise as a result of market developments. Two were important in the 2007–10 financial crisis. One is that foreign currency assets lose their value. The substantial decline in the value of U.S. dollar assets related to the U.S. housing market crisis, for instance, led to large losses for European banks. To return to their precrisis aggregate dollar exposure, therefore, banks would have to sell nondollar assets to raise dollars or would have repay (that is, not roll over) dollar liabilities falling due. Paradoxically, then, the loss of value of dollar assets may strengthen the dollar on forex markets.[8] Another is that foreign currency liabilities cannot be rolled over: the dysfunctions in interbank dollar and forex swap markets did greatly limit refinancing choices.

INDIRECT CURRENCY MISMATCHES. In general, international lending banks typically did not have currency mismatches on their own balance sheets in the early 1980s debt crisis. Their dollar loans were usually matched by wholesale dollar deposits. But many of their borrowers—particularly governments in Latin America and parts of developing Asia—were exposed to massive currency mismatches. Because dollar borrowings were typically at a floating rate, debtors also faced large interest rate risks too.[9]

The string of defaults on these international bank loans in the 1980s shook the international financial system. As a result of these losses, the international banks (often "encouraged" by their regulators) gradually moved away from cross-border lending denominated in foreign currency toward lending in local currencies via local affiliates. Dollar-denominated cross-border lending to the developing world actually declined in the five years following the Asian crisis, while local lending more than doubled (table 2-1).

It is of interest that the increased importance of local lending appears to have made global bank lending to developing countries more stable in this crisis than

8. McGuire and McCauley (2009) argue that European financial institutions were probably not rolling over their short-term dollar liabilities once they had recognized their losses on their U.S. dollar assets (mainly structured products) and that this helped to strengthen the dollar during 2008.

9. Goldstein and Turner (2004).

Table 2-1. *Consolidated Claims of Foreign Banks vis-à-vis Developing Countries, End of Year, Selected Years, 1990–2009*
U.S. $ billion

Claim	*1990*	*1995*	*1997*	*2002*	*2007*	*2008*	*2009*
Local currency claims on residents[a]	51	123	250	529	1,833	1,720	1,926
International claims[b]	528	744	980	772	2,409	2,326	2,487

Source: Bank for International Settlements.
a. Local claims comprise those of BIS reporting banks' foreign offices denominated in local currency.
b. International claims are the sum of cross-border claims in all currencies and local claims of BIS reporting banks' foreign offices denominated in foreign currency only.

it was in earlier crises. The boom-bust cycle was much more marked in international claims than in local claims (figure 2-2). In addition, the Committee on the Global Financial System (CGFS) report on funding patterns notes that large international banks that had a more decentralized multinational model were less affected by funding problems than those with more centralized funding models.[10]

Currency mismatches on the balance sheet of borrowers were the main common ingredient in all of the financial crises affecting emerging markets in the 1980s and 1990s. In the recent crisis, however, direct currency mismatches on balance sheets in the emerging markets were a major problem only in central and eastern Europe. Figure 2-3 identifies a few countries where the rise in the ratio of the external liabilities of banks to bank lending suggests a massive dependence on foreign borrowing.

But contingent and off-balance-sheet forex exposures—not all visible—were much more widespread. Corporations in Brazil, Korea, and Mexico had large exposures, often in the form of options or other derivative contracts. Some positions were nonlinear so that exposures were magnified as the currency fell through successive trigger points.[11]

In the case of Korea, for instance, these forex derivatives of corporations were largely with Korea-based banks (including foreign-owned banks). To avoid holding such exchange rate risks on their balance sheets, banks had usually sold their derivative contracts to foreign banks and hedge funds. If the corporation defaulted on its contract, however, the Korea bank would still be responsible for its losses vis-à-vis the foreign bank. When the crisis broke, banks became much more cautious, pulling back from such markets as they hoarded liquidity.

10. Committee on Global Financial System (2010b, sec. 5.1).

11. See Committee on the Global Financial System (2009, pp. 119–25) for an analysis of these exposures. For an analysis of several aspects of the policy responses in EMEs, see Bank for International Settlements (2010).

Figure 2-2. *Changes in Stocks, BIS Reporting Banks' Consolidated Lending to Emerging Economies, 2001–09*[a]

U.S.$ billion

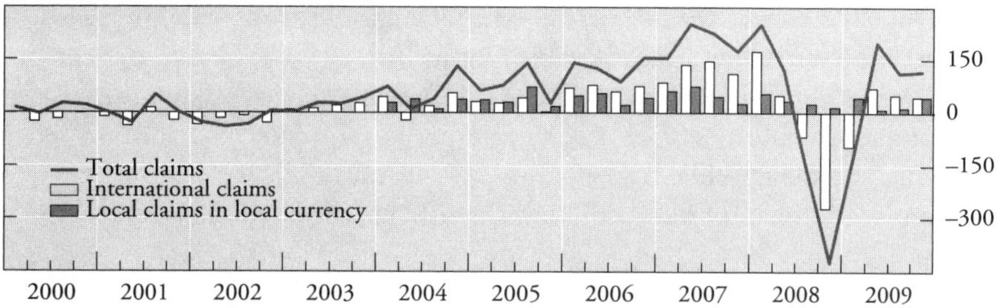

Source: BIS consolidated banking statistics on an immediate borrower basis.

a. Measures quarterly difference in outstanding stocks via the consolidated positions of banks headquartered in thirty reporting countries vis-à-vis Argentina; Brazil; Chile; China; Hong Kong, China; India; Indonesia; Korea; Malaysia; Mexico; Philippines; Poland; Russia; Saudi Arabia; Singapore; South Africa; Thailand; and Turkey. Total claims is the sum of international claims and local claims in local currency (unadjusted); international claims comprise cross-border claims in all currencies and local claims in foreign currencies; local claims relate to those booked by reporting banks' foreign offices on residents of the country in which the foreign office is located. Claims in local currencies are adjusted for exchange rate movements by converting all changes in local claims at the exchange rate prevailing in the first quarter of 2009. Total claims are computed using unadjusted local claims.

Figure 2-3. *External Liabilities to Gross Loans, Seven Countries, 2002 and 2007*[a]

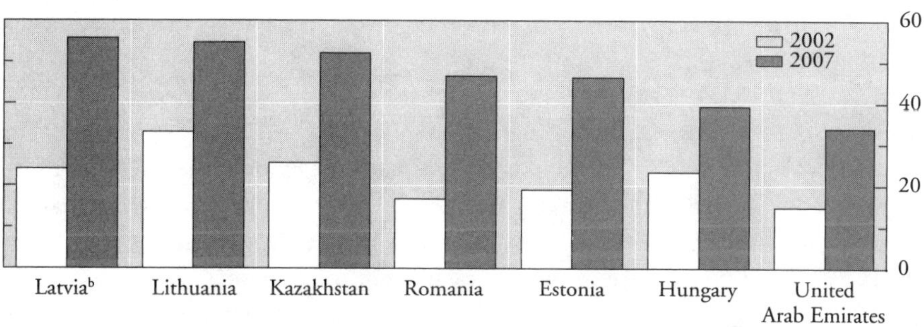

Source: FRBNY based on banking superintendency and central bank data.

a. External liabilities are for the banking sector; gross loans include both public and private sector loans.

b. 2003.

FUNDING RISKS. In addition, the international banks were exposed to funding risks. Peter Cooke explained, in the early 1980s, that the Basel Committee

> shared the concern that the rapid increase in international lending in the 1970s has increased the mismatch between banks' assets and liabilities. This gives rise to an interest rate risk and a funding risk. . . . The Committee considers that the degree of maturity transformation effected by banks in their international business is a matter of especial importance to supervisors because funding problems are not infrequently the origin of a problem bank situation. More importantly, there is the risk that the increased interdependence of banks for their liquidity management could lead to domino effects throughout the international banking system in the event of problems emerging in one corner of it.[12]

The Basel Committee on Banking Supervision, however, failed in the 1980s in its attempts to reach an accord on liquidity as it had successfully done for capital.[13] Since that time, in any case, the progressive development of money markets, in both depth and breadth, seemed to make regulatory rules about liquidity quite superfluous.

One consequence was that the exposure of international banks to funding risk grew steadily for more than twenty years. A report by the CGFS discusses in some detail two significant long-term trends.[14] First, international banks' reliance on wholesale market funding rose: between 1985 and 2006, the share of liabilities vis-à-vis nonbanks in advanced economies increased from 24 percent to 35 percent. Second, the share of intragroup funding grew from 22 percent to 30 percent, reflecting the active use of major financial centers and offshore markets as funding sources.

NO INTERNATIONAL LENDER OF LAST RESORT. A fundamental difference between foreign currency business and a bank's management of liquidity risk in its own local currency is that there is no international lender of last resort in foreign currency. International banking business involves usually three central banks: the central bank where the bank conducts this business, the central bank where the bank is headquartered, and the central bank of the currency used. Which central bank should take responsibility for emergency liquidity and exactly how this

12. Cooke (1981, p. 241).

13. Goodhart (2007). In Davies and Green (2010, pp. 98–100), the authors point out that, in the 1960s, 30 percent of British clearing bank assets were held in the form of highly liquid paper: cash, Treasury bills, or short-dated government paper. This percentage was, however, seen as too high even at that time. The banks' enormous holdings of Treasury bills—a legacy of war and immediate postwar public finance—created a risk that banks could suddenly increase lending to the private sector. This made the authorities reluctant to abolish direct controls on lending.

14. Committee on the Global Financial System (2010c).

would be provided has been long debated.[15] There was a worry in the early 1970s, when the eurodollar markets began to expand, that central banks would not be able to react quickly because of unresolved disagreements among them. After much debate, however, the G-10 central banks concluded that (with reference to the problem of the lender of last resort in the euro markets), "it would not be practical to lay down in advance detailed rules and procedures for the provision of temporary liquidity."[16]

This formal position has remained in place ever since. And the recent crisis has stimulated a renewed debate about this: see Yung Chul Park's contribution to this volume (chapter 5), advocating what he calls a "global liquidity safety net."

Markets-to-Trade Exposures across Maturities and Currencies

A bank with operations in several currencies in principle must both limit aggregate currency exposures and manage liquidity risks in each currency. In an earlier and simpler world, how a bank did this could largely be read from its balance sheet. The huge development of forex and interest rate derivative markets (including forwards, interest rate swaps, futures, and currency options) in recent decades made this much more difficult. These instruments not only gave banks powerful tools to develop lending more easily but could also help banks understate their true exposures. As documented in table 2-1, international bank claims rose from under $800 billion in 2002 to over $2,400 billion by 2007, an extraordinary expansion in just five years.

The use of ever more complete hedging markets allowed banks worldwide to borrow dollars in international markets on a massive scale. They could in effect sell their forex and maturity exposures, arising from many different business strategies, to someone else. Most of their transactions were with other banks. Often, at the end of a long interbank chain, there were institutional investors outside the banking system. The willingness of investors to take the positions that banks in aggregate wanted to shed could help to make these funding strategies resilient to shocks. Such investors include pension funds, other institutional investors, and official investors such as central banks. However, the CGFS found that many institutional investors outside the United States were also hedging their considerable U.S. dollar portfolios through the swap market, reinforcing the transatlantic funding asymmetry of the banks.[17] Also essential in sustaining these funding strategies was full confidence in the creditworthiness of the counterparties—usually banks—that wrote such contracts at very low spreads.

15. Shafer (1982) provides an excellent review of the theory of a lender of last resort in international banking markets.

16. Communiqué, G-10 Governors, September 10, 1974, Bank for International Settlements.

17. Committee on the Global Financial System (2010b).

Table 2-2. *Foreign Currency Exposure, Australian Banks, June 2001 and March 2009*
Australian $ billion

	2001 June	*2009 March*
Net balance sheet exposure	−86.0	−316.6
Foreign equity assets	30.7	22.7
Foreign currency–denominated debt assets	69.8	208.9
Foreign currency–denominated debt liabilities	186.5	548.2
Net derivatives exposure (hedging)	109.5	354.5
Derivative contracts bought with A$, principal value	435.3	1,273.6
Derivative contracts sold for A$, principal value	325.8	919.1
Net exposure after hedging (total of the above)	23.4	37.9

Source: Australian Bureau of Statistics.

One business model was for banks to use foreign wholesale markets to finance a bigger increase in lending at home than domestic bank deposits would permit. The Australian banking system illustrates this well. Australian banks in effect borrowed fixed-rate (usually medium- to long-term) dollars but swapped their exposures into floating-rate Australian dollars. This matched the nature of their lending terms to Australian residents. We can see this clearly because Australia is one of the few countries to collect and publish data from its financial institutions on off-balance-sheet forex positions. As table 2-2 makes clear, currency and maturity mismatches were thus generally avoided in the Australian case. Between June 2001 and March 2009, the foreign-currency-denominated debts of Australian banks rose by A$350 billion, financing a sizable increase in lending. As their hedging operations rose by about the same magnitude, currency mismatches were avoided. Net foreign currency exposures rose by A$14 billion. Equally, the large expansion in bank lending entailed a threefold increase in foreign currency derivative contracts, so that this business strategy was very dependent on the availability and pricing of these hedging contracts.

In other countries, however, the foreign currency liabilities used to finance (comparatively illiquid) domestic lending in local currency were of very short duration. The foreign exchange risks were also hedged using short-term instruments, usually forex swaps. Both operations required refinancing at frequent intervals and therefore depended on continued access to deep wholesale markets.

Another business model was the use of wholesale markets to fund the acquisition of higher yielding or illiquid foreign assets. Most of the activity in international interbank markets was indeed driven by this global business strategy of the large international banks. From the earliest days of what were then called the eurocurrency markets, major non-U.S. banks borrowed dollars short in order to lend long, the classic business of banking. Surplus short-term dollar funds (from other banks, central banks, money markets or asset managers, corporate treasurers, and so on) are passed through a long chain of banks. Any particular bank will not necessarily know either the initial source of funds or its ultimate (nonbank) destination. In normal times, this is a seamless market and is internationally homogeneous.[18]

In the years before the crisis, the European banks financed a sizable expansion of long-dated or less liquid dollar-denominated assets by short-term dollar borrowing (or by using forex swap proceeds). As the CGFS documents, it was this maturity mismatch that aggravated the vulnerability of the banks.[19] Unfortunately, we do not nowadays have detailed data on the maturity of banks' dollar assets and liabilities. We are forced to use what is available in the BIS's international banking statistics and do some educated guesswork. Patrick McGuire has shown much ingenuity in extracting the maximum information from these data.[20] Figure 2-4 shows the dollar-denominated positions of four European banking systems with large funding gaps in dollars (that is, longer term U.S. dollar holdings financed by short-term U.S. dollar funds). This shows a significant maturity transformation across banks' balance sheets. The lower bound estimates of the dollar-funding gap of financial firms in these countries—that is, implicitly assuming that U.S. dollar liabilities to nonbanks are longer term—peaked at well over $1 trillion in mid-2007. It fell to over $0.5 trillion at the end of 2009. On top of this, we know there are large short-term U.S. dollar liabilities to money market funds (which are counted as nonbanks in BIS statistics): $1 trillion in mid-2007; this may have fallen to $0.75 trillion by the end of the first quarter of 2010. Adding these two estimates implies a decline in the dollar funding gap from about $2 trillion in mid-2007 to over $1.25 trillion at the end of 2009. This is still very large—and there are certainly short-term dollar liabilities of other financial firms in these banking systems. The international community must do much more to plug these statistical gaps.

The dependence of non-U.S. financial firms on such a scale on wholesale, short-term, dollar-funding markets created a major systemic risk. Each individual bank may have felt that its own dependence was manageable, but the aggregate dependence of all banks globally became untenable in the crisis. The dislocations that took place in forex swap markets were dramatic (figure 2-5), particularly in the currencies of the major emerging market economies. For many currencies, swap spreads still remain above precrisis levels; they seem sensitive to adverse news, and transaction volumes have fallen.

18. For an early analysis with detailed numbers, see Ellis (1981). It is interesting that the comprehensive data he provides, for European and Japanese banks operating in London, on banks' maturity mismatches on foreign currency positions along the maturity spectrum (less than eight days, eight days to one month, one to three months, three to six months, six to twelve months, one to three years, and three years and over) are no longer available.

19. Committee on the Global Financial System (2010a).

20. See McGuire and von Goetz (2009); Cecchetti, Fender, and McGuire (2010).

Figure 2-4. *U.S. Dollar Positions, Four European Banking Systems*[a]

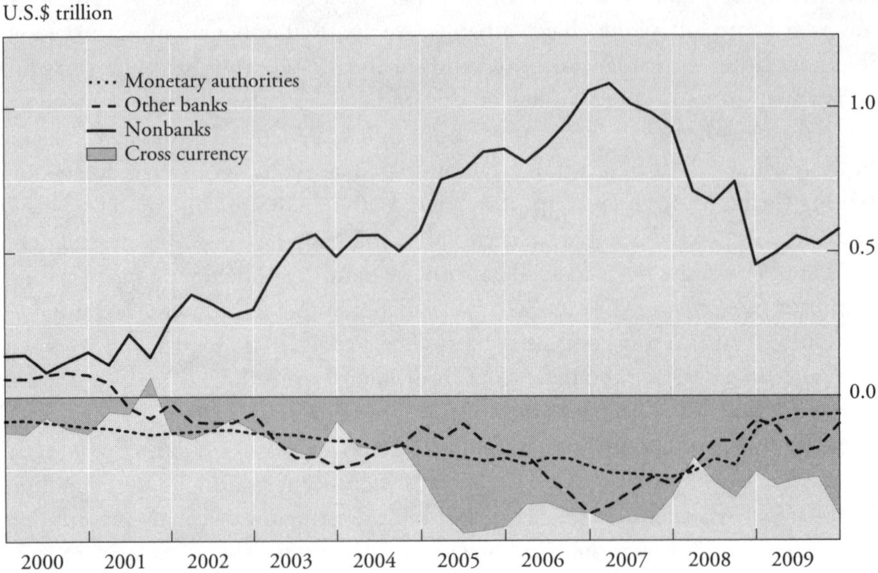

Source: BIS consolidated statistics (immediate borrower and ultimate risk basis); BIS locational statistics by nationality; Bloomberg.

a. Estimates are constructed by aggregating the on-balance-sheet cross-border and local positions reported by Dutch, German, Swiss, and U.K. banks' offices. Monetary authorities' cross-border positions are given in all currencies and local positions in foreign currencies vis-à-vis official monetary authorities. This excludes liabilities to Japanese monetary authorities placed in banks located in Japan. The other banks measure is an estimated net interbank lending to other (unaffiliated) banks. The net position vis-à-vis nonbanks is estimated as the sum of net international positions vis-à-vis nonbanks and net local U.S. positions (vis-à-vis all sectors). By construction, net claims on nonbanks is the sum of net positions vis-à-vis other banks, vis-à-vis monetary authorities, and cross-currency funding, which is the lower bound estimate of the U.S. dollar funding gap. Implied cross-currency funding (Forex swaps) equates gross U.S. dollar assets and liabilities.

Elements of Contagion during the Crisis

The most disturbing feature of the financial crisis is that the disruption of virtually all wholesale bank funding markets was on a global scale. There was a systemic seizure of funding markets. The root cause was a loss in confidence in the major bank counterparties for such contracts. Related to this, a dramatic narrowing in the quality of collateral international lending banks would accept hit asset classes worldwide in a near-indiscriminate way. The sharp rise in the dollar, particularly against major emerging market currencies, brought to light large but hidden forex exposures in several major emerging market economies. Deleveraging (or even exit) by investment banks and hedge funds accentuated the dislocations.

Disentangling the various mechanisms at work in this crisis is not easy. From the point of view of contagion mechanisms affecting liquidity, however, six elements seem to have been key.

Figure 2-5. *Implied Forex Swap Spreads, Nine Countries, 2007–10*[a]

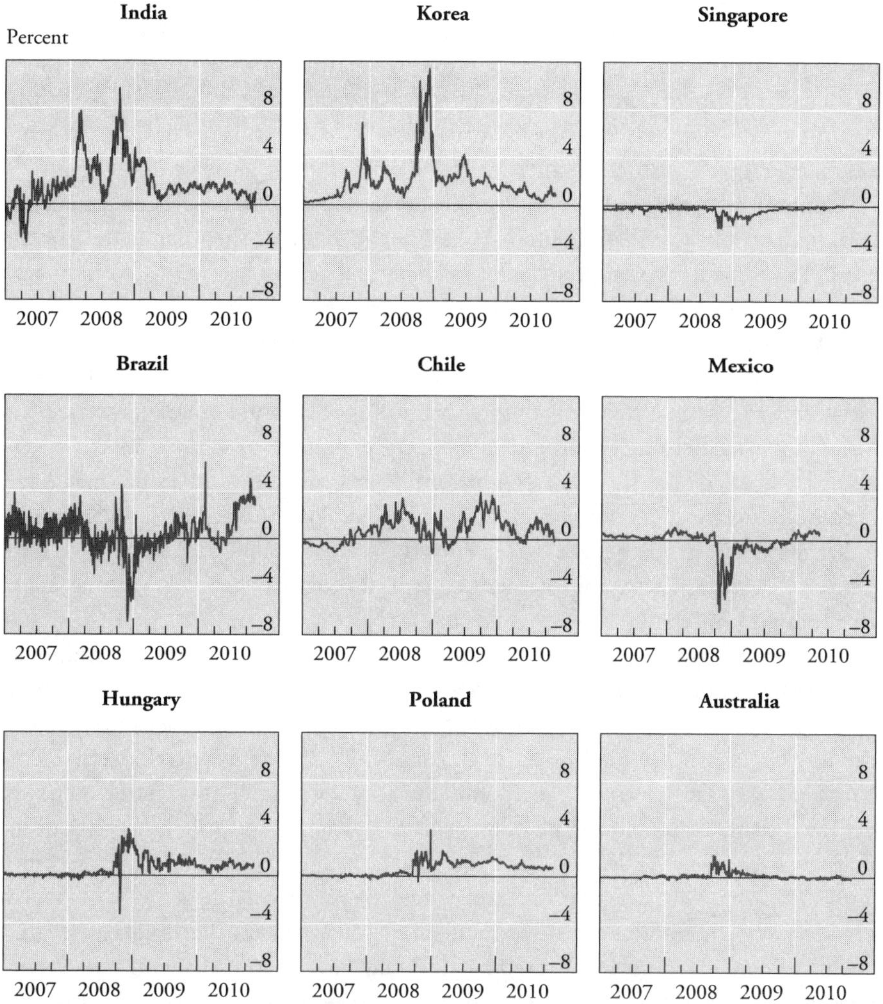

Source: Bloomberg; Datastream; BIS; authors' calculations.

a. Calculated as the difference between three-month Forex swap implied interest rate and three-month U.S. dollar Libor. The former is derived from covered interest parity condition based on the following domestic three-month interest rates: India, Mumbai interbank rate; Korea, ninety-one-day certificate of deposit rate; Singapore, interbank rate; Brazil, certificate of deposit rate; Chile, ninety-day DISCTB promissory note rate; Mexico, TIIE interbank rate; Hungary, interbank rate; Poland, Warsaw interbank rate; Australia, interbank rate.

Vulnerability of leveraged investors. Wholesale markets that are dominated by leveraged investors (such as banks and hedge funds) might well offer, in good times, impressive market liquidity on all the usual microeconomic criteria: high turnover, low spreads, and limited day-to-day volatility. But they are not resilient in the face of large macroeconomic or financial system shocks: leverage magnifies the impact of such a shock on the firm's net worth and thus on its creditworthiness. Leveraged investors can be simply forced to sell.

Counterparty risks. Deepening uncertainties about counterparty risks in interbank markets in the major centers (because the value of their exposures to, for example, subprime mortgage debt and collateralized debt obligations was unknown) led to an evaporation in liquidity in the (large) interbank cash markets. This forced banks to attempt to raise liquidity (or curb lending) in forex swap markets—which, faced with these large demands, became dysfunctional. This forced the liquidation by leveraged investors of their portfolios of emerging market assets.[21] (In some of these emerging economies, surprisingly, pockets of surplus dollars developed amid the global shortage. It is not fully clear why local investors may have become reluctant to deposit their surplus dollars with major banks U.S. banks, but it may explain the negative swap spreads in Mexico and Singapore shown in figure 2-5). Some other impediment to cross-border dollar arbitrage may have constrained local banks.

Narrowing in the quality of collateral. As the crisis deepened, international lending banks became much more demanding in the quality of collateral they would accept. A. Fostel and J. Geanakoplos demonstrate just how important is the impact of collateral practices on demand for noncore financial assets.[22] The collateral capacity of an asset depends on its volatility. If this increases (or is expected to increase), the value of an asset as collateral falls much more than its market price, because lenders demand more extreme "haircuts" (the discount applied to the asset's current market value) of more volatile assets. Leveraged investors will therefore become more inclined to buy assets that they can pledge as collateral, with minimum haircuts—and may have to forgo buying some assets regarded as underpriced (because their price has become too volatile). This narrowing in the quality of collateral hit financial assets in the emerging markets much harder than the underlying fundamentals warranted and made the financial crisis global.

Foreign exchange exposures via derivatives. Sharp currency depreciation brought to light significant forex exposures in several large emerging market countries, notably Brazil, Korea, and Mexico. Increased exchange rate volatility contributed to the virtual disappearance of many forex hedging markets.

21. See Baba, Packer, and Nagano (2008) for an explanation of this mechanism.
22. Fostel and Geanakoplos (2008).

Liquidity hoarding by banks. Most banks were well aware that they had, over many years, reduced their liquidity buffers and had become very dependent on their continued access to funding markets. Hence they had every motive to hoard liquidity once the crisis struck, thus aggravating the illiquidity in major funding markets. International banks also used their affiliates in the emerging markets to improve their dollar position at home.

Liquidity pressures in vehicle currencies. Liquidity pressures in dollar markets mean that those international financial transactions with the U.S. dollar as one component were seriously affected. This was very important in this crisis, because the U.S. dollar is more dominant as a vehicle currency in swap transactions than it is in spot markets. forex swap operations between two nondollar currencies were seriously disrupted during this crisis.

The contractionary forces set in train by these six elements reinforced each other. As banks found one market closed (or the pricing prohibitive), they sought to borrow in other markets. As a result, funding markets became very closely linked in this period of severe stress.

The CGFS explains in more detail the different channels through which disruption in one funding market is quickly transmitted to other markets. In addition, time zone differences made it harder for banks to manage their liquidity positions.

> As U.S.-based lenders became reluctant to lend early in the U.S. day (Europe afternoon) when their own liquidity positions for the day were not yet known, dollar borrowing late in the European day became more difficult. As a result, European banks increasingly sought to secure funds earlier during Asian trading hours (Europe morning). At the same time, however, the supply of U.S. dollar liquidity in the Asian and European time zones declined, as many lenders, particularly official sector lenders, reduced unsecured lending. There are also reports that some foreign banks were effectively shut out of interbank markets in other jurisdictions, particularly in Asia, as counterparty concerns took hold.[23]

Strategic Borrowing Choices for International Banks

International banks can reduce their exposure to funding market pressure in four, possibly complementary, ways. First, they can try to reduce dependence on cross-border wholesale funding by borrowing funds locally. Second, they can reduce their overall reliance on wholesale funding. Third, borrowing at longer durations can reduce the risk of near-term liquidity. And finally, banks can step up efforts to reduce (or at least more effectively manage) cross-currency maturity mismatches.

23. Committee on the Global Financial System (2010a, p. 5).

Local Sourcing of Liabilities

One natural response to the stress experienced in cross-border funding markets is to increase local sourcing of wholesale liabilities. Borrowing in local markets to finance local assets would remove the cross-currency dimension of liquidity risk. Indeed, discussions with international banks suggest that greater emphasis on local funding is one important element of adjustments in bank funding approaches.[24]

However, there are limitations to the local sourcing of funds. First, local markets for many wholesale funding instruments may lack depth or simply not exist; this is especially true in emerging market economies but also happens in small advanced economies. For example, the ability of banks to issue bonds in the local currency may be limited to short maturities if liquid instruments—usually government bonds—that can serve as the basis for the pricing of private debt are only short term.[25] In addition, certain segments of interbank markets, such as repurchase markets, may be shallow, limiting the scope for managing funding liquidity efficiently in individual currencies.[26]

Second, a simultaneous shift of all banks toward local funding would face macroeconomic constraints. The domestic funding base in many countries that are net borrowers on international interbank markets may be too small. This limited funding base may reflect many factors. It could just reflect low saving propensities caused by demographic factors. Or poor macroeconomic policies (such as large fiscal deficits and weak monetary policies) may have depressed aggregate national savings. Conversely, savings-rich economies may lack investment opportunities at home. Indeed, a substantial share of the surplus savings of capital-exporting countries is intermediated through the global banking system, especially in countries where banks traditionally play a major role. For example, banks' cross-border claims accounted for 40–50 percent of the gross external claims of Japan, Germany, Switzerland, and Belgium by the end of 2007. Banks play an analogous role for capital-importing countries (such as Australia, Spain, and Italy). In less mature markets, banks often fund local credit with cross-border intragroup transfers from the parent bank: local borrowers are often saddled with sizable currency mismatches. Persistent current account deficits may result in the buildup of large cross-border claims (as they did in central and eastern Europe).

Taken together, shallow local markets and inelastic supply of domestic savings imply that increased local funding may lead to a rise in funding costs. How banks

24. Committee on the Global Financial System (2010b).

25. Committee on the Global Financial System (2007) shows that the development of a local currency yield curve helps banks hedge maturity risks and develop instruments.

26. Immaturity and incompleteness of local funding markets might become less of a constraint over time. Banks themselves may well have greater interest in developing domestic markets and may devote more resources to domestic market activities, such as market making, or may lead efforts to lengthen maturities, standardize instruments, or develop market infrastructure. Such initiatives could foster more rapid development of domestic markets.

Figure 2-6. *Ratio of U.K. Banks' Retail Deposits to Wholesale Deposits*[a]

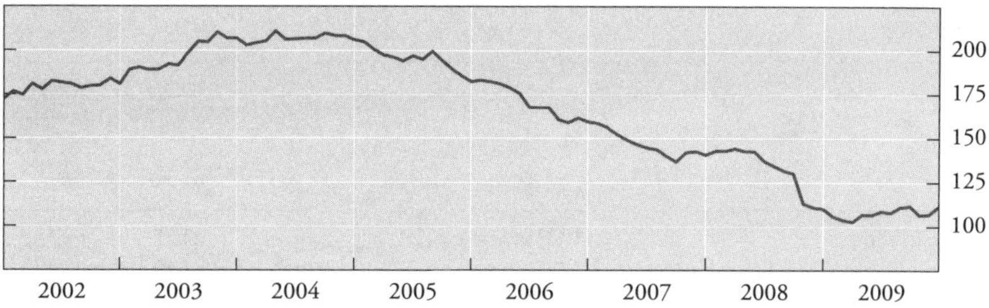

Source: Bank of England.

a. Wholesale deposits include certificates of deposit, sterling commercial paper, and other short-term paper.

would respond to tighter local funding conditions depends on their business model and risk appetite.

Shift from Wholesale to Retail Funding

Another response to the crisis experience is to reduce reliance on wholesale market funding. The use of money market funding has been identified as a major source of bank vulnerability.[27] Indeed, in discussions with the CGFS, banks said that they intend to increase reliance on retail funding.[28] In many countries, the reliance on retail deposits had fallen sharply; for example, see the U.K. case in figure 2-6. Ideally, banks need to ensure that some retail deposits are longer term maturities. A larger share of retail funding is seen as offering several benefits. First, retail funding is less exposed to changes in risk appetite in markets and, therefore, more stable than wholesale funding. Wholesale funding gives rise to concentration risks, especially in small markets. In addition, large-scale providers of wholesale funding, such as money market funds, may themselves be exposed to liquidity risk. Second, increased retail deposits will help a bank that is heavily reliant on wholesale markets to achieve a greater diversity of funding, especially when combined with geographical diversification.

Like the shift toward domestic funding, attempts to raise retail deposits face limitations. In some developing countries, a lack of trust in the health of the banking system makes it difficult for banks, even foreign banks, to raise longer term deposits. More generally, retail funding is likely to become more costly with growing competition. For instance, in the United Kingdom since the third quarter of 2008 competition among U.K. banks for retail balances has intensified.[29] This

27. Brunnermeier and Petersen (2009); European Central Bank (2009).
28. Committee on the Global Financial System (2010b).
29. Bank of England (2009).

Table 2-3. *Debt Securities and Changes in Stocks, Governments, Financial Institutions, and World GDP, 2003–10*[a]
U.S. $ billion

Entity	*2003–06*[b]	*2007*	*2008*	*2009*	*December 2009 to September 2010*[c]
Governments	1,771	1,195	2,651	4,172	3,732
Remaining maturity < 1 year	346	−52	1,500	314	−247
Longer remaining maturity	1,425	1,247	1,150	3,858	3,980
Financial institutions	3,084	4,927	2,617	516	−938
Remaining maturity < 1 year	588	808	−56	−902	−696
	2,497	4,119	2,673	1,418	−242
World GDP	43,479	55,392	61,221	57,937	60,933

Source: Dealogic; Euroclear; Thomson Reuters; Xtrakter Ltd; national authorities; IMF; BIS. The BIS endeavors to eliminate any overlap between its international and domestic debt securities statistics as far as possible. However, as two different collection systems are used (security by security collection system for IDS and collection of aggregated data for DDS) as well as two different approaches and definitions (market definitions for the IDS and statistical definitions in the DDS), some overlap and inconsistencies might remain by a margin that differs from country to country.

a. Domestic plus international issues. Exchange rate adjusted.

b. Annualized.

c. Cumulative.

represents a significant source of pressure on banks' and building societies' net interest margins and overall profitability. In addition, retail deposits might become less stable if fierce competition were to trigger more frequent shifts of deposits across institutions. Increasing competition from nonbank financial intermediaries, especially money market funds, has similar effects.

Longer Duration of Banks' Liabilities

A lengthening of the duration of liabilities reduces the exposure to rollover risk or an unexpected withdrawal of funding. But such an extension of funding maturities has costs. The incremental cost of expanding funding maturities in major currencies is high in the current environment of very low short-term interest rates and unusually steep yield curves. In this sense, monetary policies may be discouraging banks from lengthening their liabilities. Current fiscal policy does not help: high, and rising, public sector financing needs may add to upward pressure on long-term interest rates in the foreseeable future.

At the start of the 2000s, government bonds outstanding amounted to less than \$15 trillion; by September 2010, this had risen to more than \$40 trillion. Estimates by the Bank for International Settlements of global net issuance of bonds by government and by financial institutions are shown in table 2-3. Despite substantial government guarantees, long-term debt issuance by financial institutions in 2009 was $1.4 trillion, or about half of what it had been from 2003 to 2008. Net issuance was actually negative in the first three quarters of 2010.

During the past decade, several large emerging market economies have made substantial progress in developing local currency debt markets. But corporate debt markets remain shallow compared with government debt markets, making it harder for banks to borrow longer term. In some smaller emerging market countries, longer term funding may not be possible at all. As mentioned before, underdeveloped wholesale funding markets usually mean that only short-term instruments are available. In addition, the flatter yield curve environment in many emerging economies has accentuated the shortening in the maturity of bank deposits, particularly in Asia.

Enhancement of Liquidity Risk Management

Addressing shortcomings in liquidity risk management complements changes in bank funding approaches. There are several areas in which banks seem to be engaged in reforming their practices.[30] On a general level, the monitoring of liquidity risk and funding conditions may become more intense and frequent. This is likely to involve reinforcing the head office's central overview of liquidity management. For instance, a consolidated assessment of liquidity risk and coordinating access to central bank facilities at the group level requires that the head office has more information and better control over existing holdings of liquidity and collateral. Thus while one may observe further decentralization in funding, the general trend seems to be one of increasing centralization of monitoring at group headquarters.

Another area for improvement is internal fund transfer pricing in order to better reflect liquidity costs and risk. This suggests that, even for banks that to continue to rely on centralized funding, internal transfers will probably be undertaken at conditions that are closer to those prevailing in the markets. A more realistic pricing of internal fund transfers could also create incentives for local offices to raise stable funding at home and to become less dependent on intragroup funding.

While these measures will reduce the vulnerability of banks to idiosyncratic liquidity shocks, they are unlikely to address the externalities that give rise to systemic liquidity risk. More stringent and frequent stress testing may go some way in strengthening the resilience to systemwide liquidity shocks.[31] But the crisis may well have changed the endogenous dynamics of liquidity shocks in interbank markets. Any sign of interbank market strain may lead to widespread precautionary

30. See Committee on the Global Financial System (2010b) for details.
31. Senior Supervisors Group (2008).

Figure 2-7. *Ratio of International Trade and Banks' Global Claims to Global GDP, 1987–2009*[a]

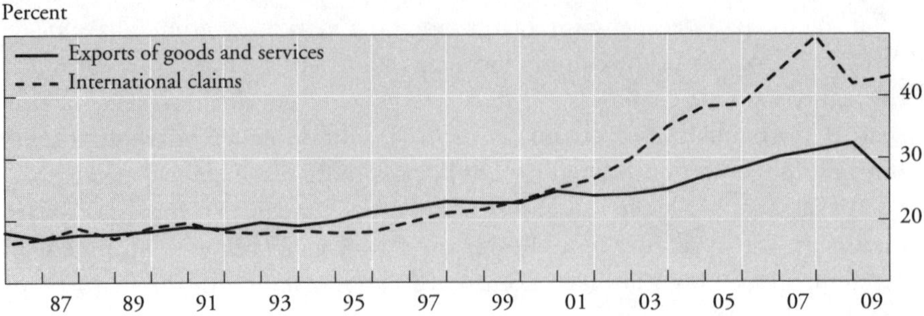

Source: IMF World Economic Outlook Database for World GDP; BIS international banking statistics.

a. The series are based on current exchange rates vis-à-vis the U.S. dollar. Foreign claims comprise cross-border claims and local claims in all currencies. Interoffice accounts are excluded.

liquidity hoarding by virtually all banks. If so, the shock-absorbing capacity of interbank markets may have been reduced permanently. As a consequence, liquidity shocks could become even larger and more abrupt.

New Constraints Shaping International Banking

As discussed above, the past decade was characterized by an extraordinarily rapid expansion of international banking activity. After the early 2000s global banking activity grew much faster than international trade, a significant change from the fifteen years before, when both had expanded more or less in lockstep (figure 2-7). However, there are questions as to whether strong growth in international banking will resume. Key factors that accommodated the growth of banks' international balance sheets include buoyant demand for securities products, the availability of hedging instruments at near-zero cost, and relatively light regulation of certain activities (such as low capital requirements on trading books or holdings of highly rated structured products).

Reforms across the whole spectrum of financial intermediation (money market, mutual funds, pension funds, insurance companies, and so on) will affect wholesale funding markets for banks. The more realistic pricing of securitization and hedging risks is likely to constrain business expansion. The more effective regulation of bank liquidity risks will be a major force.

Limited Securitization Markets

Issuance volumes of securitized products collapsed in 2007–09 (figure 2-8). As a consequence, banks had to keep on their balance sheets assets that could no longer be sold in the market. The inability to securitize assets severely constrained credit

Figure 2-8. *Global Securitization Market, Selected Countries and Regions, 1999–2009*

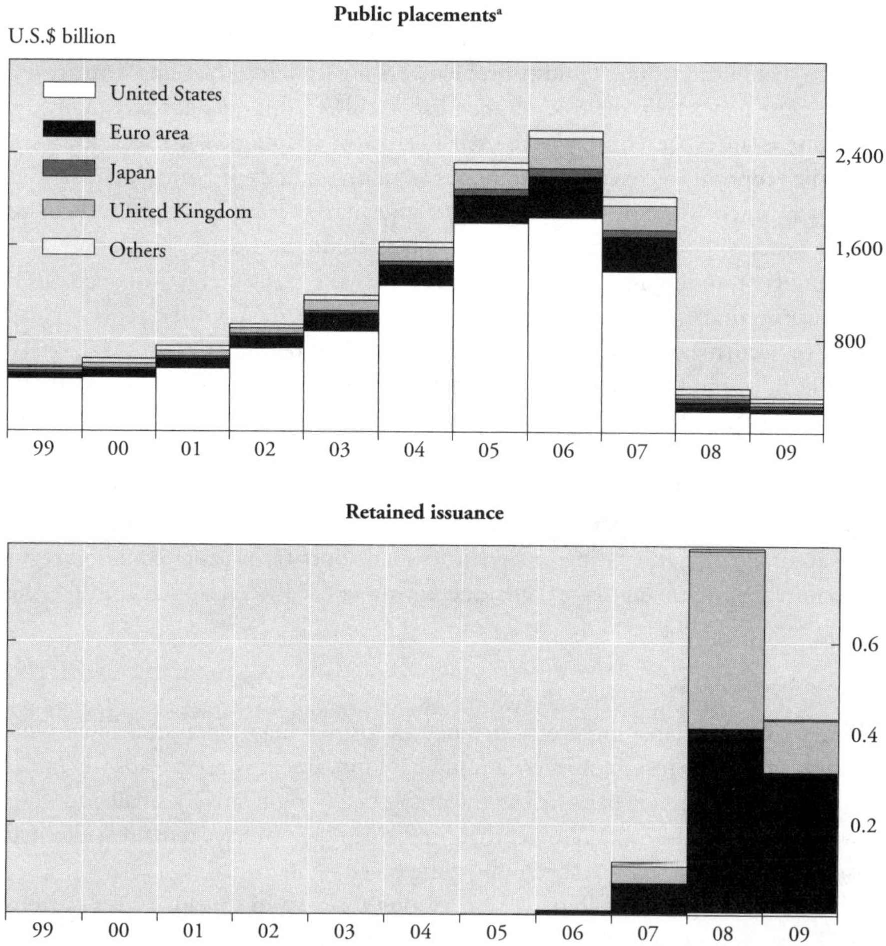

Source: Dealogic.
a. Securitizations issued by U.S. agencies are not included.

supply. Such constraints in securitization markets became visible, especially in trade finance and the syndicated loan market.[32]

The outlook for securitization markets remains uncertain. Much of the remaining market activity is still being underpinned by government and central bank support. Yet it must not be forgotten that securitization represents a technique that, properly handled, offers worthwhile benefits. Getting it restarted will probably require simpler, more standardized forms. Standardization has made headway

32. Chui and others (2010).

in the past two years but is still incomplete due to some remaining disagreements over its form; further progress is needed to improve transparency and disclosure. The experience with covered bond markets, which have held up relatively well, suggests that the double protection provided both through collateralization and through the guarantees of banks can reduce liquidity problems arising from information asymmetries. But because banks keep the risks on their balance sheet, this does not save capital.

There is an expectation of some self-healing of the market for securitization once the economic recovery gets under way and investment demands increase. But it remains uncertain how much of the previous market is likely to return through such a process. Some forms of credit—such as credit card debt (which draws on large pools of underlying debt and is short term) and trade credit—may be easier to securitize than others. Overall, however, the ability of banks to rapidly expand credit by securitization will probably be smaller than before.

One important open question is whether the greater acceptance of high-quality private sector debt products to meet regulatory requirements for liquidity could help securitization markets recover. Securitized products that are based on liabilities that are due to mature over twelve months or so would have the attractive self-liquidating properties that exchange bills had in the nineteenth century. The accuracy of credit ratings assigned to such short-term paper could be regularly tested as maturing paper falls due within short intervals, quite unlike the ratings on very long-term debt!

Higher Hedging Costs

Higher costs of managing cross-currency exposures may place additional constraints on the expansion of international banking. Forex swap spreads were near zero for many currency pairs before the crisis, including relatively small and illiquid currencies (see above). The fact that forex swap spreads have remained elevated may indicate a persistent change in hedging costs.

There is also greater differentiation among forex swap spreads across currencies. In part, this is probably attributable to perceived differences in swap market liquidity. Such differentiation should encourage a better pricing of cross-currency liquidity risk, especially if it is reflected in internal fund transfer pricing.

Changes in the Regulation of Institutional Investors

Institutional investors—money market funds, insurance firms, and pension funds—are important sources of bank funding. At times, their behavior has had strong effects on market conditions. For example, money market funds held nearly 40 percent of outstanding commercial paper in the first half of 2008, half of which was issued by non-U.S. banks. Overall, European banks appear to have relied on money market funds for about an eighth of their $8 trillion funding.[33]

33. Baba, McCauley, and Ramaswamy (2009).

It is not a surprise that the withdrawal of money market funds from short-term bank investments exacerbated strains in bank funding during the crisis.

Many institutional investors face major changes in regulatory and accounting frameworks. This could make them less willing to fund banks. New rules by the U.S. Securities and Exchange Commission (effective from May 2010) require money market funds to hold a larger share of highly liquid assets, to reduce their ability to invest in securities that bear significant credit risk, and to impose stricter maturity limits. Solvency II, the capital adequacy for European insurers scheduled to come into effect in 2012, makes the capital needs of insurance firms more sensitive to credit risk and market risk. As a result, insurance firms might review the attractiveness of investments in long-term bank bonds. Moreover, investment decisions might become increasingly sensitive to changes in bank ratings. The upshot is that one major source of long-term bank funding might become more expensive.

Regulation that leads to a better pricing of counterparty and liquidity risk should help to prevent banks' overreliance on short-term wholesale funding. And greater risk sensitivity could help to strengthen risk management and monitoring of investors in bank debt. At the same time, regulatory changes could interact, affecting banks' funding conditions in ways that are hard to predict.

Increased Host-Country Oversight

Before discussing why governments might force international banks operating in their jurisdiction to hold liquid assets locally, one issue deserves mention. Governments with large budget deficits have throughout history been tempted to force the central bank, the commercial banks, or institutional investors such as pension funds to buy and hold the debt securities they issue. These pressures frequently extend to bonds issued by government-sponsored corporate entities (including those related to mortgage finance). Such policies undermine fiscal discipline and distort the pricing of maturity risks. This issue, relevant today given the large structural fiscal deficits in many countries, needs to be kept in mind.

But it is legitimate for governments to ensure that banks operating in their jurisdictions hold some form of liquid assets to cover outflows of funds under stress and to protect local depositors. Alan Bollard's remarks in 2004, suggesting that the areas of potential divergence between home and host supervisors are likely to become most apparent in a situation of stress when the stakes are highest, look very prescient in the light of the crisis.[34]

34. Bollard said, "In times of stress, the allocation of capital and risk within the group can be crucial . . . the home and host countries may have very different views on the choice of techniques for responding to bank distress . . . and quite different perceptions of when a crisis is systemic." Alan Bollard, "Being a Responsible Host: Supervising Foreign-Owned Banks," address to the 2004 Federal Reserve Bank of Chicago Conference, Systemic Financial Crises: Resolving Large Bank Insolvencies (www.rbnz.govt.nz/speeches/0158779.html).

Host-country liquidity regulation is one traditional approach to ensure that banks hold sufficient liquid assets domestically and that these assets are not transferred to the parent in a crisis. Such regulation would be less necessary if there were an effective international agreement on bank resolution and if it were credible that the legal and political authorities in both home and host countries would actually abide by its provisions in a crisis.

Various regulatory initiatives aiming at strengthening liquidity requirements are under way. There is a strong demand for quantification: private sector counterparties dealing with opaque and complex firms argue for the publication of some benchmark measures. The Basel Committee on Banking Supervision proposed, for the first time, a global minimum standard.[35] This is designed to expand and harmonize existing approaches used by national supervisors and the banking industry (that is, liquidity coverage ratios and net liquid assets and cash capital methodologies). The definition of liquid assets includes not only cash and government bonds but also corporate bonds and covered bonds that meet certain criteria.[36] Global liquidity requirements are new, and it will take time for banks to adapt their diverse liquidity risk management practices.

From the perspective of the geographical organization of international bank funding, the scope of application of liquidity regulation is of great importance. If liquidity requirements were applied only at the level of the worldwide consolidated entity, the geographical organization of a banking group (and thus the degree of centralization) would be inconsequential. Although intended as a global standard for regulating the consolidated entity, the Basel Committee's consultative paper nonetheless gives host jurisdictions the option of applying the standards on a legal entity basis as well.

A few regulators have announced their intention to apply quantitative liquidity requirements to the subsidiaries and branches of foreign banks in their jurisdiction.[37] The main departure from current practice is that some host regulators will require quantitative liquidity ratios to be satisfied by all entities on a stand-alone basis. In some instances, such practices may be used to induce banks to buy the debt issued by host-country governments. This may well confront many foreign subsidiaries and branches active in those jurisdictions with binding constraints.

The combination of consolidated (home) and host-country regulation of banks' foreign operations can force several changes in international bank funding and liquidity management. The first is to decentralize important aspects of liquidity management. Compliance with local liquidity requirements may require

35. This is laid out in Basel Committee on Banking Supervision (2010).

36. For the precise definition of liquid assets under Basel III, see Basel Committee on Banking Supervision (2010).

37. See Committee on the Global Financial System (2010b) for details.

setting up local treasury functions for the measurement of regulatory ratios and the management of liquid asset holdings. One important drawback could be the fragmentation of liquidity holdings. While banking groups under consolidated regulation may hold liquid assets at the central treasury, local regulation could require each entity to hold liquid assets in the host country, possibly in local currency, to meet local liquidity requirements without reliance on other parts of the group.

But there are also advantages. Local liquidity regulation is likely to limit maturity and currency mismatches across the banking group. If currency and maturity mismatches offset each other to some extent when consolidated across jurisdictions, this form of diversification would no longer be recognized by host supervisors focused on the legal entity alone. Pressure to reduce mismatches at local entities may work toward lowering the overall mismatches of the consolidated group as a whole.

Global Liquidity and Its Management

This chapter explains that the term *liquidity* has very many connotations. One key dimension internationally is liquidity in global interbank markets, which remains strained. The price-based measures (Libor-OIS and implied forex spreads shown in figures 2-1 and 2-5, respectively) are described. One crude quantity-based measure, shown in the top panel of figure 2-9, is global interbank claims. This declined from a peak of almost $9 trillion at the end of the first quarter of 2008 to less than $6 trillion by the end of 2009.

The official sector has created a huge amount of liquidity globally to offset this massive private sector shift. That this has happened is beyond doubt, but defining it precisely is of course impossible. Hervé Hannoun suggests, as a rough-and-ready calculation, adding central bank assets in advanced economies (panel B) to foreign exchange reserves of the major emerging market economies (panel C).[38] On this calculation, global official liquidity rose from about $7 trillion in mid-2007 to around $12 trillion by the end of 2009.

Hannoun argues that such policies could create a "new permanent accommodative monetary policy regime" as central banks or governments seek to influence the entire length of yield curves. Therefore it will be up to international banks to reform the business strategies that, ultimately, led to the great liquidity freeze. Regulators and central banks will have to play their part in preventing an excessive buildup of liquidity risks in the global financial system.

38. Hervé Hannoun, "Unwinding Public Interventions after the Crisis," speech, IMF High-Level Conference, Washington, December 3, 2009 (www.bis.org/speeches/sp091208.htm).

Figure 2-9. *Liquidity in International Markets, 2006–10*

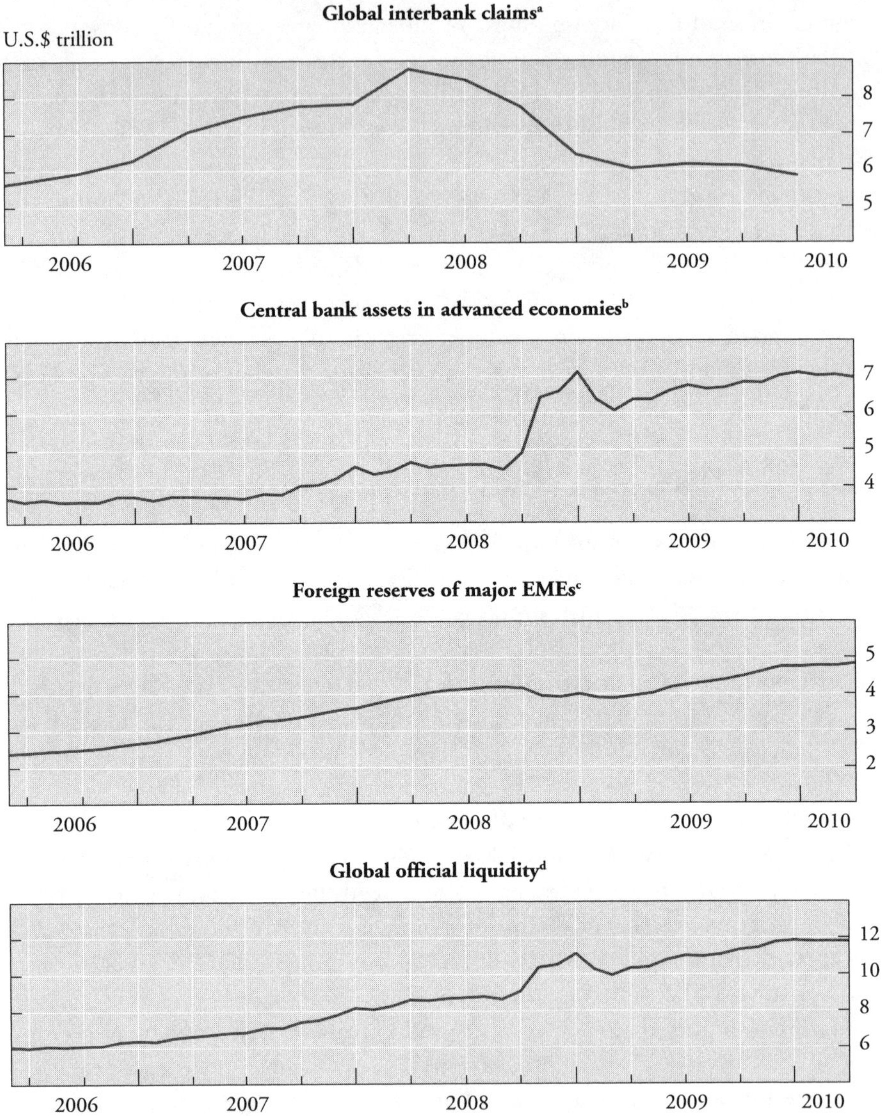

Source: Bank for International Settlements, consolidated statistics (ultimate risk basis); Datastream; national data.

a. Bank for International Settlements reporting banks consolidated foreign claims of on banks worldwide.

b. Total for the United States, the euro area, Japan, Canada, Sweden, Switzerland, and the United Kingdom.

c. Total of major emerging market economies (Brazil; China; Taipei,China; Hong Kong, China; India; Korea; Malaysia; Mexico; Russia; Singapore; Thailand; and Turkey).

d. Panels B plus C.

This chapter argues that the management and regulation of the liquidity of banks is very difficult. The discussions about liquidity ratios that took place in the early 1980s, and that failed to produce an international agreement on the regulation of bank liquidity, show this clearly. The structure of bank balance sheets that gave rise to the severe funding vulnerabilities from 2007 took years to develop; it was not just a short-lived lapse in banks' risk management. Bankers who were interviewed in the CGFS exercise were well aware of the great challenges this involves. International banks seem set to gradually increase local funding of local assets and to monitor more closely liquid reserves and liabilities at headquarters. The fact that banks in emerging market economies came through the crisis largely unscathed should not lull regulators into complacency. The financing by banks of heavy infrastructure and housing investment by short-term liabilities could expose banks in these economies to larger liquidity risks.

Policy action will have to be far-reaching and forceful. Particular attention must be paid to how new regulations for banks, for nonbank intermediaries such as money market mutual funds, for insurance companies, and for markets interact with each other. Regulation will have to be adaptable as lessons are learned about new international policies. Policymakers need to find ways both to prevent an autarkic approach to the liquidity of the affiliates of international banks and to ensure that the reliquification of the global banking system does not lead to a prolonged credit squeeze.

References

Allen, William, and Richhild Moessner. 2010. "Central Bank Cooperation and International Liquidity in the Financial Crisis of 2008–09." Working Paper 310. Basel: Bank for International Settlements.

Baba, Naohiko, Robert McCauley, and Srichander Ramaswamy. 2009. "US Dollar Money Market Funds and Non-US Banks." *BIS Quarterly Review* (March).

Baba, Naohiko, Frank Packer, and Teppei Nagano. 2008. "The Spillover of Money Market Turbulence to FX Swaps and Cross-Currency Swap Markets." *BIS Quarterly Review* (March): 73–86.

Bank of England. 1981. "The Liquidity of Banks." *Quarterly Bulletin* (March): 40–41.

———. 2009. *Financial Stability Review.* June.

Bank for International Settlements. 2009. *79th Annual Report.* June.

———. 2010. "The Global Crisis and Financial Intermediation in Emerging Market Economies." BIS Papers 54. Basel.

Basel Committee on Banking Supervision. 2010. *Basel III: International Framework for Liquidity Risk Measurement, Standards, and Monitoring.* December.

Brunnermeier, Markus, and Lasse Petersen. 2009. "Market Liquidity and Funding Liquidity." *Review of Financial Studies* 22: 2201–38.

Cecchetti, Stephen, Ingo Fender, and Patrick McGuire. 2010. "Towards a Global Risk Map." Working Paper 309. Basel: Bank for International Settlements.

Chui, Michael, and others. 2010. "The Collapse of International Bank Finance during the Crisis: Evidence from Syndicated Loan Markets." *BIS Quarterly Review* (September).

Committee on the Global Financial System. 2007. "Financial Stability and Local Currency Bond Markets." CGFS Paper 28. Basel: Bank for International Settlements.
———. 2009. "Capital Flows and Emerging Market Economies." CGFS Paper 33. Basel: Bank for International Settlements.
———. 2010a. "The Functioning and Resilience of Cross-Border Funding Markets." CGFS Paper 37. Basel: Bank for International Settlements.
———. 2010b. "Funding Patterns and Liquidity Management of Internationally Active Banks." CGFS Paper 39. Basel: Bank for International Settlements.
———. 2010c. "Long-Term Issues in International Banking." CGFS Paper 40. Basel: Bank for International Settlements.
Cooke, W. Peter. 1981. "Developments in Cooperation among Banking Supervisory Authorities." Bank of England, *Quarterly Bulletin* (June): 238–44.
Davies, Howard, and David Green. 2010. *Banking on the Future: The Fall and Rise of Central Banking.* Princeton University Press.
Ellis, John. G. 1981. "Eurobanks and the Interbank Market." Bank of England, *Quarterly Bulletin* (September): 351–64.
European Central Bank. 2009. "EU Bank's Funding Structures and Policies." May.
Fostel, Ana, and John Geanakopolos. 2008. "Leverage Cycles and the Anxious Economy." *American Economic Review* 98, no. 4: 1211–44.
Goldstein, Morris, and Philip Turner. 2004. "Controlling Currency Mismatches in Emerging Markets." Washington: Peterson Institute for International Economics.
Goodhart, Charles A. E. 2007. "Liquidity Risk Management. LSE Financial Markets Group." Special Paper 175. London School of Economics.
Goodhart, Charles A. E., and Dimitrios P. Tsomocos. 2007. "Analysis of Financial Stability." Special Paper 173. Financial Markets Group, London School of Economics.
McGuire, Patrick, and Robert McCauley. 2009. "Dollar Appreciation in 2008: Safe Haven, Carry Trades, Dollar Shortage and Overhedging." *BIS Quarterly Review* (December).
McGuire, Patrick, and Peter von Goetz. 2009. "The US Dollar Shortage in Global Banking." *BIS Quarterly Review* (March).
Sayers, Richard Sidney. 1976. *The Bank of England, 1891–1944.* Cambridge University Press.
Senior Supervisors Group. 2008. "Observations on Risk Management Practices during the Recent Market Turbulence" (www.fsa.gov.uk/pubs/other/SSG_risk_management.pdf).
Shafer, Jeffrey R. 1982. "The Theory of a Lender of Last Resort in International Banking Markets." Basel: Bank for International Settlements.
Tirole, Jean. 2008. "Liquidity Shortages: Theoretical Underpinnings." Banque de France, *Financial Stability Review* (February).
Turner, Philip. 2010. "Central Banks, Liquidity and the Banking Crisis." In *Time for a Visible Hand,* edited by Stephany Griffith-Jones, José A. Ocampo, and Joseph E. Stiglitz. Oxford University Press.

3

Macroeconomic Policy Response to the International Financial Crisis through an Indian Prism

ALOK SHEEL

It is difficult at this point in time, with little benefit of hindsight and still in the midst of crisis, to say whether we are passing through yet another of those financial crises that have punctuated economic history from time to time or whether we are indeed at a historic tipping point, a watershed that will fundamentally transform the global economy, the conduct of macroeconomic policy, financial regulation, and international financial institutions.[1] The magnitude of the macroeconomic policy response is nevertheless already apparent.

The Global Financial and Economic Crisis and the Macroeconomic Policy Response

The recent financial crisis has exposed structural imbalances in the global economy; it has underscored the need to address the blunting of macroeconomic policy tools through greater global coordination; it has exposed the limits of monetary policy, even as it pressured mainstream monetary policy to effectively target financial

This chapter has benefited from substantive comments by Y. V. Reddy, Vito Tanzi, Dipak Dasgupta, Ulrich Ubartsch, Sanjaya Panth, Joshua Felman, Eswar Prasad, M. R. Anand, and Anil Bisen.

1. On the less historic possibility, see Reinhart and Rogoff (2008). On the tipping point, see Blanchard, Dell'Ariccia, and Mauro (2010), who say that, according to the International Monetary Fund, the crisis "has exposed flaws in the precrisis policy framework, forced policymakers to explore new policies during the crisis, and forces us to think about the architecture of postcrisis macroeconomic policy," p. 16.

stability through new policy tools; it has accorded fiscal policy a new-found halo despite its checkered track record, leading to unsustainable levels of debt in developed markets—which may not be easy to exit; it has led to major initiatives to restructure the global economy and finance; and it has revived old debates and questions regarding the international monetary system.

The so-called Great Moderation preceding the crisis, characterized by unprecedented high rates of growth and accelerating economic integration across the globe (table 3-1), against an apparently benign macroeconomic backdrop of stable prices and low interest rates, turned out to be simply the proverbial calm before the storm. It seems odd, even appalling, that few economists, policymakers, and multilateral surveillance bodies saw the gathering storm, especially since the proverbial calm was associated with galloping leverage and several macroeconomic anomalies.[2]

The Great Moderation and Macroeconomic Anomalies

Accelerated and rapid globalization in the run-up to the crisis increasingly blunted both monetary and fiscal policies on account of cross-border spillages through financial and trading channels and structural changes in the global economy. Alan Greenspan, erstwhile chairman of the U.S. Federal Reserve, famously referred to the "conundrum" by which the Fed was losing control of long-term interest rates on account of large capital flows induced by globalization.[3] Large capital flows were weakening monetary policy transmission through a decoupling of short-term rates (that responded to central bank interventions) and long-term rates (that responded more to capital flows).

To a great extent this surge in cross-border flows was associated with exchange rate interventions on an epic scale (in what has come to be called Bretton Woods II) and with the consequential buildup of global imbalances, which were them-

2. Queen Elizabeth of England asked luminaries at the London School of Economics in November 2008 why nobody saw the credit crunch coming. While it is almost impossible to predict a crisis, storm clouds can certainly be discerned. Some economists, such as William White and Claudio Borio at the Bank for International Settlements, did warn of the buildup of financial instability, on account of credit expansion, and too narrow a focus on consumer price stability; see White (2006). Raghuram Rajan, in a speech at the IMF conference, Jackson Hole, August 2005, also pointed to the shift away from deposit-backed banking, the growing risk appetite of bank managers, and liquidity risks, as financial systems in advanced countries became more complex (http://imf.org/external/np/speeches/2005/082705). There was also, of course, the long-standing prophet of doom, Nouriel Roubini, who famously predicted the broad contours of the coming crisis—including the housing bust and recession but not the severity of the crisis in the financial system—in his speech at the IMF on September 7, 2006. The International Monetary Fund itself had sounded a warning on the buildup of unsustainable global imbalances as early as its 2002 *World Economic Outlook,* even before the Chinese current account surpluses; also see International Monetary Fund (2007). But imbalances were expected to lead to a disorderly collapse of the dollar, not a global financial meltdown and a strengthening of the dollar. See also McKinsey Global Institute (2010).

3. Greenspan (2007), p. 381. During the Great Moderation, however, even short-term interest rates were set at rates lower than those mandated under the Taylor rule. See Taylor (2010).

Table 3-1. *Global Growth and Globalization, 1992–2010*
Percent

			CP inflation[a]	
Year	*Global growth*	*EGS/GDP*[a]	*Advanced*	*Developing*
1992–2001	3.2	21.5	2.4	38.4
2002	2.9	23.9	1.6	6.9
2003	3.6	24.1	1.9	6.7
2004	4.9	25.0	2.0	5.9
2005	4.6	27.0	2.3	5.9
2006	5.2	28.4	2.4	5.6
2007	5.3	30.2	2.2	6.5
2008	2.8	31.2	3.4	9.2
2009	−0.6	32.4	0.1	5.2
2010	4.8	27.1	1.4	6.2

Source: International Monetary Fund, *World Economic Outlook* (2010).
a. CP = commercial paper; EGS = export of goals and services.

selves anomalous, as (contrary to economic theory) capital seemed to travel uphill from developing countries to developed countries, rather than the other way around.[4] This should have raised red flags, since this capital was not being invested in the real economy but going into leveraged consumption, just as it did in Latin America following the recycling of oil surpluses in the 1970s. Infirmities in the growing complexity of the financial systems of developed countries that intermediated this leveraged consumption, however, were not on the radar screen of the International Monetary Fund (IMF), which was firmly focused on weaknesses in the financial systems of developing countries.

Likewise, the global integration of goods and services markets through trade was changing the nature of inflation, with both monetary and fiscal policies affecting the price of domestic asset markets and nontradables much more than the price of traded goods, which mostly compose the consumer price indexes targeted by central banks.[5] Consumer prices remained low despite record growth not because of the success of inflation targeting but because of the "good deflation" triggered by the integration of large emerging markets like the People's Republic of China (henceforth referred to as China) and India into the global market for tradable goods and services. Indeed, this disinflationary impulse possibly

4. The combined account surplus of developing Asia and Middle Eastern countries rose sharply from $110 billion in 2000 to $660 billion in 2007, while that of Japan rose from $120 billion to $211 billion, and that of Germany from –$33 billion to $250 billion. The U.S. current account deficit meanwhile rose from $417 billion to $731 billion. During this period the foreign currency reserves of developing and emerging economies increased by almost $4 trillion; see International Monetary Fund, *World Economic Outlook,* October 2008. Also see Bibow (2010).

5. See Borio and Filardo (2007) on inflation.

confounded central banks to contravene the Taylor Rule and keep monetary policy unusually loose for an extended period in the run-up to the crisis. The excess liquidity spilled over into asset and commodity markets and into emerging markets in search of higher yields. Since capital could move freely across borders, but labor could not, the response of employment to a domestic policy stimulus was greatly weakened, leading to the phenomenon of jobless growth and outsourcing of production.

Fiscal policy tools in developed countries were being increasingly blunted by rising structural deficits that were reducing the cyclical space necessary to respond effectively to crises. In the United States deep tax cuts and rising defense spending were increasing fiscal deficits in the period preceding the crisis, even as age-related deficits loomed ahead. In Europe, the Maastricht fiscal framework was under increasing pressure from below-replacement birth rates and lower growth, on the one hand, and escalating age-related expenditures deriving from generous social welfare schemes, on the other. This was making it increasingly difficult to adhere to the Maastricht caps of 3 percent and 60 percent, respectively, for fiscal deficits and public debt in the absence of any serious attempt to negotiate unsustainable social compacts. Expenditures and debt levels needed to be recalibrated to growth prospects going forward, rather than to historic averages. Cyclical deficits, and sustainable levels of debt, were underestimated, since trend growth was drifting downward.

Recognizing this blunting of national macroeconomic policy instruments, the G-20 has been coordinating the policies of systemically important economies to make them more effective in combating the crisis and in addressing structural problems in the global economy.[6] It is now widely acknowledged, and eminently evident in the recent rise of the G-20, that global problems now need global solutions.

The Great Moderation, which inspired some observers to spell the death of business cycles, was therefore an indication that rapid, multilayered, global integration was redefining acknowledged relationships and challenging established economic paradigms. It should therefore not be intriguing that the proximate roots of the current global crisis lay in a sector traditionally considered nontradable. Since macroeconomic policies did not adjust to changing winds, in retrospect it is also unsurprising that the world found itself trapped in a perfect storm, now widely believed to be the greatest threat to the international economy and financial system since the Great Depression, with dramatic declines in global growth, industrial production, stock markets, international trade, and credit markets comparable with trends in the 1930s.[7]

6. Borio and Filardo (2007). For a contrarian viewpoint see Woodford (2007).
7. See the periodic updates in Eichengreen and O'Rourke (2010).

Table 3-2. *Economic Measures, Lead-Up to 2008 Recession, Selected Years, 1975–2000*
Percent change

Percent change	*1975*	*1982*	*1991*	*2009*
Output per capita (PPP)	−0.13	−0.89	−0.18	−2.50
Consumption per capita	0.41	−0.18	0.62	−1.11
Investment per capita	−2.04	−4.72	−0.15	−8.74
Industrial production	−1.60	−4.33	−0.09	−6.23
Trade	−1.87	−0.69	4.01	−11.75
Capital flows/GDP	0.56	−0.76	−2.07	−6.18

Source: International Monetary Fund, *World Economic Outlook* (2009, 2010).

The Global Financial Crisis

The recent financial crisis is quite unprecedented from the viewpoint of recent memory (table 3-2) and has several parallels with the Great Depression of the 1930s. Both had their origins in the United States and were preceded by growing imbalances and intensive globalization; both were preceded by excessive liquidity and leveraging, leading to a runaway boom in asset prices; both involved the failure, or the threat of failure, of financial institutions on a large scale; both involved a run on banks, even though the run was on conventional deposit-based institutions in the 1930s and on the capital-market-based shadow banking system during the current crisis; and like the 1930s, the current crisis threatens to culminate in a protracted period of low or negative growth, deleveraging, deflation, and deglobalization. The Great Depression was also punctuated by several temporary recoveries, when it seemed that the bottom had been reached and recovery was under way. These proved to be false dawns on each occasion, as things only kept going from bad to worse.

After initially falling more sharply than in the first twelve months of both the Great Depression and the current recession (beginning June 1929 and April 2008, respectively), global output, industrial production, equity markets, and trade turned positive again. Most developed economies are technically out of the recession, and the National Bureau of Economic Research has also certified that the U.S. recession ended in June 2009, having recorded successive quarters of positive growth after several quarters of negative growth and signs of recovery in the housing market.[8] While the recovery in advanced countries is anemic compared to the aftermath of previous recessions, and relatively jobless, dynamic emerging market economies seem to be firing on all cylinders once more, having seemingly

8. S&P Case-Shiller house price indexes (www.standardandpoors.com/indices/sp-case-shiller-home-price-indices/en/us/?indexId=spusa-cashpidff—p-us).

decoupled from OECD countries. Instead of their growth being driven by OECD countries, they seem to be driving growth in the latter.

The global economy nevertheless remains on steroids, propped up by extraordinary fiscal and monetary life support. The U.S. housing finance sector is still virtually nationalized, with most of the repayment risk ultimately devolving on government-sponsored enterprises like Fannie Mae and Freddie Mac, which are in turn backstopped by the U.S. Treasury. While large brick and mortar corporates are able to tap bond markets (which they could indeed do through the entire crisis), the shallow recovery in the banking system is hampering the traditional drivers of employment and growth of past recessions in the United States, namely, small and medium-sized enterprises.

While the banking system in developed countries has so far been unable to drive sustainable recovery of the real economy in advanced countries, it has nevertheless returned to profitability on the back of taxpayer bailouts and unprecedented monetary easing, conventional and unconventional, that has given it access to unlimited amounts of low-cost funding. Consumers are still repairing their damaged balance sheets. Housing equity in the United States that funded much of the consumption in the past continues to decline, as housing prices have resumed their downward trend after showing some signs of recovery. Although showing a declining rate, delinquency rates in residential real estate loans in the first quarter of 2011 were still around three times higher than the earlier peak recorded over the last twenty-five years for which data are available on the U.S. Federal Reserve website.[9] Credit markets in developed markets are still timid, as private deleveraging continues apace, with depository institutions continuing to park huge amounts of money with the Federal Reserve, even as total deleveraging in the system is limited by public leveraging on a scale unprecedented in peacetime.[10]

Toxic assets, much of which are now parked on the hugely expanded sheets of central banks, show few signs of recovering their former value. The market response to the new and tighter Basel-III capital and liquidity norms, including their extended phase-in, is still unclear. Despite the rapid growth of trade among emerging market intermediates, the destination of much of their final production still lies in OECD countries. It is consequently too early to definitively discount the possibility of a second dip once inventories are built up. Only when fiscal and monetary life-support systems are withdrawn and replaced by private demand can the recovery be considered assured and sustainable.

9. Federal Reserve, "Charge-Off and Delinquency Rates on Loans and Leases at Commercial Banks," release (www.federalreserve.gov/releases/chargeoff/delallsa.htm).

10. McKinsey Global Institute (2010). For continuing declines in U.S. commercial paper outstanding, see Federal Reserve release, "Commercial Paper Rates and Outstanding Summary" (www.federalreserve.gov/releases/cp). Also see Federal Reserve release (www.federalreserve.gov/releases/h3/hist/h3hist1.pdf).

While extraordinary fiscal and monetary policies adopted by G-20 countries, and forbearance in keeping markets open, are widely credited for having averted a second Great Depression, the global economy nevertheless appears to be at an inflection point.[11] It is teetering between recovery in the real economy and renewed strains in financial markets, induced by a crisis brewing in the euro zone that is threatening to boil over into the wider global economy. This disconnect between the real economy and financial markets is eerily familiar, a throwback to the confounding debate in the early stages of the global financial crisis. It was forgotten then, and is perhaps overlooked now, that the real economy lags developments in the financial sector. Financial markets eventually caught up with the real economy—and how! They could well do so again.

The origins and transmission channels of the recent global financial crisis, in which defaults in a small (subprime) segment of the American housing mortgage market pulled down the entire edifice of global finance, are too complex to detail here. Suffice it to say that most economists fall into two main camps. The first camp points to regulatory, policy, and supervisory failures, which saw a rapidly increasing proportion of financial intermediation migrate to the lightly regulated, complex, and interconnected shadow banking system, a banking system with no central bank liquidity backstops on the one hand, and excessively loose monetary policy, on the other.[12] This made it possible for a problem in a small segment of the U.S. housing market to virtually take out the entire structure of global finance.

11. WTO/OECD/UNCTAD (2010). Despite several minor protectionist steps, the World Trade Organization's assessment for the G-20 is that markets have by and large remained open. Having repeatedly sounded warnings on the catastrophic consequences of protectionism (as witnessed during the Great Depression), the G-20 can perhaps take some credit for this. The Smoot-Hawley Act of 1930 raised import duties on over 20,000 items and provoked retaliation from other countries. Global trade volumes consequently shrank sharply, from $36 billion in 1929 to just $12 billion in 1932. These tariffs are widely credited for tipping a recession into the Great Depression as U.S. exports dropped from $5.2 billion to $1.2 billion; see Chen Deming, "Protectionism Doesn't Pay," *Wall Street Journal,* February 20–22, 2009. Having said this, it would be well to keep in mind that the size and structure of world trade has changed enormously since the 1930s. While imports grew from 5 percent to 15 percent of GDP between 1929 and 2009, global production chains also mean that there are few domestic stakeholders supporting raising tariff walls, as was done during the Great Depression through the Smoot-Hawley tariffs. Protection to domestic industry is now more likely to be done through fiscal support measures, export taxes, discriminatory labor policies, aggressive exchange rate management, and other unconventional and nontariff routes. In short, fiscal and monetary policies have taken over the burden of trade policy.

12. The U.S. urban consumer price index rose by just 10 percent between June 2000 and March 2004. The U.S. Case-Shiller housing index rose by 60 percent during the same period. The Federal Reserve serially lowered the intended Fed funds rate from 6.5 percent to 1 percent over this period. Be that as it may, Fed policy was even looser than what these benign consumer inflation trends warranted, and it violated the very principles that had informed its policy over the last few decades. See *The Economist,* October 18, 2007, for graph showing the deviation of the Fed funds rate from the Taylor rule. (The Taylor rule was derived from Fed policies that had worked well during the Great Moderation.)

The second camp focuses on growing and unsustainable global imbalances, fueled by Bretton Woods II, that greatly increased global liquidity, lowered interest rates and return to capital, and fueled hyperleverage, financial innovation and excessive risk taking.

As the entire developed world slipped into synchronized recession and deflation, central banks across the globe were constrained to use their full armory of monetary policy tools, both conventional and unconventional, in a desperate attempt to pull the economy from the edge of economic Armageddon. As it became apparent that transmission channels of monetary policy, the first line of macroeconomic defense, were failing, governments supplemented central banks' efforts with fiscal expansion on a scale never seen in peacetime. Just as it appeared that the aggressive monetary, and particularly fiscal, policies may have pulled the global economy from the brink of a second Great Depression, deeper roots—which may have sprouted even before the subprime mortgage mess—were uncovered in the euro zone. Despite its aggregate external balance, monetary union in the late 1990s papered over deep internal imbalances, with southern European countries running huge current account or fiscal imbalances, which could be cheaply leveraged on the strength of the balance sheets of robust northern economies, such as Germany, France, and the Netherlands.

The globally synchronized downturn, characterized by a simultaneous deterioration in external demand and domestic revenues, exposed the frailties inherent in such internal imbalances. It now appears that European banks were hugely exposed to subprime sovereign debt in their own backyard, over and above the private exposures they may have taken. Suddenly European banks seem more vulnerable than their American counterparts, which have mostly recapitalized their losses. Financial markets eventually caught up with these economies, raising their sovereign borrowing spreads to levels that effectively mean they have been priced out of debt markets, raising fears of sovereign default and a double-dip recession. Fingers in treasuries and central banks across the globe are mostly still crossed that the global financial crisis does not morph into a full-blown sovereign debt crisis, for concerns relating to mounting deficits and public debt are no longer confined to "club Mediterranean" countries. The European Financial Stability Facility (EFSF), complemented by the IMF backstop, has failed to quell market fears regarding the health of European banks and sovereign balance sheets, as the underlying problem runs very deep and entails bold political decisions for its resolution.

As the German chancellor, Angela Merkel, sagely observed, large deficits make governments cede control to markets, since deficits need to be funded. If sovereign borrowing costs were to rise, servicing even current debt levels would become more difficult despite bold austerity measures, as some euro zone countries are discovering. Markets also fear that this might constrain central banks to keep policy rates unnaturally low and persist with quantitative easing for an extended period of time to prop up sovereign debt, fueling the kind of asset bubbles that lay behind the recent global financial crisis.[13]

The Macroeconomic Policy Response

The policy response to the recent crisis was tempered by lessons learned from macroeconomic management ever since the Great Depression, in particular the interplay between monetary and fiscal policies. Following the inflationary 1970s, and the overreliance on Keynesian economics that underscored discretionary fiscal policies to stimulate growth, monetary policy administered through independent central banks gradually came to occupy the first line of defense in stabilizing growth. According to the IMF, past experience on the use of fiscal policies indicates that they have been by and large ineffectual in developing countries, and even in developed countries they have worked only where they have been timely, temporary, and targeted, which has rarely been the case on account of the political process they need to navigate.[14] Monetary policy itself had become less discretionary and more rule based, with several central banks using variants of the Taylor rule to stabilize growth and some moving to pure inflation targeting.

MONETARY POLICY. Conventional monetary policy consists of a benchmark short-term interest rate that is transmitted along the entire yield curve. Lowering rates steepens the yield curve, thereby stimulating banks to lend more as extending credit becomes more profitable. This in turn increases the velocity of money in circulation, which stimulates economic activity. Tight monetary policy flattens the yield curve, making banks more reluctant to lend. To sum, lower short rates lead to a lower long rate, which determines GDP.

At the best of times, however, monetary policy transmission has long leads and lags and may, on its own, be inadequate in heading off a rapid deterioration in the economy. Lowering rates make deposits incrementally unattractive, while recessionary conditions make potential borrowers less creditworthy and also less willing to borrow on account of economic uncertainty. As bank balance sheets deteriorate, their capital gets overstretched, with fresh lending having a debt-restructuring bias rather than an investment bias.

As the global financial crisis deepened, it became abundantly clear that in an environment of fear monetary policy had become unusually impotent: transmission channels were failing because of frictions in the interbank market.[15] Banks were feared to be carrying indeterminate amounts of illiquid "toxic" assets both

13. George Melloan, "The Fed Has Trapped Itself on Rates," *Wall Street Journal* (Asia), June 2, 2011.

14. International Monetary Fund, *World Economic Outlook,* October 2008, chap. 5.

15. The Libor-OIS and Treasury eurodollar (TED) spreads are widely used measures of the health of interbank markets. Usually below 30 basis points in normal times, at the height of the financial crisis Libor-OIS spreads breached 400 basis points (www.bloomberg.com/apps/quote?ticker=.LOIS3:IND), while TED spreads breached 400 basis points (www.bloomberg.com/apps/quote?ticker=.TEDSP:IND); both were unprecedented.

on and off the balance sheet. This made other banks wary of lending to them.[16] There are, moreover, limits to the use of rule-based monetary policy, since interest rates cannot dip below zero. These limits are breached as inflation rates drop and the output gap grows, and there is little demand for money even when central bank discount rates are zero bound. Since banks were unwilling or unable to do so despite central banks' attempts to steepen the yield curve, central banks had to step in to compensate for the reduced velocity of money in circulation (on account of deleveraging) and to lower risk spreads. Ben Bernanke, current chair of the U.S. Federal Reserve and a historian of the Great Depression, postulates that in these circumstances central banks are constrained to resort to unconventional monetary policy, expanding money supply not only through its usual discount window but also through purchase of government (quantitative easing) or private (credit easing) assets, giving him the epithet of Helicopter Ben, as this is tantamount to dropping money by helicopter.[17] The U.S. Fed and the Bank of England did this on a massive scale to counter the effect of deleveraging on money supply.[18] By now, however, the financial crisis had morphed into a recession, and the demand for credit also declined sharply. With policy rates zero bound, and banks parking their excess funds, including the reserve money created by unconventional monetary easing, back with central banks, monetary policy in several advanced countries seemed to fall virtually into the kind of liquidity trap that Japan fell into the 1990s.

16. Estimates and definitions of toxic assets were rapidly revised upward, beginning with the original estimate of $150 billion made by Ben Bernanke in his August 2007 testimony before the U.S. Congress. The International Monetary Fund revised its estimate of potential write-downs of 2007–10 to a dramatic $4 billion in April 2009. Of this, assets originating in the United States accounted for $2.7 trillion, with the rest originating in Europe (whose banks had a big exposure to eastern and central Europe) and Japan. Nouriel Roubini's estimate was $4.6 trillion, of which $3.6 trillion was of U.S. origin. Nouriel Roubini, "The Dead Cat Bounce," *Business Standard,* April 15, 2009 (www.business-standard.com/india/news/nouriel-roubinidead-cat-bounce/355134). Although banks have since been able to mobilize capital against these toxic assets, and although their market has also risen and the IMF has consequently been progressively revising the losses downward, the current estimate of expected and realized bank write-downs nevertheless stood at $2.3 trillion in April 2010 (International Monetary Fund, 2010b). These estimates do not include provisions for losses arising out of possible sovereign defaults in southern Europe.

17. Ben Bernanke, chairman, Federal Reserve Bank, speech at National Economists Club, Washington, November 21, 2002 (www.federalreserve.gov/boardDocs/speeches/2002/20021121/default.htm).

18. Since $M * V = P * Q$ (where M = money in circulation, V = velocity of money, P = nominal price level, and Q = output), at any given money supply a reduction in the velocity of money would lead to a decline in nominal prices or a decline in output or both. Federal Reserve assets, which had increased gradually from $824 billion on November 10, 2004, to $942 billion on September 10, 2008 (before the Lehman crisis), rose dramatically by November 12, 2008, to $2.25 trillion. They stood at $2.6 trillion as of March 23, 2011, amounting to over 14 percent of GDP. The Bank of England gilt purchases in response to the crisis were also substantial, standing at 13.7 percent of the U.K. GDP at the end of the third quarter of 2010. The European Central Bank's unconventional policy was much more modest in scale, amounting to just 0.7 percent of GDP (www.federalreserve.gov/releases/h41/hist/h41hist1.pdf). See also International Monetary Fund (2010a).

The Federal Reserve's unorthodox monetary easing underwent several stages. Its balance sheet did not start expanding in the initial stages of the credit crunch from August 2007 until the collapse of Lehman Brothers. During this initial phase it off-loaded securities to accommodate the expansion of its liquidity facilities. It lent freely, at very low rather than penal rates, not only to fractional depository institutions, which it was bound to, but also to nondepositary investment banking. The time-tested Walter Bagehot rule had to be flouted, because financial institutions had become too big, interconnected, and systemically critical to be allowed to fail.

The Fed's balance sheet expanded sharply following the collapse of Lehman Brothers, as it stepped up both its liquidity support and purchase of facilities. It phased out its liquidity support facilities over the next twelve months but continued to purchase securities. It stopped buying securities in early 2010, swapping its maturing private securities (credit easing) for the purchase of government securities (quantitative easing). As monetary policy failed to gain traction, the Fed launched its ambitious $600 billion "QE 2" in November 2010. Its balance sheet now stands at three times what it was at the start of the financial crisis and is still expanding. Both the collapse of private demand and the continuing quantitative easing are keeping the yields on U.S. government securities low despite the government's huge borrowing program.

While credit easing gradually transferred much of the toxic assets from the private sector to the balance sheets of central banks, and quantitative easing supported the price of Treasury securities at a time of unprecedented fiscal easing, these could do little to stem the deleveraging under way. It is clear from table 3-3 that much of the liquidity injected by the Federal Reserve has not led to commensurate credit expansion, since most of this was parked with the central bank itself, as depository institutions just keep increasing their federal balances. In a true liquidity trap neither conventional nor unconventional monetary policy may work, as monetary policy transmission channels break down. In these circumstances macroeconomic policy is constrained to fall back on fiscal policy, as in Japan since the 1990s, and in the United States and much of the developed world recently, to pull the economy out of crisis.

FISCAL POLICY. While central banks across the globe deployed the full range of monetary tools at their command to compensate for, and revive, the sharp fall in credit and private demand, developed countries were compelled to rely increasingly on fiscal policy, even as revenues shrank consequent on negative growth. Fiscal policy was used both to support private demand and to stabilize the financial sector through capital injection and guarantees.

According to IMF estimates, overall fiscal deficits in advanced economies have increased dramatically, from –1.1 percent in 2007 to –8.8 percent in 2009 and to –8.4 percent in 2010; they are projected to be –6.7 percent in 2011. In emerging countries, which were less affected and are recovering faster, fiscal deterioration

Table 3-3. *Reserves of Depository Institutions with the U.S. Federal Reserve and the Monetary Base, 2007–11*
U.S. $ trillion

	Depository institution funds			*Monetary base*	
	Total	*Own*	*Required*	*Nominal*	*Effective (E-B)*
2007					
March	0.04	0.04	0.04	0.81	0.77
November	0.04	0.04	0.04	0.83	0.79
2008					
March	0.05	–0.06	0.04	0.82	0.77
November	0.61	–0.09	0.05	1.43	0.82
2009					
March	0.78	0.17	0.06	1.64	0.86
November	1.14	0.92	0.06	2.01	0.87
2010					
March	1.18	1.09	0.06	2.10	0.92
November	1.04	0.99	0.07	1.97	0.93
2011					
March	1.44	1.42	0.07	2.40	0.96

Source: U.S. Federal Reserve, *Statistical Release H.3. Aggregate Reserves of Depository Institutions and the Monetary Base* (www.federalreserve.gov/releases/h3/hist/).

was much more modest, rising from zero in 2007 to –4.9 percent in 2009 and to –3.9 percent in 2010; it is projected at –3.0 percent in 2011.[19]

The budget deficit figures only include up-front government financing and do not reflect the full extent of contingent liabilities taken on by advanced economies to support their financial sector through guarantees. The IMF estimates that such support to the financial sector, through liquidity provisions and guarantees, was equivalent to about 10–20 percent of global GDP.[20] The U.S. government has taken on potential liabilities of about $5 trillion (but in effect open ended) through a bailout of two government-sponsored enterprises in the housing sector, Fannie Mae and Freddie Mac. It is not clear at this point in time how much of this amount would eventually be passed on to taxpayers, as this would depend upon the extent of recovery in the prices of toxic assets.[21]

19. International Monetary Fund (2010a, p. 8; 2009b).

20. The higher figure is from International Monetary Fund (2009a), the lower figure ($6 trillion) from International Monetary Fund (2010a). It is not clear whether the latter figure includes the Fannie Mae and Freddie Mac guarantees.

21. Major Western economies are putting in place financial transaction and bank taxes to recoup some or all taxpayer costs. It is however still to be seen how such taxation measures fare or how much of the taxpayer costs would actually be recovered. The IMF's latest estimates, contained in its *Fiscal Monitor* of November 2010, are that the net direct cost is currently around $1 trillion.

The most aggressive fiscal stimulus package in overall size is that of the United States, whose budget deficit rose sharply from $161 billion (1.2 percent of GDP) in 2007 to $1.4 trillion (9.9 percent of GDP) in 2009 and to $1.3 trillion in 2010 (8.9 percent of GDP); it is projected to be $1.5 trillion in 2011 (9.8 percent of GDP), although it is rather optimistically (officially) projected to fall sharply thereafter.[22]

The IMF has come a long way from its rigid, ideological approach evident during the East Asian crisis, and these lessons are apparent in its policy guidance to the G-20 on the financial crisis.[23] It has moved away from recommending contractionary policies and fiscal rectitude in the midst of crisis and plummeting growth, which it had long advocated as the central feature of structural adjustment packages for developing countries. In a sense this marks a return to the core intellectual philosophy of its chief mentor, for it was Keynes who originally advocated the need for a global collective crisis response through an institution like the IMF, which could provide liquidity support to crisis-ridden countries to maintain full employment so as to maintain global aggregate demand in the face of contracting private demand.[24]

While most countries have so far been cautious in not repeating the cardinal policy sin of contractionary fiscal policies, which in the past aggravated the contraction in private demand, conventional wisdom on the efficacy of aggressive fiscal policies since the Great Depression is mixed.[25] There are at least two concerns, just as there were toward the second half of the 1930s. One is about the sustainability of these policies even over the medium term, on account of the sharp dip in revenue in downturns and the protracted recovery from financial crises that

22. According to the Congressional Budget Office (2010, app. I), U.S. public debt since the crisis will be double that of 2001. Projections by the International Monetary Fund (*World Economic Outlook,* April 2010) also show net public debt rising (from 42.3 percent of GDP in 2007 to 85.5 percent in 2015). Rising health care, social security, and defense costs could however change the equation, as pointed out in Cecchetti, Mohanty, and Zampolli (2010). According to their estimate, even by estimates that freeze age-related spending as a percentage of GDP at 2011 levels, debt-to-GDP could still rise to 200 percent in thirty years, much higher than crisis-riven Greece and on a par with Japan since the tsunami. Advanced countries have not had such high levels of public debt since World War II. The current economic structure is however vastly different than what it was in the 1950s, which witnessed a baby boom, a productivity boom, and a growth boom, all of which helped drive down public debt. In sharp contradistinction, Western societies are now aging and growing more slowly.

23. International Monetary Fund (2009–11), prepared for the G-20. The IMF could perhaps have learned this lesson sooner from one of its more successful structural adjustment programs in India in the 1990s. The success of India's stabilization program derived partly from its persistence in slipping in fiscal targets even as other reforms were carried through in a sequenced and calibrated manner.

24. Stiglitz (2002, p. 196).

25. The U.S. fiscal balance was positive at the onset of the Great Depression but turned sharply negative by the mid-1930s, leading to concerns about fiscal sustainability. The resultant fiscal tightening coincided with another sharp dip in GDP, which had, by 1937, almost recovered to the 1929 level.

typically keep growth rates low over an extended period. The second concern is about the ability of governments to fund large deficits without increasing interest rates, which could slow the recovery of private demand and also interfere with the smooth conduct of monetary policy.

With the return of fiscal policy to the macroeconomic high table, it is necessary to minimize the attendant pitfalls so that fiscal multipliers are greater than unity and interventions can quickly restore and sustain growth.[26] Apart from the three tests of the efficacy of fiscal interventions recently underscored by the IMF—namely, timeliness, targeting, and evanescence—in view of the extent of global integration and consequential policy spillovers, a fourth test of global coordination needs to be added to ensure that the recovery process leads to a more balanced and hence sustainable global economy: fiscal policy needs to be more aggressive in countries running current account surpluses than in those running deficits to rebalance global demand. The most aggressive use of fiscal policy, however, has so far been in the deficit countries, notably the United States.

Exit from Extraordinary Macroeconomic Policies

A protracted, tepid recovery in advanced markets, coupled with continuing deleveraging and dysfunctional financial markets, has induced the U.S. Federal Reserve to repeatedly reiterate that monetary policy would remain easy for an extended period. It has also made clear its intention to continue with nonconventional monetary policy as long as necessary. While the European Central Bank (ECB) does not usually make premature announcements of its policy stances, this is not likely to be very different from that of the U.S. Fed, especially since European governments have begun fiscal tightening in the wake of adverse market signals following the southern Europe sovereign debt crisis.

Advanced economies, struggling with the fiscal fallout of rising social welfare expenditures, found that they had limited fiscal space to sustain an aggressive countercyclical stance. Fiscal space is dynamic, since a sharp decline in private demand may create a short-term fiscal space despite the rapid fiscal slide that is a recurring feature of all episodes of sharp decline in growth on account of revenue shock and expenditure increase.[27] Indeed, even highly indebted governments may

26. This is a very contentious area. While government expenditure does increase GDP, the increase could be actually less than the amount spent. It is argued, for instance, that President Obama's ambitious $787 billion American Recovery and Reinvestment Plan not only failed to make any dent whatsoever on unemployment but that the latter climbed to levels higher than what the White House predicted it would have reached even without the stimulus. At best it shifted jobs from the private to the public sector; Veronique de Rugy, senior research fellow, Mercatus Center, George Mason University, testimony before the House Budget Committee, July 14, 2010. The design of the stimulus also matters; Romer and Romer (2007).

27. According to IMF estimates, the share of revenue loss and expenditure increase in the fiscal deterioration of fiscal balances in advanced G-20 countries is about the same; International Monetary Fund, *Fiscal Monitor,* May 14, 2010, p. 14.

be able to increase their borrowing in such circumstances without unduly impacting interest rates. The absence of such market signals during severe downturns is akin to a breakdown of the immune system in the body, as a result of which severe infections may persist without the usual red flags, such as fever. However, as private demand recovers and interest rates rise, the stock of debt could become even more unsustainable than it was before the crisis, making for a potentially inflationary outcome.[28] Over the medium to long term, fiscal space is therefore merely the flip side of debt sustainability.[29]

In view of the dangerous buildup of public debt, the IMF has advised the G-20 that fiscal exit should precede monetary exit.[30] The problem with this advice is that, even as corporates are able to tap capital markets and interbank markets (Libor-OIS and TED spreads) have normalized, credit channels are still dysfunctional in advanced markets.[31] While corporate bond markets have bounced back, securitized and commercial paper markets, which provided a substantial share of financial intermediation before the crisis, have still to recover, while banks continue to deleverage and park huge amounts of their own funds with central banks.[32]

Several developed countries, in particular the United States, may already be in a liquidity trap, and hence, instead of seeding credit markets, easy monetary policy is diverting excess liquidity to Asia, where asset prices are appreciating on the back of a robust dollar carry trade. It is difficult to see how the burden of stimulating Western economies can shift back from fiscal to monetary policy in a hurry. Advanced economies could well be trapped in some sort of a Catch-22 situation, with financial markets and the economy constraining fiscal exit and financial markets becoming dependent on continued fiscal expansion. It is fairly

28. This is the modern version of debasing currency resorted to by premodern monarchs for fiscal expansion or debt repayment and is an unfortunate downside to the movement away from the gold standard and its replacement by fiat money. This is why in macroeconomic terms inflation is nothing but another form of tax. Before the 1930s governments had no alternative to taxing their way out of public debt. In real life, however, there could be special conditions under which governments need neither default nor inflate their way out, despite theoretically unsustainable debt levels, on account of the fiscal space created by contraction in private demand. This was the case of Japan, where increase in public debt was countervailed by decline in investment. It is also the case of the issuer of the global reserve currency (that is, the United States), where the rest of the world has excessive savings, which generates a demand for holding increasing amounts of the reserve currency.

29. Sovereign debt sustainability is perhaps best captured through the Domar equation, under which the debt-GDP ratio can be stabilized if either of the two conditions are met: an increase in nominal GDP exceeds interest payments (that is, the Domar gap is positive); or the primary budget deficit (fiscal/budget deficit minus interest payments) is nominal (that is, the Domar gap is negative). If neither of these conditions is met, there is imminent danger of a runaway debt trap.

30. International Monetary Fund (2009c).

31. See www.bloomberg.com/apps/cbuilder?ticker1=.TEDSP%3aind.

32. Federal Reserve, Statistical release (www.federalreserve.gov/releases/h3/current/h3.htm).

clear that use of both fiscal and monetary tools has been exhausted, and policymakers will be hard pressed to come up with an effective policy response to either a revolt in sovereign bond markets or a second dip. Indeed, policymakers are now being called upon to address the adverse fallout of overflogging macroeconomic policy tools.

While increase in public debt is the usual aftershock of deep recessions and financial crises, structural deficits in several advanced countries were already rising before the crisis on account of aging-related expenditures. Moreover, the failure of transmission channels of monetary policy, the first line of macroeconomic response to downturns, placed a disproportionate burden on fiscal policy. There are now fears that cyclical deficits and anemic growth could push countries into a debt trap unless long-standing social compacts are renegotiated and structural reforms to raise growth kick in quickly.

Governments can either grow their way out of high levels of public debt (as in the aftermath of World War II in advanced countries, when the overall growth environment was good, and as India is at present doing) or inflate their way out (as in the 1970s, following successive oil price shocks). Since long-term growth prospects in most advanced countries look shaky, market fears regarding future inflationary outcomes will not dissipate easily.

The IMF expects policymakers to navigate a narrow, Goldilocks, policy zone that is neither too early (which would derail the recovery) nor too late (which would provoke market revolt). Emerging markets facing inflationary pressures should start exiting, which they are mostly doing, and advanced countries should exit in phases, depending on each country's fiscal and market pressures. The United States, the issuer of the global reserve currency, with few market pressures on its borrowing program, seems to echo the IMF view. Major European countries, led by the OECD and Germany, at the epicenter of the potential crisis, are in favor of a front-loaded fiscal exit.

Yet while long-term fears are real, and some advanced economies may indeed be in a debt trap, some of the short-term fears are overblown. Even as sovereign borrowing spreads have risen in southern Europe, they have fallen in major advanced countries during the same period. Paradoxically, despite being insolvent, a number of advanced sovereigns do not have a liquidity problem. Collectively, sovereign borrowing costs and liquidity problems can worsen only if private demand is on track. Markets fears regarding future inflation and sovereign default are countervailed by the current need to seek refuge in safe havens. Indeed, in such circumstances rising sovereign borrowing costs is something to look forward to, akin to a canary in the gold mine signaling the revival of private demand and the time for fiscal exit.

Therein lies a second paradox, what Keynes called the paradox of thrift. Historical experience indicates that it is indeed possible to combine fiscal consolidation with growth, especially where there is greater reliance on expenditure control than on tax increases.[33] Implementing structural reforms could also raise growth potential, making debt levels more sustainable and exercising a calming influence on markets. These medium-term issues are being addressed by the G-20 through their ambitious Framework for Strong, Sustainable and Balanced Growth.

However, it is highly unlikely that it would be possible to have fiscal consolidation during a severe and synchronized economic downturn, more so since monetary policy transmission channels are still clogged. It is difficult to compress expenditure commensurate with the compression in revenue, especially since this has to partly substitute for the steep contraction in private consumption and investment. Even so, past experience indicates that most of the fiscal deterioration in a downturn is through declines in revenue rather than through increases in automatic stabilizers or discretionary stimuli.

If there are cautionary lessons to be learned from Greece, which has recently been penalized by the market for lack of fiscal credibility, there are also lessons to be learned from Japan in the 1990s and the United States in 1937, when premature fiscal tightening resulted in both a deflationary spiral and an explosion of public debt. An undeniable virtue in normal times, fiscal chastity is of dubious value in deep recessions. Advanced countries could perhaps seek solace from the ancient Christian scholar, St. Augustine of Hippo, who famously beseeched the Lord to make him chaste, but not yet.

The situation in developing countries, especially in Asia, that have weathered the crisis far better than developed countries and accelerated the recent trend in convergence in per capita incomes between the West and Asia, is different. Unlike advanced countries, emerging markets entered the crisis with improved fiscal positions. Crisis measures in Asian economies have by and large been orthodox, focused on tried and trusted fiscal and monetary easing. Since credit markets did not freeze, and financial institutions did not collapse, there was no need to resort to either a bailout of the financial sector or the adoption of an unconventional monetary policy. Conventional measures have by and large worked, for the global recovery is led by Asia.

For this reason exit policies are being implemented first in Asia. However, unlike Western markets, where fiscal exit may precede monetary exit, the sequence could be reversed in Asia, since portfolio shifts and the sustained easy and unorthodox monetary stance in the former is drowning the latter in liquidity through a surge in capital flows and robust fiscal parameters.[34] Continuing low

33. BCA Research, "Europe: A Historical View of Fiscal Reform," *Daily Insight,* May 4, 2010 (www.bcaresearch.com/public/story.asp?pre=PRE-20100504.GIF).

34. This is so even in China, which has had the most aggressive fiscal package among developing countries. China announced a 4 trillion yuan ($585.5 billion) stimulus package in November 2008 and subsequently proposed a budgeted fiscal deficit of 950 billion yuan ($139 billion) for 2009, a record high in six decades and nearly three times the last record of 319.8 billion yuan, set in 2003. The deficit however amounted to only about 3 percent of GDP.

interest rates in developed countries could however change the outlook for monetary tightening in emerging markets, as this could aggravate capital inflows. They seem to be entering into the grip of the impossible trinity: a fixed exchange rate, free capital movement, and an independent monetary policy.

India and the Global Financial and Economic Crisis

The Indian economy was in great shape before the onset of the credit crunch in Western markets. Indeed, growth had either accelerated to above trend or, more arguably, was showing signs of shifting upward because of structural shifts in domestic savings and investment (figure 3-1).

Riding on the back of robust revenue growth consequent on high growth rates and a vastly improved and reformed tax structure that made revenues increasingly sensitive to shifts in growth, the consolidated fiscal deficit of the federal and state governments fell sharply, from around 10 percent in 2001–02 to 4.17 percent in 2007–08.

India on the Eve of the Credit Crunch

In the months leading up to the credit crunch there was an animated debate over whether the Indian economy was overheating—having hit its long-time nemesis, the infrastructural bottleneck—or whether it was simply importing inflation through rising commodity prices and capital flows, as the central bank repeatedly tightened monetary policy in response to rising consumer prices.[35]

Reeling under the twin shocks of tightening monetary policy and rupee appreciation consequent on a tsunami of capital inflows, growth rates had started to show a slightly downward trend, led by a downward-sloping industrial production index, when the first waves of the financial crisis hit India. However, Indian corporates had access to domestic equity and external commercial borrowing to soften the impact of tightening monetary policy on their borrowing costs. As a result, investment did not stall, although it dipped slightly in the second half of 2007–08. The commodity shock associated with the first-round impact of the financial crisis amplified the downward trend through an added inflationary shock.

Unlike Western markets, the shadow banking system was not a major source of funding in emerging markets, including India. Financial regulation in India was based on the antediluvian view that the financial sector should be anchored in the real economy and that financial transactions, particularly derivatives, should be based on real-economy exposures and assets. Sensing a financial boom in property prices, the Reserve Bank of India (RBI) moved to raise capital adequacy margins to cool asset prices in the run-up to the global financial crisis.

35. Both concerns have resurfaced recently.

Figure 3-1. *Macroeconomic Fundamentals, India, 2000–11*

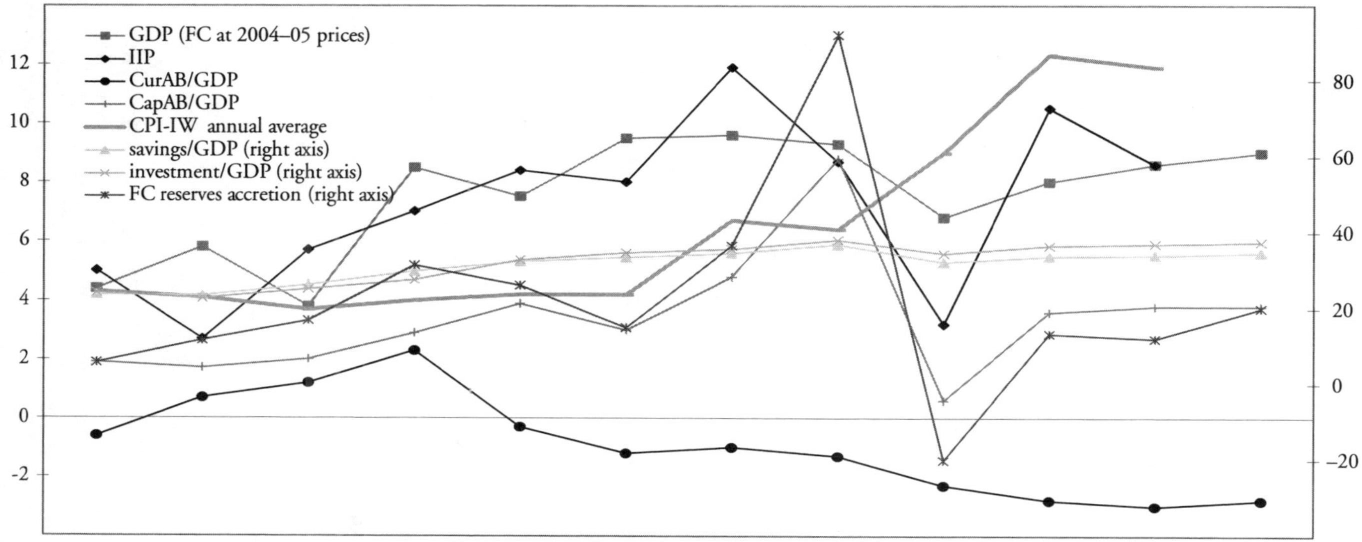

Source: Government of India, Ministry of Finance, Department of Economic Affairs, Economic Division, Economic Survey 2010–11, February 2011 (and earlier issues for historical data). Data for 2011–12 are projections from the Economic Advisory Council to the Prime Minister, Review of the Economy 2010–11, New Delhi, February 2011 (http://eac.gov.in/reports/ecoout_1011.pdf).

About 70 percent of banking assets in India are in the public sector. Since Indian banks were well capitalized, way above the Basel-II minimum norms, and had very limited exposure to the U.S. mortgage market (directly or through derivatives) or to failed or stressed financial institutions, the impact of the U.S. subprime crisis on their balance sheets was marginal. A study undertaken by the RBI in September 2007 shows that no Indian or foreign bank had any direct exposure to subprime markets in the United States or elsewhere, even though there was a small exposure to some complex and illiquid financial instruments such as collateralized debt obligations by some private sector banks, which in turn had subprime exposures. These banks suffered mark-to-market losses caused by the widening of credit spreads on these complex structured instruments.[36] The additional provisioning requirements toward mark-to-market losses were however insignificant relative to the size of their balance sheets and profit levels, and there were few concerns from the systemic point of view.

INITIAL IMPACT OF THE CREDIT CRUNCH. Since India has a huge oil deficit, the initial impact of the credit crunch was ambiguous, as the negative shock arising out of booming commodity prices was tempered by the surge in capital inflows, which led to a sharp appreciation in the value of the Indian rupee and an unprecedented bull run in the stock market (figure 3-2).[37] The policy response was to let the rupee appreciate in a smooth and orderly manner and to cushion most of the oil price shock by widening the fiscal deficit to ensure macroeconomic stability.[38] The sharp increase in the rate of reserve accretion created problems of monetary management and, along with the spike in commodity prices, added to inflationary pressures that constrained the central bank to persist with a tight monetary stance, even as the economy showed signs of weakening. While growth dipped by about 1.5 percent from the arguably above-trend growth in the preceding few quarters, the economy nevertheless chugged along at an impressive 7.75 percent in the first half of fiscal year 2008–09.

The decline in commodity prices and capital flows that began in the second half of 2008 escalated in the period following the Lehman crisis. This escalation was primarily caused by a foreign equity sell-off, a flight to quality, and the consequential repricing of risk. Indian financial institutions thus found it increasingly

36. Shri V. Leeladhar, deputy governor, Reserve Bank of India, speech at Kolkata, November 24, 2008 (www.rbi.org.in/scripts/BS_SpeechesView.aspx?Id=404).

37. While the figure shows an unmistakable direct correlation (coefficient of 0.73) between FII stocks and the Sensex between January 2007 and March 2011, asset prices rose faster than FII stocks before the financial crisis, whereas in the period following the crisis asset prices tended to lag FII stocks, indicating differences in confidence levels or animal spirits.

38. As things turned out, this quickly filled the fiscal space created in the last few years, thereby constraining the fiscal policy response to the second-round impact of the financial crisis, when growth threatened to fall sharply.

Figure 3-2. *Foreign Portfolio Stock and Asset Prices (Sensex), India, 2007–11*

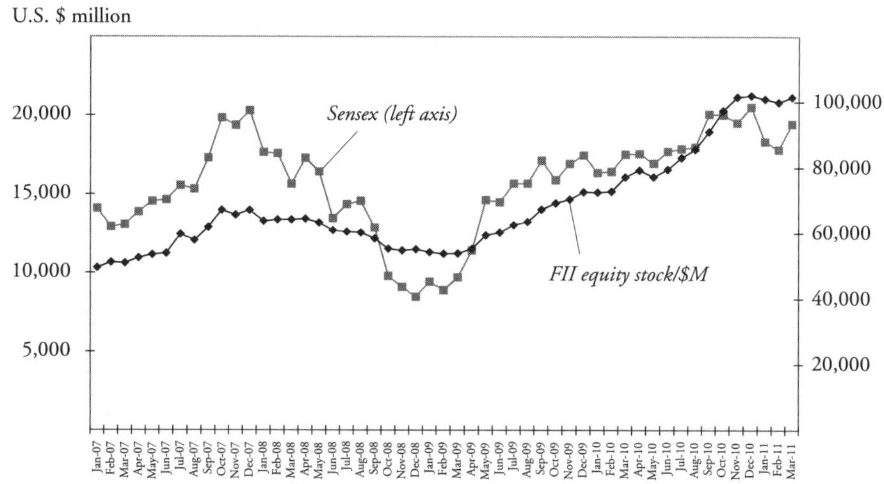

Source: Securities and Exchange Board of India, Trends in Investments, Foreign Institutional Investors Investments (www.sebi.gov.in/Index.jsp?contentDisp=Database); Bombay Stock Exchange, Archives—Indices. Sensex (www.bseindia.com/histdata/hindices.asp).

difficult to fund themselves cheaply overseas.[39] This secondary impact was transmitted to India through the pervasive sense of foreboding in domestic financial markets and the destruction of demand in Western markets.

SECOND-ROUND IMPACT OF THE CREDIT CRUNCH. Just as sharp appreciation of the rupee moderated the impact of the commodity bubble on the current account during the first-round impact, the sharp depreciation of the Indian rupee moderated the benign impact of softening oil prices in the second stage. It was mostly on account of a sharp reversal in the capital account that India's foreign currency reserves declined by $58 billion (or by about a fifth, from $299.2 billion) in fiscal year 2008–09 as of March 27, 2009, through a combination of outflows and revaluation.[40] If not for the cushion provided by the recent virtuous cycle of high growth, fiscal correction, and reserve accretion, the impact of the global financial crisis on India would have been far worse.

39. The pressure to square positions in overseas money markets in the immediate aftermath of the Lehman crisis led to a sharp rise in overnight call money rates in the domestic money market, constraining the RBI to inject large amounts of liquidity to ensure that call rates moved back within the policy rate corridor; Shah and Patnaik (2010).

40. Reserve Bank of India (1998–2011). Most of this decline was on account of revaluation of reserves denominated in various currencies. The largest outflow was on account of foreign institutional equity investors (FIIs), who took out a net of $12.1 billion between April 1, 2008, and March 31, 2009 (www.sebi.gov.in/Index.jsp?contentDisp=Database). Some of the decline was also on account of banking capital and the inability to roll over short-term debt, especially trade finance.

The international financial crisis removed the cushion that cheap external funding and equity provided against monetary tightening at home. While portfolio flows started reversing sharply from the last quarter of 2007, all forms of capital flows showed a declining trend during the third and fourth quarters of 2008, including short-term debt flow, much of which was used to finance international trade. The decline in overseas capital flows resulted in additional demand for domestic sources of funding in the near term to fill in the deficit. Practically the entire burden of adjustment fell on the banking sector, as resources raised from the domestic capital market fell sharply on account of risk aversion and tight liquidity.[41] As a result, aggregate resources (including corporate debt, initial public offerings, public and rights equity issues, private placements, and overseas issues) raised from the capital market in 2008–09 declined by 52.4 percent over 2007–08.[42]

Excessive liquidity consequent on protracted monetary easing and deleveraging in Western financial markets, combined with the revival of robust growth in emerging markets, has led to the revival of capital flows to select emerging markets, including India. By the fourth quarter of 2009, FII stocks were back to their all-time highs of late 2007, with consequential appreciation in asset markets, and have indeed increased thereafter as a result of unconventional monetary policy, such as quantitative easing, in Western markets (figure 3-2). India has a big reserve currency buffer ($303 billion as of March 25, 2011) against sharp and sudden stops or reversals in capital flows, such as what occurred in the aftermath of the Lehman Brothers crisis.

India nevertheless needs capital inflows on a continuing basis to finance its growing current account deficit, which has risen in tandem with rising energy prices, since India has a large energy deficit. Consequently, its currency has not experienced upward pressure like that experienced by the currencies of emerging economies that run current account surpluses or that are large commodity exporters, even though capital inflows in recent quarters exceeded the current account deficit. Capital inflows are critical for India's return to a high-growth trajectory not only for funding the current account deficit but also for corporates' access to cheap capital, as the cost of domestic sources of funding rises with monetary tightening. In the ultimate analysis, however, a return in India to trend growth on a sustainable basis also hinges critically on the revival of overseas demand.

Indian Macroeconomic Policy Response

Consistent with the G-20 consensus—reflected in the Washington declaration of G-20 heads of state issued in mid-November 2008 and in subsequent commu-

41. Apart from factors mentioned in the preceding note, this was also on account of the sharp increase in government borrowing.

42. Saikat Neogi, "Some Data for RBI to Chew On," *Financial Express,* New Delhi, April 17, 2009.

niqués, that greater global policy coordination was necessary to effectively address the global financial crisis—the RBI and the government of India acted in a concerted manner through major monetary and fiscal interventions to neutralize the adverse symptoms of the financial turmoil by improving liquidity and stimulating demand and investment.

MONETARY POLICY. The first-round monetary impact of the subprime financial crisis on India was to put the central bank in the grip of the impossible trinity: simultaneously trying to stabilize growth and maintain exchange rate stability in the face of rising capital inflows. With no explicit targeting of inflation or the exchange rate, India kept turning from one goal to the other, even though both were effectively determined by exogenous factors.

The most palpable result of the second-round impact of the international financial crisis on the domestic economy, which saw a sharp reversal in capital flows, was loss of both rupee and dollar liquidity for reasons that were very different from those in Western markets. Whereas the loss of liquidity in Western markets was on account of heightened perceptions of counterparty risk, rapid deleveraging, and the breakdown of transmission channels of monetary policy through the banking system, the loss of liquidity in India derived from the combination of capital flight, the inability of banks and especially corporates to fund themselves cheaply overseas and through equity markets at home outside the (relatively high-cost) domestic banking system, a growing current account deficit, and a ballooning fiscal deficit crowding out private borrowing.

Unlike Western countries, which seemed to be in the grip of a liquidity trap and where even quantitative and credit easing lost traction, monetary policy continued to be an effective macroeconomic tool in emerging economies like India.[43] The entire burden of combating recessionary forces did not, therefore, fall on fiscal policy. Indeed, the primarily publicly owned domestic banking system partially substituted for the financing space vacated by overseas borrowing and domestic equity finance. As nonbank sources of credit started drying up, bank credit actually expanded in the immediate aftermath of the Lehman crisis, until a downturn in the real economy lowered private demand and, consequently, the demand for credit (figure 3-3). In sharp contradistinction to Western economies, the channel of transmission of contagion was more from the real economy to the financial sector rather than the other way round.

In response to tightening domestic liquidity, reflected in hardening overnight rates, the central bank rapidly shifted its policy stance from tight to easy. It moved to sharply lower key policy rates and inject liquidity into the banking system. It also eased external commercial borrowing and investment policies and raised

43. Thus gross nonfood credit by scheduled commercial bank credit grew by 18.1 percent in 2008–09, only slightly lower than the 22.3 percent of 2007–08; Reserve Bank of India (2010a, table 4.5).

Figure 3-3. *Credit Extended by Scheduled Commercial Banks, 2007–11*

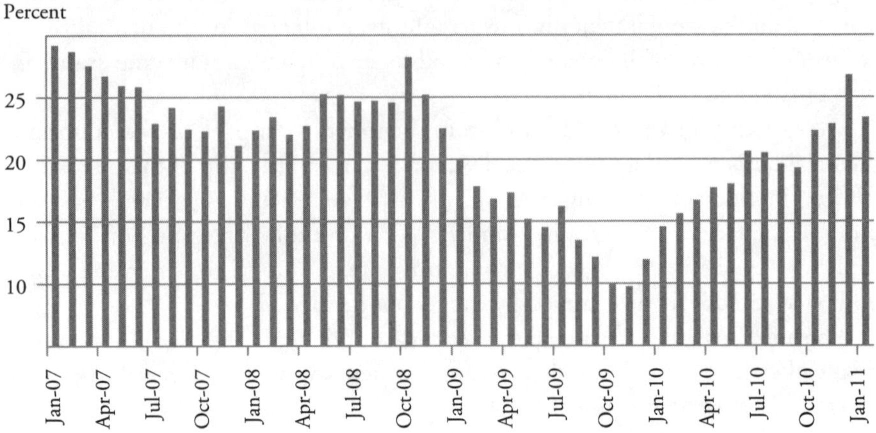

Source: Reserve Bank of India, Commercial Bank Survey (www.rbi.org.in/scripts/BS_VIEWBulletin.aspx).

deposit rates on nonresident Indian deposit schemes to reduce the friction in capital inflows. The central bank cut the benchmark overnight lending rate by 425 basis points, from 9 percent to 4.75 percent between July 29, 2008, and March 5, 2009, and also lowered the quantum of bank reserve assets to be parked with the central bank. In addition, it injected liquidity equivalent to about 9 percent of GDP by lowering bank cash reserve and liquidity requirements, unwinding sterilization measures by buying back government securities from the market and extending special refinance and liquidity facilities.[44] If these measures did not result in a commensurate increase in bank lending, this was not on account of any liquidity trap but because of renewed access to other sources of funds outside the domestic banking system and because bank credit is a lagged indicator.[45] It has since picked up smartly following the recent uptick in growth (figure 3-3).

44. Reserve Bank of India (2009b, para. 55).

45. Morgan Stanley, *India EcoView,* January 22, 2010, p. 12. Credit growth declined sharply in 2009–10 despite monetary loosening. But since this decline was accompanied by an increase in growth, it appears that corporates had accessed other sources of funding, even as banks increased their holdings of government debt (given the sharp increase in government borrowings) and also parked funds with the central bank. While nonfood bank credit decelerated sharply from its peak of over 29 percent in October 2008 to a little over 10 percent in October 2009, before picking up slightly to over 14 percent by mid-January 2010, the total flow of financial resources to the commercial sector as of January 15, 2010, was unchanged from the corresponding period of the previous year. Reserve Bank of India (2010b); D. Subbarao, governor, Reserve Bank of India, press statement (http://rbidocs.rbi.org.in/rdocs/PressRelease/PDFs/IEPR1052TQR.pdf). There are of course also residual issues regarding the transmission of monetary policy in view of illiquid corporate bond markets and key administered deposit rates. This is one reason why the central bank still uses such monetary aggregate policy tools as the statutory liquidity ratio and the cash reserve ratio, in addition to such benchmark short-term rates as the repurchase agreement and the reverse repurchase agreement.

FISCAL POLICY. Unlike Western economies, there was no need in India for fiscal intervention to support the financial sector. Fiscal policy basically worked in tandem with monetary policy to counter the contraction in private demand. Despite limited fiscal space, the Indian (central) government announced a series of major stimulus packages aggregating a net outgo of about $35 billion (Rs 160,000 crore) through three supplemental parliamentary grants, equivalent to over 3 percent of GDP, over and above the budgeted fiscal deficit of 2.5 percent, for 2008–09.[46] The fiscal stimulus instruments included enhanced outlays on social protection and employment-generation schemes, infrastructure, trade finance and promotion, and indirect tax reductions.[47] In addition state governments were given headroom for a further fiscal stimulus equal to 0.5 percent of GDP in 2008–09 and another 0.5 percent in 2009–10. The fiscal stimulus instruments also liberalized norms to improve access to resources and liquidity, both domestically and externally through equity and debt. A new automatic stabilizer, the National Rural Employment Guarantee Scheme (NREGS), made it possible to immediately ramp up consumption expenditure among the poorest sector of the population, where the multiplier impact on growth is high. Outlays on this automatic stabilizer were ramped up in the revised estimates for the 2008–09 budget, from 0.6 percent of GDP to 1.2 percent.[48] These elevated levels were maintained in 2009–10 as well.

At the onset of the global financial crisis, the central government's debt-to-GDP ratio was just above 60 percent, far higher than that of the United States, which was around 40 percent. It would therefore appear that India had far less cyclical fiscal space than the United States. Its (combined central and state governments) fiscal deficit of 4.2 percent (excluding off-balance-sheet liabilities, which would raise this figure) was also much higher than that of the United States. However, since India's trend, and hence revenue, growth is much higher than that of the United States, it is able to sustain higher levels of debt when assessed through the Domar debt sustainability equation. Fast-growing developing countries can sustain much higher levels of fiscal deficit and public debt than

46. The consolidated fiscal deficit of the central and state governments had gradually been reduced from around 10 percent of GDP in 2001–02 to below 6 percent by 2006–07; see Economic Advisory Council (2008, p. 50). This widened to 8.5 percent in 2008–09, and to 9.5 percent in 2009–10, excluding liabilities incurred off balance sheet. The consolidated fiscal deficit in 2010–11 is estimated to be 8 percent. India also has a huge public debt overhang, equivalent to 76.6 percent of GDP in 2009–10, the lagged effect of several years of high fiscal deficits, making its fiscal position one of the weakest among emerging market economies.

47. In addition, the Indian government liberalized norms, disbursed an additional $5.2 billion to help problems caused by the credit crunch, and helped recapitalize banks to enable them to expand lending. The World Bank (2009) observes that Brazil and India were the most proactive emerging market economies in trying to fill financing gaps for public-private projects.

48. This was part of the three supplementary demands for grants passed by the national parliament.

the European Maastricht Treaty norms of 3 and 60 percent, respectively. It is for this reason that India has been able to run relatively high levels of fiscal deficit and to sustain high debt-to-GDP ratios without inflationary consequences or adverse economic growth. Prudently used, this fiscal space can be used to fund the huge infrastructural and developmental backlog in such countries. However, if this space is used for increasing government consumption rather than investment, it might be difficult to sustain high growth rates over the medium to long term, and the space could rapidly shrink.

The fiscal space of fast-growing developing countries is constrained not so much structurally as by the competing demands of the private sector on the debt market. Excessive borrowing by government can crowd out private demand and exert an upward pressure on interest rates, which can lower growth and, consequently, compress fiscal space. If India's relatively high fiscal deficits have not had a significant upward pressure on interest rates, this has been largely on account of large-scale monetization consequent on the central bank's intervention in foreign currency markets and open-market operations (buying government debt in the secondary market), which would be considered a species of quantitative easing in developed markets. High levels of government borrowing, therefore, have been accompanied by quantitative easing even in non-crisis situations, as there is no firewall between fiscal and monetary policies.

The scale of fiscal expansion to finance various stimulus measures can be gauged from the fact that the government's net borrowings almost doubled in 2008–09 and rose by a further 70 percent in 2009–10. Market borrowings in 2010–11 declined slightly relative to 2009–10 only on account of a big, one-time, windfall through the auction of government assets (2G spectrum telecommunication licensing fees). The market was initially able to absorb such high levels of government borrowings without putting upward pressure on interest rates on account of the sharp contraction in private demand, the front-loading of the government's borrowing program by the central bank, and the latter's open-market operations through off-loading its stock of government securities, mostly accumulated through sterilizing the huge capital inflows in the period leading up to the crisis.[49] However, as private demand returns and the central bank's stock of government securities is depleted, the central bank may have to step up the scale of its quantitative easing program, including unsterilized interventions in the foreign exchange market, to support the government's borrowing program if the deficit is not reined in.

Fiscal expansion sustained growth during the crisis, as private consumption, exports, and investment fell (table 3-4). The increase in government final consumption expenditure partly compensated for this decline, beginning in the third quarter of fiscal year 2007–08, to prop up demand and growth. The table also

49. Reserve Bank of India (2009a); Economic Advisory Council (2009).

Table 3-4. *Quarterly Expenditure Growth Rates, India, 2007–11*[a]

Percent

	2007–08				2008–09				2009–10				2010–11			
Item	*Q1*	*Q2*	*Q3*	*Q4*	*Q1*	*Q2*	*Q3*	*Q4*	*Q1*	*Q2*	*Q3*	*Q4*	*Q1*	*Q2*	*Q3*	*Q4*
PFCE[b]	9.5	8.3	9.8	9.3	10.0	7.8	6.7	6.6	7.3	8.5	7.0	6.6	8.9	8.9	8.6	8.0
GFCE[c]	−0.4	12.2	4.1	20.9	−1.6	2.0	50.9	−2.8	21.3	37.5	9.6	6.1	6.7	6.4	1.8	5.0
Investment[d]	19.7	20.7	16.6	12.9	−1.1	0.5	−5.8	−5.2	6.1	7.1	15.2	25.3	17.4	12.1	8.2	2.2
CAB[e]	19.2	20.2	15.1	11.6	4.1	5.2	−2.0	−0.6	−0.4	0.3	8.7	19.2	17.4	11.9	7.8	0.4
Exports	2.6	0.2	13.5	7.3	29.3	28.8	8.1	−3.8	−12.9	−13.7	−3.9	9.9	11.5	10.2	24.2	24.7
Less imports	1.8	1.2	12.0	25.7	33.9	45.9	23.7	−5.8	−8.1	−15.8	1.3	19.3	15.2	11.3	0.5	10.6

Source: Government of India, Ministry of Statistics and Programme Implementation, press releases and statements (http://mospi.nic.in/Mospi_New/upload/mospi_press_releases.htm; http://mospi.nic.in/Mospi_New/site/inner.aspx?status=3&menu_id=82).

a. In constant 2004–05 market prices; growth over corresponding quarter of the previous year.

b. PFCE = Private final consumption expenditure.

c. GFCE = government final consumption expenditure.

d. Investment = Gross fixed capital formation + change in stock + valuables.

e. CAB = current account balance (exports less imports).

shows a revival in investment beginning in the second half of 2009–10 and private consumption from the first quarter of 2010–11, just as fiscal exit started. Near-quarters data, however, indicate that fiscal exit has been staggered, and while private consumption and exports are holding up, there is a sharp dip in investment (and industrial production), weakening consumption, and an upward pressure on interest rates, raising fears of crowding out.[50]

The fiscal stimulus seems to have been effective partly because it worked in tandem with monetary policy but also because it was both timely and targeted. Government fiscal expansion through additional outlays on subsidies, pay revision, a farm loan waiver, and expanded coverage of rural employment guarantee schemes—although these were not intended as fiscal stimuli—nevertheless got under way just as private demand was contracting. These expenditures were also targeted at consumption, where lead time in impact is minimal. However, for fiscal policy to be effective over the medium to long term, interventions also need to be temporary. Political exigencies apart, fiscal exit may be easier, since much of the fiscal expansion was on account of one-off expenditures, the sharp increase in revenues consequent on higher growth, and in particular through the inflation tax, which has seen an unusually large increase in nominal GDP.[51] Nevertheless, further fiscal correction hinges crucially on the policy response to rising food and oil prices and on the political resolve to contain consequential subsidies.

Indian Growth Prospects Going Forward and Exit Policies

After expanding by 9 percent in 2007–08, Indian economic growth declined to 7.8 percent and 7.5 percent, respectively, during the first two quarters of 2008–09 and fell further to 6.1 percent and 5.8 percent, respectively, in the last two quarters, yielding an annual real growth rate of 6.8 percent. Notwithstanding the sharp recession in its main export markets, India remained one of the fastest-growing economies at the peak of the global crisis.[52] This outcome can be traced to India's greater reliance on domestic demand, buoyed by a surge in rural demand consequent on a shift in terms of trade in favor of agriculture and to its timely fiscal response, including a new automatic stabilizer in low-income rural areas in the form of NREGS.[53]

50. Investment includes public investment. The share of public sector investment in total investment rose sharply in 2008–09 to compensate for the decline in private investment. Government of India, Ministry of Statistics and Programme Implementation, press release, January 29, 2010, p. 34 (http://mospi.nic.in/mospi_press_releases.htm).

51. On one-off expenditures, see Rao, "Timing the Exit Right." Some of these expenditures, such as farm loan waivers, payment of arrears on upward revisions in public sector salaries, and cleaning up accumulated off-balance-sheet liabilities, are self-limiting.

52. The United States accounts for 15 percent of India's merchandise exports (compared to 20 percent in the case of both Brazil and China), while western Europe accounts for another 23 percent. The dependence of the OECD, and particularly the U.S. market, on services exports (through which India mostly plugs its yawning merchandise trade deficit), is even greater.

53. Dev (2009).

As pointed out earlier, the cautious approach to financial regulation and the opening of the capital account, along with the abundant cushion of foreign exchange reserves, insulated the financial sector from the contagion emanating from the global financial storm, which was mostly limited to a sudden, short-term, reversal of capital flows. Growth rates picked up smartly, to 8.0 percent in 2009–10 and 8.6 percent in 2010–11 (advance estimates), on the back of a strong revival in industrial growth, exports, and investment, with the weak recovery in external demand remaining the chief constraint on return to trend growth.[54]

The return to growth since the third quarter of 2009 means that major OECD countries are technically out of recession, but the recovery is far from assured. While aggressive fiscal and monetary policies may have pulled the global economy from the brink, there is negative fallout from the protracted use of these policies; the failure to absorb the consequential liquidity appears to be spilling over into select emerging markets, on the one hand, and inflating asset bubbles, including commodities that have emerged as a distinct asset class, on the other. Thus the stock of foreign institutional investment in India has risen by over 50 percent since the middle of 2009. Rising commodity prices threaten to derail both the slow recovery in developed countries and the robust recovery in developing countries. The uptrend in global commodity prices, especially that of energy—a big deficit in India—is having a particularly deleterious impact on the Indian economy by fueling inflationary expectations and staggering the revival of savings and investment.[55] The policy dilemmas are unforgiving: if high commodity prices are passed on to consumers, the consequential adjustment will reduce private savings; if they are not, government dissavings will increase. The negative fallout on investment is compounded by unanchored inflationary expectations and continued monetary tightening. Declining investment also means that trend growth has also shifted south, at least for the time being. To get this back up again policymakers need to turn to structural policies and reform rather than rely only on macroeconomic stimulus that can never be a long-term solution to declining potential growth.

54. Even though India is not as dependent on external markets as several other developing countries, notably China, this cannot but have a dampening effect on growth. In absolute terms this dependence has risen sharply over the last decade, with its two-way merchandise trade (merchandise exports plus imports) increasing from 21.2 percent of GDP in 1997–98, the year of the Asian crisis, to 34.7 percent in 2007–08. India's financial integration with the rest of the world has increased even more steeply, with gross current and capital account flows more than doubling, from 46.8 percent of GDP to 117.4 percent over the same period. Duvvuri Subbarao, governor, Reserve Bank of India, speech at New Delhi, March 26, 2009 (http://rbidocs.rbi.org.in/rdocs/Speeches/PDFs/IGFCCII26309.pdf). The chief constraint on sustaining and increasing trend growth, however, continues to be infrastructural bottlenecks.

55. The roots of the current high rates of inflation, which mostly lie in agricultural commodities, are hotly debated. Both domestic supply and demand factors are cited as causal factors, as are the spillover effects of excessive global liquidity, since inflation has risen almost across the board in emerging markets.

Unlike Western economies, monetary exit in India preceded fiscal exit. The Reserve Bank of India was one of the first central banks, after the Reserve Bank of Australia, to signal that it would start exiting from monetary easing, even though it kept benchmark interest rates unchanged. The actual exit however began in its third quarterly review in January 2010, when the RBI raised the cash reserve ratio by 75 basis points, from 5 percent to 5.75 percent, in two stages. With food prices rising sharply and growth picking up, the RBI started raising key policy rates in steps. The repurchase rate—the rate at which the central bank lends overnight to scheduled commercial banks—has been raised, in steps, by 325 basis points, from 4.75 percent to 8 percent (as of end July 2011). The reverse repurchase rate, at which it absorbs excess liquidity overnight from banks, rose even more steeply, to 7 percent, reducing the policy corridor from 125 basis points to 100 basis points and signaling that the central bank has moved into liquidity absorption mode. It also raised the cash reserve ratio further, to 6 percent.

Despite monetary tightening, rising inflation ensures that policy rates in India remain negative in real terms, making it likely that such tightening will continue, which could severely damage growth by inhibiting both drivers of economic growth, namely consumption and investment.[56] Fiscal exit has been relatively more modest so far. The combined fiscal deficit of the central and state governments increased from 4.1 percent in 2007–08 to 8.5 percent in 2008–09 and to 9.5 percent in 2009–10, excluding off-budget liabilities. A sharp reduction in the central fiscal deficit occurred in 2010–11, from 6.4 percent to 5.1 percent, pursuant to a revenue windfall that may be difficult to sustain. However, with rising prices, it may be possible to keep budget deficits in check through the inflation tax, despite rising subsidies.

As the RBI raises policy rates to stabilize GDP, it risks aggravating the rush of external liquidity and, reminiscent of the period leading up to the global financial crisis, once again the country seems headed toward capture by the impossible trinity. The G-20 and the IMF generally advise that, since recovery is still not assured, it is too early to start exiting from extraordinary macroeconomic policies. However, weighed down by wealth losses, the threat of default, and high unemployment rates, the U.S. consumer may be retrenching permanently and returning to saving habits.[57] While this saving is currently counterbalanced by a huge surge in government dissaving, these public sector deficits are unsustainable over even the

56. Following the expectations-augmented Phillip's Curve, the trade-off between growth and inflation has become more complex, since high rates of inflation can of their own damage growth.

57. Personal consumption expenditure in the U.S., which had risen to around 95 percent of disposable personal income before the global crisis, has since reverted to its long-term postwar average of 90 percent. U.S. Bureau of Economic Analysis (www.bea.gov/national/index.htm#personal).

medium term.[58] This pattern is replicated in the euro zone, which composes a substantial chunk of the global economy, with deficit countries in the south such as Spain, Portugal, and Greece retrenching, consequent on their unsustainable fiscal deficits, and even other European countries are rushing to fiscal exit in response to market fears.

Therefore, unless global imbalances unwind substantially, there could be a permanent decline in global trend growth, as it is difficult to envisage, given current trends, that Asian consumption will increase so much so soon that it will take up the entire slack. In these circumstances there is a real danger that macroeconomic policies may overextend themselves in an attempt to overstimulate economies to precrisis levels of growth, even though potential growth may have drifted lower. Central banks and governments, in timing exit, may have to take their cue from inflationary trends rather than from perceived output gaps benchmarked to precrisis growth rates.

Macroeconomic Policy beyond the Crisis: An Indian Perspective

What lessons does the macroeconomic response to the crisis hold for India going forward? First and foremost, it exposed the limits of national macroeconomic policies and underscored the critical importance of global coordination (in view of increasing policy spillovers consequent on rapid global integration) and animal spirits in stabilizing economies. The steep fall in global economic activity during the year following the Lehman crash was sharper than during the Great Depression, but so was the dramatic recovery from the brink. This demonstrates the robustness of fiscal and monetary tools honed in the period following the Great Depression and the power of global integration, which exports both growth and woe with equal facility. The Indian experience with fiscal policy vindicates the view that, when faced with the prospect of a steep fall in economic activity, the fastest bang for the buck lies in targeting consumption. Protracted use of extreme macroeconomic policies by Western economies, however, have so far failed to stabilize them in the absence of the return of animal spirits. The removal of these macroeconomic life support systems is therefore proving challenging. Indeed, the global economy now has to deal with the adverse fallout of such policies, which may actually be derailing the recovery. Such tools should be

58. Based on their study of eight centuries of financial crises, Kenneth Rogoff and Carmen Reinhart have warned that unlike equity-financed bubbles, the fallout of debt-financed bubbles, such as the recent one, can lead to a disastrous buildup of unsustainable levels of public debt, as such losses tend to be socialized and passed on to taxpayers. In such circumstances, official debt data generally understate the magnitude of the problem on account of huge additional off-balance-sheet guarantees. See for example Kenneth Rogoff, "Spotting the Tell-Tale Signs of Bubbles Approaching," *Financial Times,* April 8, 2010.

used only in brief bursts, beyond which policymakers need to rely on structural policies and reform to boost growth.

Second, and paradoxically, even as the response to the crisis exposed the limits of macroeconomic policies, it burdens both fiscal and monetary policies with new objectives. Whether or not the global financial crisis has proved the robustness of rule-bound monetary policies, such as the Taylor rule, nevertheless monetary policy that focuses exclusively on inflation targeting is a major victim of the crisis, as loose monetary policy before the crisis inflated asset bubbles and, ipso facto, the financial crisis. Central banks in developed countries are now considering raising the inflation target to give them more policy space and are also rediscovering a long-forgotten objective of monetary policy, namely targeting financial stability. Central banks in some developing countries, such as India, on the other hand, use monetary policy to target financial stability, by cooling overheated asset prices and intervening in currency markets to cushion surges in capital inflows. The Indian central bank, frequently criticized for its attempts to resolve the impossible trinity and target asset bubbles, may well feel vindicated. Fiscal policy, too, is now burdened with the new objectives of guaranteeing financial stability and rebalancing growth, and tax policies may need to adjust appropriately. The burden of trade policy, too, is likely to fall on fiscal and monetary policies in future.

Third, in sharp contradistinction to the Great Depression, trade policy was never widely used as a macroeconomic tool to counter a downturn. It may well be the case that the lessons of the Great Depression have been absorbed by policymakers, since it is widely believed that the Smoot-Hawley tariffs simply amplified a big recession into the Great Depression. It may also be the case that policy coordination through the G-20 may have persuaded policymakers not to turn their backs on the World Trade Organization by using a politically attractive policy tool to protect domestic employment, long-term damage to multilateral institutions and their own economies notwithstanding. Be that it as it may, the big lesson from the recent crisis in this regard is that the changing pattern of global trade, which has seen the rise of global production chains, ensures that there are few domestic stakeholders to pressure governments to use tariffs as a macroeconomic policy tool to address steep recessions. This does not, however, mean that other forms of protection, such as currency devaluations and discriminatory public procurement, cannot be used as trade policy tools. In short, the burden of trade policy and protectionism may well fall on fiscal and monetary policies in the future.

Fourth, while the crisis illustrates that zero-bound interest rates do not exhaust monetary policy tools, it is not clear whether the use of unconventional tools like credit and quantitative easing is a ticket out of a liquidity trap, a lesson underscored by Japan's experience in the last decade of the last century. Drawing on the lessons from the drastic consequences of a simultaneous steep contraction in credit and money supply feeding off each other during the Great Depression, policymakers ensured that monetary contraction did not take place this time around. However, while credit easing might bail out financial institutions, it may not on its own induce them to lend, or induce others to borrow, in the absence of animal spirits. Quantitative easing, on the other hand, is simply an extension of fiscal policy at best, and by monetizing fiscal deficits it tends to blur the distinction between fiscal and monetary policies, thereby undermining the independence of central banks. With its large fiscal deficits, India has always had some species of quantitative easing in the form of the money market operations of the central bank, although, unlike in the case of reserve currencies, this does not have cross-border spillovers. But for the same reason such easing is likely to have a greater impact on domestic interest rates and inflation and so has its limitations as a macroeconomic policy tool.

Fifth, the macroeconomic response to the financial crisis has made it amply clear that only the United States has the capacity to sustain an aggressive fiscal response without triggering an adverse market response. Other countries need sound macroeconomic management in normal times so that they have the countercyclical fiscal space to use fiscal policy effectively in a crisis. As private demand contracts sharply and interest rates on fresh government debt fall on account of monetary easing, a deep recession can create the illusion of fiscal space beyond what can be sustained when normalcy returns. Nevertheless, the United Kingdom was constrained to finance 86.5 percent of its new treasury issuance in 2009 through quantitative easing, as against just 20.9 percent in the United States.[59] In 2010 the United Kingdom reversed its aggressive fiscal stance, while fiscal adjustment was forced on the euro area in the wake of the adverse market response, which resulted in a sharp rise in southern European sovereign bond yields. In sharp contrast, toward the end of 2010, the U.S. Federal Reserve embarked on another aggressive round of quantitative easing to accommodate continued fiscal expansion without any sharp market response.

This asymmetric market response to U.S. fiscal and monetary policies revived an old debate on the enormous privilege enjoyed by the U.S. dollar as the de facto world reserve currency, which enables it to fund large internal and external deficits, more so as this surge in global liquidity is widely believed to have spilled over into emerging markets through capital flows and asset price appreciation. Since Asian economies found that having accumulated reserves through the export-led Bretton Woods II insulated them against sudden stops during the crisis, they may be reluctant to shift from this tested model. Fears are therefore expressed regarding a shift from an unsustainable Bretton Woods II, where surplus savings in emerging economies funded leveraged household consumption in Western economies through runaway financial intermediation, to an equally unsustainable Bretton Woods III, where these savings are intermediated directly

59. International Monetary Fund (2010a, p. 20).

through public debt. This has led to calls for a comprehensive reform of the international monetary system.[60] The 2011 chair of the G-20, France, has consequently put reform of the international monetary system on the G-20 agenda. Academic debate and multilateral consultations notwithstanding, it is difficult at present to see how an alternative reserve currency can replace the dollar in the foreseeable future. The market has only buttressed its safe-haven status during the crisis.

Sixth, the explosion of sovereign debt across advanced countries, following the financial crisis, indicates that, while economies can put in place elaborate, publicly funded, social protection and entitlement schemes while they are young and growing fast, these become increasingly unsustainable as economies age and growth slows. Age-related expenditures were increasing structural deficits in advanced countries before the crisis, and public debt was rising. Cyclical deficits arising out of a protracted recovery from the current financial crisis may well have made this debt unsustainable relative to expected future growth rates in several major advanced countries, unless social compacts are renegotiated. These are however difficult to unwind politically. Emerging economies need to be mindful of this long-term dilemma as they put their own social protection and entitlement schemes in place.

Seventh, although the war chest of reserves provided emerging markets with insulation against a sudden stop, it could not counter the shock through trade channels, with India and China standing out as notable exceptions. Other Asian economies saw a sharp contraction in their growth rates on account of their overreliance on Western demand. The Indian economy was less affected because it is primarily domestically driven, while China was able to insulate itself through an aggressive fiscal package. The global crisis consequently underscores the virtues of externally balanced economies in an era in which rapid global integration has increased the likelihood and overall impact of external shocks. Even as the G-20 endeavors to reduce global imbalances through its signature effort to make global growth stronger, balanced and sustainable, nonreserve, issuing countries are realizing that they remain imbalanced at their peril—perhaps none more than China, its realization evident in its attempts to slowly appreciate its currency and to strengthen domestic demand through its ambitious Twelfth Plan. It is still not clear, however, how the trade-off between insulation against capital shocks and trade shocks will play out.

60. Thus Zhou Xiaochuan, the Central Bank governor of China, has called for replacing the dollar as the international reserve currency and creating an alternative that is disconnected from individual nations; Zhou (2009). While several countries resent the enormous privilege of the United States in leveraging its reserve currency status to raise virtually unlimited funds from international markets at low cost, China's fear is that the huge monetary expansion to fund growing U.S. fiscal deficits could dent the value of its substantial reserve assets denominated in dollars. Dominique Strauss-Kahn, former head of the IMF, has also called for a multiple pole reserve system, including a greater role of the SDR (www.imf.org/external/np/speeches/2010/051110.htm). There have also been some calls for a return to the gold standard (www.gold-eagle.com/greenspan011098.html).

Eighth, and finally, the external liquidity crunch notwithstanding, India's financial sector held up reasonably well during the crisis. Although its transmission channels of monetary policy were always weaker and had longer lags, than those of advanced economies, these transmission channels were nevertheless not clogged. This was largely because the Indian financial system was tightly regulated, like a public utility, which served a critical intermediating function for the real economy. Such regulation is in contrast to the lightly regulated advanced markets, which rapidly succumbed to financial contagion. India's policy has always involved an element of macroprudential regulation.[61]

It is easy to draw the wrong lesson from this. It should be borne in mind that the priorities in emerging markets, like India before the crisis, were not regulatory but developmental, with the aim of deepening and developing new markets to sustain high rates of growth in the real economy. Financial inclusion, high-cost capital (that pushes corporates to bypass monetary policy by borrowing in external markets), long-term funding instruments for infrastructure, the development of liquid bond markets to improve monetary policy transmission, among others, were financial sector priorities in India before the crisis, and nothing has happened in Indian financial markets that warrants changing these priorities. These sensitivities need to be taken into account as financial regulation in the Financial Stability Board, the Basel Committee on Banking Supervision, and other rule-setting bodies is reformed.

While a common set of principles should inform regulation, and regulatory arbitrage is clearly an issue, it is difficult to design a common regulatory framework for systems that are philosophically so different. For example, while banking capital needs to be strengthened in India, this is not on account of higher risks but because credit is projected to expand at a very fast pace to feed underlying high growth rates in the real economy. While the Indian banking system is at present adequately capitalized to meet the demanding Basel-III norms, going forward the public sector–dominated banking system would struggle to adhere to Basel-II norms while expanding credit to fuel a turbocharged economy, as the sovereign fiscal balance sheet is already overstretched. From an Asian perspective, it might be better to have a Glass-Steagall type of banking regulation, with higher capital requirements limited to investment and shadow banking that relies on volatile capital markets for funding.

To take another example, while the principle that the cost of a bailout falls on equity holders rather than on taxpayers is robust, in India large segments of the financial sector, especially banking and insurance, are mostly state owned, and equity holders and taxpayers are mostly one and the same. Therefore it is difficult

61. Duvvuri Subbarao, "Implications of the Expansion of Central Bank Balance Sheets," speech, Kyoto, January 31, 2011 (www.rbi.org.in/scripts/BS_SpeechesView.aspx?Id=547).

to see why and how a financial sector tax, which would only raise the cost of capital even further, would be appropriate.

Tight regulation in any case imposes high costs, for regulation is but a proxy for a tax, which is added to the cost of capital. In several advanced economies, however, light-touch regulation ensured that the cost of capital was kept low while systemic risks remained high, unlike in developing countries, where the cost of capital was high but systemic risks remained low. Imposing new and explicit taxes or raising capital norms and levels calibrated to risks prevailing in advanced countries, as has been agreed upon under Basel-III, on a sector where effective taxation is already high would further raise the cost of capital, and this would extract additional costs in terms of forgone growth and development. As financial markets develop, priorities could and would change, and developing countries need to be mindful of not succumbing to the same pitfalls as in advanced financial markets.

References

Bibow, Jörg. 2010. "The Global Crisis and the Future of the Dollar: Toward Bretton Woods III?" Working Paper 584. Levy Economics Institute of Bard College and Skidmore College (www.levy.org/pubs.wp_584.pdf).

Blanchard, Olivier, Giovanni Dell'Ariccia, and Paolo Mauro. 2010. "Rethinking Macroeconomic Policy." Staff Position Note 10/03. Washington: International Monetary Fund.

Borio, Claudio, and Andrew Filardo. 2007. "Globalisation and Inflation: New Cross-Country Evidence on the Global Determinants of Domestic Inflation." Working Paper 227. Bank for International Settlements (www.bis.org/publ/work227.pdf?noframes=1).

Cecchetti, Stephen G., M. S. Mohanty, and Fabrizio Zampolli. 2010. "The Future of Public Debt: Prospects and Implications." Working Paper 300. Bank for International Settlements (www.bis.org/publ/work300.pdf?noframes=1).

Congressional Budget Office. 2010. *The Budget Economic Outlook: Fiscal Years 2010 to 2020* (January) (www.cbo.gov/ftpdocs/108xx/doc10871/01-26-Outlook.pdf).

Dev, S. Mahendra. 2009. "Structural Reforms and Agriculture: Issues and Policies." *Indian Economic Journal* 57, no. 3.

Economic Advisory Council. 2008. "Economic Outlook for 2008/09" (http://eac.gov.in/reports/ecout0809.pdf).

———. 2009. "Economic Outlook for 2009/10" (http://eac.gov.in/reports/eo09_10.pdf).

———. 2011. "Review of the Economy, 2010/11" (October) (http://eac.gov.in/reports/ecoout_1011.pdf).

Eichengreen, Barry, and Kevin H. O'Rourke. 2010. "A Tale of Two Depressions: What Do the New Data Tell Us?" (March 8) (www.voxeu.org/index.php?q=node/3421).

Greenspan, Alan. 2007. *The Age of Turbulence. Adventures in a New World.* London: Allen Lane.

International Monetary Fund. 2007. "Multilateral Consultations on Global Imbalances with China, the Euro Area, Japan, Saudi Arabia and the United States." Washington (www.imf.org/external/np/pp/2007/eng/062907.pdf).

———. 2009a. "Global Economic Prospects and Effectiveness of Policy Response." Surveillance note delivered at G-20 deputies' summit, Basel, June 27 (www.imf.org/external/np/g20/pdf/070809/pdf).

———. 2009b. "Global Economic Prospects and Policy Challenges." Surveillance note delivered at G-20 leaders' summit, Pittsburgh, September 24 (www.imf.org/external/np/g20/pdf/092409.pdf).

———. 2009c. "Global Economic Prospects and Principles for Policy Exit." Surveillance note delivered at G-20 finance ministers' and central bank governors' meetings, St. Andrews, U.K., November 6–7 (www.imf.org/external/np/g20/pdf/110709.pdf).

———. 2009–11. Surveillance notes (www.imf.org/external/ns/cs.aspx?id=249). Washington.

———. 2010a. "Fiscal Exit: From Strategy to Implementation." Washington.

———. 2010b. *Global Financial Stability Report* (April). Washington.

———. Various years. *Fiscal Monitor.* Washington.

———. Various years. *World Economic Outlook.* Washington.

McKinsey Global Institute. 2010. "Debt and Deleveraging: The Global Credit Bubble and Its Economic Consequences." (January) (www.mckinsey.com/mgi/publications/debt_and_deleveraging/index.asp).

Reinhart, Carmen M., and Kenneth S. Rogoff. 2008. "This Time Is Different: A Panoramic View of Eight Centuries of Financial Crises." Working Paper 13882. Cambridge, Mass.: National Bureau of Economic Research (www.nber.org/papers/w13882).

Reserve Bank of India. 1998–2011. "Weekly Statistical Supplement" (www.rbi.org.in/scripts/WSSViewDetail.aspx?TYPE=Section&PARAM1=2).

———. 2007–11. *Bulletin* (www.rbi.org.in/script//BS_ViewBulletin.aspx).

———. 2009a. "Second Quarter Review of Monetary Policy for the Year 2009–10" (http://rbi.org.in/scripts/NotificationUser.aspx?Id=5326&Mode=0).

———. 2009b. "Third Quarter Review of Monetary Policy, 2008–09" (rbi.org.in/scripts/NotificationUser.aspx?Id=4796&Mode=0).

———. 2010a. "Report on Trend and Progress of Banking in India, 2008–09" (http://rbidocs.rbi.org.in/rdocs/Publications/PDFs/CHP04201009.pdf).

———. 2010b. "Third Quarter Review of Monetary Policy, 2009–10."

Romer, Christina D., and David H. Romer. 2007. "The Macroeconomic Effects of Tax Changes: Estimates Based on a New Measure of Fiscal Shocks" (March) (www.econ.berkeley.edu/~cromer/RomerDraft307.pdf).

Shah, Ajay, and Ila Patnaik. 2010. "Why India Choked when Lehman Broke." Working Paper 63. New Delhi: National Institute of Public Finance and Policy (www.nipfp.org.in/working_paper/wp_2010_63.pdf.

Stiglitz, Joseph E. 2002. *Globalization and Its Discontents.* Norton.

Taylor, John B. 2010. "Does the Crisis Experience Call for a New Paradigm in Monetary Policy?" CASE Network Studies and Analyses 402/2010. Warsaw: Bishkek Kyiv Tbilisi Chisinau Minsk (http://www.case-research.eu).

White, William R. 2006. "Is Price Stability Enough?" Working Paper 205. Bank for International Settlements (www.bis.org/publ/work205.pdf?noframes=1).

Woodford, Michael. 2007. "Globalization and Monetary Control." Working Paper 13329. Cambridge, Mass.: National Bureau of Economic Research (www.nber.org/papers/w13329).

World Bank. 2009. "Private Participation in Infrastructure Design" (http://ppi.worldbank.org/features/march2009/200903PPIFinancialCrisisImpact.pdf).

WTO/OECD/UNCTAD. 2010. *Report on G-20 Trade and Investment Measures.* Various issues.

Zhou Xiaochuan. 2009. "Statement on Reforming the International Monetary System." Council on Foreign Relations (www.cfr.org/publication/18916/zhou_xiaochuans_statement_on_reforming_the_international_monetary_system.html).

PART II

Macroprudential Regulation

4

Macroprudential Approaches to Banking Regulation: Perspectives of Selected Asian Central Banks

REZA SIREGAR

The past two decades have witnessed a high frequency of banking and financial crises. The blame for these crises is often laid upon macroeconomic policies, especially fiscal and exchange rate policies. Many also passionately argue that bank regulators could do more to ward off crises in the banking system. Borio, in particular, underscores the urgency to strengthen two core and integrated components of prudential regulation.[1] The first one is the microprudential element, which concentrates on the stability of the individual bank. The second, the macroprudential component, is concerned with preventing systemic crisis in the banking system.

In the past, many (including Borio) have argued that regulation has hitherto focused too much on the micro and too little on the macro. Understanding macrofinancial linkages is also concerned with the twin objectives of monetary and financial stability. The increasing competition and integration of financial sectors globally have been emphasized as driving factors behind the surging interest in this twin stability.[2] One outcome of the debate is the acceptance of the concept of macroprudential policy, which takes into account the interconnectedness of financial systems as well as between the financial system and the overall economy, often referred to as macrofinancial linkages.

1. Borio (2003).
2. Borio (2006).

Table 4-1. *Financial Soundness Indicators, Selected Asian Countries, 2007 and 2009*
Percent

	Nonperforming loans as share of bank loans		*Risk-weighted capital adequacy ratio*		*Bank return on assets*	
Country	*2007*	*2009*	*2007*	*2009*	*2007*	*2009*
Cambodia	3.4	6.1 (Sep)	23.6	32.2 (Sep)	. . .	. . .
Fiji Islands	6.0	3.3 (Sep)	13.2	16.2 (Sep)	. . .	. . .
Indonesia	4.0	3.9 (Oct)	19.2	17.5 (Oct)	2.8	2.7 (Apr)
Korea	0.6	1.2 (Sep)	12.0	14.3 (Jun)	1.1	0.5 (Dec)
Malaysia	6.4	4.6 (Apr)	13.2	14.1 (Nov)	1.5	1.5 (Dec)
Mongolia	3.2	16.5 (Sep)	14.2	7.5 (Sep)	. . .	. . .
Myanmar	2.4	2.6 (Sep)	43.4	57.3 (Sep)	. . .	. . .
Nepal	10.3	3.6 (Sep)	–1.7	4.3 (Jun)	. . .	. . .
Papua New Guinea	1.7	1.4 (Jun)	. . .	. . .	. . .	. . .
Philippines	4.5	3.3 (Sep)	15.9	15.5 (Mar)	1.3	0.8 (Mar)
Singapore	1.5	2.3 (Sep)	13.5	16.5 (Sep)	1.3	1.1 (Dec)
Sri Lanka	5.0	8.6 (Sep)	13.6	14.1 (Sep)	. . .	. . .
Taipei,China	1.8	1.4 (Sep)	10.8	11.6 (Sep)	0.1 (Dec)	0.3 (Jun)
Thailand	7.3	5.3 (Sep)	15.4	16.4 (Sep)	. . .	1.0 (Dec)
Viet Nam	1.5	2.2 (Sep)	. . .	. . .	. . .	. . .

Source: Siregar and Lim (2010).

For Asian policymakers, the intricate links between macroeconomic performance and financial stability have been recognized and appreciated since the 1997 financial crisis. Numerous reforms of the financial sector were initiated during the past decade. By and large, the outcomes have been encouraging and have contributed to a much healthier financial sector, especially the banking sector. The capital position, liquidity position, and profitability of banks in major Asian economies in fact strengthened tremendously in the years 2007–09 (table 4-1).

However, no two crises are exactly alike. New lessons, challenges, and debates emerged from the recent subprime crisis. While macro-orientation is in fact not new, and has always been in the classic tool kit of the central bank for ensuring financial stability, the current explicit articulation and specification of such a tool as a global standard is new. The primary objective of this chapter is to present a broad review and analysis of the efforts of the central banks of key Asian emerging markets to strengthen their prudential regulations, particularly the macroprudential component.

Macrofinancial Linkages

In the decade before the 2007–09 subprime financial crisis, central bankers and monetary authorities around the globe grew confident that they could manage economic fluctuation, including inflation.[3] Their overall success in achieving single-digit inflation led central bankers to believe not only that they had conquered inflation but also that they could indeed flatten the business cycle. Financial imbalances were however hidden within the stable inflation environment. The deepening of financial liberalization and the tightening of financial integration around the globe made it more difficult not only to detect imbalances but, more important, to contain the spread of the financial crisis. Therefore, in these changing financial landscapes, the success of monetary policy and macroeconomic policies in general hinges on the ability of policymakers to design monetary policies that explicitly take into account macrofinancial linkages.

The importance of macrofinancial linkages to Asian central banks is shown by how swiftly they adopted financial stability as one of their primary objectives. A score of countries—among them Malaysia, Singapore, Sri Lanka, and Taipei, China—adopted financial stability as one of their central banks' statutory objectives. Similarly, central banks in Asian countries like the Philippines and Republic of Korea proposed amendments to their central bank acts to include financial stability as one of their mandates.

In a 2007 work, D. Gray, R. C. Merton, and Z. Bodie argue that existing monetary policy frameworks are ill suited to their task, since their focus is limited to the monetary system.[4] Their view is clearly not new and has been expressed by many earlier studies. A. Houben, J. Kakes, and G. Schinasi, for instance, maintain that a financial system is in a range of stability whenever it is capable of facilitating (rather than impeding) the performance of an economy, and dissipating financial imbalances that arise endogenously or as a result of significant adverse and unanticipated events.[5] This broader definition moves beyond that of the monetary system, which simply focuses on individual banks, to the system in its entirety and linkages between the financial system and the real economy.[6]

One straightforward framework (figure 4-1) to observe the transmissions and implications of the macrofinancial linkage is provided by a 2008 paper by T. Bayoumi and O. Melander. The study applies this macrofinancial linkage to explain the recent subprime crisis in the United States. The authors assume the occurrence of an adverse shock, which led to a deterioration in the quality of bank capital and its capital adequacy. In turn, banks were forced to make some adjustments in their lending standards. A credit crunch followed, and eventually resulted in

3. During the same period there has been an increase in the number of countries adopting an inflation-targeting policy as the anchor of their monetary policies, especially among emerging markets. Before the 1997 Asian financial crisis, only five economies had adopted an inflation-targeting policy, and none of them were emerging markets. By the end of 2006 twenty-six economies, more than half of them developing economies, committed to inflation-targeting policies.

4. Gray, Merton, and Bodie (2007).

5. Houben, Kakes, and Schinasi (2004).

6. Woolford (2001).

Figure 4-1. *Conceptual Framework of Crisis*

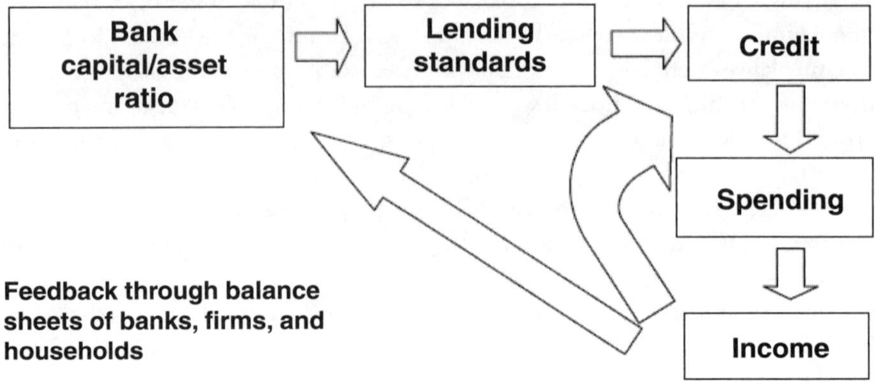

Source: Bayoumi and Melander (2008).

the weakening of investment and spending, causing income to fall. The study also emphasizes the second-round, or feedback, effect. A slowdown in economic growth would weaken demand for credit. Concurrently, the deterioration of collateral during an economic crisis would further worsen the quality of a bank's capital. Hence, more rounds of macrofinancial linkages would likely take place, depending on the severity of the economic and financial crisis.

Accepting such a macrofinancial linkage is arguably the least difficult part. Estimating the impacts of these feedback loops is however not a straightforward task. During a crisis period in particular, a few rounds (vicious circles) of adverse feedback between the macroeconomic environment and the financial condition are common. The consequences of macrofinancial linkages on the effectiveness of monetary policy in particular have also been known to be amplified by the procyclical nature of the financial system. Financial institutions have demonstrated that they are vulnerable to the collective impulse to lend aggressively when times are good only to excessively cut lending when the economic cycle experiences a downturn. This behavior amplifies the impact of the economic cycle on bank lending and is termed *procyclicality.* The recent subprime crisis underscores the boom-and-bust consequences of the procyclical feature of bank lending in particular and the activities of financial institutions in general.

To expose procylicality, several studies estimate the degrees of correlation between credit growth and GDP growth. As explained by R. S. Craig, E. P. Davis, and A. G. Pascual, real GDP growth has long been considered a standard measure of the business cycle, while real credit growth reflects the role of the financial sector in the cycle.[7] Based on data from eleven Asian economies, their study further claims that the correlation of credit to GDP is much stronger on average

7. Craig, Davis, and Pascual (2006).

Figure 4-2. *Annualized Credit Growth and GDP Growth, Indonesia*

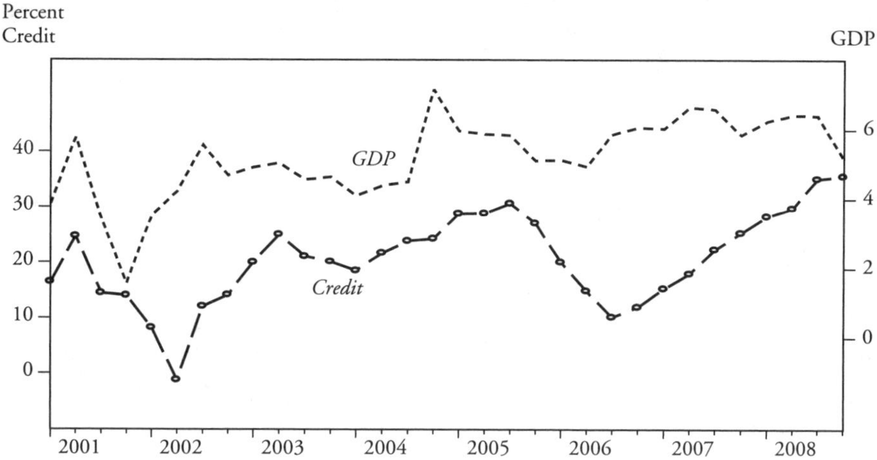

Source: CEIC database; author's calculations.

when growth is weak, suggesting that procyclicality is greater during a recession. Figure 4-2 demonstrates that relationship for the case of Indonesia.[8] Similar trends can also be found in other parts of Asia.[9] In addition, procyclicality can also be confirmed by the established relationship between accumulations of household debt to GDP growth rates (figure 4-3). A simple regression equation relating the two variables indicates that the rise in GDP (PPP) per capita contributes positively and significantly to the rise in the household debt-to-GDP ratio across the seventeen countries shown.

A similar message on the procyclical nature of the financial sector can also be captured by the relationship between credit growth and asset price (particularly real house prices). As shown in figure 4-1, the robust supply of bank loans to credit stimulates rapid spending, especially during years of soaring economic growth rates. In Asia the property sector, in particular, has long attracted a fair share of consumer/household and commercial loans. Consequently, the availability of these loans during strong economic growth fueled concerns about the emergence of bubbles in this sector. Figure 4-4 illustrates the possible link between loan availability and house price in Taipei,China. Similarly, the booms and busts of property prices in major Asian economies such as Taipei,China, Singapore, and the Philippines, in particular, have been found to be closely linked to economic

8. Unlike past economic and financial crises, financial institutions in Indonesia and most neighboring countries had an overall strong capital position and good liquidity during the peak of the subprime financial crisis. The strong balance sheet of the banking sector, in particular, minimized the procyclicality of the economic slowdown.

9. The comovement of GDP and credit growth can also be seen in other Asian economies. For the sake of brevity, we only demonstrate the case of Indonesia.

Figure 4-3. *Household Debt-to-GDP Ratio and Log GDP (PPP) per Capita, 2008, Given the Equation* $y = 28.915\text{Ln}(x) - 215.81$, $R^2 = 0.87$

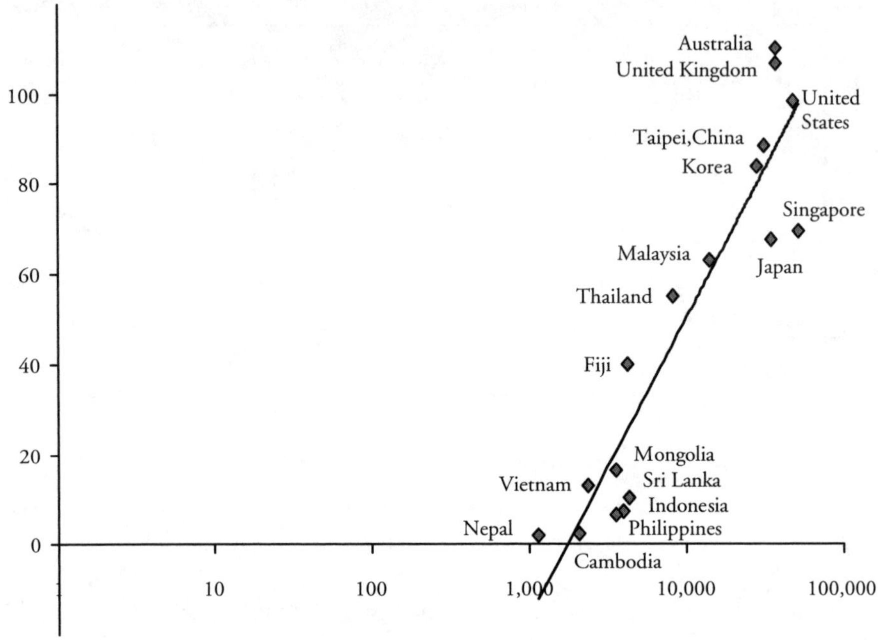

Source: Nakornthab (2010).

Figure 4-4. *Loan to Real GDP and House Price Booms and Busts, Taipei,China, 1989–2009*

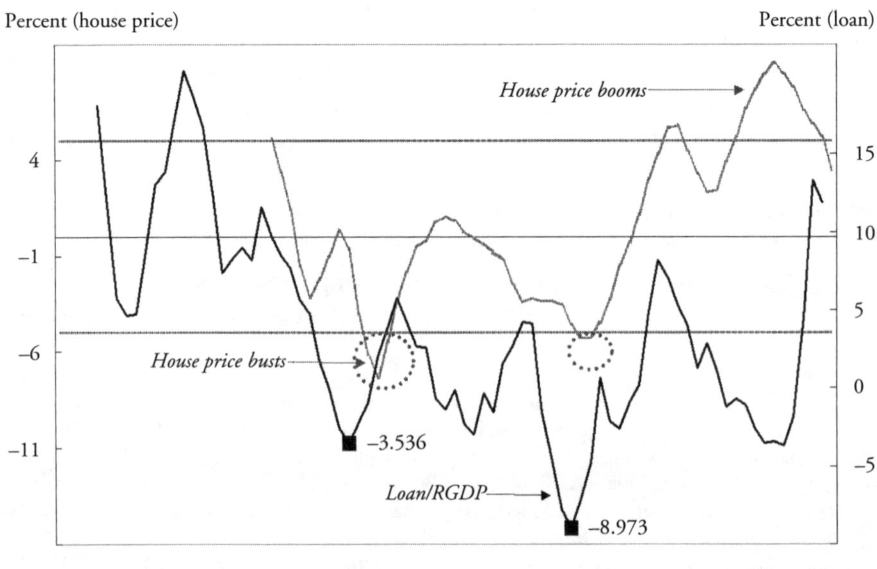

Source: Ho (2010).

Table 4-2. *GDP Growth and External Rating, 1992–2006*
Percent

Year	*GDP growth*	*Upgrades*	*Downgrades*
1992	0.30	0.00	0.00
1993	2.10	0.00	0.00
1994	4.40	0.00	0.00
1995	4.70	0.00	0.00
1996	5.80	9.09	9.09
1997	5.20	3.03	3.03
1998	–0.60	0.00	18.75
1999	3.40	3.70	14.81
2000	4.00	7.69	15.38
2001	1.80	4.35	26.09
2002	4.40	4.76	14.29
2003	4.90	7.69	7.69
2004	6.40	0.00	8.33
2005	4.90	9.09	9.09
2006	5.40	6.67	0.00

Source: Prenio (2008).

cycles.[10] Moreover, Craig, Davis, and Pascual warn that correlations between property price and credit growth are often asymmetrical over economic cycles in Asia. Their study shows that property prices are more highly correlated with credit during the downturn. Interestingly, the recent subprime crisis is the exception, largely due to the strong balance sheet of the domestic banking sector, which contributed to sustained credit expansion. Thus the correlation between economic downturn and falling property prices was not severe in some Asian economies, particularly Southeast Asian economies.

A study by J. Y. Prenio reviews the external rating on banking assets in the Philippines during several economic cycles (table 4-2). The study demonstrates that the percentage of banking assets that experienced downgrades shot up at the outset of the 1997 financial crisis. Downgrades continued to dominate until 2002 but stabilized and declined marginally from 2003 onward, when the country's GDP was in a period of stable rapid growth. Fortunately, less than 12 percent of the universal banking assets of the Philippines at that time were subject to external ratings under the Basel II regulation. Hence the economic downturn and a downgraded rating had a rather limited impact on a bank's capital requirement. The case could arguably be different under the circumstance wherein a major share of bank assets is exposed to external credit ratings. The downgrade could have adversely affected the capital adequacy position of the banks, which in turn would result in a reduction of lending and real economic activity.

10. Nakornthab (2010).

The globalized banking system is another factor that needs to be recognized when estimating the consequences of the linkages between macroeconomic policies and the financial market. Studies show that, while lending by small banks appears to be highly responsive to monetary policy shocks, the same is not true of large banks. One plausible explanation stems from the presumed greater ability of large banks to substitute reservable deposits with other external sources of funds.[11] Large U.S. banks with a global network are shown to be insulated from domestic monetary policy shocks. However this does not necessarily imply that monetary policy transmission has weakened completely. Rather, the lending channel of U.S. monetary policy is easily underestimated if one examines its impacts on the local economy only. The response of the foreign offices of these U.S. banks to a change in domestic monetary policy is consistent with an international mechanism of transmission of monetary policy. A later study demonstrates that adverse liquidity shocks to developed country banking, such as those that occurred in the United States in 2007 and 2008, reduce lending in emerging markets through contractions in cross-border lending to banks and private agents and also through contractions in parent banks' support of foreign affiliates.[12] In short, the feedback effects of macrofinancial linkages could easily be complicated further by multiple and concurrent shocks from both local and external sources.

The globalization of the banking system is indeed not new to Asia and has deepened significantly during this past decade. R. Y. Siregar and K. M. Choy find that the size of international bank lending from private banks in seven Organization for Economic Cooperation and Development countries to nine Asian economies fluctuated in tandem with the economic performance of the recipient countries.[13] Accompanying the collapse of economic growth in major Asian economies was a sharp decline in loans from commercial banks based in these seven OECD countries. The hardest hit economies—namely, Indonesia, Malaysia, the Philippines, Thailand, and South Korea—which had experienced net private inflows averaging from around $160 billion a year in 1995 and 1996, saw total foreign liabilities drop by around 45 percent in 1998, as international banks were unwilling to roll over existing loans. Siregar and Choy examined a number of plausible push and pull factors in OECD banks' claims on these countries. Bilateral trade between the Asian countries and the OECD economies, for example, contributed significantly to the flows of cross-border bank lending, underscoring again the importance of macrofinancial linkages.

By end of 2008, arguably the peak of the subprime financial crisis, some Asian economies turned from being net debtors to being net creditors. The gap between international interbank liabilities and assets has significantly widened since Sep-

11. See Cetorelli and Goldberg (2008).
12. Cetorelli and Goldberg (2009).
13. Siregar and Choy (2010).

tember 2007. Individually, Australia, Korea, Indonesia, Malaysia, Korea, and Viet Nam saw a significant buildup of net international interbank debt, suggesting capital inflows in this category; Japan, Hong Kong, China, Singapore, and Taipei,China saw significant outflows. The significant roles of foreign banks in local economies combined with the roles of local banks in global financial markets complicate efforts to estimate the feedback effects of macrofinancial linkages.

Forging Ahead with Macroprudential Regulations in Asia

Under the present global financial landscape, macroprudential regulations are a key option for consideration. The importance of these instruments is increasingly recognized as it becomes clear that conventional policy interest rate manipulation is too blunt an instrument. Microprudentialists have long argued that, for the financial system to be sound, it necessary that each individual institution be sound. Naturally, the proximate objective of the microprudential approach is to limit distress on individual institutions. This approach assumes that risk is exogenous, a partial equilibrium view. In contrast, macroprudentialists maintain that there are situations where what is rational for an individual institution could result in undesirable aggregate outcomes. Based on the belief that risk is in part endogenous to the financial system, the objective of the macroprudential approach is to limit the risk of financial distress while accepting that there will be significant losers in the economy as a whole.

Despite the different views, macro- and microprudential instruments are closely intertwined. The key aim of macroprudential instruments is to fit into existing microprudential tools. In general, macroprudential measures can be categorized into three primary groups. In the first group are price- and quantity-based measures designed to limit credit expansion. Reserve requirements and credit ceilings are typical measures. The second group of regulations aims at maintaining the quality of loans. Typical measures are loan-to-value ratios, debt-to-income rules, limits on currency mismatches, and improved credit information. The third group of measures focuses on strengthening the resilience of the banking system to balance-sheet shocks (both assets and liabilities). Capital adequacy requirements and rules on the composition or type of foreign borrowings fall into this category.

The Committee on the Global Financial System further classifies macroprudential instruments by type of vulnerability in the financial system.[14] Some of the macroprudential instruments used to manage the leverage position of the banking system are capital ratios, risk weights, provisioning, credit growth, loan-to-value caps, and maturity caps. As for dealing with liquidity risk and market risk, authorities can consider one or a combination of the following macroprudential

14. Committee on the Global Financial System (2010).

instruments: a liquidity or reserve requirement, a foreign exchange lending restriction, and a currency mismatch limit. Last but not least is the vulnerability arising from interconnectedness. To mitigate this exposure, concentration limits, a systemic capital surcharge, and a strict policy on bank subsidiaries are instruments to be considered.

The enforcement of macroprudential measures to manage credit cycles is not a new phenomenon in Asia (table 4-3). Particularly after the 1997 financial crisis, authorities in the region collectively enforced both macro- and microprudential regulations to supplement their monetary policy measures. One aim of these policies has often been to manage loan or credit extensions to the property sector. Given the typical significant profit margins from property credit and loans, policy rate adjustments have long been found to be insufficient to address strong credit expansions. The overall primary objective of these prudential measures has also been to prevent systemic risks for overall financial stability, as experienced during the 1997 financial crisis.

These macroprudential measures were adopted by the authorities to supplement macroeconomic policy measures and to gradually shift away from the generally expansionary policy stances of the peak of the subprime crisis. Instead of relying on interest rate policy adjustments, the Bank of Indonesia enforced a combination of the loan-to-deposit ratio and the reserve requirement policy to manage credit growth and risk taking in the domestic banking sector. As in the past, the primary objectives of recent macroprudential measures are to manage procyclicality and to reduce interconnectivity and systemic risk. Generally, Asian central banks, as with many other central banks, closely monitor procyclical movements in debt and leverages, especially those related to such asset markets as the real estate sector. A key objective of the Singapore government, for example, is to ensure a stable and sustainable property market, where prices move in line with fundamentals. In February 2010 the loan-to-value limit for housing loans extended by financial institutions was lowered to 80 percent. To discourage speculative flipping of properties, a seller's stamp duty on all residential properties bought and sold within one year was introduced. In August 2010 the holding period for imposition of the seller's stamp duty was increased from one year to three years. The Singapore government also tightened measures to ensure that public housing was utilized as intended—that is, for owner occupation.

Bangko Sentral ng Pilipinas has also enforced a loan-to-value ratio as a tool to limit the risk exposure of the banking sector to the real estate sector. To moderate any excessive investments and speculative activity in the residential property market, effective November 3, 2010, new housing loans approved by financial institutions and development financial institutions to borrowers who already hold two outstanding housing loan accounts are subject to a maximum loan-to-value ratio of 70 percent. The adjusted loan-to-value cap has also been applied by the Bank of Thailand in recent years.

Table 4-3. *Credit Booms, by Prudential Measure, Selected Asian Countries*[a]

Country	*LTV*	*Capital*	*Provision*	*Exposure limit*	*Lending criteria*
Cambodia	. . .	2009	. . .	2008	. . .
People's Republic of China	2001, 2005, 2006	. . .	. . .	. . .	2004
Hong Kong, China	1991, 1997	. . .	. . .	1994–98	. . .
India	. . .	2005, 2008, 2009	2005, 2006, 2007	2006	2007
Indonesia	. . .	2008	. . .	2004, 2005	. . .
Korea	2003, 2006–08	. . .	. . .	. . .	2006
Malaysia	1995–98	2005, 2008, 2009	. . .	1997–98	1995–97
Mongolia	. . .	2008	. . .	. . .	. . .
Nepal				2010	
Papua New Guinea	. . .	2003	2003	2000, 2001, 2003	. . .
Philippines	1997, 2010	. . .	. . .	2010	. . .
Singapore	2010	. . .	. . .	2010	. . .
Sri Lanka	. . .	2008	. . .	2007	. . .
Taipei,China	2010	Pre-2007	. . .	Pre-2007	Pre-2007
Thailand	2003	. . .	. . .	. . .	2004–05
Viet Nam	. . .	2010	2010	2010	. . .

Source: SEACEN Centre survey, October 2010.

a. LTV = loan-to-value ratio; capital = capital requirements/reserve requirement; provision = loan provisioning rules; exposure limit = credit exposure to a sector; lending criteria = limits on debt repayment-to-income, debt repayment-to-debt, or credit line-to-income ratio.

To manage interconnectivity and risk exposure, Bank Indonesia monitors the daily liquidity positions of banks, especially those institutions with systemic implications. Commercial banks in Indonesia are also prohibited from extending loans to a single affiliated party by more than 10 percent of the capital. A prohibition on complex derivative asset trading has also been enforced by a number of Asian central banks. Nepal Rastra Bank, for instance, imposes limits on investments except for government and central bank securities. Another typical prudential measure to manage interconnectivity is limiting sectoral credit, including interbank placements.[15] The Central Bank of Sri Lanka introduced the Direction on Maximum Amount of Accommodation regulation in 2007, with the main objective of limiting a bank's credit exposure to any single individual or company or to any group of individuals or companies.

Macroprudential regulations have also been implemented to manage and address surges of capital inflow, especially since the second half of 2009. To reduce short-term volatility, Bank Indonesia introduced a one-month holding period for its certificate (SBI) purchased in both primary and secondary markets in June 2010. Before this, Bank Indonesia made a concerted effort to shift the maturity structure from a one-month tenure to three-month and six-month tenures and from weekly to monthly auctions. Longer maturity SBIs (nine and twelve months) were being considered in late 2010, with the purported aim of lengthening the maturity profile of investors. In November 2009 authorities in Korea imposed tighter regulations on currency trading, including new standards for foreign exchange liquidity risk management, restrictions on currency forward transactions of nonfinancial companies, and mandatory minimum holdings of safe foreign currency assets by domestic banks. These policies followed an earlier move to curb speculative foreign exchange transactions. In July 2010 the minimum amount of deposits for foreign currency margin trade was raised to 5 percent of transaction value, from 2 percent, in an effort to clamp down on speculative foreign exchange trading by individual investors.

Stress Testing

Stress testing has been accepted in recent years as one of the most integral macroprudential tools and, increasingly, a risk management tool. The term *stress testing* is used to describe the various techniques and procedures employed by financial firms to gauge their vulnerability to exceptional but plausible events.[16] These techniques and procedures are used by financial institutions to assess their risk and by supervisory authorities to assess the stability of the banking system. U.S. Federal Reserve Bank chairman Ben Bernanke argues that "stress tests are a good

15. The Bank of Papua New Guinea has imposed a prudential standard on limits on interbank placements.

16. Blaschke and others (2001); Sorge (2004).

way to augment models and other standard quantitative techniques for risk management. And they force bankers to think through the implications of scenarios that may seem relatively unlikely but could pose serious risks if those scenarios materialized."[17]

Basic Framework

Stress testing is an integral part of both pillars of Basel II. Under the first pillar, on the minimum capital requirement, stress testing is a vital instrument to assess credit risk, market risk, and operational risk. Furthermore, it requires that banks using the internal models approach to determine market risk capital have in place a rigorous program of stress testing. Similarly, banks using the advanced and foundation internal ratings-based approaches for credit risk assessment are required to conduct credit risk stress tests to measure the robustness of their internal capital and capital cushions above the regulatory minimum. Under the second pillar, on the supervisory review process, stress testing is required to measure interest rate risk, credit concentration risk (potential overexposures to a specific class of asset, borrower, industry, or region), and counterparty credit risk.

In principle, there are two stress test techniques. The basic one is known as a sensitivity test, and the more popular one today is referred to as a scenario analysis. The sensitivity test focuses on the effect on a portfolio's value of a particular risk factor, such as interest rate or exchange rate risk, individually. One frequently mentioned shortcoming of this approach is lack of plausibility. Furthermore, critics point to the difficulties in separating one risk from another: more often than not a financial institution faces multiple risks simultaneously.

Scenario analysis is recognized as the better stress test technique because of its several advantages over sensitivity analysis. This technique is more realistic as it considers a number of risk factors simultaneously. Furthermore, it takes into account a range of plausible scenarios. One of them is the historical scenario, which replicates historical episodes of stress, such as Black Monday in 1987, the 1997 Asian crisis, and the 9/11 terrorist attacks. One obvious shortcoming of this technique is that no single past crisis has actually been repeated. A hypothetical scenario is another option. This involves considering a plausible event that has not yet happened. The advantage of this approach is its flexibility, allowing it to be relevant to the individual bank's risk profile. The downside, however, is that constructing a hypothetical scenario that is realistic and comprehensive can be a challenge.

In addition, stress testing can be carried out in two ways, top down and bottom up (table 4-4). The top-down approach is conducted by the supervisor of the banking sector. Using the data supplied by member banks to the supervisor,

17. Ben Bernanke, speech, Federal Reserve Bank of Chicago, 46th Annual Conference on Bank Structure and Competition, May 6, 2010.

Table 4-4. *Stress-Test Approaches*

	Top-down approach	*Bottom-up approach*
Tool developer	Central banks or supervisory agencies develop the tools	Individual banks develop their own tools or using their internal model
Data supplier	Uses aggregate data of each bank or banking system available at the central bank	Uses subportfolio/portfolio-level data or the customer data of its individual bank
Impact analysis	Assesses the impact of stress scenario on individual banks and banking system's portfolio quality and capital position	Assesses the impact of stress scenario on financial statements of each customer then aggregates the impacts to find overall impacts on each bank's portfolio and capital position
Pro	Effective in examining credit risk. Stress test results can be compared across banks. It covers broader perspectives, including feedback effects from the financial system to the macroeconomy, and contagion.	Due to its tailor-made and richer data sets, better reflects the market and liquidity risk profiles of each bank's portfolio.
Con	Results may not reflect each bank's risk profile well.	With different methodologies used by each bank, it is difficult to compare results across banks.

Source: Power point presentations by M. Subhaswadikul, "Stress-Testing: The Experience of Bank of Thailand," and H. Zhu, "An Introduction of Stress Testing," Third SEACEN–Deutsche Bundesbank Intermediate Course on Banking Supervision and Financial Stability, Kuala Lumpur, May 11, 2010.

stress tests can be performed to measure the credit risk exposures of both individual banks and the overall banking system. Since the tests are designed and executed by a single institution (the supervisor of the banking sector, for instance), the results are comparable. Furthermore, given the source of the data, this approach should able to capture contagion effects.

Bottom-up stress testing is carried out by the individual banks, with scenarios defined by the supervisory authority. The advantage of this approach is the richer data that the bank has and also the bank's more comprehensive understanding of its market and liquidity risks. Comparing the outcomes of the bottom-up approach, however, can be difficult, since each bank selects its own methodology and applies it to its own unique data base. For instance, poorly capitalized banks react more sensitively than do well-capitalized banks.[18] If the financial stability of individual banks differs, the transmission of monetary policy is likely to be adversely affected.[19] Furthermore, this approach, due to data limitation on the

18. Kishan and Opeila (2000).
19. De Graeve, Kick, and Koetter (2008).

Box 4-1. *Bank of Thailand, Stress-Testing Activities, 2007–10*

2007—The Bank of Thailand participated in the stress-testing component of the Financial Sector Assessment Program, a joint undertaking by the International Monetary Fund and the World Bank. It also developed a macroeconomic credit risk model to be used in top-down assessments of macrocredit.

2008—The bank presented supervisory scenarios to its commercial banks for their assessments of effects, using a bottom-up approach. Scenarios featured subprime, macrocredit, and market and liquidity issues.

2009—The bank required foreign banks' branches in Thailand to perform liquidity stress testing. It also issued pillar 2 guidelines, which include stress testing.

2010—The bank developed examination guidelines on credit risk, market risk, and interest rate risk in book and liquidity stress testing. It also began developing several sectoral credit risk models: a corporate model, a personal loan model, a real estate loan model, and a housing loan model.

Source: M. Subhaswadikul, Powerpoint presentation, "Stress Testing: The Experience of Bank of Thailand," Third SEACEN–Deutsche Bundesbank Intermediate Course on Banking Supervision and Financial Stability, Kuala Lumpur, May 11, 2010.

overall banking system and its focus on the individual bank, will not be able to capture the contagion effect or the macrofinancial feedback effect. Therefore, the standard practice would be to perform both top-down and bottom-up techniques.

In short, three prerequisites will ensure a production stress test. One, a high level of high-quality data is imperative to conduct any meaningful test. Two, selecting plausible scenarios and building appropriate models that capture feedback effects govern the outcome and the relevancy of the stress test. Three, follow-up measures to address the outcomes of the stress test, such as adjustment in capital adequacy positions and other regulatory actions, are vital.

Joining the Bandwagon: Selected Experiences of Asia

In many developing economies, including those in Asia, stress testing is still in its infancy. Major Asian economies, such as Indonesia, Malaysia, the Philippines, Taipei,China, Thailand, Singapore, and Hong Kong, China, all underwent sensitivity tests immediately after the 1997 financial crisis. In fact, some Asian countries have conducted macroprudential surveillance (financial sector assessment programs with macro stress testing as an essential component) of their financial systems jointly with the International Monetary Fund and the World Bank. At the early stages of implementation, the stress testing was done externally by the IMF team. However, since late 2006 the central banks and monetary authorities have begun to implement basic modifications of the assessment program model. The case of Thailand is summarized in box 4-1. This case represents the general

Table 4-5. *Macroeconomic Scenarios for Credit Risk Stress Testing, Selected Asian Countries*

Country	*Scenario*
Hong Kong, China	Ranges for baseline and stress scenario via domestic GDP growth rate, GDP growth rate of mainland China, interest rate, and property price
Indonesia	A shift in credit collectability to lower level by 20% each, a rise in the interest rate by 100 bps, rupiah depreciation by 20% from the foreign exchange maturity profile of less than three months, price of government bond drop by 20%, and drops in real domestic GDP growth rate
Malaysia	Macroeconomic parameters that are comparable to such historic worst levels as the 1997 East Asian financial crisis, the 2001 dot.com bubble, and the 2003 SARS outbreak; and external factors such as prolonged slowdowns of global and regional economies
Philippines	Domestic GDP growth rate, interest rate, inflation rate, remittance growth rate, and exchange rate (against the U.S. dollar)
Singapore	Various macroeconomic shocks, shocks to the global economy, dividend payouts, and earning projections over stress horizon
Taipei,China	Fall in revenues of corporate borrowers, decline in real income of household borrowers, and decline in real estate collateral
Thailand	Domestic growth rates of GDP and its various components, interest rate, inflation rate (core and headline), exchange rate (against the U.S. dollar), crude oil price, and trading partner GDP growth rates

Source: Financial stability reports of central banks and monetary authorities; SEACEN Centre survey, October 2010.

process that applies also to Indonesia, Malaysia, and the Philippines. In addition, a number of SEACEN central banks have embarked on a similar effort. The central bank of Sri Lanka for instance officially launched its quarterly stress testing in 2009, and the central bank of Nepal initiated trial stress testing on commercial banks in early 2010.

It is worth highlighting that before 2007 the sensitive stress-testing technique was predominantly employed by the central banks and monetary authorities of East and Southeast Asia. Not until 2008 and 2009 were other scenarios explored; these scenarios tested various risks, like credit, liquidity, and market. For credit risk, a number of scenarios are shared by these countries (table 4-5). Furthermore, the implementation of a foundation internal rating base for examining credit risk in major economies in Asia and the Pacific in general is still in a very early stage (table 4-6). For the most part the standardized approach has been used.

Similarly, the sophistication of the financial sector clearly governs the selection and design of the scenarios for other types of shock. The scenario for the trading

Table 4-6. *Time Table, Implementation of Foundation Internal Rating Base, Selected Asian Countries*

	Credit risk			Operational risk		
Country	*Standardized approach*[a]	*Foundation IRB*	*Advanced IRB*	*Basic indicators approach*	*Standardized approach*	*Advanced measurement approaches*
Australia	2008	2008	2008	2008	2008	2008
China	Not permitted	2010–13[b]	2010–13[b]	Undecided	Undecided	Undecided
Hong Kong, China	2007	2007	2008	2007	2007	Not permitted
India	2008–09[c]	2012–14	2012–14	2008–09[c]	2012–14	2012–14
Indonesia	2009	2010[d]	2010[d]	2009	2010[d]	2011[e]
Japan	2007[f]	2007[f]	2008[f]	2007[f]	2007[f]	2008[f]
Korea	2008	2008	2009	2008	2008	2009
Malaysia	2008	2010	2010	2008–10[g]	2008–10[g]	Undecided
New Zealand	2008	2008	2008	2008	2008	2008
Philippines	2007[h]	2010	2010	2007[h]	2007[h]	2010
Singapore	2008	2008	2008	2008	2008	2008
Taipei,China	2007	2007	2008	2007	2007	2008
Thailand	2008[d]	2008[d]	2009[d]	2008[d]	2008[d]	Not permitted

Source: H. Zhu (2010).

a. Minimum capital requirements.

b. Permitted only for internationally active banks; banks can implement an IRB approach as early as December 31, 2010, but it must be implemented by December 31, 2013.

c. For Indian banks with a foreign presence and foreign banks operating in India—March 31, 2008; for all other banks—March 31, 2009.

d. December 31.

e. June 30.

f. March 31.

g. For banks adopting the standardized approach for credit risk—2008; for those adopting an IRB approach for credit risk—2010.

h. July 1.

risk component of market risk and liquidity risk is influenced by the financial assets being traded. In the case of Hong Kong, China, for instance, the scenarios would include a sharp shock to prices of a structured financial asset, while for most of the emerging markets in Southeast Asia, the offering of structured products has so far been either tightly regulated or prohibited completely.[20]

There are several immediate challenges to the overall improvement of stress testing by Asian central banks and commercial banks, particularly in emerging markets. One challenge is the quality of the data. A lack of high-frequency and long time-series data at disaggregated levels prevents expansion of scenarios that can be tested and, therefore, the comprehensiveness of the analyses that can be generated.

Another limitation of the stress testing in Asia is with the models used. As indicated before, the choice of model is still simplistic. They are mostly linear model equations, which may be suitable to examine risk exposures in a normal economic environment but not in a crisis. Furthermore, the models do not incorporate feedback effects, and risks are still frequently treated and evaluated separately. As discussed earlier, the absence of feedback effects suggests that the stress testing did not take into account second-round effects and critical systemic effects. Data and model limitations are the fundamental weaknesses in infrastructure and have been found to limit the ability of banks to identify and aggregate exposures across the wider financial system.[21]

Another critical shortcoming of stress testing by commercial banks in emerging markets in Asia is the lack of appreciation and commitment on the part of the senior management of these banks. This weakness however is global and not unique to Asia. According to the Basel Committee, "Prior to the crisis, stress testing at some banks was performed mainly as an isolated exercise by the risk function with little interaction with business areas. This meant, amongst other things, business areas often believed that the analysis was not credible."[22] It is often the case that commercial banks carry out internal stress testing mainly to comply with requests by the supervisory authority. In July 2008 the Institute of International Finance published its *Final Report of the IIF Committee on Market Best Practices: Principles of Conduct and Best Practice Recommendations.* The report underscores that, for stress testing to have a meaningful impact on business decisions, the board and senior management ought to have an active role in evaluating the results and the impacts on a bank's risk profile.

20. To promote product transparency and consumer protection, Bank Indonesia has prohibited banks from offering structured products, including foreign exchange transactions against the local currency, the rupiah.

21. Basel Committee on Banking Supervision (2009). It is recognized however that the complexity and sophistication of the models do not guarantee the comprehensiveness of the results.

22. Basel Committee on Banking Supervision (2009, p. 8).

By the same token, for the stress test to be a credible one, monetary authorities must ensure the transparency of the whole process. An important aspect of stress testing is disclosure of results.[23] Stress test results may be disclosed to the public in one of three ways.[24] The first way is release of detailed information about the methodology and the banks' specific outcome. The second is release of detailed information but without the specific results of individual banks. The third is release of aggregate results with forward-looking assessments of the overall financial system.

How far would Asian central banks or bank regulators publicly disclose the process and the outcome of stress testing? Would they go as far as publishing the test results for each individual bank (as in the case of the Supervisory Capital Assessment Program in the United States during the first quarter 2009) or would they just release the aggregate results of the test without revealing how individual banks fared (as in the case of the European Union stress test results in 2009)? One thing is certain, though: the disclosure of stress test results can increase the understanding of financial markets.

However, it is also important to realize that disclosure can be damaging, especially for economies that are heavily reliant on the role of banks as financial intermediaries (such as in Europe and Asia, versus in the United States).[25] Due to the complexity of stress test results, industry practitioners caution against the risk of their misinterpretation by the public. If the support mechanisms are not made explicit beforehand, making the results of stress tests public would not be recommended, as it could lead to uncertainty and could even destabilize markets.[26] On the other hand, P. M. Nagy points out that past experiences demonstrate that market reaction to stress test results has been positive.[27] D. K. Tarullo also argues that the more frequent the release of stress test results, the better for the market, as frequent and detailed disclosure can result in fewer unpleasant surprises.[28]

Table 4-7 reveals some of the features of participation, frequency, and dissemination of stress testing among selected SEACEN economies. As expected, a range of stress-testing practices are used by these countries. To ensure comprehensive testing, at least 60 percent, and as much as 100 percent, of a country's commercial banks are required to participate. Thailand and Taipei,China carry out the

23. To restore confidence in European banks, European Union leaders agreed in June 2010 to publish the results of the bank stress tests in July 2010.

24. Tarullo (2010).

25. Nagy (2009).

26. A. Kirchfeld and S. Clark, "Deutsche Bank CEO Says EU Stress Tests Could Be 'Dangerous,' " *Bloomberg News* (www.bloomberg.com/news/2010-06-10/ackermann-says-publishing-bank-stress-tests-data-could-be-very-dangerous-.html).

27. Nagy (2009).

28. D. K. Tarullo, speech, Federal Reserve Board, International Research Forum on Monetary Policy, Washington, March 26, 2010.

Table 4-7. *Participation, Frequency, and Dissemination of Stress Test Results, Selected Asian Countries*

Country	*Institutions participating*	*Frequency*	*Public dissemination of results*
Indonesia	All	Monthly for credit, market and liquidity risk, quarterly for macrorisk analysis	Partial disclosure (no name of institution) via financial stability review report
Malaysia	All financial institutions under the supervision of Bank Negara Malaysia	Quarterly by financial institutions, semiannually by Bank Negara Malaysia	Partial disclosure (no name of institution) via financial stability review report
Philippines	Top ten (of thirty-eight) universal and commercial banks, or around 62% of the country's banking system in March 2010	Quarterly	Partial disclosure (no name of institution) via financial stability review report
Singapore	20% of banks, or more than 65% of banking system	At least annually	No
Sri Lanka	All commercial banks	Quarterly	No
Taipei,China	92% of domestic banks, covering 98% of total domestic bank assets	Annually	No
Thailand	All local banks, covering 80% of total portfolio of each bank	Annually	No

Source: Financial stability reports of central banks and monetary authorities; SEACEN Centre survey, October 2010.

testing on an annual basis, while others have chosen more frequent examinations (quarterly and monthly). Based on the survey conducted by the SEACEN Centre, a fair share of SEACEN central banks still have no plans to publicly disseminate the results of the testing. Bank Indonesia, Bank Negara Malaysia, and the Central Bank of the Philippines partially disclose the aggregate results via their financial stability reports.

Furthermore, given the interconnectivity of the financial sector with the corporate and household sectors, should the central bank/monetary authority also consider conducting stress testing on those two sectors as well? In particular, recognizing the rising trend of household and corporate debt and the exposure to the banking sector, Bank of Thailand for instance has started to conduct stress testing on the household and corporate sectors to enhance their capacity to achieve and manage financial stability.

A comprehensive analysis of stress-testing results may also require systems thinking beyond national borders by taking into account international linkages and dynamics. As the recent case of structured credit and credit derivatives markets shows, the scale of cross-border banking is becoming increasing large, which has the potential to transmit shocks from one country to another on a large scale. Currently, stress test modeling has not reached that level of sophistication to take into account cross-border dynamics. However, supervisors can share vital cross-border information regarding their domestic financial situation.

Supervision: Beyond the Borders

Having comprehensive information on the exposures of a bank's balance sheet to shocks from both macroeconomic conditions (internal and external) and the activities of other financial and nonfinancial institutions is vital for the overall success of stress testing, both at the individual level of the bank and at the overall level of the banking system. Recent efforts, therefore, to address this need will strengthen the apparatus for the supervision of financial institutions.

For the Asian economies affected by the 1997 financial crisis, the struggle to enhance the supervision of financial institutions started immediately after the crisis. Following the 1997 financial crisis, the debate centered on the need for an integrated domestic financial supervisory system to keep up with the advances in the banking sector.[29] Banks no longer provide conventional services (such as savings and loans). Instead they provide investment and insurance services. Furthermore, the challenges facing the central bank as bank supervisor include possible inconsistencies among monetary policy objectives, the objectives of prudential supervision, and the promotion of a sector of the financial service industry.

Past financial crises, including those experienced by the developed economies, teach us that the last objective is often dominant. In the 1980s massive losses were incurred in the U.S. thrift industry partly because the industry's prudential supervisor, the Federal Home Loan Board, was also charged with promoting the housing industry. The 1997 Asian financial crisis highlights efforts to bail out institutions, which resulted in a sudden and severe rise in the rate of inflation and in the meltdown of local currencies, particularly in Indonesia. In many Asian emerging markets the central bank is still playing a critical role of agent for development (there has always been strong political pressure to support small and medium-sized enterprises). A careful assessment of this policy should be carried out to prevent future losses.

29. Siregar and James (2006).

The recent U.S. experience highlights the need to strengthen coordination among domestic financial supervisory agencies.[30] The U.S. Securities and Exchange Commission is responsible for setting accounting policies to assist investors in making informed decisions. The SEC believes that reported net income in each period should fairly reflect the results of the firm's operation for that period. The Federal Reserve's regulatory agencies, on the other hand—which are responsible for the prudential supervision of commercial banking—believe that banks should build up loan loss reserves during good periods to cover losses that are likely to be incurred during weaker economic conditions. The two conflicting approaches could easily lead to inconsistent reporting.[31]

Coordination among financial supervisors has arguably improved in Asia during the past decade. The Bank of Korea conducts a regular examination of financial institutions through the Financial Supervisory Service, an independent, integrated, financial institution, established in 1998. The Central Bank Act of Indonesia, introduced in 1999, stipulates the commitment of Bank Indonesia, jointly with the Ministry of Finance, to establish an independent and integrated financial supervisory institution by the end of 2010. In Malaysia, the Central Bank Act of 2009, which came into force in November 2009, provides a consolidated supervisory mandate for the central bank, Bank Negara Malaysia. Provisions of the act include the power to require relevant information for the purpose of measuring financial stability among both banks and nonbanks.

Furthermore, in countries such as the Philippines and Indonesia a financial sector forum plays a major role in improving coordination among the supervisory agencies of financial institutions. The forum aims to facilitate regular consultations and an exchange of information among its members relating to the supervision and regulation of financial institutions. The members are the central bank, the securities and exchange commission, and the deposit insurance agency. In Indonesia, the ministry of finance is also a member of this forum.

The recent global financial meltdown pushed the envelope on the issue of banking supervision and regulation. The presence of multinational banks, including emerging regional multinational banks, forced central banks to get involved in cross-border supervisory arrangements. As discussed, globalized banks play a crucial role in the international transmission of monetary policies and economic shocks. Naturally, cross-border cooperation and coordination will become increasingly vital as banking systems become even more globally integrated.[32] The effec-

30. Wall (2009).

31. A number of U.S. banks, including Sun Trust (a large regional bank), were caught between the two regulators (Wall, 2009). The U.S. Congress eventually had to step in and mediate the policy conflicts between these two key regulatory agencies.

32. As the subprime crisis shows, the lack of information on cross-border risk exposure resulted in an underappreciation of systemic risks and connections by supervisors and regulators (Kodres and Narain, 2009).

tiveness of various prudential measures to supervise cross-border financial institutions must therefore be enhanced with adequate cross-country supervisory cooperation and coordination to avoid loopholes, such as currency substitution or switching from domestic lending in foreign currency to direct foreign credit.

One potentially effective method to facilitate cross-border policy cooperation and coordination is through the college of supervisors, defined as a "permanent, although flexible, structure for cooperation and coordination among the authorities of different jurisdictions responsible for and involved in the supervision of the different components of cross-border banking groups."[33] As a general rule, the establishment of a supervisory college should be considered for significant financial institutions, taking into account their size, their interconnectedness with other components of the financial system, and their role in the market (whether they can systemically affect the country's financial system).

A recent survey identifies a number of regional and global banks with a strong presence in major Asian economies.[34] The Hong Kong Shanghai Banking Corporation, the Citibank, and the Standard Chartered Bank are the three major international banks that have wide and intensive networks of branches in Asia (table 4-8). The region has also witnessed the emergence of its own multinational banks. In Malaysia, Maybank, the CIMB Group, and the RHB bank have expanded their networks beyond the major Southeast Asian countries. A number of Singapore banks, namely the Development Bank of Singapore, the United Overseas Bank, and the Overseas Chinese Bank Corporation, have achieved a similar success in their efforts to become regional banks.

Beginning in May 2010 a number of major central banks in Asia have been invited to participate in colleges of supervisors. Bank Negara Malaysia for instance is involved in the colleges of supervisors organized by the Financial Stability Agency of the United Kingdom for the Standard Chartered Group, the BaFIN for the Deustche Bank group, and the OFSI for Bank of Nova Scotia Group. Similarly, the Monetary Authority of Singapore and the Central Bank of the Philippines have also participated in a number of colleges of supervisors organized for major European and U.S. banks. However, as of June 2010 there has not been any arrangement for supervisory colleges for Asian regional multinational banks, such as those for Malaysian and Singaporean banks discussed earlier.

A number of issues and challenges were recognized by the Asian central banks and monetary authorities during their participation in various colleges of supervisors. Some of these challenges are not specific to Asian central banks but are shared by many others globally. To start, it is imperative that information exchange be a two-way process and that it reflects the needs of all the authorities

33. Committee of European Banking Supervisors (2010, p. 1). As of September 2009 there were more than thirty colleges to supervise these institutions.

34. Siregar and Lim (2010).

Table 4-8. *Significant Asian Financial Institutions*

Central banks	*Top 3 domestic foreign institutions in jurisdiction with significant presence in the region*	*Top 3 foreign institutions in jurisdiction from SEACEN member countries*	*Top 3 other foreign institutions (apart from SEACEN member countries) with significant presence in country*
Ministry of Finance, Brunei Darussalam	Domestic banks have a presence only within the country	Maybank (Malaysia), UOB (Singapore), RHB Bank Berhad (Malaysia)	Citibank, HSBC, Standard Chartered Bank
Bank Indonesia	Bank Mandiri, Bank BRI, BCA	CIMB Niaga (Malaysia), Bank International Indonesia (MayBank Malaysia controls around 43%)	Citibank, HSBC, Standard Chartered Bank
Bank of Korea	None	DBS (Singapore), UOB (Singapore), OCBC (Singapore)	Citibank, HSBC, Standard Chartered Bank
Bank Negara Malaysia	Maybank, CIMB Group, Public Bank	OCBC (Singapore), UOB (Singapore), Bangkok Bank (Thailand)	Citibank, HSBC, Standard Chartered Bank
Bank of Papua New Guinea	Bank South Pacific	Maybank (Malaysia)	ANZ Bank (Australia), Westpac Bank (Australia)
Bangko Sentral ng Pilipinas	Metropolitan Bank Corporation (Metrobank), Philippine National Bank (PNB)	Chinatrust (Taipei,China), Maybank (Malaysia), Korea Exchange Bank (Korea)	Citibank, HSBC, Standard Chartered Bank
Monetary Authority of Singapore	DBS Bank Limited, OCBC, UOB	Maybank (Malaysia), Bangkok Bank (Thailand), RHB Bank (Malaysia)	Citibank, HSBC, Standard Chartered Bank
Central Bank of the Republic of China (Taipei,China)	Bank of Taiwan,[a] Taiwan Cooperative Bank,[a] Mega International Commercial Bank	DBS (Singapore), OCBC (Singapore), Bangkok Bank (Thailand)	Citibank, HSBC, Standard Chartered Bank
Bank of Thailand	Bangkok Bank, Kasikorn Bank, Siam Commercial Bank	UOB (Singapore), CIMB Thai (Malaysia), OCBC (Singapore)	GE Capital, ING, Standard Chartered Bank

Source: Siregar and Lim (2010).

a. A financial institution in the ADB member referred to as "Taipei,China."

involved to ensure effective prudential supervision. However, supervisors may be under various legal and constitutional constraints on sharing such vital information. Furthermore, given the sensitivity of the information, supervisors need to weigh national interests. In some circumstances, when problems surface there may be a divergence of interests. Either the home or the host supervisor may seek to ignore problems at the national level and, hence, impede the detection of group-wide, cross-border problems. Some central banks in Asia have also expressed concern over differing levels of supervisory and manpower capacity.

The home country versus host country issue may also arise due to the importance of the relevant financial institution. For instance, a global financial institution may be deemed systemic and significant by the host supervisor of country A. Yet the home supervisor may consider its presence insignificant given its global activities.[35] In such a case, one may apply the principle of proportionality.[36] The principle of proportionality gives a more prominent role to entities that figure prominently in their jurisdictions (for example, in terms of asset size). In this way, incentive problems can be reduced.

Liquidity Risk Management

The importance of liquidity for the functioning and stability of the financial sector is underscored by past financial crises.[37] The recent subprime crisis reaffirms the importance of liquidity. The massive and rapid provision of liquidities to interbank markets during the crisis by central banks and monetary authorities around the world has been credited with the economic recoveries of recent months. The role of the central bank as provider of market liquidity during times of disorderly and illiquid markets has been referred to as market maker of last resort. In a recent study, W. H. Buiter compares and contrasts the effectiveness of these policies across a number of central banks in developed economies, namely the European Central Bank, the Bank of England, and the Federal Reserve.[38] Policy measures to manage liquidity during the crisis period have indeed been costly. Provision of liquidity in the interbank market against credit-risky collateral has placed central banks' balance sheets at risk. The experiences of central banks of small, open economies throughout Latin America demonstrate that systemic liquidity provision can lead to sharp depreciation of the exchange rate and, in the

35. For instance, Citibank NA, the biggest foreign bank in Indonesia, has only 0.29 percent of the total assets of Citigroup. Given this, Bank Indonesia has had difficulty soliciting sufficient information on the overall soundness of this group from Citigroup's home regulator.

36. J. C. Trichet, "Towards the Review of the Lamfalussy Approach: Market Developments, Supervisory Challenges and Institutional Arrangements," speech, First CEBS Conference, London, May 9, 2007.

37. The discussion in this section benefits greatly from Subhanij (2010) and from the research project on measurement and management of liquidity conducted by SEACEN Centre in 2009.

38. Buiter (2008).

long run, to inflation.[39] A similar experience has been reported in Indonesia during the 1997 financial crisis.[40]

Given the high cost of liquidity provision, it is in the interest of any central bank to reduce systemic liquidity stresses. The objective of this section is to take stock of the challenges facing the management of liquidity in the financial sector and, more important, to evaluate what has been done by central banks in Asia to enhance their capacities and to conform to the initiatives on liquidity management introduced by the Basel Committee.

When discussing the liquidity of financial sector, three broad types of liquidity should be considered. One type is funding liquidity. It refers to the ability of banks to meet their liabilities and their due obligations.[41] A second type is market liquidity. This refers to the ability to trade an asset on short notice, at low cost, and with minimal impact on its price.[42] The third type is central bank liquidity. This one is the least discussed, but during a crisis the ability of the central bank to inject liquidity into the market is detrimental to the overall functioning and stability of the financial sector, as witnessed during the recent subprime crisis.

A survey conducted by the SEACEN Centre of a number of central banks in Asia highlights various factors affecting the liquidity of the financial sector (table 4-9). The most common source of funding liquidity is the liquidity mismatch between assets and liabilities (that is, assets being less liquid than liabilities). This is not a surprise, given the basic function of a bank—namely to transform liquid short-term deposits into illiquid long-term loans. The second most dominant source of the liquidity problem is inadequate liquidity risk management. Concurrently, this same factor appears as the most crucial root cause of market illiquidity. This finding accentuates the urgency to develop comprehensive stress-testing practices to strengthen liquidity risk management capacity. Shifts in monetary policy and supervisory regulation have also been listed as major factors in funding liquidity, especially for newly emerging markets, such as Cambodia. Requirements for larger reserves and capital are examples of amendments to the supervisory regulations.

For the more advanced and open Asian economies (Korea, Malaysia, Philippines, Thailand, Taipei,China, and Indonesia), global financial crises and the contagion effect are the factors that financial institutions and central banks have to closely monitor in their management of liquidity. Following the subprime crisis, the impact was felt in the bond markets, where the outflow of foreign investment led to a shortage of liquidity in the Korean bond market. High loan-to-deposit

39. Jacome (2008).
40. Siregar (2005).
41. Basel Committee on Banking Supervision (2008).
42. Sarr and Lybeck (2002).

Table 4-9. *Factors Affecting Funding and Market Liquidities, Selected Asian Countries*

Type of liquidity	*Countries*
Funding	
Inadequate liquidity risk management	Cambodia; Malaysia; Nepal; Sri Lanka; Thailand; Taipei,China; Indonesia; Brunei Darussalam; Viet Nam
Lack of contingency funding plan	Malaysia, Nepal, Sri Lanka, Indonesia
Regulatory changes	Cambodia, Malaysia, Nepal, Philippines, Thailand
Stresses in local financial market	Malaysia, Nepal, Philippines
Contagion effect	Korea; Malaysia; Philippines; Taipei,China; Thailand; Indonesia
Asset-liability mismatch	Cambodia; Korea; Malaysia; Myanmar; Nepal; Philippines; Sri Lanka; Taipei,China; Thailand; Indonesia; Brunei Darussalam; Viet Nam
Lack of alternative funding	Korea, Malaysia, Nepal, Sri Lanka, Indonesia, Viet Nam
Loss of confidence	Cambodia; Malaysia; Taipei,China; Thailand; Indonesia
Market	
Inadequate liquidity risk management	Malaysia; Nepal; Sri Lanka; Taipei,China; Brunei Darussalam; Viet Nam
Global financial crisis	Korea, Malaysia, Philippines, Thailand, Indonesia
Stresses in local financial market	Korea, Malaysia, Philippines, Indonesia
Changes in monetary policy	Malaysia, Nepal, Sri Lanka, Thailand
Lack of liquidity in interbank and bond markets	Korea, Malaysia, Nepal, Philippines, Thailand, Indonesia
Loss of confidence	Korea; Taipei,China; Thailand; Indonesia
Contagion effect	Philippines; Taipei,China; Thailand

Source: SEACEN Centre survey, December 2009; M. Subhaswadikul, "Stress-Testing: The Experience of Bank of Thailand," Powerpoint presentation, Third SEACEN–Deutsche Bundesbank Intermediate Course on Banking Supervision and Financial Stability, Kuala Lumpur, May 11, 2010.

ratios and a reliance on bond issuances further fueled foreign investors' loss of confidence in Korea.

Unlike the 1997 financial crisis, however, the banking sectors of Asian countries were in a much better position during the recent crisis. Funding liquidity appears to be abundant in most parts of the region. Deposits continue to grow, with the exception of Thailand. Strong deposits contribute to a healthy loan-to-deposit ratio of 70–80 percent. Banks in the region hold a large amount of excess reserves, so that liquid assets are more than adequate to cover short-term liabilities. Furthermore, the ratio of excess to required reserves ranges from 20 percent

Table 4-10. *Funding Liquidity, Selected Asian Countries, June 2009*
Percent

Country	*Excess to required reserves*	*Loan to deposit ratio*	*Deposit growth rate*	*Liquid asset to short-run liabilities*
Cambodia	220.00	83.00	2.44	46.00
Korea	2,304.00	108.12	3.42	122.60
Malaysia	324.00	81.00	1.61	24.78
Nepal	23.00	71.00	12.60	. . .
Philippines	23.40	69.10	10.20	51.80
Sri Lanka	–0.73	78.50	8.30	34.70
Taipei,China	304.40	76.80	11.50	28.31
Thailand	399.10	102.80	–1.62	29.90

Source: SEACEN Centre survey, December 2009; M. Subhaswadikul, "Stress-Testing: The Experience of Bank of Thailand," Powerpoint presentation, Third SEACEN–Deutsche Bundesbank Intermediate Course on Banking Supervision and Financial Stability, Kuala Lumpur, May 11, 2010

to 2,000 percent, while the ratio of liquid assets to short-term liabilities is also well above the minimum targets of 25–125 percent (table 4-10).

Reform initiatives taken immediately after the outset of the 1997 financial crisis contributed significantly to the strength of the banking sectors of these Asian economies. Liquidity ratio, cash flow projections, and minimum quantitative limits such as liquid asset and reserve holdings have become common instruments for liquidity management for commercial banks (table 4-11). In addition, these banks are required to report their liquidity positions on a regular basis to supervisory institutions (table 4-12). It is important to underline here, however, that the quality and the enforcement of these regulations vary from one jurisdiction to another. In the Philippines for instance, the required reserve is the highest in the region, at 19 percent, reflecting in part authorities' concern about the health of the banking system. Classifications of liquid assets also vary from one country to another. For example, in Cambodia, liquid assets include only cash and bank accounts. In Malaysia, apart from securities issued by the government and Bank Negara Malaysia, other securities such as those issued by recognized government-linked institutions, banker's acceptance, negotiable certificates of deposit, residential mortgage-backed securities, and equities are also considered liquid assets. Efforts to align classification and reinforcement regulations with the international standard are certainly warranted.

Going forward, a number of new initiatives have been considered and passed by the Basel Committee on Banking Supervision. In September 2008 bank regulators issued a revised set of principles on how banks should manage liquidity.[43]

43. Basel Committee on Banking Supervision (2008).

Table 4-11. *Banks' Liquidity Management Instruments, Selected Asian Countries*

Instrument	*Countries*
Minimum holdings of liquid assets	Korea; Malaysia; Nepal; Philippines; Sri Lanka; Taipei,China; Thailand; Indonesia; Brunei Darussalam; Viet Nam
Minimum holdings of reserves	Cambodia; Korea; Malaysia; Nepal; Philippines; Sri Lanka; Taipei,China; Thailand; Indonesia; Brunei Darussalam; Viet Nam
Liquidity ratio	Cambodia; Korea; Malaysia; Philippines; Sri Lanka; Taipei,China; Thailand; Indonesia; Brunei Darussalam; Viet Nam
Limits on concentration of funding	Cambodia; Korea; Malaysia; Sri Lanka; Taipei,China; Thailand; Indonesia
Cash flow projections	Cambodia; Korea; Malaysia; Sri Lanka; Taipei,China; Thailand; Indonesia; Brunei Darussalam; Viet Nam
Maximum cash outflow	Korea; Malaysia; Nepal; Philippines; Sri Lanka; Taipei,China; Thailand; Indonesia; Brunei Darussalam; Viet Nam

Source: Subhanij (2010); SEACEN Centre survey, December 2009.

These principles impose supervisory expectations on a framework for banks' liquidity risk management. The principles consist of the following elements: board and senior management oversight; the establishment of policies and risk tolerance; the use of liquidity risk management tools such as comprehensive cash flow forecasting, limits, and liquidity stress testing; the development of contingency funding plans; and a buffer of high-quality liquid assets to meet contingent liquidity needs. Supervisors are expected to evaluate both the sufficiency of a bank's liquidity risk management and its liquidity exposure. Moreover, supervisors are expected to address a bank's risk management inadequacies or excess exposure, so as to protect depositors and ensure financial stability.

A number of Asian economies, such as Malaysia, the Philippines, Sri Lanka, Indonesia, Brunei Darussalam, and Viet Nam, require contingency funding planning (CFP) by their local commercial banks. Others, such as Cambodia, Korea, Taipei,China, and Thailand, have incorporated CFP into their prudential liquidity guidelines. There is, however, a noticeable difference in enforcement of CFP from one country to another. In Korea, banks follow multistage contingency plans, wherein banks undertake appropriate responses to a fall or rise in liquidity indicators. In Sri Lanka, however, only a few banks fully adhere to CFP.

Following the recommendation of the G-20 to establish by 2010 a global framework for stronger bank liquidity buffers, the Basel Committee released, in December 2009, a consultative document on an international framework for

Table 4-12. *Frequency of Liquidity Disclosure to Central Banks, Selected Asian Countries*

Country	*Deposit concentration*	*Loan-to-deposit ratio*	*Short-term liabilities breakdown*	*Maturity gap report*	*Liquid assets breakdown*	*Liquidity ratios*	*Liquidity gap report*
Cambodia	Monthly	Monthly	Monthly	Monthly	Monthly	Monthly	Monthly
Korea	NR	NR	Monthly	Monthly	Monthly	Weekly	Monthly
Malaysia	Monthly	Monthly	Monthly	Monthly	Monthly	Monthly	Monthly
Philippines	Monthly and quarterly	Monthly and quarterly	Monthly and quarterly	Monthly and quarterly	Monthly and quarterly	Monthly and quarterly	Monthly and quarterly
Sri Lanka	Weekly	NR	NR	Monthly	NR	Monthly	NR
Taipei,China	Monthly	Monthly	NR	Monthly	Monthly	Monthly	Monthly
Thailand	Monthly	Monthly	Monthly	Monthly	Monthly	Monthly	Monthly
Indonesia	Daily	Weekly and monthly	Daily	Daily	Daily	Daily	Monthly
Viet Nam	NR	NR	NR	NR	NR	Daily and weekly	NR

Source: SEACEN Centre survey, December 2009; M. Subhaswadikul, "Stress-Testing: The Experience of Bank of Thailand," Powerpoint presentation, Third SEACEN–Deutsche Bundesbank Intermediate Course on Banking Supervision and Financial Stability, Kuala Lumpur, May 11, 2010.

NR = No reporting required.

liquidity risk measurement, standards, and monitoring.[44] Banks are expected to meet these standards and also to adhere to all the principles set out in September 2008. In effect, there are two standards for liquidity risk, namely the liquidity coverage ratio and the net stable funding ratio. The liquidity coverage ratio specifies the amount of high-quality liquid assets a bank can use to offset the net cash outflows it experiences under severe, short-term, stress. This ratio is meant to ensure that banks have adequate, high-quality, liquid resources to survive a month of extreme stress.[45] The net stable funding ratio, on the other hand, sets a minimum acceptable amount of stable funding to survive a year. The objective is to promote resiliency over a long time horizon by creating incentives for banks to aim for stable funding.[46]

To further strengthen and improve consistency in international liquidity risk supervision, the Basel Committee also developed tools to be used by supervisors to monitor the liquidity risk profiles of banks globally. The proposed tools include the following: contractual maturity mismatch (provides an initial, simple baseline of contractual commitments), concentration of funding (involves analyzing concentrations of wholesale funding), available unencumbered assets (measures the amount of unencumbered assets a bank could use as collateral for secured funding), market-related monitoring tools (includes monitoring marketwide data on, among others, asset prices and liquidity, credit default swap spreads, and equity prices).

New Capital Standards under Basel III

Basel III represents a new era for global capital standards, with an emphasis on increasing both the quality and level of banks' capital.[47] Recognizing the procyclical nature of banking activities and the close connectivity of macroeconomic and financial sector conditions, the primary objective of the new capital standard is to enhance the quality and the level of banks' capital. On September 2010 the Group of Governors and Heads of Supervision (the Basel Committee's governing body) announced higher global minimum capital standards for commercial banks. This followed the agreement reached in July 2010 on the overall design of the capital and liquidity reform package—referred to as Basel III.

The tier 1 minimum capital requirement, which includes common equity and other qualifying financial instruments based on stricter criteria, will be

44. Basel Committee on Banking Supervision (2009).

45. Liquidity coverage ratio = stock of high-quality liquid assets/net cash outflows over a thirty-day time period $\geq$ 100 percent.

46. Net stable funding = available amount of stable funding/required amount of stable funding $>$ 100 percent.

47. J. Caruana, "Macroprudential Policy: Could It Have Been Different This Time?" speech, People's Bank of China Seminar, Shanghai, October 18, 2010.

Table 4-13. *Components of New Capital Framework*
Percent

	Common equity	*Tier 1 capital*	*Total capital*
Minimum	4.5	6.0	8.0
Conservation buffer	2.5	. . .	. . .
Minimum + conservation buffer	7.0	8.5	10.5
Countercyclical capital buffer	1–2.5	0–2.5	. . .

Source: Danske Markets (2010).

increased to 6 percent, compared to a minimum ratio of 4 percent under Basel II (table 4-13). Under the new standard, a higher minimum capital requirement in terms of common equity is raised from 2 percent to 4.5 percent of risk-weighted assets. Furthermore, a broader and stricter definition of risk-weighted assets was imposed, particularly with the restrictive treatment of trading book, counterparty risk, and securitizations. With the new tighter treatment, the common equity minimum capital increased effectively from roughly 1 percent to 4.5 percent. Hence the new capital requirement is expected to increase not only the level of capital adequacy but also the quality of loss-absorbing capital.

To improve further the resilience of the banking sector, a 2.5 percent capital conservation buffer (CCB) was added on top of the 4.5 percent minimum capital requirement in the category of common equity, pushing the top-quality equity capital requirement to 7.0 percent, compared to just 2 percent under Basel II standards. There is also flexibility in the CCB, as it can be drawn down in times of losses, thus mitigating procyclicality in times of stress for individual banks. The CCB has a macroprudential dimension, as it can impact credit supply.[48]

Another important aspect of the systemwide approach is the countercyclical buffer (0–2.5 percent) of common equity or other fully loss-absorbing capital, in addition to the CCB, to ensure that systemically important financial institutions possess loss-absorbing capacity beyond the common standards. The cyclical buffer, aimed at achieving the broader macroprudential goal, is based on private sector credit, as excess aggregate credit growth has often been associated with systemic risk. It is up to national supervisors to exercise judgment on the common point of reference and determine when it is necessary to impose such a buffer.[49] There is no cost for withdrawal, in contrast to the CCB, which imposes some costs if it is drawn down. These costs might include restrictions on earning distributions to stakeholders for banks approaching the regulatory minimum requirements.

48. Caruana, "Macroprudential Policy."

49. However, the Basel Committee on Banking Supervision expects the national authority to invoke this requirement only infrequently.

Table 4-14. *New Minimum Capital Requirements, 2013–19*
Percent

	2013	*2014*	*2015*	*2016*	*2017*	*2018*	*2019*
Minimum common equity ratio	3.5	4.0	4.5	4.50	4.50	4.50	4.5
Capital conservation buffer	. . .	. . .	. . .	0.63	1.25	1.88	2.5
Common equity plus capital conservation buffer	3.5	4.0	4.5	5.13	5.75	6.38	7.0
Minimum tier 1 capital	4.5	5.5	6.0	6.00	6.00	6.00	6.0
Total capital	8.0	8.0	8.0	8.00	8.00	8.00	8.0
Total capital plus conservation buffer	8.0	8.0	8.0	8.63	9.13	9.88	10.5

Source: Bank for International Settlements; Danske Markets (2010).

Last, a nonrisk-based leverage ratio (that is, tier 1 capital divided by total assets, with no risk weighting), which acts as a backstop (that is, as a last resort), is proposed to address the risk of buildup of excessive leverage in the system.[50] The backstop leverage ratio ensures that resulting distortions, if any, are kept within a certain range if risk-based capital rules are found to be wrong. In general, the minimum total capital ratio remains at 8 percent, but the additional CCB increases this ratio to 10.5 percent of risk-weighted assets, of which 8.5 percent must be tier 1 capital. Member countries will start implementing Basel III on January 1, 2013, with the phase-in period extending in some cases to January 2019 (table 4-14). For example, the phasing-in period for the CCB is between January 1, 2016, and year-end 2018, becoming fully effective on January 1, 2019. However, national authorities may shorten the phasing-in period where appropriate.

In general, Asian commercial banks are well capitalized (table 4-1). With the exception of Nepal and Mongolia, they have been maintaining a capital adequacy ratio (CAR) well above the Basel II requirement of 8 percent. By the end of March 2010, commercial banks in Malaysia maintained systemwide risk-weighted and tier 1 capital ratios at around 14.9 percent and 13.2 percent, much higher than the Basel II regulatory minimum of 8 percent and 4 percent. The monetary authority of Singapore has in fact enforced a minimum tier 1 CAR of 6 percent and a total CAR of 10 percent. In addition, a number of Asian central banks and monetary authorities encourage banks to hold more capital than the minimum requirement through incentives measures. In Taipei,China, for instance, the Financial Supervisory Commission requires a CAR well above 10 percent if banks want to establish foreign branches and subsidiaries or buy back their own shares from the stock market. The central bank in the Philippines allows a bank to expand its operation if it maintains a CAR higher than 10 percent.

50. Caruana, "Macroprudential Policy."

Furthermore, major central banks have gradually moved from minimum prescriptive loan loss provisioning to an approach based on current asset impairment. Bank Negara Malaysia adopted this approach at the end of 2009, in line with International Accounting Standard 39. The forward-looking risk assessment is also being considered by many Asian central banks in their efforts to improve their estimation of capital adequacy.

However, Mervyn King, governor of the Bank of England, suggests that the Basel III framework did not raise the capital requirement sufficiently to prevent another crisis.[51] He bases his conclusion on three criteria. First, a much higher level of capital than that proposed is needed to counteract a change in sentiment during times of stress. Second, the Basel risk-weights approach is based on estimates during normal periods, and in times of stress these valuations become very poor estimates of underlying risk. Third, the Basel framework still concentrates on the asset side of a bank's balance sheet and is, thus, inadequate to deal with risks arising from liquid assets and the risky structure of liabilities. As the financial sector system becomes more sophisticated, as is the case in the more advanced economies, banks rely less on deposits for their lending and investment activities. Liquidity mismatches may thus arise, as the net stable funding ratio can be lower than required.[52] More explicit elaboration is arguably needed for Basel III on this liquidity issue.

A. S. Blinder argues that Basel III does not fully address the issue of overreliance on credit ratings.[53] He asserts that rating agencies, which have performed poorly on rating mortgage-backed securities and collateralized debt obligations, will still play a major role in the risk-weighting process under Basel III. Furthermore, he argues, letting banks use their own internal model to measure risk remains in Basel III, and this has proven to be disastrous for Basel II. There will be challenges in implementing Basel III for supervisors across different jurisdictions.[54] However, it is fair to say that Basel III is attempting to address systemic issues more methodically. The integrated approach, which includes resolution regimes, will take into account a combination of capital surcharges, contingent capital, and bail-in debt.

51. M. King, "Banking: From Bagehot to Basel, and Back Again," speech, Second Bagehot Lecture Buttonwood Gathering, New York, October 25, 2010 (www.bankofengland.co.uk/publications/speeches/2010/speech455.pdf).

52. NFSR = stable funding (capital, deposit, etc.)/assets*haircut ratio according to liquidity of assets. This ratio should be higher than 100 percent. See Ito (2010).

53. A. S. Blinder, "Two Cheers for the New Bank Capital Standards: Why Do We Still Rely on the Rating Agencies, and Why Are We Still Allowing Lehman Brothers Levels of Leverage," opinion, *Wall Street Journal* online.

54. Slaughter and May (2010).

Closing Remarks

The outlook for most Asian economies indeed appeared much more upbeat in the first quarter of 2010 than a year earlier. Growth rate projections for 2010 and 2011 reported by market analysts and multilateral agencies have for the most part been more buoyant than those of the government of the country. This partly reflects the swift and strong return of market confidence, as capture by the falling emerging market bond index and credit default swap rates, especially after the second half of 2009. Along with the return of market confidence is the surge of capital flows into these countries. Management of these capital flows will indeed be critical to the overall strength of the economic recoveries of these countries and also to the overall stability of their financial sectors.

One immediate challenge for most central banks in this region is to unwind the stimulus packages implemented during the height of the subprime crisis. The central banks of Malaysia and the Philippines have raised their policy rates, while the monetary authority of Singapore has expanded the ban for an appreciation of the local currency to cool down inflationary pressure. While domestic economic landscapes should influence the exit strategy, external factors remain a critical consideration for the central banks in the region. The outcome of any exit strategy will likely have an impact on capital flows and therefore the management, particularly regarding risks, of these much-needed but volatile flows.

Like past crises, the recent subprime crisis challenges financial stability in particular and monetary policy in general. This chapter discusses a number of lessons and recent initiatives in the area of macroprudential regulations. Some of them are still in the very early stages of implementation and will likely continue to undergo adjustments and improvements. Stress testing for instance has indeed been recognized as a useful tool, but it remains to be seen how practical it is, especially for emerging markets. Similarly, the globalized banking system accentuates the urgency to push forward with colleges of supervisors. Skeptics however point to mounting challenges for central bankers, especially from emerging markets, to move forward and take an active role. Despite the challenges going forward, the lessons from past crises are very clear: that the repercussions from inaction are very costly. The major economies in Asia benefited from strenuous reforms that were put in place at the outset of the 1997 financial crisis.

References

Basel Committee on Banking Supervision. 2008. "Principles for Sound Liquidity Risk Management and Supervision." September.

Bayoumi, T., and O. Melander. 2008. "Credit Matters: Empirical Evidences of US Macro-Financial Linkages." Working Paper 08/169. Washington: International Monetary Fund.

Blaschke, E., and others. 2001. "Stress Testing of Financial Systems: An Overview of Issues, Methodologies, and FSAP Experiences." Washington: International Monetary Fund.

———. 2009. "Principles for Sound Stress Testing Practices and Supervision." January.

Borio, C. 2003. "Toward a Macroprudential Framework for Financial Supervision and Regulation." Working Paper 128. Basel: Bank for International Settlements.

———. 2006. "Monetary and Financial Stability: Here to Stay?" *Journal of Banking and Finance* 30: 3407–14.

Buiter, W. H. 2008. "Central Banks and Financial Crises." Paper prepared for the Federal Reserve Bank of Kansas City symposium, Jackson Hole, Wyo.

Cetorelli, N., and L. S. Goldberg. 2008. "Banking Globalization, Monetary Transmission, and the Lending Channel." Working Paper 14101. Cambridge, Mass.: National Bureau of Economic Research.

———. 2009. "Globalized Banks: Lending to Emerging Markets in the Crisis." Staff Report 337. Federal Reserve Bank of New York.

Committee of European Bank Supervisors. 2010. "Colleges of Supervisors: 10 Common Principles." London.

Committee on the Global Financial System. 2010. "Macroprudential Instruments and Frameworks: A Stocktaking of Issues and Experiences." Working Paper 38. Basel.

Craig, R. S., E. P. Davis, and A. G. Pascual. 2006. "Sources of Procyclicality in East Asian Financial Systems." In *Procyclicality of Financial Systems in Asia,* edited by S. Gerlach and P. Gruenwald. Washington: International Monetary Fund.

De Graeve, F., T. Kick, and M. Koetter. 2008. "Monetary Policy and Financial (In)Stability: An Integrated Micro-Macro Approach." *Journal of Financial Stability* 4: 205–31.

Gray, D., R. C. Merton, and Z. Bodie. 2007. "New Framework for Measuring and Managing Macrofinancial Risk and Financial Stability." Working Paper 13607. Cambridge, Mass.: National Bureau of Economic Research.

Ho, D. C. 2010. "Asset Price Bubbles and Challenges to Taipei,China's Central Bank." In *Asset Price Bubbles and Challenges to Central Banks,* edited by J. H. Kim. Kuala Lumpur: SEACEN Centre.

Houben, A., J. Kakes, and G. Schinasi. 2004. "Toward a Framework for Safeguarding Financial Stability." Working Paper 04/101. Washington: International Monetary Fund.

Ito, T. 2010. "Banking Behaviour in the Midst of Financial Reform." Paper prepared for the SEACEN–Bank Indonesia High Level Seminar for Deputy Governors on Optimal Central Banking for Financial Stability. Bali, December 9–11.

Jacome, L. 2008. "Central Bank Involvement in Banking Crises in Latin America." Working Paper 08/135. Washington: International Monetary Fund.

Kishan, R. P., and T. P. Opiela. 2000. "What Do a Million Observations on Banks Say about the Transmission of Monetary Policy?" *American Economic Review* 90, no. 3: 407–28.

Kodres, L., and A. Narain. 2009. "What Is to Be Done?" *Finance and Development* 46, no. 1.

Nagy, P. M. 2009. "Stress Testing of Banks and Policy Implications." London: European Bank for Reconstruction and Development (www.ebrdblog.com/wordpress/2009/07/stress-testing-of-banks-and-policy-implications).

Nakornthab, D. 2010. "Household Indebtedness and Its Implications for Financial Stability." Research project paper. Kuala Lumpur: SEACEN Centre.

Prenio, J. Y. 2008. "Overview of the Philippine Banking System." In *Understanding and Addressing the Pro-cyclicality Impact of Basel II in the SEACEN Countries,* edited by P. P. Wibowo. Kuala Lumpur: SEACEN Centre.

Sarr, A., and T. Lybeck. 2002. "Measuring Liquidity in Financial Markets." Working Paper 02/232. Washington: International Monetary Fund.

Siregar, R. Y. 2005. "Interest Rate Policy and Its Implication for the Banking Restructuring Programs in Indonesia during the 1997 Financial Crisis: An Empirical Investigation." In *Institutional Change in Southeast Asia,* edited by F. Sjoholm and J. Tongzon. Routledge.

Siregar, R. Y., and K. M. Choy. 2010. "Determinants of International Bank Lending from the Developed World to East Asia." *IMF Staff Papers* 57, no. 2: 484–516.

Siregar, R. Y., and W. E. James. 2006. "Designing an Integrated Financial Supervision Agency: Selected Lessons and Challenges for Indonesia." *ASEAN Economic Bulletin* 23, no. 1.

Siregar, R. Y., and C. S. Lim. 2010. "The Role of Central Banks in Sustaining Economic Recovery and in Achieving Financial Stability." *Journal of Advanced Studies in Finance* 1 (Summer).

Slaughter and May. 2010. "Basel 3: Agreement at Last but Questions Remain." London (www.slaughterandmay.com/media/1466594/basel_3_agreement_at_last_but_questions_remain.pdf).

Sorge, M. 2004. "Stress-Testing Financial Systems: An Overview of Current Methodologies." Working Paper 165. Basel: Bank for International Settlements.

Subhanij, T. 2010. "Liquidity Measurement and Management in the SEACEN Countries." Research project paper. Kuala Lumpur: SEACEN Centre.

Wall, L. D. 2009. "Prudential Discipline for Financial Firms: Micro, Macro, and Market Structures." Working Paper 176. Tokyo: Asian Development Bank Institute.

Woolford, I. 2001. "Macro-Financial Stability and Macro-Prudential Analysis." *Reserve Bank of New Zealand Bulletin* 64, no. 3.

5

The Role of Macroprudential Policy for Financial Stability in Asia's Emerging Economies

YUNG CHUL PARK

Episodes of financial crises in both advanced and emerging economies over the past decade leave little doubt that the stability of consumer prices does not necessarily ensure financial stability. Although there is no universally accepted definition and operational measure of financial stability, wide swings in asset prices and the boom-bust credit cycles during much of the Great Moderation bear witness that price stability is not a sufficient condition for financial stability anywhere—in either advanced or emerging economies. Asia is no exception. As shown in the appendix, prices of stocks and housing display wide swings, whereas consumer prices have remained relatively stable. These divergent movements cast doubt on the presumption that price stability ensures stability of financial markets and institutions.

In the run-up to the 1997–98 Asian financial crisis, the boom in real estate markets in many emerging economies in the region—a boom fueled in part by capital inflows—piled up financial imbalances that were manifested in soaring asset prices, a large increase in leverage in financial institutions and corporations, deterioration of the currency, and maturity mismatches in the balance sheets of both banks and other financial institutions. The cumulative effects of these imbalances eventually touched off a financial meltdown.

In the aftermath of the crisis, Asian economies—in particular those hit by the crisis—made concerted efforts to improve the efficiency and stability of their

The author is grateful to Giovanni Dell'Ariccia, Eswar Prasad, Ilhyock Shim, Hyun Song Shin, and Philip Turner for their comments on drafts of this chapter.

financial systems. Both banks and nonbank financial institutions strengthened risk management, improved governance, and fortified themselves with equity capital more than that required by the Bank for International Settlements (BIS). On the macroeconomic policy front, these countries embraced more flexibility in managing the exchange rate system. To complement these reforms they also amassed large foreign exchange reserves for insurance against future crises.

Yet ten years after recovering from the 1997–98 crisis—that is, in 2009—some of these countries again fell victim to a global economic crisis. As it turned out, they were as vulnerable to reserve currency liquidity shortages as they had been in 1997. When foreign lenders and investors liquidated their investments in domestic financial assets or refused to renew their loans to Asian banks in the second half of 2008, countries like Republic of Korea and Singapore had to seek a currency swap line with the U.S. Federal Reserve to avoid a liquidity crisis.

Most Asian emerging economies are yet to develop policy instruments effective in sustaining financial stability. In countries adopting inflation targeting, the main tool of monetary policy—the policy rate—has been tied up in anchoring expectations about the future rate of inflation. Fiscal policy, on the other hand, is mostly reserved for countercyclical aggregate demand management. In realization of the limited scope of monetary and fiscal policy for securing financial stability, the BIS advocates macroprudential policy—a recalibration of microprudential regulations for macroeconomic purposes—as a means of safeguarding the economy against the accumulation of financial imbalances.

The purpose of this chapter is to analyze—in the context of the Asian economy—the role and scope of macroprudential policy in controlling financial institutions' management of their assets and liabilities in a manner that will prevent market failures. For this purpose, the chapter identifies two major sources of financial instability that plague many of Asia's emerging economies: speculation and the boom-bust cycle in the housing market. These and balance-sheet mismatches were at the top of the list of the financial frailties of Asia's emerging economies at the time of the 1997–98 financial crisis.

Financial Instability in a Low-Inflation Environment: Systemic Risk and Macroprudential Policy

Before a series of financial crises wreaked havoc on a number of emerging economies in Asia and other parts of the world in the late 1990s and early 2000s, the dominant view had been that financial stability, however defined, was predicated on price stability.[1] When examining the history of financial instability in the

1. According to Schwartz (1995), one of the major causes of financial instability is fluctuations in the inflation rate, which tend to amplify the uncertainty in estimating the potential real returns on investments; most severe episodes of instability occurred typically in a disinflationary environment.

United States from 1789 to 1996, together with the experiences of the United Kingdom and Canada, Michael Bordo and David Wheelock agree with A. J. Schwartz by saying that a monetary policy that focuses on limiting fluctuations in the price level would tend to promote financial stability.[2]

Why Is Price Stability Not Enough?

Since the early 2000s, however, this view has come under growing skepticism as it has become evident that financial imbalances in the form of boom and bust, excessive leverage in financial institutions and households, and deterioration in maturity and currency mismatches in the balance sheets of banks and other financial institutions could build up in a noninflationary environment and that the unwinding of these imbalances could destabilize the financial system and even trigger a financial crisis.

In describing the divergence between price and financial stability, a series of papers published by the BIS staff coins a new terminology, a "paradox of financial instability" in which "the financial system looks strongest when it is most fragile."[3] Two of these authors ask, for instance, "Why has the full peace dividend of the war against inflation ostensibly not materialized?"[4] Another claims that the 2008–09 crisis is another proof that achieving stability of consumer prices through monetary policy is not enough to ensure financial stability.[5] What is then the causal nexus between price and financial stability?

During the Great Moderation, a low and stable rate of inflation in an environment of great economic predictability fostered a false sense of financial stability. Together with a low cost of borrowing brought about by price stability, this feeling of security led to a lowering of the aversion to risk taking, which in turn resulted in an excessive leverage in financial institutions and households. When combined with procyclicality of lending at banks and other financial institutions, the greater appetite for risk culminated in high price volatility and in a boom-bust cycle in real and financial asset markets.

A low rate of inflation may not guarantee financial stability, but a high rate of inflation may coincide with falling asset prices. This means that the effectiveness of policies for financial stability hinges on a clear understanding and empirical identification of the nexus between price and financial stability. But such identification has been complicated by the difficulty of defining and measuring financial stability. There is no general agreement on an operational definition of finan-

2. Bordo and Wheelock (1998).

3. See Borio and Drehmann (2009, p. 9).

4. Borio and White (2004, p. 1).

5. J. Caruana, "Macroprudential Policy: Working toward a New Consensus," presentation at the high-level meeting, the Emerging Framework for Financial Regulation and Monetary Policy, BIS Financial Institute, April 2010. See also Barrio and Lowe (2002); White (2006); Borio and Shim (2007).

cial stability appropriate for policy purposes. Unlike price stability, which can be represented in terms of a price index, financial stability defies such a precise measurement. For the purpose of this chapter, a qualitative measure, such as the stability of key financial institutions and markets, will suffice.[6]

Systemic Risk and Macroprudential Policy

According to a BIS paper, systemic risk is "a risk of disruption to financial services that is caused by an impairment of all or parts of the financial system and has the potential to have serious negative consequences for the real economy."[7] Claudio Borio and Hervé Hannoun identify two types of disruption that could cause the accumulation of financial imbalances.[8] One type is the financial cycle—the procyclicality over the business cycle of lending by banks and other financial institutions. Another type is a cross-dimensional disruption arising from direct exposure of financial institutions to a set of common shocks or risk factors (as in the case of holding the same or similar assets) or indirect exposure through network linkages (as in the case of assuming counterparty risks).[9]

Although monetary policy should be an integral component of any policy framework for managing systemic risk, it has its limitations, in particular when consumer prices and asset prices move in opposite directions. In economies adopting inflation targeting, the policy rate is not an efficient tool to restrain excessive leverage and risk taking. For example, a higher policy rate may be able to stabilize high asset prices, but when speculation sets in, it is likely to do so at the cost of a larger output gap, if consumer price inflation is below the target rate.[10] This limitation has aroused interest in macroprudential policy and brought on efforts to develop and refine such a policy as a means of managing excessive leverage, procyclicality in bank lending, and real and financial asset speculation.

Macroprudential policy is defined as "the use of prudential tools with the explicit objective of promoting the stability of the financial system as a whole, not necessarily of the individual institutions within it."[11] To be more specific, it has two objectives: one is to mitigate the financial cycle or procyclicality over time, and the other is to make the financial system more resilient, given the cycle, by

6. Other definitions include one by the European Central Bank, which defines financial stability as "a condition whereby the financial system is able to withstand shocks without giving way to cumulative processes, which impair the allocation of savings to investment opportunities and the processing of payments in the economy" (Padoa-Schioppa, 2003, p. 1).

7. Bank for International Settlements (2010, p. 2).

8. Borio (2009); Hannoun (2010).

9. On the procyclicality of lending, see Crockett (2000); Borio (2003); and White (2004).

10. Blanchard, Dell'Ariccia, and Mauro (2010).

11. Clement (2010, p. 65).

moderating systemic risk caused by "interlinkages between the common exposures of all financial institutions" at a point in time.[12] To be sure, the objectives are not mutually exclusive, as a greater resilience in the financial system would enable it to moderate financial cycles better.

A large number of microprudential instruments could be recalibrated for macroeconomic objectives that would sustain financial stability.[13] These tools are basically designed and implemented to contain the distress of individual financial institutions, but one author argues that they could be used to mitigate systemic risk, as they can complement the instruments of monetary policy.[14] Some of the instruments that may be used to strengthen financial system resilience include capital and liquidity requirements and restrictions on leverage in particular types of lending and currency mismatches. In particular, regulatory authorities can separate out vital requirements to reflect their potential threat to the stability of the financial system.[15]

A host of microprudential tools may also be reoriented to help lessen procyclicality. They include countercyclical capital charges; forward-looking provisioning for loan losses; capital conservation rules for banks that ensure prudent profit retention; changes in the loan-to-value ratio, in the repayment period, and in margin requirements; capital requirements against real estate lending; and a countercyclical adjustment of exposure to the real estate sector. These tools would be tightened in the upswing phase and loosened in the downswing phase.[16] They could be adjusted frequently and quantitatively. (This categorization is based on broad correspondence between the instruments and the two objectives of macroprudential policy, as some of these instruments—such as the loan-to-value ratio—can not only improve the resilience of the financial system but also serve as an automatic stabilizer for the financial system.)[17]

12. Hannoun (2010, p. 6). See also Bank for International Settlements (2010, pp. 1–2).

13. Bank for International Settlements (2010) and Hannoun (2010) provide a list of these instruments, categorized by the disruptions to the financial system they constrain. The bank discusses how to design macroprudential frameworks and reviews experiences in a range of countries.

14. Hannoun (2010).

15. Borio (2009) proposes a top-down approach in employing prudential tools in which the contribution of each institution to the systemwide risk in calculated. On the basis of this information, higher standards are imposed on institutions with a larger contribution.

16. Hannoun (2010). These instruments can be complemented by dynamic provisioning, but with caution, because the dynamic provisioning scheme may have an inherent bias against small and medium-sized firms and households, which account for an increasing share of bank customers. Large firms have access to international as well as domestic capital markets for financing their investments. If denied credit at banks, they could issue commercial paper, bonds, and equities to raise the funds they need. These financing alternatives are often not available to small and medium-sized firms. During an economic boom, dynamic provisioning may discriminate against small and medium-sized firms, which are likely to be perceived as high-risk clients.

17. Bank for International Settlements (2010).

Boom-Bust Cycle in Real Property Markets

The two episodes of financial crisis over the past decade are evidence that the markets for real properties and equities are prone to speculation and bubbles and that this susceptibility has been one of the most damaging frailties of Asia's financial system.[18] In the run-up to the 1997–98 Asian financial crisis, investment exceeding the average in housing and other types of real estate—much of which was financed by foreign capital inflows—set off speculation in real assets. The subsequent boom fed into bubbles, which eventually burst, exacerbating the crisis. In the past few years, the People's Republic of China, Singapore, and Hong Kong, China have witnessed soaring housing prices, which are seen as a sign of new speculative bubbles in the making. Thus the housing market provides an interesting case study for examining the effectiveness of macroprudential policy.

Characteristics of the Real Estate Market

Real estate includes land, residential housing, and commercial real estate. Although housing and other types of real estate have traditionally served as investment vehicles for wealth accumulation, many households and firms hold them for their services rather than for portfolio investment.[19] The absence of a standard unit of real estate hampers market transactions, and largely for this reason the markets for land, housing, and commercial real estate are heterogeneous, illiquid, and segmented. Such heterogeneity and market segmentation suggest that different classes of real estate are likely to be poor substitutes for one another and for financial assets. As a result, the price of each class of real estate is largely determined by its supply and demand and is mostly unaffected by changes in the prices of other types of real and financial assets. These features may provide a rationale for policy authorities to intervene in these markets when they see signs of speculation; they may intervene by tightening microprudential regulations (to curtail bank financing for real estate investment) and by taxing property transactions, rather than changing the stance of macroeconomic policies such as monetary policy.

Substitutability between Housing and Financial Assets

Before the onset of the financial liberalization that began in the early 1980s—and that has spurred the expansion and diversification of housing finance—there was no unified national housing market in Asia's emerging economies. In fact there were many heterogeneous housing markets, segmented by region and differenti-

18. According to Glindro and others (2008), speculation in the housing market is considered one of the major sources of systemic risk. Zhu (2006) also points to booms and busts in the real estate market as having played a crucial role in triggering and worsening the 1997–98 Asian crisis.

19. In many Asian emerging economies that have suffered from high and unpredictable inflation, housing has been one of the most sought-after assets for wealth accumulation. In Korea, for example, the total market value of housing was estimated to be three times as large as GDP in 2006.

ated by type of housing. With the continuing expansion and diversification of the housing financial system, however, these segmented markets have increasingly been integrated into a unified national housing market, which in many Asian emerging economies is large and liquid. This market integration was instrumental in lowering transaction costs and increasing market liquidity, which have in turn made housing a tradable asset and a good substitute for financial assets.

As a result, housing demand has become more sensitive to changes in macroeconomic variables, such as the prices of bonds and equities and the exchange rate. One BIS study finds a strong positive relationship between prices of real estate and those of equities, suggesting that, in countries with a well-developed and efficient mortgage market, the two assets are likely to be good substitutes for each other.[20] The same study also provides evidence that changes in the exchange rate have a significant impact on housing prices in countries that adopt flexible exchange rate systems, where currency appreciation is associated with a housing boom and depreciation with a market contraction. It is also seen that during the boom period foreign investors move heavily into Asian property markets and retreat en masse when a downturn begins, as they did during the 1997–98 Asian financial crisis.

For an analysis of the dynamics of housing market speculation, it is convenient to divide buyers of housing into two types. The first type are buyers who enter the market for consumption of housing services; the second type enters for speculative investment. Buyers in the first category live in the houses they purchase. Buyers in the second group invest in housing for capital gains.

On the supply side, available housing consists of existing houses on the market for sale and the inventory of newly built houses. Since it takes time to build new houses and most house owners are not likely to put up their houses for sale in response to the housing market boom, the supply of housing tends to be insensitive to changes in house prices in the short run. An exogenous increase in demand, therefore, does not elicit much of a supply response and is likely to raise housing prices more than in other financial markets, suggesting that much of the market clearing takes place through price changes.

Financial Accelerator and Extrapolative Expectations in Housing Markets

When there exists a well-developed housing finance system, investments in housing are mostly financed by loans originated by banks and other mortgage lenders, for which real estate properties are pledged as collateral. This availability and diversification of housing finance result in a positive correlation between housing prices and the supply of bank credit. This correlation establishes a strong linkage between the housing price and bank credit cycles.[21] This linkage then activates the

20. Zhu (2006). See also Borio and McGuire (2004) for strong linkages between equity price and house price movements.

21. Zhu (2006) finds that bank credit is positively related to house prices in all the countries he examined.

financial accelerator mechanism, which could put the housing price on a path to creating a bubble.[22]

The collateral value of houses increases with an increase in their price. This increased collateral allows housing investors to secure more mortgage loans, with favorable terms, than before. That is, the rise in house prices lowers the cost and increases the availability of mortgage credit to house buyers, as their financial positions measured by their house collateral values improve. The borrowers in the first category may then be able to extract additional equity to finance their next house, and for the same reason speculative buyers will be able to purchase more houses. Because of these secondary and cumulative effects of the increase in housing finance and demand, housing prices continue to soar.

When the financial accelerator mechanism is set in motion, changes in current housing prices are likely to be determined by their previous changes in addition to deviations from the fundamental housing values and the contemporaneous adjustment to changes in the fundamentals. That is, an initial price increase induces an additional demand for housing for investment purposes, as it generates an expectation of a continuous increase in housing prices to attract speculative buyers, pushing up house prices further and thereby setting off a price dynamic that could build a bubble. The financial accelerator mechanism may then explain that investors in the housing market are likely to be guided by an extrapolative expectation.

Role and Effectiveness of Macroprudential Policy in Stabilizing the Housing Market

In order to discuss the scope and effectiveness of macroprudential policy in subduing financial cycles, I consider a situation in which consumer prices are not expected to rise beyond a target range but in which there are signs of incipient speculation, which may create a bubble in the housing market. Faced with growing instability in the housing market, the central bank could increase the policy rate to suppress unwarranted high expectations of capital gains, but it would be reluctant to do so unless the speculation could increase inflationary pressure. Fiscal authorities may raise the property tax rate and impose additional taxes on property transactions and transfers, but these types of taxation may not be desirable, as they distort property markets to impair their efficiency.

As a third alternative policy measure, the financial regulatory authorities may consider imposing microprudential regulations on mortgage lending at banks and nonbank financial intermediaries for the macroeconomic purpose of stabilizing

22. On the financial accelerator, see Ben Bernanke, "The Financial Accelerator and the Credit Channel," conference, Monetary Policy in the Twenty-First Century, Federal Reserve Bank of Atlanta, June 2007.

the housing market. In this regard, the regulatory authorities could employ two types of macroprudential instrument. The first includes some of the microprudential instruments adjusted to control the supply of credit to a particular sector like housing; these instruments include loan-to-value (LTV) and debt-to-income (DTI) ratios. The second type comprises tools for controlling the supply of aggregate bank credit, such as countercyclical capital charges, dynamic loan-loss provisioning, and capital conservation rules for banks. These tools are usually used to moderate procyclicality in bank lending. Implementation of these two types of instrument entails quantitative control, rather than price control, of the availability of bank credit, sectoral as well as aggregate.

Fungibility of Money and Selective Credit Control

Suppose that, in an effort to stave off a housing market boom, regulatory authorities lowered the two microprudential ratios, LTV and DTI, without changing monetary policy. The squeeze on mortgage lending would likely discourage borrowing for consumption demand—the purchase of houses for their services—but not necessarily the purchase of houses for investment demand. Under these circumstances, as long as total bank lending is unchanged, banks will be able to extend more of other types of business and consumer loans with the funds released by curtailing housing finance. But if the expected real return on housing investment is perceived to be higher than the return on other assets, many of the borrowers taking out other nonmortgage bank loans are likely to invest in housing.[23] This results from the fungibility of money and imperfections in ex post loan use monitoring.

Given the fungibility of money, it appears that, in countries where housing has become a good substitute for financial assets and banks dominate financial intermediation and the financial system as a whole, restrictions on mortgage lending alone may not be effective in preventing a housing market bubble. Restrictions need to be complemented by an overall cutback of aggregate bank credit through, for instance, an increase in loan-loss provisioning. But once housing speculation gathers force (as shown by the Korean experience, discussed below), even a simultaneous squeeze on the sectoral and aggregate supply of bank credit may not be effective. This is because, despite the tightening of bank credit, some of the loans extended to nonhousing borrowers could be invested in housing, as long as real property speculation picked up speed.

Macroprudential and Monetary Policy: Are They Independent?

In the preceding discussion, a tightening of macroprudential policy is shown as likely to move banks to raise interest rates on their loans. It will also drive many

23. A housing market boom often coincides with land speculation. Business borrowers may decide to use a fixed investment loan to build a plant on a larger site of land than otherwise.

of their loan customers out of the bank loan market and into money and capital markets for direct financing. This increase in debt and equity financing will then increase market interest rates.

If this happens, contractionary macroprudential policy will dampen the aggregate demand for goods and services (with a possible exception of construction investment), as many borrowers without access to the capital market will be rationed out of the bank loan market. The policy will not, however, suppress housing market speculation. Tighter macroprudential policy may therefore widen the output gap, depending on the extent to which bank loans are shifted to housing finance. Macroprudential measures may strengthen the financial system but will not necessarily enhance financial macroeconomic stability. It follows then that, if the policy rate is a poor tool for dealing with financial market instability, so are macroprudential tools for moderating financial cycles.

The preceding discussion raises an important question as to whether the division of labor in policy management—in which the central bank follows an interest rate rule in conducting monetary policy for price stability, whereas regulatory authorities are engaged in quantitative control in managing macroprudential policy for financial stability—is a viable institutional arrangement. This question arises because most macroprudential instruments that have an effect on financial cycles work through changes in the availability of sectoral and aggregate credit; in this respect, they are similar to reserve requirements. That is, macroprudential tools operate through effects on bank lending: changes in bank loans cause investment and consumer spending to change. Since this bank-lending channel is one of many channels of monetary policy, it follows that, in emerging economies where the banking system dominates financial intermediation as far as the channel of transmission is concerned, macroprudential policy geared to controlling procyclicality in bank lending and monetary policy targeted for price stability are one and the same. They do have, however, different objectives.

Korea's Experience with Macroprudential Policy

A recent survey by the BIS on the use of macroprudential instruments in thirty-three countries shows that in most cases the objective was to enhance the resilience of the financial system rather than to moderate financial cycles; the evidence on the effectiveness of macroprudential measures is not conclusive.[24] In part these findings are supported by the recent experience with managing the real estate boom in Korea. Over a seven-year period, beginning in 2001, the Korean government tightened monetary policy and on twelve occasions imposed various macroprudential and tax measures to end real estate speculation.

In October 2003 Korea not only increased the policy rate but also lowered the LTV ratio to 40 percent from 60 percent on mortgage loans, with maturity of less

24. Bank for International Settlements (2010).

than ten years for apartment purchases.[25] But control of the LTV ratio turned out to be less than effective, because of leakage: banks were able to extend mortgage loans with maturity longer than ten years to avoid the restriction. To plug this loophole, two years later mortgage lending was tightened further by lowering the LTV ratio on those loans with maturity longer than ten years for the purchase of an apartment valued at more than 600 million won (or approximately $600 thousand). At the same time the DTI ratio was lowered below 40 percent for apartment financing in some of the districts of the Seoul metropolitan area, where there were signs of real estate speculation. In 2009 this restriction was extended to all apartment financing in those areas.

Despite the implementation of these macroprudential measures, housing speculation did not subside. It was clear that stronger doses of antispeculation measures were needed. These stronger measures included a registration requirement and the imposition of transfer and transaction taxes on properties; these measures eventually ended the boom in the housing market. In retrospect it is unclear whether real estate speculation would have been brought under control if the government had not resorted to direct-control measures. It is difficult to examine empirically the extent to which the 20 percentage point reduction in the LTV ratio contributed to slowing down (if not stopping) the speculation. In retrospect it was more of a symbolic move on the part of the financial supervisory service (FSS) to signal that it was serious about stabilizing expectations on future prices of apartments, although it is unclear as to how successful the signaling was.

In general, the effectiveness of macroprudential tools depends on the circumstances in which they are implemented. When the consumer price index and asset prices move in the same direction, it is likely that the stance of both monetary and macroprudential policies are the same: they reinforce each other to restore both price and asset market stability.[26] On the other hand, when movements of consumer and asset prices diverge, the two policies run into conflict with each other, as in the case of a stable consumer price index and rising asset prices (discussed above).

In particular, the conflict between the two policies appears to be more severe if rising consumer prices are accompanied by stagnation in the housing market, as shown by the recent experience in Korea. In August 2010 the central bank raised the policy rate, as it was concerned about the buildup of inflationary pressure. At the same time, regulatory authorities raised the DTI ratio on specific mortgage

25. In Korea there is a liquid market for apartments, which are standardized in terms of size and actively traded. Smaller ones in particular are easily marketable, making them a tradable investment asset and a good substitute for financial assets.

26. A recent BIS report argues that the use of macroprudential policies targeting the real estate sector in Asian countries helped make banking systems more resilient to real estate downturns but did not make much difference either to the strength of the boom or to the depth of the bust. See Bank for International Settlements (2010).

loans to revive the sagging demand for housing loans. Although it is too early to judge, the higher DTI ratio did not seem to have elicited any positive housing market response.[27]

Macoprudential tools such as the LTV and DTI ratios are rather inflexible instruments: they cannot be fine-tuned frequently to alter price expectations in real property markets. The fungibility of money makes the effectiveness of these ratios at best ambiguous. Macroprudential policy for controlling the quantity of aggregate credit needs to be coordinated with the conduct of monetary policy, but given the different policy objectives and approaches to policy management of the monetary and regulatory authorities, such a coordination would be difficult to institutionalize.[28] The financial regulatory authorities would find it difficult to decide on the timing and the extent of an adjustment of their tools. For an effective management of macroprudential policy, regulatory authorities should be able to detect signs of real-asset speculation well before it gets out of control and to identify the turning point in cyclical developments in the economy. Equipping regulatory authorities with this macroeconomic forecasting function would mean entrusting them with a role in the conduct of monetary policy. It is not clear what that role should be.

Currency and Maturity Mismatches as a Source of Financial Instability

Another source of financial instability that has caused much anguish to many Asian emerging economies is the propensity of their financial institutions to hold assets and liabilities mismatched in terms of maturity and currency.[29] The twin mismatches are typical of the systemic risk in a cross-sectional dimension that many emerging economies are exposed to. When banks and other financial institutions hold long-term and low-liquidity assets—such as long-term loans in both domestic and foreign currencies and funded by borrowing from both domestic and external wholesale funding markets—they expose themselves to a liquidity and solvency crisis when market liquidity in both domestic and reserve currencies suddenly evaporates. If banks commit similar mismatches across the board, an external shock such as a sudden reversal in capital flows could endanger the safety of the entire financial system.

27. During the first seven months of 2010, consumer prices rose by about 1 percent, whereas housing prices in some parts of the Seoul metropolitan area began to fall in the second quarter of 2010.

28. Regulatory authorities may not have developed the expertise or culture of macroprudential policy, while the central bank cannot exercise supervisory control at the level of individual institutions. These institutional constraints could hamper coordination between the two policy authorities.

29. This section draws on Park (2009).

During the 1997 Asian crisis, currency mismatches between foreign currency assets and liabilities in bank balance sheets were at the top of the list of financial vulnerabilities of Asian banks that exacerbated, if not triggered, the financial meltdown. A number of studies attribute their causes to the market failures associated with asymmetric information and moral hazard.[30] This chapter argues that there were more mundane causes.

In the run-up to the 2008–09 global economic crisis, it appears that the currency mismatch of Asian financial institutions was moderate compared to the massive deterioration before the 1997–98 crisis, although this may not be the case for the maturity mismatch. The 2008 global economic crisis highlights the gravity of the maturity mismatch as a major cause of the crisis in not only emerging but also advanced economies.[31] As shown below, in emerging economies with foreign currency liabilities, maturity mismatches create a more serious systemic risk, as they are invariably accompanied by currency mismatches. This section discusses how financial imbalances stemming from the twin mismatches arise and whether they could be mitigated through macroprudential policy.

Scale and Pervasiveness of Maturity and Currency Mismatches

Morris Goldstein and Philip Turner constructed a measure of currency mismatch known as the aggregate effective currency mismatches (AECMs).[32] Figure 5-1 presents the AECMs of Asia's emerging economies.[33] A negative number for the AECM, which results from a negative position on net foreign currency assets, indicates a high degree of mismatching. The estimates show that Indonesia, Korea, the Philippines, and Thailand all let their currency mismatch deteriorate below a negative level before the 1997–98 crisis.

Since then it has eased up, as the AECM has remained in positive territory in most countries; although reflecting the decline in net foreign assets caused by the 2008 global economic crisis, it slipped in all sample Asian countries in 2008. The deterioration is most pronounced in Korea: its AECM slid since 2005, turning into a negative figure in 2008 due to a sharp decline in capital inflows.

Even when the AECM is positive, as noted earlier, a country could run into a financial crisis if reserve currency liquidity vanishes when it is exposed to a large

30. Goldstein and Turner (2004) argue that all prominent financial crises in emerging economies in the 1990s and the early 2000s share one striking characteristic: a large currency mismatch. See also Chang and Velasco (2000); Corsetti, Pesenti, and Roubini (1999); and Rodrik and Velasco (1999).

31. Brunnermeier and others (2009) point out that one of the most critical lessons of the 2008–09 crisis is that the maturity mismatch, short-term funding of long-term assets with potentially low market liquidity, has been the main source of financial instability.

32. Goldstein and Turner (2004). According to the authors, AECM = NFCA/XGS (FC/TD), where NFCA = net foreign currency assets (+) or liabilities (–), XGS = exports of goods and services (national income account) when NFCA is negative, MGS = imports of goods and services (national income account) when NFCA is positive, and FC/TD = foreign currency share of total debt.

33. Recent figures are provided by Philip Turner at the Bank for International Settlements.

Figure 5-1. *Currency Mismatches, Selected Asian Countries, 1994–2008*

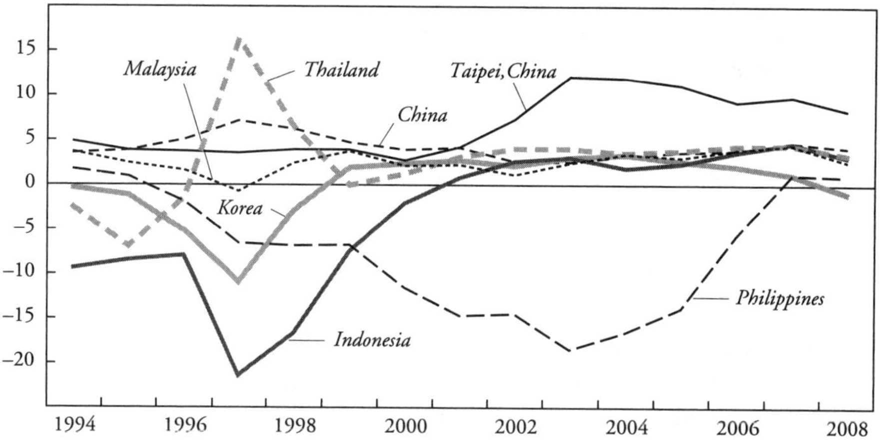

Source: Goldstein and Turner (2004).

maturity mismatch between foreign currency assets and liabilities. To be a useful predictor or an early-warning indicator for a financial crisis, therefore, the AECM may need to be adjusted for the maturity mismatch. In the absence of the banking data needed for the construction of a measure of the maturity mismatch, Yung Chul Park examines changes in the loan-deposit ratio and short-term foreign liabilities relative to foreign exchange reserves for a qualitative assessment of the extent of the mismatch.[34] In general, a rise in the loan-deposit ratio indicates that banks rely more on both domestic and foreign wholesale market funding than on core deposits. This will cause an increase in the maturity mismatch.

Likewise, an increase in short-term foreign liabilities relative to foreign exchange reserves is likely to aggravate the maturity mismatch, since it means that banks secure more external funding from the short end of global financial markets. Here one could use volume of total foreign liabilities rather than level of foreign exchange reserves as a scale variable, but the latter provides additional information on a country's vulnerability to a liquidity crisis, as the ratio of short-term foreign liabilities to foreign exchange reserves is often regarded as a barometer for an adequate amount of foreign exchange reserves to be held in emerging economies.

Park shows that between 2000 and 2008 loan-deposit ratios were stable and stayed well below 100 percent in most countries except Korea and Thailand, where the 2008 ratios were 135 and 105 percent, respectively. On the external liability side, short-term foreign liabilities as a proportion of foreign exchange reserves in Asian countries where data are available were well below the maximum

34. Park (2009).

level allowed for by the Greenspan-Guidotti-Fischer rule, which prescribes an amount of reserves equal to the country's short-term foreign currency liabilities.

The two ratios, together with changes in the AECM, suggest that all Asian countries under review appeared to have been in a much stronger financial position than in 1997, allowing them to withstand and remain outside the danger zone of a currency crisis. During the fourth quarter of 2008, after the collapse of Lehman Brothers, however, Korea came close to facing insolvency of many of its financial institutions.

Causes of Twin Mismatches

Regardless of their nationality, banks are open to maturity mismatching for a number of inherent characteristics of bank intermediation. One such characteristic is the debt maturity transformation they are engaged in. Another is procyclicality in their lending and borrowing. A third is relationship banking, in which banks establish long-term relationships with their loan customers.

All banks, whether they are operating in advanced or emerging economies, earn a substantial share of their profits by borrowing from the short end of the financial market (as in the case of accepting short-term deposits and issuing certificates of deposit) and by lending long (as in the case of financing business long-term investment in addition to short-term working capital).[35] The maturity mismatch "reflects the underlying structure of the economy in which individuals have a preference for liquidity but the most profitable investment opportunities take a long time to pay off. Banks are an efficient way of bridging the gap between the maturity structure embedded in the technology and liquidity preference."[36]

From the perspective of an individual bank, it would be reasonable to assume that, under normal circumstances, it would have an adequate deposit base and access to wholesale funding markets to finance its long-term loans and its investments in securities. Any temporary difficulties in short-term funding markets in domestic currency could easily be dealt with by the central bank. But dependence on foreign currency funding is quite different. When reserve currency liquidity dries up, the central bank can meet only a limited amount of the increase in the demand for reserve currency liquidity.

To be sure, some individual banks may be able to avoid a liquidity crisis, but the financial system as a whole cannot when it is faced with a sharp decrease in net capital inflows. Even when banks in emerging economies lend in reserve currencies, they may not be able to avoid the currency mismatch, because local borrowers include not only exporters with cash flows in dollars and euros but

35. Brunnermeier and others (2009) argue that there are many caveats to this generalization and that the mismatch is a matter of degree.

36. Allen and Gale (2007, p. 59).

also importers from the nontradable sector without cash flows in major reserve currencies.

As Turner points out, the massive aggregate dependence of non-U.S. financial firms on wholesale, short-term, dollar-funding markets created a major systemic risk in 2008.[37] When depositors left the banks en masse and liquidity in short-term funding markets disappeared rather suddenly, the entire banking sector of emerging economies suffered from severe shortages in dollar liquidity. In some countries the liquidity crisis threatened the solvency of their banking industry. It should be noted that, unlike their counterparts in emerging economies, financial firms from reserve currency countries (the United States and members of the Economic and Monetary Union) and engaged in cross-border financial intermediation are largely immune to such a liquidity drought.

Banks are, in general, relationship lenders. They nurture close, long-term relationships with their loan customers, relationships that help improve the screening and monitoring of lenders by mitigating the asymmetry in information. Banks routinely roll over loans to their customers with good credit. They also know that most of their loan customers are so accustomed to the loan rollover that they would not be prepared to repay their loans even when they are due, not to mention before they are due. Therefore, even when banks are faced with liquidity shortages, they would not refuse renewal of most of their household and business loans for fear of losing customers.

Procyclicality over the business cycle is another characteristic of banking that exacerbates the twin mismatches. During the cyclical upturn the yield curve gets steeper, creating incentives for banks to rely on short-term funding for the growing demand for their loans. In particular, banks may borrow more in volume and from the short end of international money markets if domestic interest rates are higher. As a result, both the maturity mismatch and the currency mismatch deteriorate. When a cyclical downturn sets in, foreign investors unload their holdings of domestic securities, and foreign banks refuse to renew their short-term loans. Domestic banks and other financial institutions find it increasingly difficult to recall foreign currency loans held by local customers or to liquidate their foreign currency assets. A subsequent decline in net capital inflows exacerbates currency mismatching and, depending upon the magnitude of the currency mismatch, could provoke a reserve currency liquidity crisis.[38]

During the downturn, the central bank is expected to loosen monetary policy to prevent credit contraction. Although an expansionary monetary policy of cutting the policy rate is called for to forestall deflation, cutting the rate could deepen

37. Turner (2010).

38. As shown by Kaminsky, Reinhart, and Vegh (2004); Contessi, DePace, and Francis (2008); and Cardarelli, Elekdag, and Kose (2009), capital flows in emerging markets tend to be procyclical.

the liquidity crisis as it weakens the currency and hence could induce further capital outflows. Over the business cycle, there is a limit to what monetary policy can do to mitigate an increase in the twin mismatches. This limitation may provide the rationale for strengthening macroprudential policy, in cooperation with the monetary authorities, but as argued in the following section, its effectiveness remains unclear.

Twin Mismatches and Macroprudential Policy

Goldstein and Turner propose setting limits on net foreign exchange positions, foreign exchange liabilities, and banks' holdings of foreign currency–denominated securities.[39] They also recommend introducing more restrictive rules for liquidity risk management and a higher reserve requirement on foreign currency deposits. Requirements on foreign currency loan to deposit may be added to this list.[40] In this section it is argued that these regulations could distort resource allocation and that, in a crisis situation, are likely to be ineffective, as the Korean experience shows.

Could Mismatches Be Mitigated by Prudential Regulation?

A strict regulatory restriction designed to prevent currency mismatches would dictate that bank lending and debt contracts be made in the currencies in which deposits and foreign funding are denominated and in which borrowing customers earn revenues. In an extreme case, loans to local customers who earn only in a local currency should be excluded from banks' foreign currency lending. Would such a regulatory restriction be efficient or, more important, enforceable?

Such a regulation is not efficient because banks are likely to discriminate in foreign currency lending against those borrowers from the nontradable sector without foreign currency revenues. Compliance with the currency mismatch regulation would mean that banks would lend in foreign currency mostly to borrowers from the tradable sector. If banks lend to firms in the nontradable sector, they may charge a higher premium. Therefore, the regulation is likely to distort resource allocation and even retard development of the nontradable sector.

Is such a regulation enforceable? To alleviate the twin mismatch problem, Korea's FSS imposes a foreign currency liquidity regulation, by which banks are required to relend in foreign currencies to local borrowers at least 85 percent of

39. Goldstein and Turner (2004).

40. Hannoun (2010). In addition, these regulatory restrictions may be complemented by two measures limiting maturity mismatching: linking the class of assets for which short-term funding is secured to the maturity of the funding, such as restricting banks to hold only short-term safe and liquid assets for short-term funding; and imposing a higher capital charge on financial institutions with funding liquidity risk stemming from holding long-term assets with low market liquidity funded by short-term liabilities. See Brunnermeier and others (2009).

their foreign currency funds maturing within three months (15 percent for domestic currency loans). The maturity of the local foreign currency loans must also be less than three months. The FSS also enforces a liquidity restriction by which banks are required to keep a positive ratio between net short-term foreign currency assets that mature within seven days and total foreign currency assets. They must be more than minus 10 percent for maturity of less than thirty days. On their balance sheets banks do comply with these regulatory measures, but not in reality. Indeed, if these prudential measures had been observed to the letter, one might argue that Korea could have avoided the run on the central bank reserves during the fourth quarter of 2008. But it could not.

In reality it appears that banks' compliance has not prevented, or even moderated, the pervasiveness of the two balance-sheet mismatches, largely because banks kept on renewing their domestic and foreign currency loans regardless of their maturities, with the expectation that banks would have continuing access to global wholesale funding markets. This laxity in contingency planning for lining up liquidity in a crisis does not necessarily reflect a serious moral hazard on the part of Korean banks, because their experience with the 1997–98 financial crisis must have taught them that the government could not come to their aid in a crisis caused by the drought in reserve currency liquidity. Instead, the laxity may have more to do with relationship banking and may reflect the fact that compliance means loss of competitiveness vis-à-vis their foreign competitors in global financial intermediation.

If regulatory restrictions prove to be ineffective, governments of emerging economies may invoke more direct measures, such as providing government guarantees on foreign loans and imposing capital control. To restore foreign investors' confidence, on October 12, 2008, the Korean government issued sovereign guarantees on new foreign loans up to $100 billion and maturing before the end of June 2009. Similar guarantees had failed to allay fears of financial meltdown at the beginning of the Asian crisis in 1997, and they failed again. As in 1997, market participants simply ignored the guarantees. Foreign creditors simply do not believe government promises when its official reserves are inadequate to meet foreign debts that are coming due.

As for direct-control measures, there is an emerging consensus on the need to conduct reserve intervention and impose taxes and other restrictions on short-term capital inflows. Even the International Monetary Fund (IMF) has softened its opposition to intervention in the foreign exchange market and to imposing capital control.[41] Whatever the benefits and costs of capital control and foreign exchange market intervention, national policy authorities would not refrain from

41. Blanchard, Dell'Ariccia, and Mauro (2010); Ostry and others (2010).

invoking these measures if the volatility of the exchanges rate rises to a level that endangers the stability of the domestic financial system.[42]

A Global Liquidity Safety Net

The United States is largely free from currency mismatches because the dollar is used for a high proportion of international banking business. Its central bank can always print more money to thwart any impending liquidity crisis caused by an increase in maturity mismatches. The rise of international banking created a need for a lender of last resort in the euro currency markets.[43] But G-10 central banks could not agree on how to create such an institution in the 1970s, leading them to decide not to establish any rules and procedures for the provisioning of short-term liquidity.[44] During the 2008 economic crisis, the four foreign central banks of Canada, Japan, Switzerland, and the United Kingdom, together with the European Central Bank, had unlimited dollar-swap lines with the Federal Reserve. Most central banks of emerging economies were given no such access.

All this puts banks in advanced countries at a competitive advantage in international financial intermediation. This means that, even during the tranquil period, the international monetary and financial systems do not provide a level playing field for emerging market economies in global finance. From their point of view, this bias—which is equivalent to a nonreserve currency discount—raises the issue of fairness and even questions the rationale for these economies to integrate into the global financial system to the extent that it weakens their competitiveness.

As argued in the preceding section, there are few effective measures that emerging economies can take to prevent or alleviate the consequences of a currency mismatch. The problem instead calls for multinational efforts to institutionalize a global system of reserve currency liquidity support, at both regional and global levels, a system of support that can be activated in a crisis situation—that is, when participating members suffer from short-term, reserve currency, liquidity shortages. The U.S. dollar has been a de facto global currency; the euro has emerged as a distant second candidate, although the recent euro crisis has put its future in doubt.

42. Only when Korea secured a swap line of $30 billion from the U.S. Federal Reserve on October 30 did the foreign exchange market settle down somewhat—but not for long. Three weeks after the swap was announced, the won-dollar exchange rate depreciated by more than 15 percent. The Fed's liquidity support was apparently not enough to remove uncertainties about Korea's ability to service its foreign debt. Korea also secured, on December 13, local swap lines with the central banks of China and Japan, each amounting to an equivalent of $30 billion. This additional support, together with the indication that the Fed would renew the swap agreement, improved foreign investors' confidence in the Korean economy. Stability in the foreign exchange market returned toward the end of the first quarter of 2009.

43. Shafer (1982).

44. Turner (2009).

As the providers of global media of exchange and stores of value, reserve currency countries need to take responsibility for controlling and stabilizing the global supply of liquidity. In assuming their global role, the U.S. Federal Reserve and the European Central Bank may consider constructing a global currency swap network to supply liquidity in a crisis, such as when banks and other financial institutions retreat from the market. The swap network membership could include, in addition to current members, emerging economies that are active in international financial markets. The swap network could then support them in case they need an infusion of short-term dollar or euro liquidity to prevent a contagion of liquidity shortages.[45] At the same time, the swap network could be complemented by new credit facilities at the IMF, such as the flexible credit line, and by an expansion and consolidation of regional liquidity support arrangements, such as the Chiang Mai Initiative's multilateralization among the ASEAN+3.

Concluding Remarks

In the wake of the 2008–09 global financial crisis, there has been a growing concern about destabilization of the financial system in a low-inflation environment. One of the lessons of the Great Moderation is that price stability is not a sufficient condition for financial stability, although it remains true that sustained inflation encourages speculation and that an abrupt decline in the rate of inflation could cause an increase in financial institution failures and significant financial stress throughout the economy. Monetary policy, as it is targeted to price stability, may not be an effective means to prevent a financial crisis or to manage it better when it does occur. Fiscal policy is traditionally reserved for the management of aggregate demand.

Harnessing financial stability therefore requires an additional instrument, and the reorientation of microprudential regulations has been promoted as such a measure. This chapter examines the extent to which regulatory tools, which are basically designed to safeguard the soundness of individual financial institutions, could be implemented to moderate the boom-bust cycle in the real estate market by changing sectoral and aggregate volumes of bank credit. The chapter argues that macroprudential policy operates through the bank credit channel, as does monetary policy, and that its effectiveness is thus ambiguous. As far as the transmission mechanism is concerned, the two policies are one and the same.

Traditionally, banks specialize in asset transformation. As such they are exposed to maturity mismatches in their balance sheets and, hence, to a liquidity crisis, which often provokes a bank run. In emerging economies, banks active in

45. There is concern that the expansion of the swap network could create moral hazard problems in emerging economies. But it is difficult to believe that emerging economies would be disposed to laxity in managing their macroeconomic policy simply because they have access to the swap lines.

international financial intermediation are open to another risk that could undermine their soundness, namely the currency mismatch that occurs as they finance their local currency lending by borrowing in foreign currencies. Various regulatory restrictions may not be effective in preventing banks from committing the mismatch, because as long as banks are entrenched in long-term-relationship banking, which systemizes the rollover of loans as a routine practice, they find it difficult to comply with regulatory supervision. If these regulations are strictly enforced, there is the danger that they could limit the scope of banks' asset-to-liability management and hence could undermine their competitiveness in international financial intermediation vis-à-vis their counterparts from advanced or reserve-currency countries, which are not subject to a similar constraint.

When a sudden reversal in capital flows occurs, even well-regulated and sound banks in emerging economies are likely to be faced with solvency risk as they are denied access to external wholesale funding markets. This risk is one of the main reasons that many emerging economies hold excessive amounts of foreign exchange reserves and may need to intervene in the foreign exchange market and impose capital controls. Since holding large amounts of reserves is costly and could exacerbate global trade imbalances, a global liquidity safety net, one that could meet short-term reserve currency liquidity needs, would serve as a more effective means of preventing reserve-currency liquidity crises in emerging economies.

Appendix: Consumer Price Index and Prices of Housing and Stocks, Seven East Asian Countries, First Quarter, 2005–10

Figure 5A-1. *People's Republic of China*

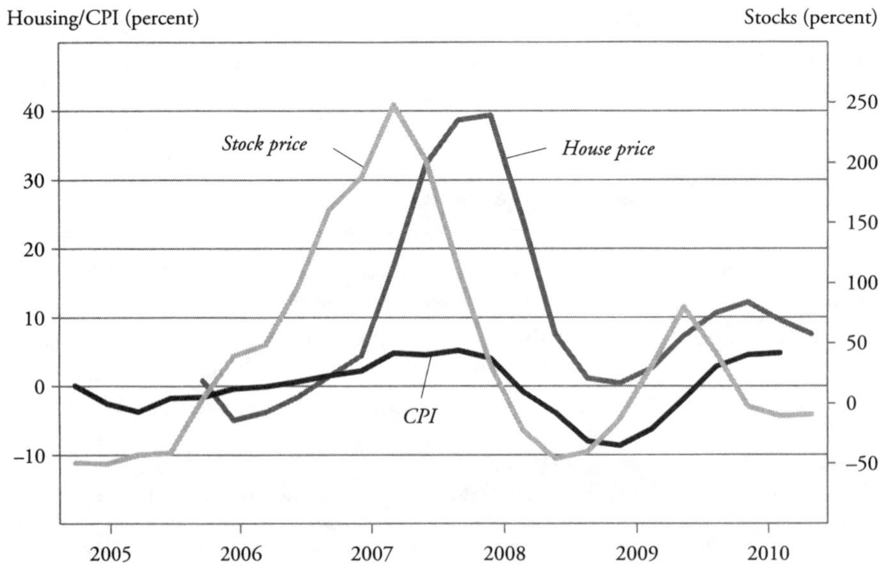

Source: National Bureau of Statistics of China; Shanghai Stock Exchange.

Figure 5A-2. *Hong Kong, China*

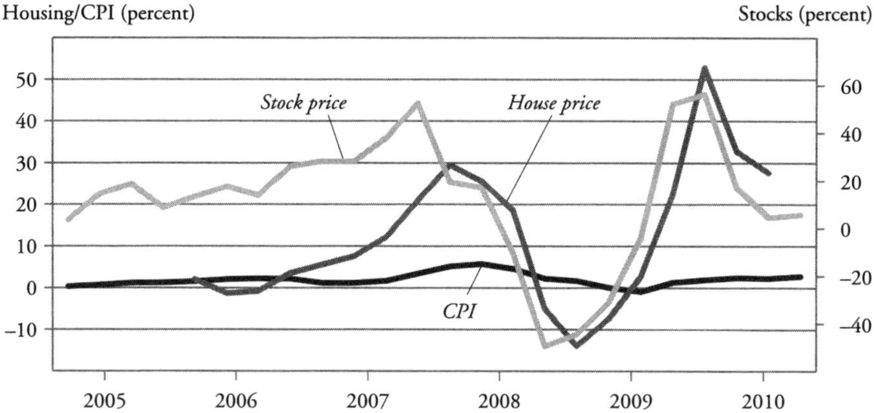

Source: Census and Statistics Department, Hong Kong Special Administrative Region; Hang Seng Stock Exchange.

Figure 5A-3. *Indonesia*

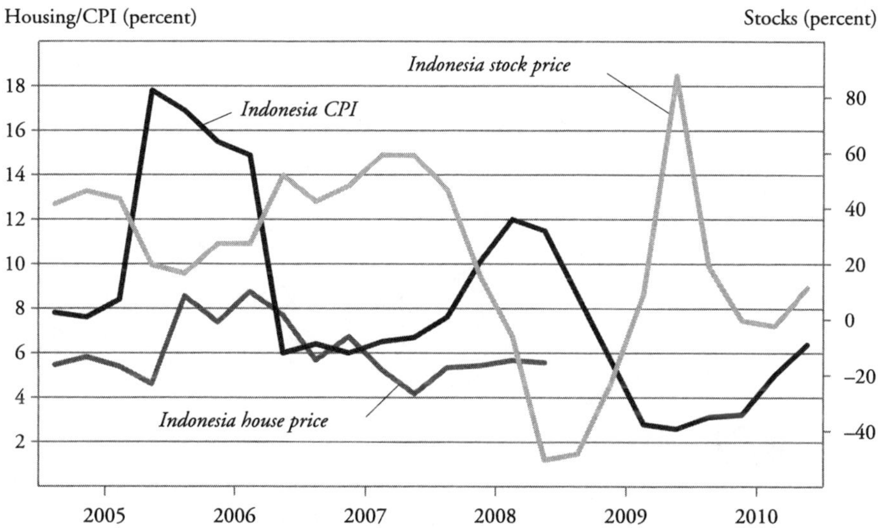

Source: Bank Indonesia; Statistics Indonesia; Indonesia Stock Exchange.

Figure 5A-4. *Korea*

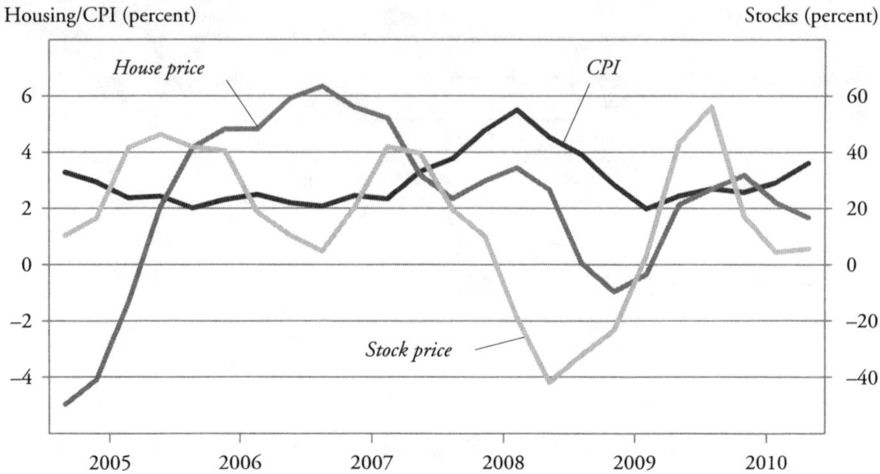

Source: Korea National Statistical Office; Koomin Bank Korea; Korea Composite Stock Price Index.

Figure 5A-5. *Malaysia*

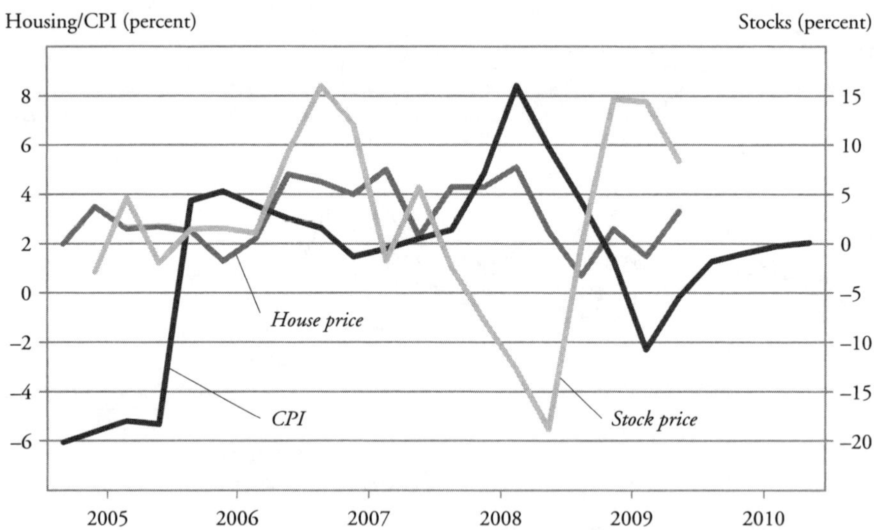

Source: Bank Negara Malaysia; Kuala Lumpur Stock Exchange.

Figure 5A-6. *Singapore*

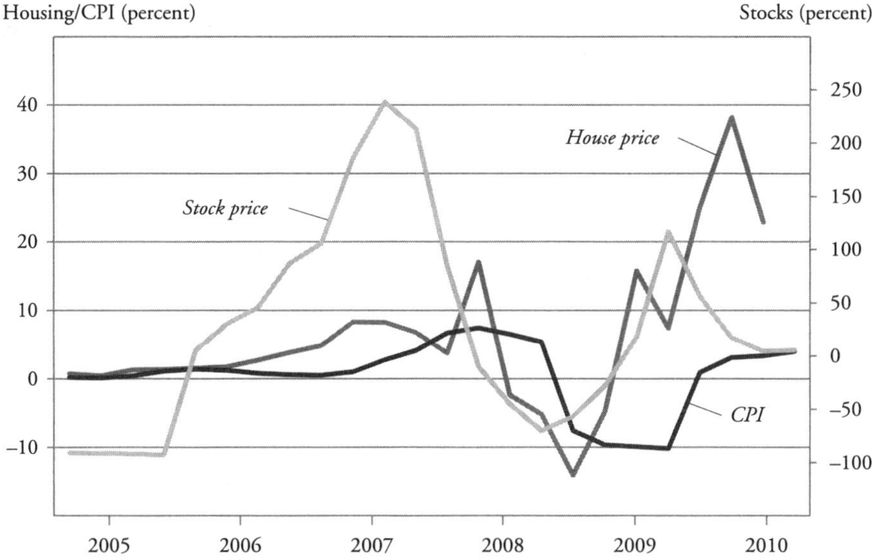

Source: Singapore Department of Statistics; Urban Redevelopment Authority Singapore; Singapore Exchange.

Figure 5A-7. *Thailand*

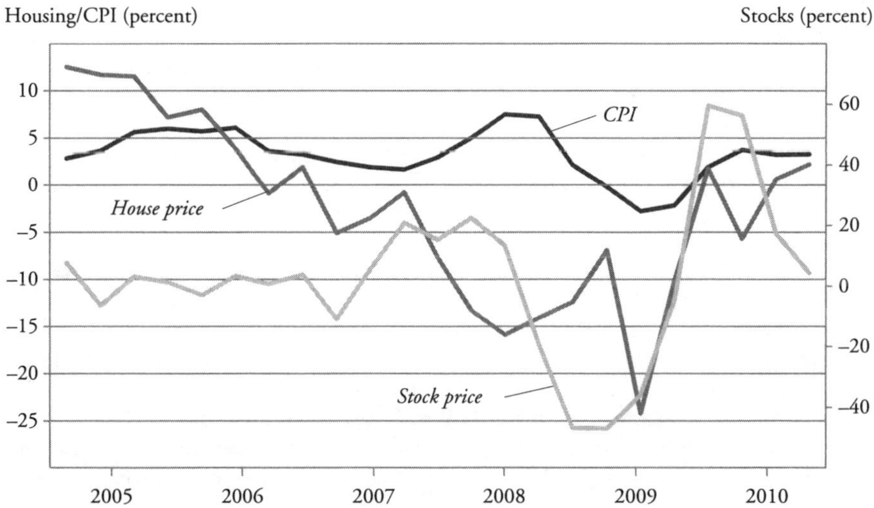

Source: Bank of Thailand; Stock Exchange of Thailand.

References

Allen, Franklin, and Douglas Gale. 2007. *Understanding Financial Crises.* Clarendon Lecture in Finance. Oxford University Press.

Bank for International Settlements. 2010. "Macroprudential Instruments and Frameworks: A Stocktaking of Issues and Experience by Committee on the Global Financial System." Paper 38. Basel.

Blanchard, Oliver, Giovanni Dell'Ariccia, and Paolo Mauro. 2010. "Rethinking Macroeconomic Policy." Paper prepared for the KDI/IMF Workshop on Reconstructing the World Economy. Seoul, February 25.

Bordo, Michael D., and David C. Wheelock. 1998. "Price Stability and Financial Stability: The Historical Record." *Federal Reserve Bank of St. Louis Review.*

Borio, Claudio. 2003. "Towards a Macroprudential Framework for Financial Supervision and Regulation?" Working Paper 128. Basel: Bank for International Settlements.

———. 2009. "Implementing the Macroprudential Approach to Financial Regulation and Supervision." Banque de France, *Financial Stability Review* 13 (September).

Borio, Claudio, and Mathias Drehmann. 2009. "Towards an Operational Framework for Financial Stability: 'Fuzzy' Measurement and Its Consequences." Working Paper 284. Basel: Bank for International Settlements.

Borio, Claudio, and Philip William Lowe. 2002. "Asset Prices, Financial and Monetary Stability: Exploring the Nexus." Working Paper 114. Basel: Bank for International Settlements.

Borio, Claudio, and Patrick McGuire. 2004. "Twin Peaks in Equity and Housing Prices?" *BIS Quarterly Review* (March): 79–93.

Borio, Claudio, and Ilhyock Shim. 2007. "What Can (Macro-) Prudential Policy Do to Support Monetary Policy?" Working Paper 242. Basel: Bank for International Settlements.

Borio, Claudio, and William R. White. 2004. "Whither Monetary and Financial Stability? The Implications of Evolving Policy Regimes." Working Paper 147. Basel: Bank for International Settlements.

Brunnermeier, Markus, and others. 2009. "The Fundamental Principles of Financial Regulation." Geneva Report on the World Economy 11.

Cardarelli, Robert, Selim Elekdag, and M. Ayhan Kose. 2009. "Capital Inflows: Macroeconomic Implications and Policy Responses." Working Paper 09/40. Washington: International Monetary Fund.

Chang, Robert, and Andrés Velasco. 2000. "Banks, Debt Maturity, and Financial Crisis." *Journal of International Economics* 51: 169–94.

Clement, Piet. 2010. "The Term 'Macroprudential': Origins and Evolution." *BIS Quarterly Review* (March).

Contessi, Silvio, Pierangelo DePace, and Johanna Francis. 2008. "The Cyclical Properties of Disaggregated Capital Flows." Working Paper 2008-041. Federal Reserve Bank of St. Louis.

Corsetti, Giancarlo, Paolo Pesenti, and Nouriel Roubini. 1999. "What Caused the Asian Currency and Financial Crisis?" *Japan and the World Economy* 11: 305–73.

Crockett, Andrew. 2000. "Marrying the Micro- and Macro-Prudential Dimensions of Financial Stability." Paper prepared for the Eleventh International Conference of Banking Supervisors. Basel, September 20–21.

Glindro, Eloisa, and others. 2008. "Determinants of House Prices in Nine Asia-Pacific Economies." Working Paper 263. Basel: Bank for International Settlements.

Goldstein, Morris, and Philip Turner. 2004. "Currency Mismatches at Center of Financial Crises in Emerging Economies." Washington: Peterson Institute for International Economics.

Hannoun, Hervé. 2010. "Towards a Global Financial Stability Framework." Paper prepared for the Forty-Fifth SEACEN Governors' Conference. Siem Reap Province, Cambodia, February.

Kaminsky, Graciela L., Carmen M. Reinhart, and Carlos A. Vegh. 2004. "When It Rains, It Pours: Procyclical Capital Flows and Macroeconomic Policies." Working Paper 10780. Cambridge, Mass.: National Bureau of Economic Research.

Ostry, Jonathan D., and others. 2010. "Capital Inflows: The Role of Controls." Staff Position Note 10/04. Washington: International Monetary Fund.

Padoa-Schioppa, T. 2003. "Central Banks and Financial Stability." Jakarta (www.ecb.int/press/key/date/2003/html/sp030707.en.html).

Park, Yung Chul. 2009. "Global Economic Recession and East Asia: How Has Korea Managed the Crisis and What Has It Learned?" Working Paper 209. Institute for Monetary and Economic Research, Bank of Korea.

———. 2010. "Reform of the Global Regulatory System: Perspectives of East Asian Emerging Economies." In *Lessons from East Asia and the Global Financial Crisis,* edited by Justin Yifu Lin and Boris Pleskovic. Washington: World Bank.

Rodrik, Dani, and Andres Velasco. 1999. "Short-Term Capital Flows." Paper prepared for Annual World Bank Conference on Development Economics, Washington, June.

Schwartz, Anna J. 1995. "Why Financial Stability Depends on Price Stability." *Economic Affairs* (Autumn): 21–25.

Shafer, Jeffrey R. 1982. "The Theory of a Lender of Last Resort in International Banking Markets." Central Banking Series 381. Basel: Bank for International Settlements.

Turner, Philip. 2009. "Central Banks, Liquidity, and the Banking Crisis." In *Time for a Visible Hand: Lessons from the 2008 World Financial Crisis,* edited by Stephany Griffith-Jones, Jose Antonio Ocampo, and Joseph Eugene Stiglitz. Oxford University Press.

———. 2010. "The Great Liquidity Freeze: What Does It Mean for International Banking?" Paper prepared for the ADBI-IMF-CBRC conference, Banking Regulation and Financial Stability in Asian Emerging Markets. Beijing, May.

White, William R. 2004. "Making Macroprudential Concerns Operational." Paper prepared for Netherlands Bank symposium on financial stability. Amsterdam, October.

———. 2006. "Is Price Stability Enough?" Working Paper 205. Basel: Bank for International Settlements.

Zhu, Haibin. 2006. "The Structure of Housing Finance Markets and House Prices in Asia." *BIS Quarterly Review* (December).

6

Macroprudential Approach to Regulation: Scope and Issues

SHYAMALA GOPINATH

Explicit pursuit of macroeconomic and financial stability can be said to be the single most significant takeaway from the recent financial crisis. More than in the specifics, the importance of this mandate lies in decisively effecting a course correction with regard to the approach and philosophy for regulation of the financial system. It is now being acknowledged that a macroprudential perspective is critical in designing and pursuing microprudential regulation of institutions and markets.

Underlying Constructs

Two distinct but highly interrelated constructs have come to epitomize this postcrisis framework: systemic risk management and macroprudential regulation. Both these concepts are philosophically appealing and conceptually sound but operationally quite challenging. Understanding the nuanced interplay between them is crucial in designing an efficient operative framework for financial stability.

Systemic risk management is a much broader concept than macroprudential regulation, implying the probability of sudden disruption to a large part of the financial system, reflected in the failure of multiple institutions and a freezing of markets, triggered by a common shock and propagated through interconnected exposures and correlated positions. Any framework for containing systemic risks would need to include the following elements:

—Strengthening the financial system's resilience to economic downturns and other adverse aggregate shocks.

—Monitoring common, correlated exposures among financial institutions arising out of network linkages.

—Developing measures to quantify the contribution of individual institutions to systemic risk.

—Minimizing the moral hazard associated with failure of systemically important financial institutions (SIFIs).

—Creating mechanisms to restrict the contagion impact of failing institutions during a crisis.

Macroprudential regulation, as it has come to be generally interpreted, essentially envisages that the key instruments of prudential regulation—capital, liquidity, and provisioning—vary dynamically according to macroeconomic circumstances. Macroeconomic triggers could be set off either by changes in the normal economic cycle or by sharp asset price movements. Conceptually, this is supposed to be in addition to stricter prudential standards for capital, liquidity, and leverage across the board.

Broad Objectives

The dynamics of macroprudential regulation are evident when seen in terms of its broad objectives. One of these is to address procyclical elements in the financial system: the basic idea is that cushions should be created during upswings so as to be in place when the rough times arrive—the countercyclical approach. The key measures under consideration, which have countercyclical characteristics and could act as automatic stabilizers, are as follows:

—Buffers built through capital conservation based on simple capital conservation rules. The objective is to ensure that banks that have depleted capital buffers rebuild them by reducing discretionary distribution of earnings. A buffer range will be established above the regulatory minimum capital requirement, and distribution constraints will be imposed on the bank when capital falls within this range.

—A countercyclical capital buffer, which will sit on top of the conservation buffer. It will establish a range according to the macrofinancial environment in which banks operate. This buffer will be triggered only when excessive credit growth, compared to the long-term trend, is judged to be associated with the buildup of systemwide risk. This buffer has to be combined with jurisdictional reciprocity to be effective. The upside of this will be that capital will not be a constraint to maintain the flow of credit to the economy during a period of stress.

—Forward-looking provisions that come about through accounting standards using the expected loss approach. Current standards do not take into account credit losses based on events that are expected to occur in the future.

Credit Risk and Price Bubbles

Major causes of the recent crisis were the general euphoria of the precrisis boom period and the severe underpricing of risks in the financial sector. In a risk-based capital regime, during booms this directly implies lesser capital for risky activities and hence increased lending to risky sectors and increased trading volumes in risky instruments. It was only after the crisis had set in that the true extent of risk underpricing became evident. The situation swung to the other extreme after the crisis. Macroprudential tools, including the leverage ratio, are meant to address situations like this by influencing the costs of credit exposures dynamically—that is, to provide a mechanism to correct the inherently skewed pricing of credit risk.

Asset price booms have invariably been identified with a precrisis economic configuration both symptomatic and causative. Earlier, though, the policy approach was that of benign neglect of asset prices as policymakers saw little role either for the monetary policy or for prudential policy in addressing these. The recent crisis however has forced a rethinking in this regard. There is now a broad consensus on the need to use credit as a macroprudential instrument.

The Basel III framework announced in December 2010 incorporates some of the above elements, particularly those affecting capital requirements. Starting in 2016 banks will be required to build up, over a three-year period (through 2018), a capital conservation buffer of 2.5 percent as well as a countercyclical buffer varying between zero and 2.5 percent of risk-weighted assets, depending on the extent of the buildup of systemwide risk. With regard to countercyclical capital buffers, a broad framework is laid out based on deviations in the credit-to-GDP ratio from its long-term trend. Recognizing the differing jurisdiction contexts, each national supervisor is expected to apply judgment in setting the buffer, using the best information available to gauge the buildup of systemwide risk. However, the framework does not envisage addressing sectoral credit issues through such countercyclical measures.

The challenge, particularly in the growing emerging market economies, will be to reconcile this approach with the risk of credit constraints, given supply-side issues that are qualitatively very different from those of the advanced economies. Generalized credit increases, higher than the trend, may not in themselves be a matter of systemic concern in view of the changing structure of economies. The framework in these countries would therefore have to have a more nuanced, sectoral focus. There are challenges in trying to influence asset prices through the credit channel. First, it is really difficult to set an optimum level of asset prices as a target. Second, only bank-financed exposures to asset markets can be influenced through macroprudential tools, and these may not be the dominant funding

Table 6-1. *Risk Weights and Standard Assets, Commercial Real Estate, India, 2004–07*
Percent

Date	*Risk weight*	*Provisions on standard assets*
December 2004	100	0.25
July 2005	125	0.25
March 2006	125	0.40
May 2006	150	1.00
January 2007	150	2.00

Source: Reserve Bank of India.

source: there have been instances in which a buildup of asset prices was due to leverage outside the banking sector. Third, a sectoral approach will inevitably involve an element of regulatory judgment and discretion.

In this context, it would be pertinent to recount the Indian experience in applying macroprudential elements in view of apparently excessive credit to certain sectors, particularly commercial real estate, which has been the cause of most banking crises.

Indian Experience

During the expansionary phase (since 2004), the Reserve Bank of India adopted various measures to counter procyclical trends. The impact of high credit growth in some sectors and asset price fluctuations on banks' balance sheets at various points in time were contained through preemptive countercyclical provisioning and differentiated risk weights for certain sensitive sectors.

In October 2004 the rapid growth in housing and consumer credit was flagged for the first time as a concern and as a temporary countercyclical measure; the risk weight applicable to these loans was increased by 25 percentage points. In October 2005, in the context of continuing high credit growth, the limitations of the prudential framework in capturing the ex-ante risks of procyclical bank credit were explicitly recognized, triggering an across-the-board increase in the provisioning requirement for standard assets.

The possibility of an asset bubble in addition to concerns about credit quality led to a risk weight on banks' exposure to the commercial real estate and to the capital market being increased from 100 percent to 125 percent in July 2005 (table 6-1). In May 2006, given the continued rapid expansion in credit to the commercial real estate sector, the risk weight on exposure to this sector was increased to 150 percent. In April of that year the general provisioning requirement on standard advances in specific sectors—that is, personal loans, loans and advances qualifying as capital market exposures, residential housing loans beyond Rs 2 lakh, and commercial real estate loans—was increased from 0.40 percent to 1 percent. On January 31, 2007, it was increased to 2 percent.

Box 6-1. *Factors Leading to Preemptive Action in the Real Estate Sector, India*

On-site inspections of banks uncovered indications of negative fallout from the general euphoria, such as lax underwriting standards and fraud.

Signs of the underpricing of risks emerged as real estate prices spiraled, fueled by ample liquidity and the wealth effect transmitted from the stock market boom. Tax incentives encouraged the use of stock market gains to buy real estate. Anecdotal evidence pointed to too much inventory.

Land prices rose steeply, according to auction results. Large real estate companies monetized huge land banks based on booming stock market valuations and the simultaneous increase in bank lending for commercial real estate.

While contemplating the measures, policymakers did not have any disaggregated statistical data or evidence to support their concerns about the risks of rising bank exposures to real estate. However, a trend in significant year-to-year increases in aggregate bank credit was clear. The Indian financial system is still largely a bank-intermediated system, and for this reason the bank credit channel is a key monetary policy transmission instrument. Thus growth in aggregate bank credit has always formed an important variable in the conduct of monetary policy. The credit-deposit ratio, particularly on an incremental basis, has been an important indicator.

In view of the rapid credit expansion in the period 2003–06, in addition to the countercyclical measures taken, the Reserve Bank explicitly indicated in April 2006 that growth of nonfood bank credit—including investments in bonds, debentures, and shares in public sector undertakings and the private corporate sector and commercial paper—was to be calibrated to decelerate to around 20 percent during 2006–07, from a growth of above 30 percent. Inflationary expectations also started firming up, and as part of monetary management, the repurchase rate was increased, in stages, by 175 basis points—to 7.75 percent by April 14, 2007, from its level of 6 percent in September 2004. Further, the cash reserve ratio was raised by 200 basis points, in stages, from 4.5 percent in September 2004 to 6.5 percent. From a regulatory perspective, the key factors that tilted the balance in favor of preemptive sectoral action, aimed primarily at preparing the banking sector to better manage potential downsides, are shown in box 6-1.

In this environment, it was decided to make it costlier for banks to finance loans backed by real estate. It was felt that the usual sector-neutral monetary policy instruments would not be effective without posing significant costs to the economy generally. So while monetary policy instruments were indeed used, the objective of this gradual tightening was quite different from the requisite stronger action in respect to bank exposures to sectors such as real estate.

It needs to be appreciated that, in the Indian context, the sharp rise in bank credit to the real estate sector was per se not a clear indicator of any asset price bubble, given the inherent demand-supply dynamics in the economy and the genuine needs of an economy on a high-growth path. A confluence of positive factors contributed to this development: a decline in inflation and stable inflationary expectations, a decline in both nominal and real interest rates, and the availability of ample systemic liquidity (contributed by the rising tide of capital flows). Concomitantly, there was a shift in funding by corporates to nonbank sources, including external borrowing, which forced banks to look at diversifying their lending portfolios. This shift also helped in meeting the demands on the commercial real estate front, including office space to accommodate the information technology boom and the gradual expansion of organized retail to smaller cities.

The objective, I must underline, was not to address the asset price bubble per se or to curtail the genuine credit needs of the economy but to prepare the banking sector to better manage any downside related to selective sectors. In other words, the bank adopted what is now called expected and unexpected loss approaches.

Since the crisis, sectoral provisioning and risk weight requirements have been modulated in sync with the emerging conditions. (The raising of risk weights has second-order impact on bank advances to commercial real estate in terms of reversing its growth rate.) In the immediate aftermath of the crisis—in November 2008—provisioning requirements were brought back to a uniform 0.40 percent (figure 6-1). However, in view of the large increase in credit to the commercial real estate sector and of restructured advances in this sector, the following year—in November 2009—the provisions required on standard assets in the commercial real estate sector were increased from 0.40 percent to 1 percent to create a cushion against deterioration in asset quality. The measures had their intended effect.

Recently, the risk weights on residential housing loans of Rs 7.5 million and above have also been raised to 125 percent. In addition, a minimum loan-to-value ratio of 90 percent has been prescribed for all mortgage loans of more than Rs 2 million (80 percent for lesser amounts).

As yet another unconventional macroprudential measure, banks have been required to build provisions against nonperforming assets, including floating provisions, of 70 percent. There was a realization that, from a macroprudential perspective, banks should use part of their profits to shore up provisions held against these assets when profits were good so that they can be used for absorbing losses in a downturn. It was felt that the graded system of provisioning, based on the period of delinquency and the extent of collateralization of the nonperforming assets, captured the risks only partially, particularly in respect to substandard and restructured assets.

Figure 6-1. *Time-Varying Risk Weights and Provisioning for Commercial Real Estate, 2004–11*

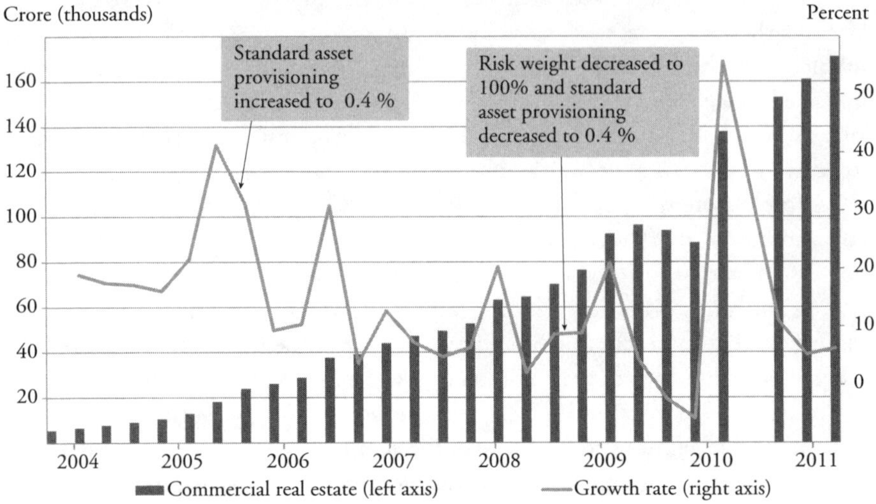

Source: Reserve Bank of India.

What are the key lessons from the Indian experience? First, the harmonization of monetary policy objectives and prudential objectives can give a more complete picture of the financial landscape than might be possible if banking supervision is separate from central banks. Two, macroprudential policy is no substitute for monetary tightening but should rather act as a complement to monetary policy. Three, supervisors need to have the independence and flexibility to act in a timely way on the basis of the available information, albeit incomplete.

Beyond Macroprudential Regulation

As with all ideas that gain currency and wide acceptance in a short period of time, macroprudential regulation runs the risk of being overapplied. However, there is an equally strong risk of making it too narrow in focus. It must be reiterated that macroprudential regulation is just one element of a broader macroprudential approach and needs to be supplemented with other tools to address systemic risk issues. Such tools could be in the form of additional prudential measures applied to all institutions with a systemic objective. It may be difficult to make a binary distinction between microprudential and macroprudential policies, as ultimately all macrorisks translate into microrisks for financial institutions. The critical thing is the incorporation of a systemic perspective into the policy design.

A survey conducted by the Committee on the Global Financial System on macroprudential frameworks in various countries finds that, though conceptions of macroprudential policy aims and objectives were fuzzy, many countries had kept the broad systemic perspective in mind.[1] The survey also notes far more extensive use of macroprudential policies in emerging market economies as opposed to advanced economies.

The survey also shows that emerging markets were open to target-specific sectors. The most widely used instruments are measures to limit credit supply to sectors prone to excessive credit growth. These include limits calibrated to borrower risk characteristics (caps on loan-to-value ratios or debt-income ratios) as well as aggregate or sectoral credit growth ceilings and limits on exposures by instruments. Many emerging economies, given their specific context, already had adopted measures to address specific risks. Among these are loan-to-deposit limits, core funding ratios, reserve requirements for liquidity risk, and limits on open currency positions or on derivative transactions.

The nature and sources of systemic risks are different in emerging market economies from those in advanced economies. This part of the world has seen many systemic crises over the past two decades, and each of these crises demonstrates the importance of prudential policy to minimize risks to financial stability and to reduce the impact from disturbances domestically and globally. Financial markets in emerging markets tend to be less well developed and resilient than such markets in advanced economies. This makes the system more vulnerable to even small disturbances and increases the criticality of macroprudential safeguards. It therefore becomes imperative, from the systemic stability perspective, to guide other realms of the economic policy framework as well.

In the Indian context, this perspective was writ large on most of the elements of the policy framework. The approaches adopted in three areas—the prudential regulation of institutions, the capital account management framework, and the management of sovereign borrowings—illustrate the systemic perspective in the policy sphere.

Regulatory Framework for Banks

The regulatory framework for banks aims to address interconnectedness and forex liabilities. To address interconnectedness, prudential limits are placed on aggregate interbank liabilities for banks as a proportion of their net worth, the overnight uncollateralized funding market is restricted only to banks and primary dealers, and there are ceilings for both lending as well as borrowing by these entities. In addition, investment by banks in the subordinated debt of other banks is assigned 100 percent risk weight for capital adequacy purposes. Also, the bank's aggregate investment in tier II bonds issued by other banks and financial institutions is

1. Committee on the Global Financial System (2010).

limited to 10 percent of the investing bank's total capital. Exposure limits apply to exposures between banks and nonbank finance companies.

For forex liabilities there are limits on the proportion of wholesale foreign currency liabilities intermediated through the banking system (other than for lending for exports). Retail foreign currency deposits from nonresidents are subject to minimum maturity requirements and interest rate caps. Banks are required to hold a minimum of 24 percent of their liabilities in the form of liquid domestic sovereign securities. This stipulation has worked both as a solvency and as a liquidity buffer.

Credit conversion factors used for calculating the potential future credit exposure for off-balance-sheet interest rates as well as exchange rate contracts were doubled across all maturities in 2008. This was done since it was felt that credit conversion factors, per Basel norms, did not fully capture the volatility in the interest rate and forex markets in the Indian context. Profits on the sale of assets to a special purpose vehicle under securitization are not recognized immediately on sale but over the life of the pass-through certificates issued by the vehicle. Any rated liquidity facility by the originator or a third party is treated as an off-balance-sheet item; it attracts a credit conversion factor of 100 percent and is risk weighted per its rating.

Capital Account Management

Excessive volatility of capital flows imposes significant costs to the economy beyond the obvious exchange rate impact. There are implications for financial stability in the form of induced risks of asset price bubbles and excessive foreign currency exposures in the financial system and in external debt in general. Experience shows that the most volatile components of capital flows are portfolio flows. These flows, as well as debt flows, are also procyclical.

While the capital account regime in India has accorded substantial freedom to equity flows—both foreign direct investment and portfolio flows—debt flows have been modulated contextually through the regulatory framework, with a combination of quantitative and price-based measures. Calibration of debt flows into sovereign and corporate debt is the instrument most commonly used for this purpose.

Management of Sovereign Borrowings

Since the automatic monetization of government debt stopped in the 1990s, market borrowing by the government has been a critical variable in the macroeconomic framework. The stipulation of a statutory liquidity ratio for banks needs to be seen in this context. Banks have been permitted to hold this mandated investment to maturity.

Another critical factor that buffered India's sovereign balance sheet from the global crisis is that India does not borrow on the foreign currency market and depends very little on foreign investors in respect to its domestic currency debt. Its strong domestic investor base (apart from banks), in the form of insurance and pension or provident funds, has enabled India to lengthen the maturity of its domestic debt. The experience in general of emerging market countries has been that foreign investors in sovereign debt prefer short-term investments.

Systemically Important Financial Institutions

The universally accepted postcrisis approach with regard to the management of systemic risks in the financial system accords primacy to the issue of banks that are too big to fail. The view is that resolution of the problems presented by these institutions, short of a publicly funded bailout, is at the heart of the too-big-to-fail issue. SIFIs exaggerate the negative externalities and correlated exposures within the financial system. Their scale, complexity, and interconnectedness also implies that their resolvability is extremely difficult.

In November 2010 the Financial Stability Board issued its report, "Reducing the Moral Hazard Posed by Systemically Important Financial Institutions." The report sets out a framework for addressing the moral hazard risks associated with SIFIs. The report, favoring a calibrated approach, focuses on global SIFIs—institutions of such size, market importance, and global interconnectedness that their distress or failure would cause significant dislocation in the global financial system and adverse economic consequences across a range of countries. The report's recommendations are given in box 6-2.

The real challenge will be to have a nondiscretionary framework for quantitatively defining SIFIs. In November 2009, G-20 finance ministers agreed on the criteria for identifying institutions and markets of systemic importance, based on the joint proposals of the International Monetary Fund, the Bank for International Settlements, and the Financial Stability Board.[2] Three main criteria are proposed: size, lack of substitutability, and interconnectedness. Size, for the purposes of systemic risk identification, is an exhaustive notion covering the exposures, or balance-sheet and off-balance-sheet risks, of the entity in question. Lack of substitutability involves assessing the financial system's relative dependence on the financial services provided by that entity to measure the system's immunity to the disappearance of said entity. Interconnectedness requires looking at the direct and indirect links between financial institutions that will contribute to the spread of systemic risk and its contagiousness for the real economy.

The Financial Stability Board and the Basel Committee on Banking Supervision have started work on developing a broad methodology for the identification of global SIFIs. National supervisors will make these assessments based on not

2. G-20 Communiqué, meeting of finance ministers and central bank governors, London, November 7, 2009.

Box 6-2. *Financial Stability Board Recommendations for Systemically Important Financial Institutions*

The policy framework for systemically important financial institutions should include the following:

—Measures to ensure that financial issues can be resolved safely, quickly, and without destabilizing the financial system and exposing the taxpayer to risk.

—A requirement that these institutions' capacity to absorb loss is equal to the risks they pose to the global financial system.

—Intensive supervisory oversight.

—Infrastructure that reduces risk of contagion from a single failed institution.

—Supplementary prudential requirements as determined by the national authorities.

Additionally, home jurisdictions should

—Require international supervisory colleges to make rigorous and coordinated assessments of the risks facing these institutions.

—Mandate international recovery and resolution planning and negotiate institution-specific crisis cooperation agreements within cross-border crisis management groups.

—Subject institutions' policy measures to review by the proposed peer review council.

Source: Financial Stability Board (2010).

only quantitative criteria but also their own judgment using ancillary indicators and other supervisory knowledge. A critical issue in this regard is the moral hazard associated with disclosing the names of SIFIs. However, markets would always be able to infer their identity fairly well from, for example, their level of capital and buffers. The factor that may make it harder to make accurate guesses is if banks operate well above the minimum requirement of capital and buffers. What is important is that there be a clear communication of policies to markets so that markets understand the intent behind the identification of SIFIs and the regulatory approach in dealing with them.

Work is also under way to improve authorities' ability to resolve the problems such institutions present, without interrupting their vital economic functions and without exposing taxpayers to loss. In particular, the focus is on a couple of changes: the imposition of a loss-absorbency capacity higher than the minimum level agreed to in Basel III and more intensive and coordinated supervision and resolution planning.

Improved Resolution Regime

Problems arising in all financial institutions should be resolvable in an orderly manner, without taxpayers' support, and within the applicable resolution regimes in the jurisdictions in which they operate. Various approaches that have gained traction in policy deliberations for improving resolution capacity include limits on the complexity of internal structures (that is, a preference for stand-alone subsidiaries); recovery and resolution planning; use of contingent capital and other instruments to absorb losses as a going concern; a special resolution regime for SIFIs that makes their shareholders and creditors share losses; and a bailout fund, contributed to by the entities expecting to be bailed out. In the United States, the Dodd-Frank Wall Street Reform and Consumer Protection Act envisages a resolution regime that allows the government to impose losses on shareholders and creditors, unlike the normal bankruptcy provisions for other firms, where the aim is to reorganize or liquidate a failing firm "for the benefit of its creditors."

Stressed environments often reveal weaknesses in supervisory frameworks and methods that are not apparent in times of stability. Regulators and supervisors should be better equipped to not just identify but also take appropriate action preemptively to address risks that have the potential to destabilize the system. It is in this context that the critical factor of supervisory space becomes significant. It is possible that, at times, supervisory assessments will be useful mainly for their anecdotal evidence rather than conclusive evidence. In such a scenario, supervisors would be prone to making either a type I error or a type II error in judgment; that is, they may either raise false red flags or ignore genuine red flags. It is for the broader political economy and policy setup to provide the tolerance for each of the two errors. This would largely determine the decisionmaking framework and provide the necessary space for the regulators to make timely decisions, given that dynamic judgment is necessary to deal with system risk that is constantly changing.

The singular area of attention in this regard is the move of much of the over-the-counter derivatives market to a central clearing model. There is broad agreement in this regard, though a few important concomitant issues arising out of risk concentration in CCPs will need be addressed carefully, including cross margining across CCPs or across different products.

There is also the issue of implicit or explicit liquidity support by the banking system to central counterparties in the form of lines of credit or to intermediaries such as brokers and market participants in the form of margins for trades, payment commitments, or other forms of guarantee. It is likely that the risk of transactions undertaken through central counterparties sits in the books of banks or regulated financial entities either directly or indirectly. If so, these entities need to be subject to prudential norms. Ideally, regulators of these parties should prefer collateral in the form of liquid securities rather than bank deposits or guarantees.

Equally important, issues relating to market practices also have a bearing on financial stability. One fundamental issue is the indisputable faith that markets will experience ever-increasing volumes and liquidity. Shifting to central counterparties is only shifting the risks. There is a need to regulate all derivatives markets in interest rate, credit, and forex products from a systemic perspective; if this is done, then market regulation as practiced by many emerging countries may not be so anachronistic.

The regime for credit rating agencies is another such area. In spite of the systemic risk inherent in ratings, current efforts to regulate rating agencies focus mainly on microprudential issues and typically aim at reducing conflicts of interest and cliff effects by lowering their use in regulatory and supervisory frameworks. One moral hazard created by rating agencies is the use of support ratings, wherein implicit sovereign support available to SIFIs is taken into account to upgrade ratings. It may be necessary to require agencies to provide ratings without this assumption of support. Addressing financial stability issues relating to potential procyclicality and systemic risk stemming from rating agencies is an agenda for future work.

Another important issue, which will be accentuated by the move toward central counterparties and collateral support arrangements, is the increasing collateralization of bank balance sheets. Leverage is one part of this aspect—a recent IMF paper clearly points out the risks inherent in widespread rehypothecation of collaterals in many of the developed markets.[3] The other part is the impact on bank balance sheets of procyclical collateralization regimes. If a large part of the good-quality collateral on banks' books is locked up for their trading operations, what does it do to the resolvability issues in times of crisis and burden sharing? Both regulation of markets and close monitoring of interconnected exposures would be required to address the underlying risks.

India and SIFIs

The financial system in India is largely bank dominated; banks are the parents of most of the large financial conglomerates. These conglomerates are not owned by holding companies. Since 2004 there has been a framework in place to closely monitor certain large financial conglomerates. This framework aims at reducing the probability of failure among institutions considered too big to fail. It also aims to address problems of contagion.

The supervision of these conglomerates includes off-site surveillance through quarterly returns, regular interactions with the CEOs of parent companies and other entities in the group, and periodic reviews by a technical committee made up of sectoral and financial market regulators. Off-site surveillance and periodic interfaces with the conglomerates have afforded quite robust assessments of the risks faced by these SIFIs. From time to time these groups have been advised to improve their corporate governance processes and risk management systems, especially with respect to the management of credit concentration risks and liquidity risks on a groupwide basis.

3. Singh and Aitken (2010).

Recently other initiatives have also been launched for further strengthening regulatory and supervisory approaches for the identified conglomerates. Discussion with the main auditor of the group by the lead regulator is being contemplated. Steps are already being taken to tighten the capital adequacy norms for these conglomerates to ensure that the amount of capital that the group possesses on a consolidated basis is adequate not only for the discretionary risks that the group entities take but also for nondiscretionary risks—operational, reputational, and strategic, especially those arising from fiduciary activities.

The above approach for large financial conglomerates is focused primarily on an intensive supervisory process aimed at capturing risk concentrations within the group. A differential prudential framework for SIFIs has not been considered necessary, as the regulatory framework for banks in general addresses issues of excessive risk taking by individual institutions. The financial system is considerably less complex than most developed markets, as many complex, high-risk products are not allowed or are regulated.

The sole metric of size has not been found to be much help as—apart from the largest bank, which is state owned, and a large private sector bank with a relatively low market share—the market share of the other larger banks is not that significant. Relative to the needs of the growing economy and the rapid growth in nonfinancial conglomerates, emerging countries require a larger number of banks of optimal size to meet increasing demands. The focus has therefore been on differential and intensive supervision of large banks that are conglomerates (which includes the size metric).

The real concern, from the interconnectedness perspective, arises from the nonbanking financial sector, which is regulated by regulators for such sectors as insurance, securities broking, mutual funds, venture capital, and housing finance. All other nonbanking financial activities are regulated by the Reserve Bank of India as part of a separate regulatory framework. Many of these institutions are significantly large. Through their interaction with other financial market segments, they could pose systemic risk. For these entities, a stricter prudential framework like that for banks has been put in place. Still, going forward, India will have to consider a range of policy levers to address problems arising from these institutions.

Conclusion

Macroprudential regulation is essentially an inexact science. It has its limitations and needs to be used in conjunction with other policies to be effective. To correct for the buildup of imbalances, a combination of monetary and macroprudential policies is required. If inflation risks are emerging, macroprudential measures cannot take the place of interest rate increases. Macroprudential measures are well suited to enhance the resilience of the financial system, but their effect on aggregate demand and inflationary expectations are weak compared to interest rates.

It is also important to acknowledge what macroprudential regulation cannot do. It cannot manage economic cycles or target asset prices. It can only provide instruments to respond to these developments to cushion the financial system from stresses. It is in this context that the imperative for involvement of central banks becomes evident, as otherwise the required synergy between monetary management and macroprudential management will be lost.

The real challenge of macroprudential regulation is strong resistance to countercyclical actions during booms. A rule-based approach will to a large extent obviate this problem, but this approach has its own limitations. It is difficult to lay down simple rules, as the financial system and markets are evolving and banks continue to be the dominant source of funding. The suitability of tools can of course change as the structure of the economy and financial system changes. Regulators may have to rely on their own discretion.

As the global policy stance remains highly accommodative, there are concerns that the current two-speed recovery implies short-term volatile capital flows or an accentuation of carry trades, which increase the foreign currency mismatches in the nonfinancial sector. Emerging market economies will have to address these issues with a range of policy tools. A realistic assessment may be required about what capital regulations can do. Banks need capital for lending and for resilience against shocks, so it is important to focus on the business model and to continuously monitor leverage and liquidity risks.

Going beyond macroprudential regulation, an issue that will be of critical importance to emerging market economies from a stability perspective is the presence of foreign financial institutions. They will determine the exposure of domestic financial systems to the risk of proxy contamination with problems in global markets. A recent Bank for International Settlements paper attempts to make a distinction between multinational banks and international banks primarily based on their funding models.[4] It argues that, from the perspective of bank exposures to borrowers, local funding (as in the case of multinational banks) is more stable during the crisis than funding across borders and currencies (as in the case of international banks). For the host country, the key relevant issue from a market disruption perspective is the destabilizing spillovers on local lending decisions as a result of problems in the global wholesale funding and swap markets. This fear actually materialized for many borrowing countries during the recent crisis.

In India the banking sector is currently at a crucial regime-shift point, and the way ahead will be significantly contingent on the evolving thinking in regard to SIFIs. Policymakers are weighing the various options in respect to two areas: one, increasing competition and furthering financial inclusion through permitting new banks domestically; and two, giving further space for foreign banks to expand their

4. McCauley, McGuire, and von Goetz (2010).

operations. Increasing competition can indeed help reduce the systemic significance of existing institutions, provided it is accompanied by the requisite measures to strengthen the legal and institutional framework.

References

Committee on the Global Financial System. 2010. "Macroprudential Instruments and Frameworks: A Stocktaking of Issues and Experiences." Working Paper 38. Basel.

Financial Stability Board. 2010. "Reducing the Moral Hazard Posed by Systemically Important Financial Institutions." Basel.

McCauley, Robert, Patrick McGuire, and Peter von Goetz. 2010. "The Architecture of Global Banking: From International to Multinational?" *Bank for International Settlements Quarterly Review* (March).

Singh, Manmohan, and James Aitken. 2010. "The (Sizable) Role of Rehypothecation in the Shadow Banking System." Working Paper. Washington: International Monetary Fund.

7

Macroprudential Lessons from the Financial Crises: A Practitioner's View

KIYOHIKO G. NISHIMURA

In this chapter, I focus on the issues of financial stability and central bank policies based on two episodes of financial crisis: one dating from twenty years ago in Japan and the other from three years ago in the United States. I first present one stylized account from a macroprudential perspective of the buildup in financial imbalances that led eventually to the financial crisis in the late 1980s in Japan. Then I illustrate the startling similarities between the recent U.S. subprime-triggered experience and that of Japan in the 1980s. Examining these two crises, I draw four implications for macroprudential policy, which are likely to be universally relevant, particularly for emerging economies. The message is simple and straightforward: Beware. So-called macroprudential measures may not always be sufficient. For example, if investors are excessively optimistic, a modest increase in capital requirements and leverage restraints may not be effective to curb such unwarranted optimism. This leads to the final topic, the role of monetary policy during the buildup of financial imbalances, a role that I would argue is, in a word, crucial.

Letting financial imbalances balloon and then collapse may be too costly to bear, if such imbalances lead to wasteful irreversible investment. Moreover, there remains substantial uncertainty about the effectiveness of regulatory reforms and other macroprudential measures in the real world. It is therefore wise to use monetary policy to address the issue of financial imbalances in tandem with macroprudential measures, if, first, substantial imbalances are building up and, second, regulatory policies have proved to be insufficient.

Financial Imbalances in 1980s Japan: A Stylized Account

This account, of the buildup to financial imbalances in Japan in the late 1980s, is from a macroprudential perspective.[1] It is intended to be descriptive and schematic in the way that macroprudential issues are highlighted. It is admittedly simplistic, but I believe this is a good starting point for discussion.

Deregulation-Induced Financial Innovations and Financial Anomalies

A number of financial innovations introduced as a result of deregulation appear to have played a role in the late 1980s bubble in Japan. Under the designation of financial liberalization, deregulation sparked the arrival of new products such as commercial paper (CP) and large time deposits with unregulated rates, which nourished the atmosphere of profit seeking through these "financial technology" products.[2]

Financial liberalization was a gradual process; it started in the late 1970s and spanned twenty years. Around 1986 signs of financial anomalies emerged, brought about by innovations associated with financial liberalization. The most notable anomaly was the apparent no-risk arbitrage opportunity for large nonfinancial corporations. In 1985 banks were allowed to offer large time deposits with no regulation on their rates. Banks then offered short-term, large, time deposits to major nonfinancial corporations with rates higher than the corresponding term CP rates. Thus large nonfinancial corporations could profit from raising funds by issuing CPs and depositing them in these unregulated, large, time deposits.[3] By a similar token, three-to-six-month unregulated time deposit rates were substantially higher than short-term prime lending rates (figure 7-1).

These anomalies were often explained as banks' investment in customer capital in large nonfinancial corporations. These large nonfinancial corporations, which were once good customers of the banks, had gained increasingly good access to capital markets through deregulation. If the banks could obtain and keep long-term customer relations with these corporations, the banks could profit from their clients' increased financial and other activities through increased fees and commissions. This was not mere wishful thinking at that time, since the banks themselves were being gradually deregulated and allowed to expand their business into securities markets and other activities, in order to accommodate the various financial needs of these large nonfinancial corporations.

Favorable Capital Market Conditions and Looser Lending Standards

At the same time, banks' profits surged and their capital positions strengthened, as shown in figure 7-2. Banks tapped capital markets to raise capital easily, and

1. This account is partly based on Hattori, Shin, and Takahashi (2009).
2. These technologies were known at the time as *zai-teku* in Japanese.
3. Bank of Japan (1989).

Figure 7-1. *Time Deposit Rates and Prime Lending Rates, Japan, 1980–95*[a]

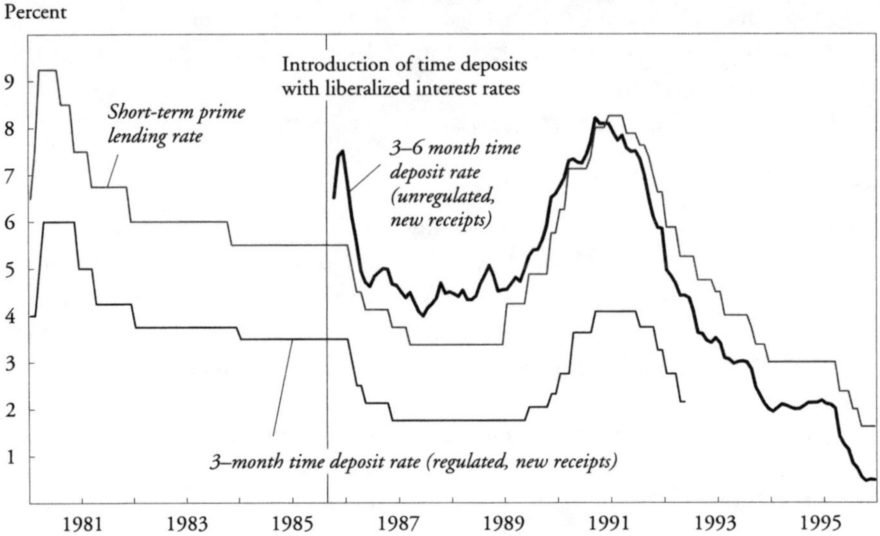

Source: Bank of Japan, Economic Statistics Annual, various years.

a. The three- to six-month time deposit rate (unregulated, new receipts) is the average interest rate on newly received time deposits with unregulated interest rates of terms between three and six months. The three-month time deposit rate (regulated, new receipts) is the interest rate set by the regulation on newly received three-month time deposits. Regulations on time desposit interest rates were abolished in 1993. The end-of-month data for the three-month time deposit rates are available only until May 1992.

Figure 7-2. *Net Income and Loss, Japanese Banks, 1983–93*

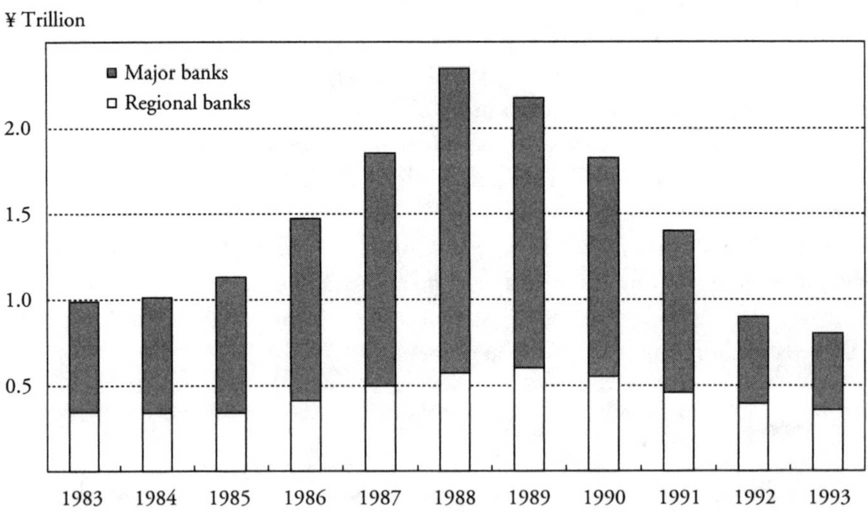

Source: Bank of Japan.

Figure 7-3. *Leverage, Assets, and Loans, Japan, 1975–95*[a]

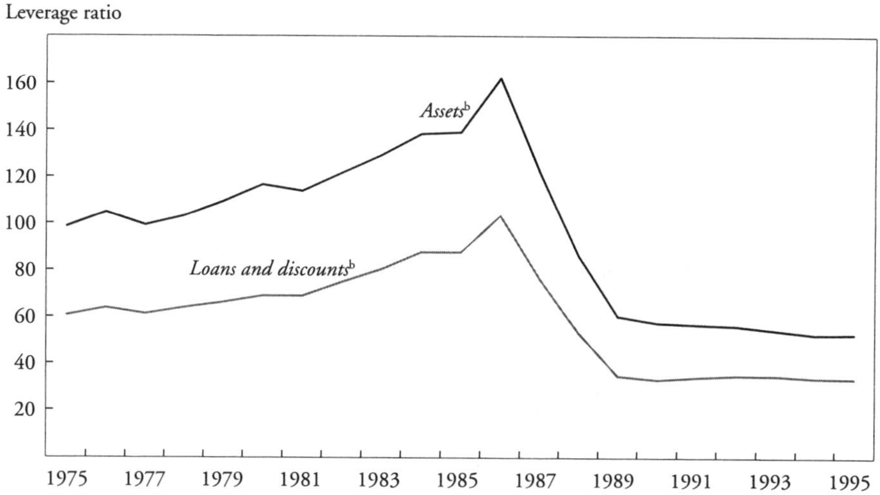

Source: Bank of Japan, Economic Statistics Annual, various years.

a. Figure includes all domestically licensed banks, excluding member banks of the Second Association of Regional Banks.

b. Common stock and capital reserves.

their leverage ratio declined dramatically, from around 160 in 1986 to around 60 in 1989, as shown in figure 7-3.

With strong profit positions, loosened capital constraints through new equity issues, and substantial inflows of time deposits from large nonfinancial corporations, bank lending to real estate–related sectors surged, as did lending to small enterprises (figures 7-4 and 7-5), partly compensating for lackluster growth in lending to large nonfinancial corporations. Around this time, anecdotal evidence also emerged to suggest that banks had loosened their lending standards. Some banks transferred their loan examination function from the loan examination division of their headquarters to their loan-making divisions. Hence the ratio of loan examination officers at headquarters declined sharply in the 1980s, as shown in figure 7-6.

Overlooked Signs of Excessive Optimism

Around this time, there were signs of excessive optimism among investors, especially in property markets. Figure 7-7 illustrates the price-to-rent ratio in residential property markets in Tokyo, based on hedonic price and rent price indexes of condominiums and taking due account of vast differences in quality.[4] (Rents here are market-determined, new contract rents, not institutionally rigid, continuing

4. See Shimizu, Watanabe, and Nishimura (2010a).

Figure 7-4. *Corporate Borrowers, Japan, by Size, Selected Years 1975–90*[a]

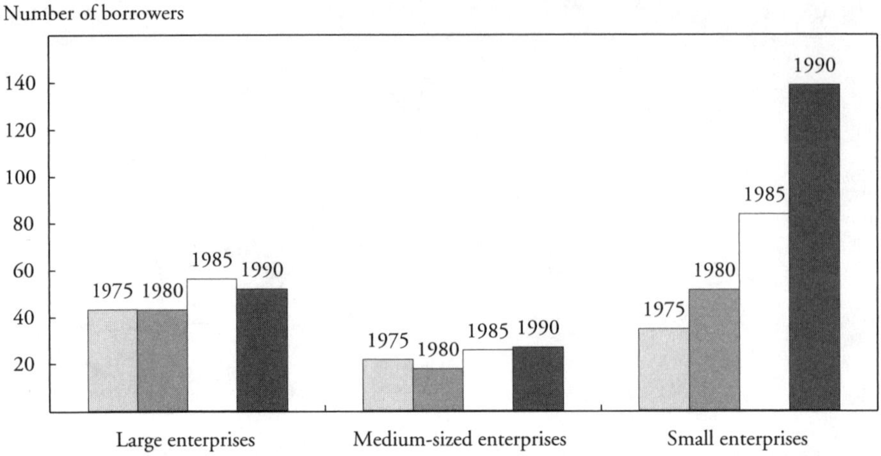

Source: Bank of Japan, Economic Statistics Monthly, various issues; Statistics Bureau, National Accounts.

a. Includes all banks, excluding member banks of the Second Association of Regional Banks. Total outstanding loans used for calculations are outstanding loans and discounts to domestic corporate borrowers, excluding overdrafts. Large enterprises are corporations with capital of 1 billion yen or more and more than 300 regular employees. For the wholesale trade industry, the criterion for the number of regular employees is more than 100 persons. For the retail and service industries, it is more than 50 persons. Small enterprises are unincorporated enterprises as well as corporations with capital of 100 million yen or less or with regular employees of 300 persons or fewer. For the wholesale trade industry, the definition is corporations capitalized at 30 million yen or less or with 100 regular employees or fewer. For the retail trade and service industries, it is corporations capitalized at 10 million yen or less or with 50 regular employees or fewer. Outstanding loans for medium-sized enterprises are calculated by excluding those for small enterprises and large enterprises from total outstanding loans. Figures are deflated by GDP deflators. Total borrowings in 1975 in real terms = 100.

contract rents.)[5] This ratio surged in one year (1986) from around 23, which in retrospect looks like the long-run average, to around 40, suggesting substantial overheating in property markets. After a short pause, the price-to-rent ratio shot up to a peak of around 50 in the fall of 1990 (even after the collapse of the stock markets).

However, it should be noted here that this quality-adjusted, price-to-rent ratio has only recently become available. In the late 1980s only appraisal price indexes for residential and commercial lands were available, with a substantial lag of half a year. There were no reliable rent data. Thus there were no contemporaneous hard data showing investors' excessive optimism in property markets, though there were lots of anecdotes of property investors' excessive optimism. Moreover,

5. There is sizable rigidity in continuing rents, partly because of institutional factors. The consumer price index rent is the weighted average of market-determined, new-contract rents and institutionally rigid continuing rents, with more weight on the latter. See Shimizu, Watanabe, and Nishimura (2010c).

Figure 7-5. *Bank Lending to Real Estate–Related Sectors, Japan, Selected Years 1975–90*[a]

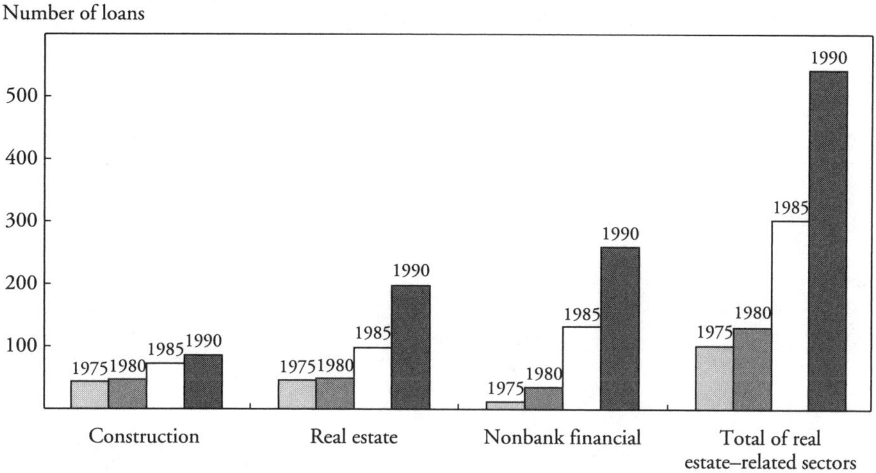

Source: Bank of Japan, Economic Statistics Monthly, various issues; Statistics Bureau, National Accounts.

a. Includes all banks, excluding member banks of the Second Association of Regional Banks. Real estate–related sectors include real estate, construction, and nonbank financial. Total outstanding loans used for calculations are outstanding loans and discounts to domestic corporate borrowers, excluding overdrafts. Outstanding loans to the nonbank financial industry are the sum of those to the other financial industry and the lease industry. Figures are deflated by GDP deflators. Total lendings in 1975 in real terms = 100.

Figure 7-6. *Ratio of Examining Officers at Headquarters, Japan, by Bank Type, Fiscal Years 1980–2000*

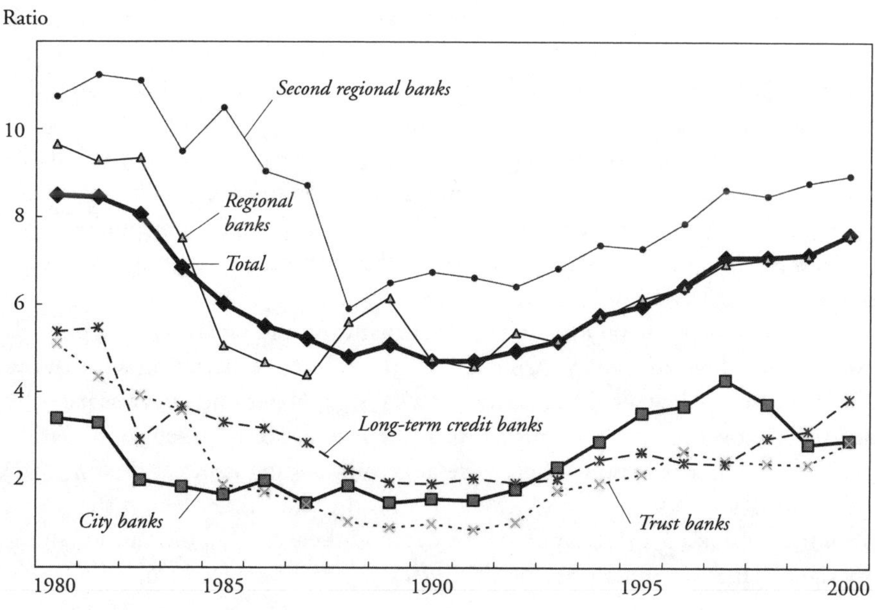

Source: Fukao and others (2005, fig. 1).

Figure 7-7. *Price-to-Rent Ratio, Tokyo Residential Area, 1986–2008*

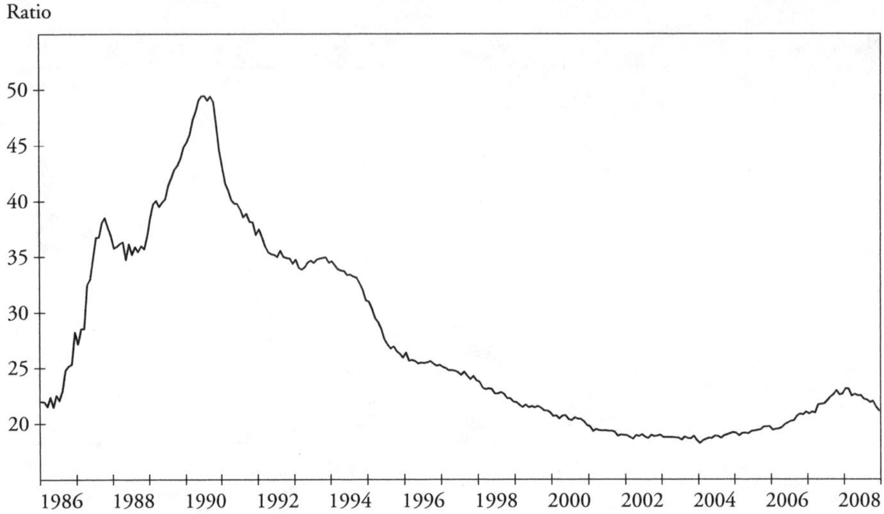

Source: Author's calculation.

in retrospect, the government itself was overly optimistic: it anticipated a substantial scarcity of office space partly because of internationalization of the Japanese financial markets in its Metropolitan Reconstruction Plan (1985) and the Fourth National Comprehensive Development Plan (1987).

Central Bank Policy

Facing investors' excessive optimism and banks' loose lending standards, the Bank of Japan used its then-conventional window guidance to control banks' lending volumes. Although direct control of lending through the practice of window guidance was criticized as a discretionary measure contrary to market principles, window guidance at a time of seemingly excessive optimism could be interpreted as a macroprudential measure, albeit a crude one, to dampen excessive optimism through the exercise of moral suasion. However, as financial deregulation got under way, window guidance proved to be ineffective and failed to curb loans outstanding in the late 1980s.

What was the monetary policy stance at that time and what were the public's expectations about the policy? Around 1986 the market's expectation was that the easy monetary policy would continue for a substantial period. This was partially due to the government's commitments in the international policy coordination pledged during that period. There were also confounding issues at the time: the fallout of Black Monday (October 19, 1987), the fear of a recession stemming from the substantial appreciation of the yen, and the lack of significant inflationary signs in the consumer price index. In fact, the policy rate was cut from 5 percent in December 1985 to 2.5 percent in February 1987 and remained unchanged for more than two years.

Then, as we know only too well, the stock market began to drop in January 1990, falling from more than 38,000 to around 16,000 in two and a half years.[6] The quality-adjusted Tokyo condominium price index continued to climb, until October 1990, to triple the price of 1986 and then declined by about 30 percent in three years.[7] It continued declining through the 1990s, with the price in 2000 being approximately the same as that of 1986.

Recent U.S. Experience and Japan's 1980s Experience

When considering this stylized account, one cannot help noticing the similarities between Japan's experience in the 1980s and recent events in the United States triggered by the subprime mortgage crisis.

First, financial innovations were at least partly responsible for the buildup of financial imbalances. Securitization was thought to improve risk allocation, as risk was now borne by those who were more able to bear it. This reduced risk premiums (equilibrium or sustainable) for previously very risky investments, such as subprime mortgages. The financial sector could earn substantially higher profits from originating and distributing these securitized products. Taking advantage of this and other innovations, banks' profits increased and their capital market standing became more solid.

Second, there were signs of financial anomalies and loose lending standards. For example, collateralized debt obligation squares (CDO^2s) based on collaterized debt obligations (CDOs), which were in turn based on subprime mortgage pools, sometimes had a thick AAA tranche. It was argued that their pricing was based on a model proven to track the history well, but the history was usually too short to ensure the model's sustained reliability. Again as we know only too well, their assumed correlations turned out to be wrong. In addition, there were reports of "low doc loans" and "no doc loans," especially in subprime mortgages.[8]

Third, there seemed to be signs of excessive optimism, at least in the booming United States, though not as obviously as in Japan in the late 1980s. Unlike Japan then, semicontemporaneous house price indexes were available in the United States, including those of the Office of Federal Housing Enterprise Oversight (now the Federal Housing Finance Agency) and Case-Shiller indexes, taking account of vast differences in the quality of housing stock. In some parts of the United States, notably Los Angeles and Miami, price increases accelerated in

6. The Nikkei index was 38,915 on December 29, 1989, and 15,951 on June 30, 1992.

7. These quality-adjusted house price indexes are in Shimizu, Watanabe, and Nishimura (2010a).

8. "Low doc loans" and "no doc loans" are mortgage loans that require less than full documentation of income, employment, and assets.

Figure 7-8. *Real House Prices, United States (1998–2010) and Japan (1998–2008)*

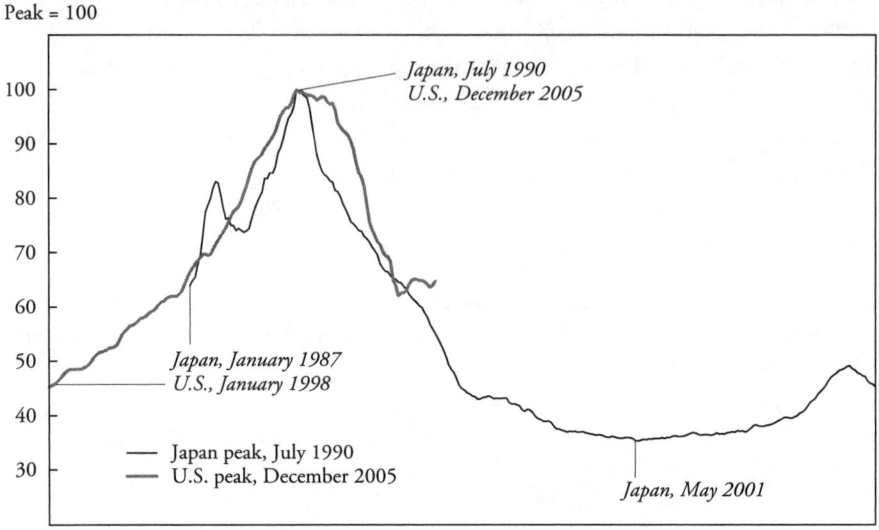

Source: S&P Case-Shiller indexes; residential rental price indexes; consumer price indexes.

the early 2000s and more than doubled from 2001 to 2006. Unfortunately, there were no corresponding (new contract) rent data, comparable to Japan's, with which to gauge excessive investor optimism by calculating price-to-rent ratios. However, since there was no report showing substantial rent increases relative to the consumer price index in these areas, it might be appropriate to assume that the real price change coincided with the change in the price-to-rent ratio. The real house-price change in ten large U.S. cities (whose residents constitute roughly 10 percent of the U.S. population) was comparable to that in Tokyo (where a similar percentage of the Japanese population lives) in the late 1980s, as shown in figure 7-8.

The course of central bank policy in the United States is well known, and I will not repeat it in detail here. I will just point out that, first, whatever macroprudential measures were implemented at that time were inadequate to curb excessive optimism and that second, monetary tightening was "measured" and long-term rates remained relatively low, stirring debates about this "conundrum."

Anomalies and Excessive Optimism: Implications for Macroprudential Policy

So what lessons should we draw from these two episodes? Each crisis seems different from every other, so I should avoid oversimplification. However, the following four points are likely to be universally relevant, and especially so from the perspective of emerging economies.

First, financial innovations often provide fertile ground for financial excesses or imbalances. This may not be surprising, since innovations sometimes make old knowledge obsolete: veterans become novices and pros become amateurs. The old prudential measures look out of date. We are told that "this time is different" and that we should embrace these new ways of thinking. Often, these new ways of thinking disguise excessive optimism, as exemplified by the two episodes discussed.

Financial innovations are not different from Schumpeterian product innovations. Financial innovators capture previously unnoticed, unexploited opportunities in the allocation of risks, as product innovators do in the allocation of resources. The first-mover advantage ensures sizable excess profits initially. However, market discipline follows, as competition intensifies, and the first-mover advantage dissipates accordingly, leaving better resource-risk allocation with normal profits. Thus the key is to enhance market discipline, not to suffocate innovations, to balance the benefits of innovations versus their risks.

Second, in the process of the buildup of imbalances, there are often signs of anomalies. In the past, these anomalies were often ignored as being isolated and having no macroeconomic significance or were explained as rational choices, such as investment for future returns. But if these anomalies are found to coexist with other signs of excessively optimistic investor forecasts, these are likely signs of the buildup of financial imbalances.

This point is especially relevant if the signs are found saliently in property markets. Property market anomalies are important in two respects. On the one hand, property investment is often irreversible, and its failure will exert lingering negative effects for a long time, as I explain in the next section. The cost of failure in rectifying market excesses is large. On the other hand, property markets usually move slowly, compared with more volatile stock markets, implying their low signal-to-noise ratio. This means to spot market anomalies is relatively easier in property markets than in stock markets, though only in relative terms. Thus the "return" from the macroprudential policy is sizable in property markets.

Third, timely information about excessive investor optimism is of utmost importance in this regard. Price-to-rent ratios in property markets are one indicator of investor sentiment. Whereas information about price-to-earnings ratios is easily available in stock markets, corresponding (properly quality-adjusted) price-to-rent ratios in property markets are not easily available. This poses a serious problem for macroprudential policy, especially for emerging economies, where property markets are becoming increasingly important.

To have timely information about proper price-to-rent ratios, or at least price indexes that are reliable and internationally comparable, is not only important for assessing the magnitude of financial imbalances that need rectifying but also vital to communicate with the public, both inside and outside of the country. In this respect, it is highly recommended that price indexes be constructed consistent with the Handbook on Residential Property Price Indices, and that these indexes be published regularly in a timely manner.[9] The Japanese price-to-rent ratios presented are calculated from large data sets using hedonic regression methods and are available monthly with approximately two weeks' lag.

Fourth, if investors are excessively optimistic, a modest increase in capital requirements and leverage restraints may not be sufficient to curb such unwarranted optimism. The case in point is the increase in banks' new stock issues in Japan in the late 1980s and the dramatic decline of their leverage ratio during the buildup of the financial imbalances. This point is also relevant in contemplating maximum loan-to-value ratio requirements as macroprudential policy. When the price doubles in a few years, it is relatively easy to comply with seemingly stringent maximum loan-to-value requirements, since the property's assessed value increases in tandem with market prices.

To curb excessive loans, it is important to have measures to restrain leverage. But at the same time we should better understand their limitations. They may be effective in some cases, especially for rather small buildups of financial imbalances, but perhaps not in other cases.

Excessive Optimism and Policy Expectations: Implications for Monetary Policy

Finally, let me turn to the role of monetary policy during the buildup of financial imbalances and consider the implications of the analysis so far.

There are two strands of thought on this issue. One strand emphasizes that monetary policy is a blunt instrument affecting activity across a wide variety of sectors, many of which may not be experiencing speculative activity. To dampen speculative bubbles may require substantial changes in interest rates, which may hurt unaffected sectors. So in principle, it is better to use macroprudential measures, rather than monetary policy, to counter financial imbalances.[10]

The other strand of thought points out that letting financial imbalances balloon and then collapse may be too costly to bear, depending on the magnitude of these imbalances. Moreover, although regulatory reforms and other macroprudential measures are now under consideration in addressing the issue of the buildup of financial imbalances, there remains substantial uncertainty about their

9. On September 29, 2009, G-20 finance ministers and central bank governors directed the Inter-Secretariat Working Group on Price Statistics to write a handbook on real estate price indexes. Under these auspices, a team of experts, designated at the Eurostat, completed the final draft of "The Handbook on Residential Property Price Indices (RPPIs)" in March 2011. The conceptual framework of the handbook is expected to be followed by all members of the G-20 as well as by other countries.

10. This view has been expressed notably by many Federal Reserve officials in the past.

effectiveness in the real world. It is therefore not wise to rule out categorically the use of monetary policy to address the issue of financial imbalances. Monetary policy could be used in tandem with macroprudential measures if, first, substantial imbalances are building up and, second, regulatory policies have proved to be insufficient.[11]

In retrospect, events in Japan in the late 1980s seem to support the second view. In particular, that episode satisfied the two requirements for the use of monetary policy in addition to macroprudential measures to counter the buildup of financial imbalances.

Let me summarize what the stylized account of late 1980s Japan shows from the perspective of monetary policy. Around 1986, investors' expectations of investment returns were substantially elevated, especially in property markets, though grossly erroneously in retrospect. And at the same time, market expectation was that monetary easing would continue and that the policy rate would remain low for a substantial period. This combination of elevated investment-to-return expectations and market expectation of continuously low policy rates accelerated property investment, both residential and commercial, though especially the latter.

Property investment is a long-term, irreversible investment. It is a lengthy process, from starting to find a lot to final dedication, and once built for a particular purpose, it is difficult to change usage. This is especially important in Japan, where urban redevelopment can take years. Thus not only the current policy rate but also the expectations of its future course have a significant effect on investment decisions. Consequently, the expectation of continuing monetary easing significantly encouraged property investments, and particularly those in commercial properties.

Because of the inherent irreversibility, the excessive optimism inflicted a huge scar on Japanese commercial property markets. The quality-adjusted commercial land price index of Tokyo's central business districts was 2.161 in 1999 (1975 index = 1), down from its height of 16.556 in 1990.[12] It is mind boggling to imagine how this 87 percent decline in commercial land prices in the heart of Tokyo, which is the center of the Japanese economy, affected business activity in general. The same is true for residential property markets, though to a lesser extent. Moreover, since investment in industrial sectors is often long term and irreversible, these sectors also suffered serious overcapacity and misallocation problems caused by the excessive optimism of the late 1980s and its subsequent collapse.

In retrospect, taking account of the devastating effects of excessive optimism and also the ineffectiveness of macroprudential measures (in particular, window guidance), few would disagree that monetary policy should have played a role in

11. This view is articulated in White (2006).
12. See Shimizu and Nishimura (2006, fig. 1).

attempting to rein in excessive optimism, provided that this had been detected at the time. This episode teaches two lessons about the role of monetary policy and its relation to macroprudential measures in the buildup toward financial imbalances.

First, when excessive optimism prevails in the market, macroprudential measures alone may prove to be insufficient, and we may need monetary policy on top of these measures to rein in such excessive optimism. When investors are overly optimistic, asset prices go up to make it easy for banks to comply with, for example, increased capital buffer requirements and more stringent loan-to-value ratio requirements. Moreover, when financial imbalances are sizable, they are likely to broadly affect many sectors of the economy, as exemplified by 1980s Japan, and this may justify the use of monetary policy.

Second, when excessive optimism prevails and investment-to-return expectations rise erroneously, the central bank should be careful to avoid nourishing expectations of prolonged low interest rates relative to their long-run, sustainable levels. These expectations are likely to fuel investment activities further, especially in property markets. This increases the magnitude of possible future winding down.[13]

In this respect, there is an important informational factor through which the central bank's action or inaction influences market expectations. When excessive optimism emerges, a lack of action by the central bank may convey the wrong signal to the public. The central bank is responsible for the price stability that ultimately ensures the stability of economic activity. If there is no correspondent increase in prospects for economic growth, a sharp increase in investment-to-return expectations may lead to strong pressure on prices, raising concerns over inflation. If the central bank does not show concern over inflation when investment-to-return expectations are raised, this may be interpreted as a sign that the central bank has also raised its expectations for growth potential and is thus "underwriting" market expectations.

In practice, the most difficult task in combating excessive investor optimism and the buildup of financial imbalances is to detect the excess early and in a transparent way. Unfortunately, at the time of writing, conventional macroeconomic models are of little help in detecting excesses, though progress has been made in incorporating some characteristics of financial imbalances and thus in explaining their propagation mechanism. Taking account of this state of our understanding, it seems to me that significant efforts in the following two areas are needed from the practitioner's viewpoint.

13. In the semiannual "Outlook Reports of the Bank of Japan," the Policy Board examines this possibility routinely in the second perspective of the two-perspective examination of economic conditions.

First, it may be desirable to develop and operationalize so-called early-warning indicators, to detect signs of a buildup in financial imbalances and to rein them in early before it is costly to do so. Attempts to develop early-warning indicators are sometimes criticized ad hoc because of their lack of microeconomic foundations, so to speak. However, what we face are "tail risk" phenomena or, more precisely, unknown unknowns, where past regularities apparently no longer hold true. In this respect, though atheoretical, the development and continuing improvement of early-warning indicators are valuable in discerning factors that might be important though somewhat overlooked in conventional thinking.

Second, it is important (though admittedly not easy) to have timely and persuasive market information related to the possible buildup of financial imbalances, particularly information about investor optimism. As has been shown before, the Japanese government (or more precisely, some of its divisions) was partly responsible for the excessive optimism of the late 1980s. This suggests that it is not an easy task at all to convince the market (and parts of the government) otherwise, plagued as they are by excessive optimism. Many central banks and international institutions are working to obtain first-hand, broad, asset market information that is reliable and timely. Here, market intelligence plays an important role in detecting signs of anomalies in these markets. In doing so, we should also duly recognize heterogeneity among regions. These are challenging tasks for emerging economies' central banks, especially with respect to property markets, which are traditionally not the main focus of central bank business, and anomalies originating in financial innovations, which often "mutate" and "disguise" themselves in subtle ways.

We usually regard financial crises as rare events, and most of the time our model of the economy evolves from some form of economic equilibrium in a linear, though stochastically stable, way. In reality, however, we too often find—very painfully—that these rare events are not in fact rare and that the economy moves rather drastically from stability to instability in a short period of time. The case of Japan in the late 1980s and the recent U.S. case highlight dramatically this pattern. To contemplate best practices in macroprudential and monetary policy, we should take proper account of our intellectual limitations in modeling the real economy, and at the same time we should be practical in coping with the many-faceted problems of financial crises.

References

Bank of Japan. 1989. "Shouwa 63 nendo no kinyuu oyobi keizai no doukou" [The financial markets and economy in 1988] [in Japanese], *Chosa Geppo* (May): 1–61.

Fukao, K., and others. 2005. "Japanese Banks' Monitoring Activities and the Performance of Borrower Firms: 1981–1996." *International Economics and Economic Policy* 2: 337–62.

Hattori, M., H. S. Shinm, and W. Takahashi. 2009. "A Financial System Perspective on Japan's Experience in the Late 1980s." Discussion Paper 2009-E-19. Tokyo: Institute for Monetary and Economic Studies.

Shimizu, C., and K. G. Nishimura. 2006. "Biases in Appraisal Land Price Information: The Case of Japan." *Journal of Property Investment and Finance* 24: 150–75.

Shimizu, C., T. Watanabe, and K. G. Nishimura. 2010a. "House Prices in Tokyo: A Comparison of Repeat Sales and Hedonic Measures." *Journal of Economics and Statistics* 6, no. 230: 792–813.

———. 2010b. "Residential Rents and Price Rigidity: Micro Structure and Macro Consequences." *Journal of Japanese and International Economies* 24: 282–99.

White, W. 2006. "Is Price Stability Enough?" Working Paper 205. Basel: Bank for International Settlements.

PART III

Financial Development

8

Financial Deepening and Financial Integration in Asia: What Have We Learned?

RAYMOND ATJE

The 1997 Asian financial crisis revealed the weaknesses of the region's financial sectors. It had devastating impacts on the banking sector in some countries, most notably Indonesia, Thailand, and Republic of Korea. At the center of the crisis were currencies mismatches and maturity mismatches throughout the region. A currency mismatch occurs when residents of a country have assets in the local currency but liabilities in a foreign currency. Such was the case in many economies in Asia at the onset of the crisis. Banks and corporations with liabilities in dollars were not adequately hedged against a possible change in the exchange rate. In addition, many of them also had large short-term liabilities relative to their assets. So when the region's local currencies experienced large depreciations against the dollar their assets were no longer sufficient to service their liabilities.

Introduction

It should be noted that, before the crisis, most economies in the region adopted fixed exchange rates. Such an exchange regime provided holders of dollar-denominated liabilities with an implicit guarantee against a sudden and large depreciation of local currencies vis-à-vis the dollar. Hence banks and corporations borrowed only in dollars, without adequately insuring themselves against exchange rate volatility. Moreover, they often borrowed short term to meet their

The author would like to extend thanks to Widdi Mugijayani for excellent research assistance.

long-term investment needs and, therefore, created a double mismatch: currency and maturity mismatches.

In contrast, the recent global financial turmoil has had relatively mild impacts on Asian financial sectors. It signifies a number of things. First, it suggests limited exposures of the region's financial institutions to subprime mortgage-related securities. This in turn reflects, in part, the relatively low level of financial deepening or financial development, especially among the region's emerging economies. In the case of Indonesia, for instance, none of the country's banks have a significant, if any, presence abroad. In addition, these banks do not undertake significant investment activities—for example, issuing and selling securities in capital markets. Second, it may also suggest an improved soundness of the region's financial institutions, especially in the aftermath of the Asian financial crisis.

The finance literature indicates that financial development—that is, increased provision of financial services with a wider choice of services available to all levels of society—seems to be linked to real development. Yet the exact nature of the link remains unclear. The question about the direction of causation and the exact way by which one variable influences the other are not altogether resolved. One would expect that causation runs both ways. Consider the effect of the real side on finance. It seems natural to assume that a rich financial structure is a general good: wealthier societies will tend to set up more sophisticated financial arrangements. Nowadays even banking has become highly technological. Sophisticated technology is being used in a wide range of banking activities, such as payments and assets transfer, calculation of the pricing of complex financial instruments, processing of data and their application to market transactions, and risk management.

But there may be another reason for the line of causation to run from the real to the finance side. Richer societies tend to use more complex technology, so that investment opportunities are more specialized, which in turn leads to greater information gaps between borrowers and lenders. Greater information gaps may dictate the need for more elaborate financial arrangements.[1] Another way to think of it is that an advanced economy with a set of specialized investment opportunities needs a well-informed financial sector that will channel funds to best users.

The reverse direction of causation from the financial to real side is better understood. A well-developed financial system raises the rate of return to savings in most states of the world and for that reason also induces people to save.[2] Moreover, in addition to allowing risk diversification on the part of savers, financial markets facilitate risk diversification for projects that will effect technological change.

1. This line of reasoning is captured in Obstfeld (1994). He argues that growth depends on the availability of an ever-increasing array of specialized but inherently risky production inputs and that this requires portfolio diversification.

2. However, because of income and substitution effects, the effect of a higher return to savings on saving rates is indeterminate.

Financial development tends to evolve only slowly. Hervé Hannoun identifies four stages of financial deepening.[3] The first stage is the emergence of banks that are good at dealing with asymmetric information. At this stage, banks play a leading role in mobilizing savings, allocating capital, and providing risk management instruments. The second stage involves stock market development based on an arm's-length relationship between companies and investors and, hence, requires companies to publicly disclose their business activities. The next stage involves the development of fixed income markets: bond markets and money markets in which large corporations manage their short-term cash needs. The last stage involves the development of derivatives markets and securitization.

The severity of the Asian financial crisis has prompted governments in the region to undertake the necessary steps to strengthen their financial sector, the banking sector in particular. In addition, they also decided to promote greater financial integration at the regional level. The aim is to reduce financial vulnerabilities as well as to provide conduits for recycling the region's excess savings. One such attempt is the creation of the Asian bond market with help from the Asian Development Bank.

In another development, the ASEAN+3—that is, the ten ASEAN member countries plus the People's Republic of China (henceforth referred to as China) (including Hong Kong, China), Japan, and Korea—has launched a multilateral currency swap, drawn from a foreign exchange reserves pool worth $120 billion. The swap was initiated in Chiang Mai, Thailand, hence the name Chiang Mai Initiative Multilateral (CMIM). Its main purpose is to allow member countries to manage their short-term liquidity problems.

A number of conclusions can be drawn from this experience. First, in a certain way, most financial systems in the region are still dominated by banks. In Japan, the region's most developed economy, the banking sector is still the largest in terms of asset sector, much larger than its equity and bond markets. Recently, there have been some notable improvements in the region's banking performance: lower nonperforming loans, a higher capital adequacy ratio, and notwithstanding the global financial crisis, a higher return on assets in almost all of the countries of the region. Meanwhile, there has been a change in the intermediary function of the banking sector, as well. The share of credit going to the corporate sector has fallen in some countries, such as Indonesia, Korea, and Malaysia, while lending to the household sector has increased significantly. In addition, the loan-to-deposit ratio is relatively low in many economies, suggesting that, for whatever reason, banks throughout the region seem to have turned more risk averse in recent years.

3. Hervé Hannoun, "Financial Deepening without Financial Excesses," speech, 43rd SEACEN Governors Conference, Jakarta, 2008.

Second, stock markets are increasingly becoming an important source of investment funds through both primary and secondary issues. In general there has been a move toward improving corporate governance in the region's stock markets. This includes protection of minority shareholders and improvement in transparency through disclosure. There are two basic models of regulatory systems: disclosure based and merit based. Hong Kong, China, Singapore, Malaysia—and to a lesser extent Korea, Indonesia, and Thailand—have adopted the disclosure-based system, whereby the issuers and intermediaries offering securities are required to provide sufficient, accurate, and timely information pertaining to the company's business, finances, prospects, and terms of the securities to allow investors to make informed decisions. Meanwhile, China and the Philippines are still following a merit-based system. Another important development is the demutualization of a number of stock markets in the region, including Hong Kong, China, Indonesia, Malaysia, the Philippines, and Singapore.

Finally, unlike bank and capital markets, the bond market is relatively new for many of these countries. Its development is prompted by the severity of the crisis. While the primary markets have grown significantly, the growth in some markets has been led by quasi-government issuers or issuers with some form of credit guarantee. Moreover, issuers in some markets, such as Malaysia, still concentrate at the high end of the credit quality spectrum. Secondary bond markets have developed even more slowly than primary markets. Some markets are relatively small and, hence, seem to lack investor diversity. Foreign investors, including global financial intermediaries, have avoided these markets, discouraged by, among other things, withholding taxes and the lack of deep markets for hedging instruments.

Economic Growth Nexus: A Brief Review

The idea of associating economic growth and financial development is not new. John Gurley and Edward Shaw argue that a highly organized and broad system of financial intermediation is typical of the developed economies but not of the developing ones.[4] The primary function of financial intermediaries is to facilitate the flow of funds from savers to investors. In this process intermediaries issue indirect debt to depositors and absorb direct debts from investors. By doing so, they enhance the efficiency of trade through space and time (intertemporal).

The benefits of well-developed financial markets are familiar. For instance, the financial market is the most important means of channeling funds to their highest return uses. Well-developed financial markets ensure investors against idiosyncratic risk, and since more productive investments tend to be riskier, they also induce investors to shift their portfolios toward higher return investment. Fur-

4. Gurley and Shaw (1955).

ther, they generate more information about investment projects and are therefore able to channel investors' funds to more productive use. In other words, they disseminate information about profitable and productive investment opportunities and, hence, enhance the efficiency with which capital is allocated. These effects raise the rate of return to economywide investment.[5]

Well-developed financial markets also provide liquidity and allow risk sharing through the diversification of portfolios of assets and liabilities. They allow individuals and households to smooth their consumption through borrowing and lending and to undertake profitable investments that would otherwise not be possible. Finally, well-developed financial markets allow for greater specialization; specialization requires more transactions, which are costly, but well-developed financial markets tend to lower such transaction costs. This increases the production technologies available for adoption.[6]

In an influential paper, Robert King and Ross Levine study financial development in eighty countries over the period 1960–89.[7] To measure overall financial development they use the liquid liabilities of the financial system: currency plus demand and interest-bearing liabilities of banks and nonbank financial institutions divided by GDP. They employ other financial development indicators to measure the degree to which banks provide credits as well as private sector domestic liabilities. They find a positive correlation between GDP growth during the period under consideration and all of these financial development indicators. In particular, they find that, as a financial market moves from an underdeveloped level to a more developed one, it raises the rate of economic growth by almost a percentage point. This is a large number.

Ross Levine and Sara Zervos study the relationship between stock market development and economic growth, capital accumulation, and productivity growth in forty-two countries over the period 1976–93.[8] They construct numerous measures of stock market development. The study finds positive correlations between, on the one hand, real per capita GDP growth, real per capita capital growth, and productivity growth and, on the other, stock market turnover. However, the study fails to find a robust correlation between the size of the stock market and growth. One may conclude from this study that, with regard to capital market development, what matters to economic growth is not the size of the market or market capitalization but its liquidity.[9]

5. See for instance Goldsmith (1969); Greenwood and Jovanovic (1990).

6. Greenwood and Smith (1997).

7. King and Levine (1993).

8. Levine and Zervos (1998).

9. It is likely however that market activity and market size are mutually reinforcing. Active capital markets will attract more companies and investors than less active ones. Hence, properly measured, market activity and market size are likely to be correlated. Recent literature on internationalization of financial activities (Levine and Schumukler, 2005) seems to support this assertion.

Meanwhile, Geert Bekaert and his colleagues examine the impact of capital market liberalization on economic growth.[10] The idea is that equity market liberalizations give foreign investors an opportunity to invest in domestic equity securities and domestic investors the right to transact in foreign equity securities. To measure equity market liberalization they use the official equity market liberalization indicator. The variable takes the value of one when it is possible for foreign portfolio investors to own equity in a particular market and zero otherwise. The authors find that, after controlling for a host of variables, capital market liberalizations lead to, on average, a 1 percent increase in annual real economic growth. Once again, this is a large number. Peter Henry argues that, from a neoclassical perspective, such a large growth effect is difficult to fathom unless equity market liberalization also induces growth in total factor productivity.[11] Bekaert and colleagues also find that the positive effect on growth is largest when the quality of institutions and the level of financial development are high.

Raghuram Rajan and Luigi Zingales approach the finance and growth issue from a different vantage point.[12] They want to test the validity of the idea that the costs of external finance drop with financial development. To do this they examine whether industrial sectors that are more dependent on external finance develop disproportionately faster in countries with more developed financial markets. Their study confirms this assertion for a large number of countries during the 1980s. In other words, according to the study, by providing external financing to sectors that need it the most, financial development, in essence, promotes economic growth.[13]

One of the most binding constraints faced by firms is financial constraint. In a firm-level study, Inessa Love wants to know whether financial development helps alleviate financing constraints faced by firms.[14] In particular, she wants to find out whether financial development eases financial constraint that firms otherwise face. For this purpose she estimates the Euler equation for investment using firm-level data from forty countries and finds a strong negative relationship between the extent of financial market development and the sensitivity of investment to availability of internal funds. In other words, the more developed a financial market the less dependent firms in that particular market are on internal financing. She also finds that small firms are disproportionately more disadvantaged in less-developed financial markets than are large firms. In addition, she finds that an improvement

10. Bekaert, Harvey, and Lundblad (2005).

11. Henry (2007).

12. Rajan and Zingales (1998).

13. It should be noted, however, that some of the industries that, according to the authors, are in need of substantial external financing, such as pharmaceuticals and electronics, also require a high degree of research and development as well as highly skilled workers, which only industrialized countries can provide in a sustainable manner.

14. Love (2001).

in the efficiency of the legal system means less risk of appropriation and corruption; a better accounting system also helps alleviate financial constraint.

Meanwhile, an early study by Asli Demirgüç-Kunt and Vajislav Maksimovic also is done at the firm level.[15] The study focuses primarily on the use of external debt or external equity by firms to expand their activities. In particular, the authors ask whether the underdevelopment of legal and financial systems in some countries prevents their firms from undertaking potentially profitable investment opportunities. A well-developed financial market has two important roles—as a source of capital for firms and as a source of information regarding firms' activities for potential investors. In effect, the presence of a well-developed and active capital market in a country will make it easier for firms in that country to raise long-term capital. The study shows that both an active stock market and a well-developed legal system are important in facilitating a firm's growth. It also supports Levine and Zervos's claim that, for firms, the size of the capital market is not as important as the firm's activities in mobilizing capital.

Finally, some recent studies focus on issues concerning capital account liberalization, financial development, and economic growth. One such study by Aghion and others investigates the interaction between exchange rate volatility and productivity growth, and the role of financial development.[16] The authors argue that it is important to look at the interaction between exchange rate volatility and both financial development and macroeconomic shocks. They find that real exchange rate volatility could conceivably be costly to long-term productivity growth. In particular, they find that for countries with relatively low levels of financial development, exchange rate volatility reduces growth but that there is no significant effect for financially developed countries.

Financial Development in East Asia

East Asian financial markets have experienced major changes since the 1997 financial crisis. In particular, countries in the region have turned their attention to developing their bond markets. Meanwhile, their capital markets have made a remarkable recovery from their virtual collapse during the crisis. But the banking sector continues to dominate the region's financial intermediation activities (table 8-1).

Banking Sectors

To prevent another financial crisis, countries in the region have undertaken some measures to improve the soundness of their banking industries. As a result, there has been notable improvement in prudential as well as performance indicators of

15. Demirgüç-Kunt and Maksimovic (1999).
16. Aghion and others (2006).

Table 8-1. *Indicators of Financial Intermediation Development, Selected Countries, 2000, 2007, and 2008*
Percent of GDP

	Domestic credit provided by banking sector			*Market capitalization of listed companies*			*Bond market capitalization*		
Country	*2000*	*2007*	*2008*	*2000*	*2007*	*2008*	*2000*	*2007*	*2008*
China	120	132	126	48	184	65	15	44	49
Hong Kong, China	136	125	125	369	561	218	26	25	23
Indonesia	61	41	37	16	49	19	31	19	20
Japan	309	294	293	68	102	66	126	199	204
Korea, Republic of	89	102	113	32	107	53	73	107	112
Malaysia	179	113	115	125	174	84	78	90	93
Philippines	67	46	N.A.	34	72	31	29	35	32
Singapore	89	78	84	165	212	99	42	55	54
Thailand	138	132	131	24	79	38	26	51	57
United States	201	241	224	155	145	83	145	172	177

Source: Bank for International Settlements (siteresources.worldbank.org/INTRES/Resources/FinStructure_2008_v4.xls).

N.A. = Not available.

the region's banking systems. Between 2000 and 2008 the ratio of nonperforming loans to total loans in the banking system has declined significantly. Meanwhile, the global financial crisis notwithstanding, return on assets also noticeably increased in almost all of the counties in the region (table 8-2).

The emerging Asian economies have also built up their banks' capital buffers. This is evident from the substantial increase in the risk-adjusted capital adequacy ratios of the region's banks since 2000. By 2008 the ratios were well above the minimum Basel II standard of 8 percent (figure 8-1). In most Asian countries, commercial banks have either increased or maintained their capital adequacy ratios. It should nevertheless be noted that a change in a bank's capital adequacy ratio does not solely depend on additional capital but also on its choice of risk level of its assets. In practice, regulatory pressure does not always induce banks to increase their capital but rather to adjust their risk levels instead.

In addition to capital buffers, Asian banks have also built up their liquidity buffers, as indicated by the relatively low loan-to-deposit ratios. The ratio ranges between 50 percent and 100 percent, except for Korea and Thailand (figure 8-2). As a comparison, in the United States and the United Kingdom, the loan-to-deposit ratio exceeds 110 percent. One way to interpret this is that Asian banks have been overcautious; they prefer to maintain stable funding and remain largely free of liquidity risk.

Table 8-2. *Structural Indicators, Selected Countries, 2000, 2007, and 2008*[a]
Percent

	Nonperforming loans			*Capital assets ratio*			*Return on assets*		
Country	*2000*	*2007*	*2008*	*2000*	*2007*	*2008*	*2000*	*2007*	*2008*
China	22.4	6.2	2.4	13.5	8.4	12.0	0.2	0.9	1.0
Hong Kong, China	7.3	0.8	1.2	17.8	13.4	14.8	0.8	1.9	1.8
Indonesia	21.8	4.1	3.2	21.6	19.3	16.8	0.3	2.8	2.3
Japan	6.1	1.4	1.6	12.2	12.3	12.4	0.3	0.3	–0.2
Republic of Korea	8.9	0.7	1.1	10.5	12.3	12.3	–0.6	1.1	0.5
Malaysia	15.4	6.5	4.8	12.5	13.2	12.7	1.1	1.5	1.5
Philippines	24.0	5.8	4.5	16.2	15.7	15.5	0.4	1.3	0.8
Singapore	3.4	1.5	1.7	19.6	13.5	14.7	1.3	1.3	1.1
Thailand	17.7	7.9	5.7	11.9	14.8	13.8	–0.2	0.1	1.0
United States	1.1	1.4	2.9	11.7	12.8	12.8	1.2	0.8	0.0

Source: International Monetary Fund (2008).

a. Nonperforming loans as percent of total loans, capital assets ratio as a percent of risk-weighted assets.

Figure 8-1. *Risk-Weighted Capital Adequacy Ratios, Selected Asian Countries, 2000, 2007, 2008*

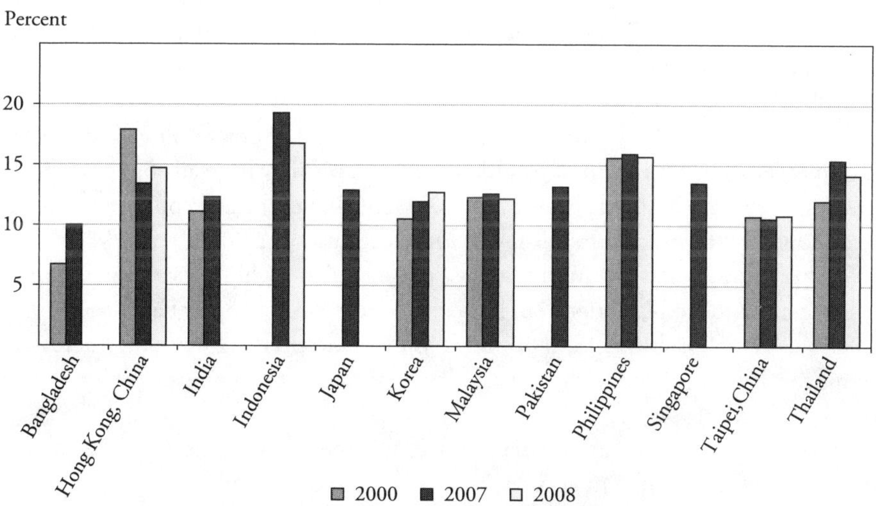

Source: Asia Regional Integration Center (http://aric.adb.org/aric_database.php).

Figure 8-2. *Bank Loan-to-Deposit Ratio, Selected Asian Countries*

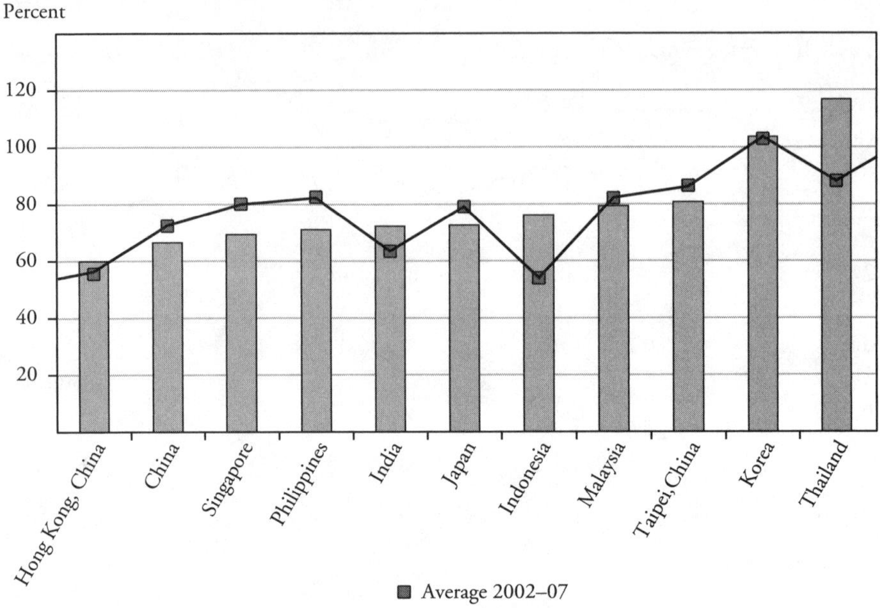

Source: International Monetary Fund (2010) (www.imf.org/external/pubs/ft/reo /2010/apd/eng/areo 1010.htm).

As noted earlier, after the crisis, the financial health of the region's banking systems improved. Sizable prudential cushions have been built, as new capital has been injected into the system. However, bank lending to private business remains subdued, and credit ratings remain relatively weak. Charles Adams identifies the following key changes in the region's banking sectors after the 1997–98 financial crisis.[17]

First, concentration in the banking systems increased as a result of restructuring (merger and acquisition of troubled banks). This may have advantages as well as disadvantages. On the one hand, to the extent that there are economies of scale and scope, concentration might lower unit costs and improve efficiency. But on the other hand, based on international experiences, a highly concentrated banking system tends to be riskier than less concentrated ones. Larger banks are prone to moral hazard problems. Second, both foreign and private ownership increased significantly because of the change of rules concerning foreign participation in the domestic banking sector.

According to Sasidaran Gopalan and Ramkishen Rajan, the Asian countries have followed two different approaches with regard to foreign participation in the banking sector.[18] On the one hand, there are countries like Indonesia, Korea,

17. Adams (2008).
18. Gopalan and Rajan (2009).

Thailand, and the Philippines that have aggressively opened up their financial sector, their banking sector in particular, to foreign investors. As a result, foreign bank penetration in these countries has increased dramatically, especially in Indonesia and Korea but somewhat less in Thailand and the Philippines. On the other hand, China, India, and to a lesser extent, Malaysia have been more cautious in liberalizing their financial sectors. In China, for instance, the share of foreign banks in total banking assets was only around 2.3 percent in 2007. Meanwhile, in Malaysia, which has maintained restrictions on foreign participation in the banking sector, the share of foreign banks' assets increased only slightly, from 21.6 percent in 1997 to 23 percent in 2008.

Change is also evident in market structure, although there are significant differences across the region. Banking systems in Hong Kong, China, China, Singapore, and Korea are relatively more competitive than those in Thailand, Indonesia, and the Philippines. Another change is the movement into investment banking, particularly for banks in more advanced economies. In the past, banks' activities have been concentrated on their core business of providing liquid loans to business and households, financed by liquid deposit liabilities. Nowadays, banks' activities include securities underwriting and trading, securitization, derivatives, and insurance. There has also been a shift toward household and real estate lending; in fact, the bulk of household lending has been mortgage related. Several factors may have influenced this shift, such as financial sector deregulation, government efforts to encourage domestic demand, and weak business credit demand. In addition, unsecured lending, including credit card finance, has also picked up in Asian countries.

Another noticeable change in the region's banking practices concerns banks' intermediary role. The banking system used to mainly collect depositors' funds and pass them as credits to corporations or use them to purchase government bonds. In 2005, though, the share of credit going to the corporate sector in Indonesia, Korea, and Malaysia fell from over 60 percent in 2000 to below 50 percent. Meanwhile, lending to the household sector increased, currently hovering between 25 and 50 percent of total bank credits.[19]

Furthermore, credit to the business sector has been weak or contracted, with its share in domestic assets falling since the 1997–98 financial crisis.[20] In contrast, the share of the household sector increased sharply in several countries. While banks have been expanding their retail business through increased mortgage and credit card lending, households have been more willing to finance their consumption and residential investment through bank credit. There is both a demand-side and a supply-side explanation of this phenomenon. Demand-side factors include, one, weak corporate demand for credit, which led banks to seek alternative

19. Mohanty and Turner (2010).
20. Mohanty, Schnabel, and Garcia-Luna (2006).

investment opportunities, particularly as they were awash with liquidity in an easy monetary environment; and two, increased risk aversion and the associated tendency among banks to hold liquid assets. Supply-side factors include, one, increased securities issuance through, for example, large government borrowing in countries where fiscal deficits remain high; and two, issuance of more government debt to develop the domestic bond market (for instance, in Singapore) or to facilitate central banks' sterilized intervention (for instance, in India). Yet another factor (for instance, in Indonesia and Turkey) is the recent effort to recapitalize banks or to restructure their bad debts by issuing government securities.

When the global financial crisis of 2008, because of the subprime mortgages problem, occurred in the United States, the impact on Asian banks was substantially less than that of the 1997–98 financial crisis. The reasons are as follows:[21]

—Asian banks rely on traditional banking services, with revenues from fixed income, currency, and commodities business accounts forming a significantly smaller portion of their income than for Western banks.

—Asian banks are less involved in structured credit and related derivative products, because they are still at an early stage in the securitization process.

—Regulators in more developed countries such as Japan, Singapore, and Hong Kong, China have had a more proactive role in ensuring that smaller local banks have sufficient risk management capacity before they start investing in complex structured products.

—Bank lending has been profitable in many Asian economies.

Moreover, in response to the global financial crisis in 2008, East Asian governments have taken action to provide expanded coverage of deposits. For instance, Taipei,China, Hong Kong, China, Singapore, and Malaysia provided an unlimited guarantee of all deposits on a temporary basis. Meanwhile, the Indonesian government took a more cautious approach and only increased the deposit guarantee from IDR 100 million to IDR 2 billion per individual. Cindy Marks and Walter Yao argue that this policy has advantages in the short term because it could strengthen confidence in local and regional banking markets.[22] Yet in the long term it could lead to additional costs for banks, depending on how governments intend to pay for such programs. Blanket guarantees, combined with other recent government actions, could also create moral hazard issues within the banking industry. Nonetheless, most of the recent changes made to deposit coverage terms are temporary, and policymakers have given themselves room to reverse expanded coverage in the future.

In recent years, Indonesia and Malaysia, two countries with large Muslim populations, have introduced the Islamic, or sharia, banking system. Sharia banking targets primarily, but not exclusively, Muslim communities in countries that want

21. International Monetary Fund (2008).
22. Marks and Yao (2009).

to adhere to the Islamic teaching that prohibits usury. In terms of assets, a sharia bank is relatively small. In Malaysia the average share of a sharia bank's assets in total banking assets between 2007 and 2010 was 15 percent, while in Indonesia it was less than 4 percent (figure 8-3). There are at least two reasons that may explain the relatively modest growth of the sharia bank in the two countries. First, the sharia bank has not proved itself as a serious alternative to conventional banks. Second, most people do not understand how a sharia bank operates. In particular they do not know what to expect if they put their money in a sharia bank.

As Ishrat Husain notes, education and public awareness is important to develop the Islamic financial system.[23] Besides, Islamic banking still faces several challenges, such as ineffective enforcement of contracts, an inefficient system for early recovery, ineffective code of conduct for professionals, lack of development of sharia-compliant government securities, weak research and development in the field of Islamic finance and economies, and weak human resource development and training for bank staffs.

Capital Markets

With regard to capital markets, emerging East Asian stock markets have become an important source of investment funds through both primary and secondary issues. In 2006, for instance, the total amount of funds raised in the region's stock markets reached $105.9 billion, of which primary issues were $65.9 billion and secondary issues were $40 billion. In 2007 the total amount jumped by around 90 percent, to $201 billion, comprising $112 billion of initial public offerings and $88 billion of secondary public offering (table 8-3). In terms of market capitalization, the region's two largest markets, namely, Shanghai and Hong Kong, China stock markets, accounted for around 60 percent of East Asian emerging markets capitalization.

Of the region's emerging markets, capital markets in China, Korea, Singapore, and Taipei,China were among the most active in 2008, as shown by a relatively higher turnover ratio in those markets than in other markets in the region (table 8-4). Turnover ratio is a measure of market liquidity. The Philippines stock market was one of the least active in the region during the past decade.

Ismail Dalla notes that there has been a general move toward improving corporate governance in East Asian stock markets, including protection of minority shareholders and improvement in transparency through disclosure.[24] There are two basic models of regulatory systems: disclosure based and merit based. Hong Kong, China, Singapore, Malaysia, and to a lesser extent, Korea, Indonesia, and Thailand have adopted the disclosure-based system, whereby issuers and inter-

23. Ishrat Husain, "Evolution of Islamic Banking," speech, Meezan Bank seminar on the evolution of Islamic banking, Karachi, September 2, 2010 (www.nzibo.com/IB2/Evolution.pdf).
24. Dalla (2005).

Figure 8-3. *Islamic and Commercial Bank Assets, Malaysia and Indonesia*[a]

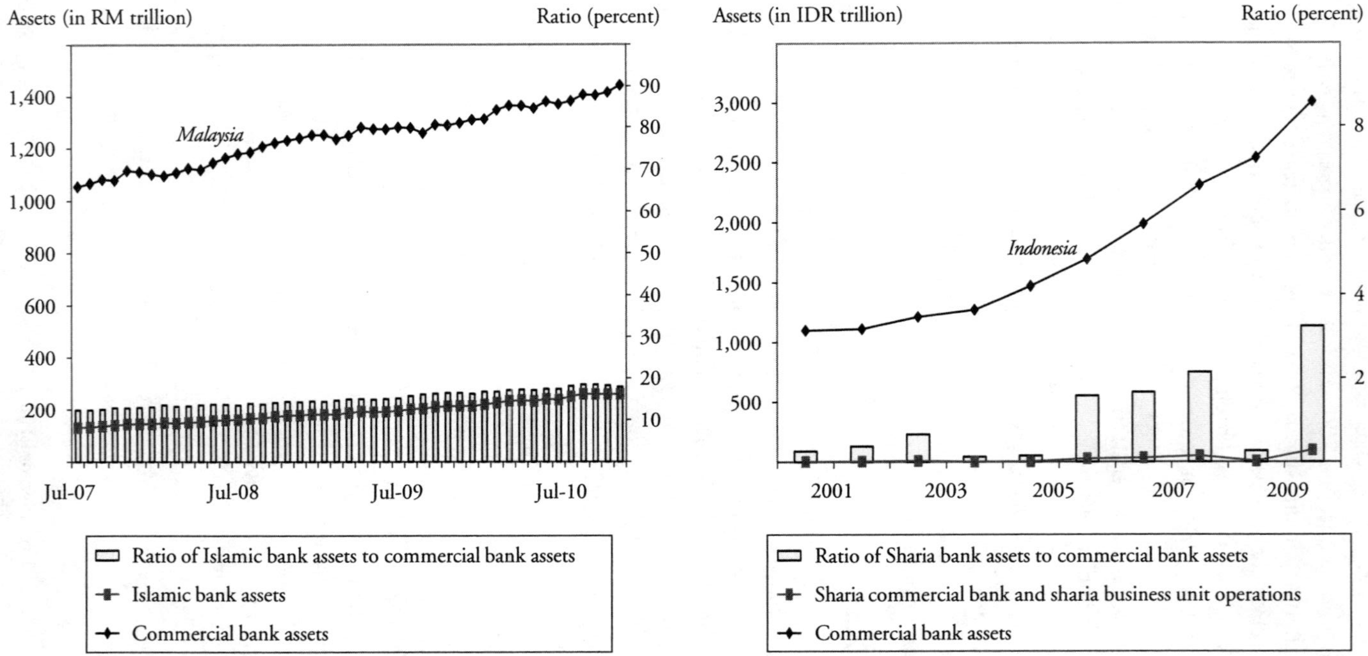

Source: Bank Negara Malaysia; Bank Indonesia.

a. Islamic bank assets comprise Islamic bank, Islamic banking system of commercial banks, and Islamic banking system of investment or merchant banks.

Table 8-3. *Market Capitalization and New Capital, Selected Stock Exchanges, 2006 and 2007*

U.S.$ billion except as indicated

	2006					*2007*				
Stock exchanges	*Initial public offerings*	*Secondary public offerings*	*Total IPO and SPO*	*Market capitalization*	*IPO and SPO per market capitalization (percent)*	*Initial public offerings*	*Secondary public offerings*	*Total IPO and SPO*	*Market capitalization*	*IPO and SPO per market capitalization (percent)*
Shanghai S.E.	11,817.7	4,734.6	16,552.3	917,507.5	1.8	57,770.0	29,395.5	87,165.5	3,694,348.0	2.4
Hong Kong exchanges	42,972.4	24,465.0	67,437.4	1,714,953.3	3.9	37,485.9	36,541.4	74,027.3	2,654,416.1	2.8
Shenzhen S.E.	2,029.1	3,937.9	5,967.0	22,7947.3	2.6	5,670.7	7,405.6	13,076.3	784,518.6	1.7
Korea Exchange	2,853.3	2,473.3	5,326.6	834,404.3	0.6	3,170.0	3,806.9	6,976.9	1,122,606.3	0.6
Taiwan S.E. Corp.[a]	751.5	1,361.0	2,112.5	594,659.4	0.4	566.1	1,550.2	2,116.3	663,716.0	0.3
Singapore Exchange	4,800.2	924.1	5,724.3	384,286.4	1.5	5,159.8	4,588.3	9,748.1	539,176.6	1.8
Bursa Malaysia	322.9	645.3	968.2	235,580.9	0.4	317.4	2,157.5	2,474.9	325,290.3	0.8
Indonesia S.E.	364.9	1,464.7	1,829.6	138,886.4	1.3	1,976.3	3,446.5	5,422.8	211,693.0	2.6
Thailand S.E.	474.4	3,498.1	3,972.5	140,161.3	2.8	332.6	606.1	938.7	197,129.4	0.5
National Stock Exchange India	4,534.9	9,610.1	14,145.0	774,115.6	1.8	7,874.1	2,5470.1	33,344.2	1,660,096.9	2.0
Bombay S.E.	5,600.5	1,320.2	6,920.7	818,878.6	0.8	9,642.8	2,074.0	11,716.8	1,819,100.5	0.6
NYSE Group	37,130.1	66,040.1	103,170.2	15,421,167.9	0.7	60,385.8	76,598.4	136,984.2	15,650,832.5	0.9

Source: World Federation of Exchange (various years).

a. A stock exchange in the ADB member referred to as "Taipei,China."

Table 8-4. *Stock Market Turnover, Selected Countries, Various Years 1995–2009*[a]
Ratio

Country	*1995*	*1998*	*2002*	*2005*	*2008*	*2009*
China	1.18	1.23	0.72	0.75	N.A.	N.A.
Hong Kong, China	0.35	0.60	0.45	0.42	N.A.	N.A.
Indonesia	0.22	0.48	0.43	0.51	0.82	1.31
Japan	0.34	0.38	0.74	1.06	1.60	1.77
Korea	1.02	1.20	3.17	1.68	1.94	2.18
Malaysia	0.34	0.30	0.22	0.28	0.78	1.40
Philippines	0.25	0.29	0.08	0.17	0.51	N.A.
Singapore	0.41	0.54	0.55	0.38	1.85	3.26
Taipei,China	2.05	3.42	2.42	1.39	2.22	2.86
Thailand	0.40	0.62	1.03	0.72	0.42	0.33
United States	0.74	0.98	2.29	1.27	2.72	3.51

Source: Financial structure data (siteresources.worldbank.org/INTRES/Resources/FinStructure_2008_v4.xls).

a. Stock market turnover is ratio of value of total shares traded to average real market capitalization; the denominator is deflated using the following method: Tt/P_at/{(0.5)*[Mt/P_et + Mt-1/P_et-1] where T is total value traded, M is stock market capitalization, P_e is end-of-period CPI, P_a is average annual CPI.

N.A. = Not available.

mediaries offering securities are required to provide sufficient, accurate, and timely information regarding the company's business, finances, prospects, and terms of the securities, to allow investors to make informed decisions. Meanwhile, China and the Philippines are still following the merit-based system. Another important development is the demutualization of a number of stock markets in the region, including Hong Kong, China, Indonesia, Malaysia, the Philippines, and Singapore.

Some studies concerning stock market development focus on a phenomenon known as internationalization. In recent years an increasing number of firms in emerging markets, most notably in Latin America, have turned to international markets, such as New York and London, to raise capital. It seems that most of the firms in question had hitherto been listed in their respective domestic markets. When they turned to international markets they either cross-listed their firms on domestic and international markets or delisted their firms at home. This phenomenon has raised concern because it has an adverse effect on domestic markets. In particular, there has been a reduction in the domestic trading of firms that cross-list, as trading migrates from domestic to international markets. Further, as a corollary, there has been a reduction in the liquidity of the domestic market and, hence, less liquidity for the remaining firms in the domestic market.[25]

25. Levine and Schumukler (2005).

Interestingly, most of the migrating firms are from more developed emerging markets, with sound macroeconomic policy, more efficient legal systems, better protection of shareholders (including minority shareholders), and greater openness. Firms in such markets are able to attract foreign investors and will turn to international markets if they are certain they will be able to attract these investors.[26] This has led Stijn Claessens and colleagues to tentatively conclude that large-scale internationalization may make it difficult to sustain fully fledged local stock markets and, as a consequence, may adversely affect medium-sized firms. Medium-sized firms are less likely to go directly overseas but, at the same time, may find it difficult to float their shares in shrinking local markets.

It seems from the foregoing discussion that firms use domestic markets as "showrooms" to attract foreign investors' attention. Without home markets it would be difficult for them to gauge their ability to attract foreign investors. It will be interesting to see how many firms from emerging markets bypass local markets altogether and go directly to international markets to raise capital.

Data suggest that East Asian economies have a relatively low rate of firm migration compared to Latin American economies. In 2000 the ratio of value traded abroad to value traded domestically was 122.4 percent for Latin American economies and only 4.0 percent for East Asian economies. Meanwhile, during the same year, according to Augusto de la Torre and colleagues, the ratio of capital raised abroad to capital raised domestically was 91.9 percent for Latin American economies compared to 17.1 percent for East Asian economies.[27] The authors do not, however, explain what differentiates Latin America from East Asia or what led to the far greater rate of internationalization of the former than of the latter.

This issue is important for policymakers in East Asia who have to formulate proper responses to the internationalization phenomenon. The question of whether national financial institutions and markets still matter once domestic agents have access to foreign markets has become very important from a policy perspective.

To answer the above question, Luigi Guiso and colleagues investigate the effect of differences in local financial development within an integrated financial market.[28] They try to answer the question as to whether domestic financial markets become irrelevant in the increasingly integrated financial markets throughout the world. Their finding shows that, even in a fully integrated country like Italy, local financial development still matters. Local financial development, they find, not only enhances the probability that an individual will start his own business but also favors entry, increases competition, and promotes growth of firms. In short, local financial development matters, especially for small firms, even in the absence

26. Claessens, Klingebiel, and Schumukler (2006).
27. De la Torre, Gozzi, and Schumukler (2007).
28. Guiso, Sapienza, and Zingales (2002).

of restriction on capital movements. It is perhaps one reason that Western European countries, which are highly integrated with the global economy and whose capital markets have declined in importance relative to where they were a century ago, still retain their capital markets.

Bond Markets

Unlike bank and capital markets, the bond market is relatively new for many countries in East Asia. In the aftermath of the East Asian financial crisis, policymakers in the region widely recognized the importance of the bond market in avoiding currency and maturity mismatches in the financial system as well as in providing a reliable source of long-term finance to the corporate sector. In addition, the growth of a country's bond market improves the resilience of its financial system. The bond market's intermediary role becomes critical when banks and capital markets falter or fail. In other words, with multilayer financial intermediation in place, financial intermediation activities can continue, even if the primary intermediation is in distress.

From this perspective, banks, which are East Asia's primary intermediation institutions, capital markets, and bond markets are considered complementary. Moreover, the availability of alternative channels of financial intermediation will enhance the efficiency of the financial system as whole and, therefore, will promote economic growth and development. Following the crisis, members of the EMEAP (Executives' Meeting of East Asia Pacific Central Banks) launched the Asian Bond Fund (ABF), which aimed at broadening and deepening domestic and regional bond markets.[29] In June 2003 the EMEAP launched the first stage of ABF (ABF1), which invests in a basket of dollar-denominated bonds issued by Asian sovereign issuers in EMEAP economies (except Australia, Japan, and New Zealand). In 2005 EMEAP introduced nine funds: the Pan Asian Bond Index Fund (PAIF) and eight single-market funds, one for each of the following markets: China, Hong Kong, China, Indonesia, Korea, Malaysia, Philippines, Singapore, and Thailand. Whereas PAIF invests in sovereign and quasi-sovereign local currency–denominated bonds issued in all of the eight markets, each of the eight single-market funds invests in sovereign and quasi-sovereign local currency–denominated bonds issued in the local market.[30]

With regard to corporate bonds, primary markets in East Asia have grown significantly. Nevertheless, Jacob Gyntelberg and colleagues note that growth in some markets has been led by quasi-government issuers or issuers with some form

29. EMEAP members are Reserve Bank of Australia, People's Bank of China, Hong Kong Monetary Authority, Bank Indonesia, Bank of Japan, Bank of Korea, Bank Negara Malaysia, Reserve Bank of New Zealand, Banko Sentral ng Pilipinas, Monetary Authority of Singapore, and Bank of Thailand.

30. Leung (2006).

of credit guarantee.[31] One possible explanation is that investors have had little access to information that would enable them to evaluate the credit risks of the issuers. Moreover, issuers in some markets still concentrate at the high end of the credit-quality spectrum. In Malaysia issuers with the equivalent of triple-A ratings account for around 40 percent of the market and issuers with the equivalent of double-A ratings account for another 40 percent. In Korea issuers with the equivalent of triple-A ratings control around 60 percent of the market. Gyntelberg and colleagues argue that it is likely that institutional investors in these markets have internal guidelines to invest only in high-quality securities.

Table 8-5 depicts market activities in selected Asian bond markets. Most of the region's emerging markets experienced a substantial increase in activities between 2005 and 2007. However, in 2008 some of the markets experienced a decline in activities, presumably because of the global financial turbulence. In terms of issuers, the public sector still dominates in the region's emerging markets. Meanwhile, a small number markets, most notably Hong Kong, China's, have also been trading foreign bonds. This is consistent with Jonathan Batten and colleagues' observation that foreign borrowers, which have overwhelmingly high-quality credit and comprise sovereigns, supranational, and major financial institutions, enter a market at a later stage of bond market development.[32] Meanwhile, the long-term viability of foreign bond markets appears to be linked to highly liquid foreign exchange and derivatives markets, benchmark issues, and competitive pricing among markets.

Secondary bond markets have developed even more slowly than primary markets. A number of factors have been identified as possible reasons for the illiquidity of secondary markets. One is that some East Asian markets seem to lack investor diversity. In particular, foreign investors, including global financial intermediaries, seem to have avoided those markets. According to Gyntelberg and colleagues, they have been discouraged by, among other things, withholding taxes and the lack of deep markets for hedging instruments. The introduction of ABF2 has helped to address these issues. Meanwhile, John Burger and Francis Warnock argue that bond markets in developing countries tend to be more volatile and exhibit significantly more negative skewness than developed country bond markets, whether returns are hedged or not.[33] These are factors that, according to them, U.S. investors shun. They also argue that improving macroeconomic stability can help mitigate these problems.

In one study, Barry Eichengreen and Pipat Luengnaruemitchai focus on impediments to bond market development in Asia.[34] In particular, they attempt

31. Gyntelberg, Ma, and Remolona (2006).
32. Batten, Hogan, and Szilagyi (2009).
33. Burger and Warnock (2007).
34. Eichengreen and Luengnaruemitchai (2004).

Table 8-5. *Value of Bonds, Asian Exchanges, 2005, 2007, 2008*
U.S.$ million

	2005				
Stock exchange	*Total*	*Domestic private sector*	*Domestic public sector*	*Foreign*	*Total*
Bombay S.E.	18,297.6	2,515.6	15,781.9	0.0	33,273.5
Bursa Malaysia	1,391.5	1,391.5	0.0	0.0	3,270.5
Hong Kong exchanges	55,464.2	9,639.4	23,117.8	22,707.0	54,866.2
Indonesia S.E.	N.A.	N.A.	N.A.	N.A.	59,282.6
Korea Exchange	714,294.7	106,149.7	607,892.7	252.3	887,652.3
National Stock Exchange of India	344,223.0	10,917.0	333,207.4	98.6	504,021.8
Osaka Securities Exchange	4,807,649.7	12,177.2	4,795,472.5	0.0	5,118,717.1
Shanghai S.E.	181,588.8	16,940.5	164,648.3	0.0	274,799.1
Shenzhen S.E.	2,734.5	2,290.8	443.7	0.0	3,384.7
Singapore Exchange	245,460.5	N.A.	N.A.	N.A.	380,377.0
Taiwan S.E. Corp.[a]	95,720.0	6.5	95,652.7	60.9	108,844.8
Thailand S.E.	18,791.8	6,870.4	11,921.4	0.0	113,219.8
Tokyo S.E. Group	4,730,812.1	15,693.2	4,715,118.8	0.0	N.A.

Source: World Federation of Exchange (various years).
N.A. = Not available.
a. A stock exchange in the ADB member referred to as "Taipei,China."

to identify factors that constrain the growth of the region's bond markets. They argue that one such factor is the size of the economy. Larger economies tend to have bond markets with larger capitalization relative to the size of the economy (GDP) than do smaller ones. Many of the countries in the region have relatively small economies. Other factors that tend to prevent the local bond market from growing are failure of the countries to adhere to international accounting standards, corruption, and low bureaucratic quality. The authors also note that capital control tends to discourage participation in domestic bond markets, which in turn inhibits further development of the bond market in question.

Regional Financial Integration

In the aftermath of the 1997–98 financial crisis, countries in the region attempted to promote regional financial integration. One way to promote such integration was to take up the problem of mismatches (maturity and currency) in debtors' balance sheets. To address this issue, regional governments, with assistance from the ADB, created Asian bond markets to foster local currency debt markets. Another course of action was to recycle the region's excess savings within the region; that is, to invest them directly in the region. So far Asians had been sending large

2007			2008			
Domestic private sector	*Domestic public sector*	*Foreign*	*Total*	*Domestic private sector*	*Domestic public sector*	*Foreign*
33,273.5	0.0	0.0	N.A.	N.A.	N.A.	N.A.
3,270.5	0.0	0.0	1,184.3	1,184.3	0.0	0.0
15,304.5	23,160.7	16,401.1	53,415.3	16,784.8	21,839.0	14,791.6
8,417.9	50,864.7	N.A.	54,927.0	6,698.1	48,228.9	0.0
101,252.3	786,346.6	53.4	654,831.7	173,118.4	481,713.3	0.0
24,149.5	479,745.5	126.9	514,645.2	27,872.8	486,669.5	102.9
5,626.7	5,113,090.6	0.0	6,289,353.1	4,628.4	6,284,724.6	0.0
22,570.9	252,228.2	0.0	263,514.8	38,995.9	224,518.9	0.0
2,966.8	417.9	0.0	6,664.4	5,528.4	1,136.0	0.0
N.A.	N.A.	N.A.	397,654.5	N.A.	N.A.	N.A.
0.2	108,844.6	0.0	114,175.8	0.0	114,175.8	0.0
11,618.7	101,601.1	0.0	115,234.6	14,871.8	100,362.8	0.0
14,718.3	N.A.	0.0	6,298,364.6	13,640.2	6,284,724.4	0.0

amounts of their savings abroad, especially to the United States. The savings would then come back to the region in the form of foreign direct investment and portfolio investment.[35]

As noted earlier, the region also established the CMIM under the auspices of the ASEAN+3. The CMIM is a self-managed, reserves-pooling, arrangement governed by a single contractual agreement. The total size of the reserve pool is $120 billion, to which China, Japan, and Korea contribute 80 percent. The breakdown is as follows: China together with Hong Kong, China, $38.4 billion (32 percent); Japan, $38.4 billion (32 percent); and Korea, $19.2 billion (16 percent). The ASEAN countries together contribute $24 billion (20 percent) to the pool.

The purpose of greater regional financial cooperation is twofold: to prevent or, perhaps more accurately, to reduce the likelihood of a systemic financial crisis and, in case of a crisis, to mitigate its impact. With regard to the purpose of the CMIM, there is the desire, in the event of a crisis, to be able to quickly disburse funds with minimal conditionality. The desire for a quick response is understandable. A failure to promptly respond to a demand from a country that

35. See Hannoun, "Financial Deepening."

is facing a crisis may end up costing more than if the crisis and contagion were prevented in the first place.

Minimal conditionality poses a dilemma, however. Countries may run into financial problems due to various causes and, therefore, require different approaches. On the one hand, a country with a sound overall economic system may face a dire financial problem because it has been subjected to a large unanticipated external shock. In this situation, it would be unfair to impose strict conditionality. On the other hand, countries' financial problems may be of their own making. The current crisis in Greece is a case in point. The country ran into financial problems because of government economic mismanagement—that is, a budget deficit too high relative to economic output. In such a case, stricter conditionality was deemed necessary.

Strict conditionality has two main purposes. First, it may compel the government in question to undertake the necessary corrective actions to address the root causes of the problem at hand. Second, it minimizes the likelihood of a similar problem reappearing in the future. To achieve this, the CMIM should have a strong, credible, and independent regional surveillance mechanism. For this purpose, the ASEAN+3 countries have established the ASEAN+3 Macroeconomic Research Office (AMRO) to serve as a regional surveillance unit. AMRO will monitor members' economic conditions and convey its findings to the respective governments. The process of regional financial integration essentially implies opening up a country's financial market to players from neighboring economies and, at the same time, allowing local residents to access the financial services available in neighboring economies.

Regional financial integration provides a number of benefits to countries involved. First, a regional market expands the scale and opportunities for financial intermediation. One advantage of a larger market is that, other things equal, it is more cost efficient than a smaller one. Second, a regional market can introduce efficiency in a local market by fostering competition, thus lowering the price of financial products and services. Third, a regional market is more able to cope with idiosyncratic risks by allowing for greater diversification of assets and markets for individual investors.[36]

Notwithstanding all the attempts, the regional financial integration process has been advancing only slowly; regional markets remain fragmented. A study by Soyoung Kim and Jong-Wha Lee compares the degrees of real integration and financial integration in East Asia using price as well as quantity measures.[37] The idea is that, in fully integrated regional real markets, goods can move freely within the region. More specifically, in fully integrated markets the price should be equalized across countries (law of one price). Also, because of the interdependence

36. Wakeman-Linn and Wagh (2008).
37. Kim and Lee (2008).

through trade, one would expect to observe an increased comovement of the countries' outputs. Similarly, in fully integrated financial markets, traders can transact financial assets freely within the region. In particular, one would expect to observe the equalization of returns to equivalent financial assets across the region. Meanwhile, better risk sharing resulting from the integration tends to increase the comovement of consumption across the region.

Kim and Lee find that, on the one hand, real integration has been accelerating, as evidenced by increasing intraregional trade among countries in the region. In particular, they find that real integration based on output linkages increased substantially both regionally and globally following the East Asian financial crisis. On the other hand, regional financial integration clearly lags behind. More specifically, East Asian financial markets are integrated relatively more with global markets than with each other. In another study, Lee utilizes the gravity model to investigate the patterns and determinants of financial integration in East Asia.[38] He finds that holding of bilateral assets (equity portfolio and debt securities) is lower in East Asia than in Europe. He attributes this phenomenon to an underdeveloped financial infrastructure, low capital account liberalization, and high exchange rate volatility.

In an earlier study, Barry Eichengreen and Yung Chul Park ask the question as to why there has been less financial integration in Asia than in Europe.[39] The study focuses on cross-border bank claims, which are available on a bilateral basis. They observe that cross-border bank claims in Europe account for around 33.9 percent of GDP, compared to a mere 3.5 percent in Asia. However, they further note that cross-border bank claims are strongly related to per capita income. The authors therefore conclude that the difference between the two regions in cross-border bank claims is largely the result of their very different levels of economic development as well as differences in factors such as geography and language. The authors also suggest that since intraregional exports as a percentage of GDP are only a third of what they are in Europe, Asia needs additional cross-border finance to support further intraregional trade.

Financial Deepening: The Way Forward

It is clear from the foregoing discussion that financial development is at least correlated with economic development. While the exact nature of the link remains unclear, it is also obvious that a sound and sophisticated financial system promotes the efficiency of investment and hence economic growth and that a poorly functioning financial system can inhibit economic growth.

38. Lee (2008).
39. Eichengreen and Park (2003).

It is therefore important that East Asian economies continue to deepen their financial sector. With regard to the banking sector, further improvements are called for, even though in some respects the sector has achieved significant progress. In Indonesia, for instance, net interest margin—the difference between loan and deposit interest rate—has been persistently high since the East Asian crisis. At the end of 2010 the net interest margin was around 5 percent. This indicates some degree of inefficiency in the country's banking sector. At the beginning of 2011 there were 122 banks in Indonesia, with the 4 largest banks accounting for around 46 percent of the country's total bank assets. It may seem paradoxical, but further consolidation in the sector may be necessary to improve its efficiency. The banking sector in other economies may require different measures, but the bottom line is the same. They all need to increase their efficiency. Unless this deficiency is adequately addressed, East Asians will continue to send their savings abroad, investing them in more liquid, high-quality foreign assets.

The quality gap and the relative shallowness of East Asian financial markets, argues Hervé Hannoun, have led to financial intermediation being done abroad.[40] Indeed, the efficiency of the region's capital markets also needs further enhancement. Some markets need to increase their transparency through disclosure by requiring the issuers and intermediaries offering securities to provide sufficient, accurate, and timely information pertaining to the company's business, finances, prospects, and terms of securities to allow investors to make informed decisions. China, for instance, also needs to gradually liberalize the capital account of the balance of payments and develop a market-based monetary policy. The overall aim is to establish well-regulated competitive capital markets. This requires improvements in the regulatory systems in which the markets operate and in the provision of information to market participants. It also requires reasonable legal and accounting systems to be in place.

In recent years more and more foreign investors entered the region's capital markets and have become major players in some of the markets. Meanwhile, there are also benefits for allowing domestic firms to have access to global capital markets. While there may be a legitimate concern that some firms may migrate to international financial centers such as New York and London, thereby reducing the liquidity of domestic markets, yet the experience of other countries seems to suggest that, even in highly integrated economies such as those in Western Europe, domestic capital markets still have roles to play, not the least of which is to provide financial services to small and medium-sized enterprises that otherwise would find it difficult to obtain such services abroad.

As noted, the bond market is relatively new to many of the countries in the region. Many of the constraints identified as inhibiting bond market development, such as the relatively small size of the market, are external in nature. But there are

40. Hannoun, "Financial Deepening."

factors that tend to discourage participation in domestic markets—such as failure to adhere to international accounting standards, corruption, low bureaucratic quality, and capital control—that the government can remedy. As with the capital market, foreign investors are necessary for further development of the bond market. The governments of the region should address these issues if they hope to develop their bond markets. Emerging markets also tend to be relatively more volatile, and this may be addressed by seeking macroeconomic stability. In the longer term, countries in the region may need to develop foreign exchange and derivatives markets as well as ensuring competitive pricing among alternate market segments.

References

Adams, Charles. 2008. "Emerging East Asian Banking Systems Ten Years after the 1997/1998 Crisis." Working Paper on Regional Economic Integration 16. Manila: Asian Development Bank.

Aghion, Philippe, and others. 2006. "Exchange Rate Volatility and Productivity Growth: The Role of Financial Development." Working Paper 12117. Cambridge, Mass.: National Bureau of Economic Research.

Batten, Jonathan A., Warren P. Hogan, and Peter G. Szilagyi. 2009. "Foreign Bond Markets and Financial Market Development: International Perspectives." Working Paper 173. Tokyo: Asian Development Bank Institute.

Bekaert, Geert, Campbell R. Harvey, and Christian Lundblad. 2005. "Does Financial Liberalization Spur Growth?" *Journal of Financial Economics* 77, no. 1: 3–55.

Burger, John D., and Francis E. Warnock. 2007. "Foreign Participation in Local Currency Bond Markets." *Review of Financial Economics* 16: 291–304.

Claessens, Stijn, Daniela Klingebiel, and Sergio L. Schumukler. 2006. "Stock Market Development and Internalization: Do Economic Fundamentals Spur Both Similarly?" *Journal of Empirical Finance* 13, no. 3: 316–50.

Dalla, Ismail. 2005. "Deepening Capital Markets in East Asia." East Asian finance study. Washington: World Bank.

De la Torre, Augusto, Juan Carlos Gozzi, and Sergio L. Schumukler. 2007. *Financial Development: Maturing and Emerging Policy Issues.* Oxford University Press for International Bank for Reconstruction and Development.

Demirgüç-Kunt, Asli, and Vojislav Maksimovic. 1999. "Institutions, Financial Markets, and Firm Debt Maturity." *Journal of Financial Economics* 54: 295–336.

Eichengreen, Barry. 2004. "Financial Instability." Paper prepared for conference, Copenhagen Consensus, Copenhagen, May 25–28.

Eichengreen, Barry, and Pipat Luengnaruemitchai. 2004. "Why Doesn't Asia Have Bigger Bond Markets?" Working Paper 10576. Cambridge, Mass.: National Bureau of Economic Research.

Eichengreen, Barry, and Yung Chul Park. 2003. "Why Has There Been Less Financial Integration in Asia than in Europe?" Political Economy of International Finance paper. Institute of European Studies, UC Berkeley.

Goldsmith, Raymond W. 1969. *Financial Structure and Development.* Yale University Press.

Gopalan, Sasidaran, and Ramkishen S. Rajan. 2009. "Financial Sector Deregulation in Emerging Asia: Focus on Foreign Bank Entry." Working Paper 76. Institute of South Asian Studies, National University of Singapore.

Greenwood, Jeremy, and Boyan Jovanovic. 1990. "Financial Development, Growth, and the Distribution of Income." *Journal of Political Economy* 98, no. 1: 1076–07.

Greenwood, Jeremy, and Bruce D. Smith. 1997. "Financial Markets in Development and the Development of Financial Markets." *Journal of Economic Dynamic and Control,* no. 21: 145–81.

Guiso, Luigi, Paola Sapienza, and Luigi Zingales. 2002. "Does Local Financial Development Matter?" Working Paper 8923. Cambridge, Mass.: National Bureau of Economic Research.

Gurley, John, and Edward Shaw. 1995. "Financial Aspects of Economic Development." *American Economic Review* 45, no. 4: 515–38.

Gyntelberg, Jacob, Guonan Ma, and Eli Remolona. 2005. "Developing Corporate Bond Markets in Asia." Paper 26. Basel: Bank for International Settlements.

Henry, Peter Blair. 2007. "Capital Account Liberalization: Theory, Evidence, and Speculation." *Journal of Economic Literature* 45 (December): 887–935.

International Monetary Fund. 2008. "Regional Economic Outlook, Asia and Pacific." Washington.

Kim, Soyoung, and Jong-Wha Lee. 2008. "Real and Financial Integration in East Asia." Working Paper 17. Manila: Asian Development Bank.

King, Robert G., and Ross Levine. 1993. "Finance and Growth: Schumpeter Might Be Right." *Quarterly Journal of Economics* 108: 713–37.

Lee, Jong-Wha. 2008. "Patterns and Determinants of Cross-Border Financial Asset Holding in East Asia." Working Paper 13. Manila: Asian Development Bank.

Leung, Julia. 2005. "Developing Bond Markets in Asia: Experience with ABF2." BIS Paper 26. Basel: Bank for International Settlements.

Levine, Ross, and Sergio L. Schumukler. 2005. "Internationalization and Stock Market Liquidity." *Review of Finance* 10, no. 1: 153–87.

Levine, Ross, and Sara Zervos. 1998. "Stock Markets, Banks, and Economic Growth." *American Economic Review* 88, no. 3: 537–58.

Love, Inessa. 2001. "Financial Development and Financing Constraints: International Evidence from the Structural Investment Model." Policy Research Working Paper 2694. Washington: World Bank.

Marks, Cindy, and Walter Yao. 2009. "Recent Developments in Asian Deposit Guarantee Programs." Asia Focus report. Federal Reserve Bank of San Francisco (http://frbsf.org/publications/banking/asiafocus/20. . .Insurance_Oct_08.pdf).

Mohanty, M. S., and Philip Turner. 2010. "Bank and Financial Intermediation in Emerging Asia: Reforms and New Risks." Working Paper 313. Basel: Bank for International Settlements.

Mohanty, M. S., G. Schnabel and P. Garcia-Luna. 2006. "Banks and Aggregate Credit: What Is New?" BIS Paper 28. Basel: Bank for International Settlements.

Obstfeld, Maurice. 1994. "Risk-Taking, Global Diversification, and Growth." *American Economic Review* 84, no. 5: 1310–29.

Rajan, Raghuram G., and Luigi Zingales. 1998. "Financial Dependence and Growth." *American Economic Review* 88, no. 3: 559–86.

Wakeman-Linn, John, and Smita Wagh. 2008. "Regional Financial Integration: Its Potential Contribution to Financial Sector Growth and Development in Sub-Saharan Africa." Paper prepared for conference, African Finance for the Twenty-First Century, Tunis, March 4–5 (www.imf.org/external/np/seminars/eng/2008/afrfin/pdf/wakemanlinn.pdf).

World Federation of Exchange. Various years. *Annual Report and Statistics* (www.world-exchanges.org/reports).

9

The Development of Local Debt Markets in Asia: An Assessment

MANGAL GOSWAMI AND SUNIL SHARMA

Since the regional crisis of 1997–98, Asian emerging markets have focused considerable attention on developing domestic debt markets to reduce foreign exchange mismatches in their financial systems and to decrease the concentration of credit and maturity risks in banks.[1] Besides building large foreign exchange reserve buffers, much of their effort has gone into local currency bonds, since such bonds constitute a significant share of emerging bond markets, especially in Asia (figure 9-1). Liquid and deep domestic debt markets are seen as vehicles for diversifying the funding of governments, households, and corporations; for attracting the financing required for huge infrastructure needs; for broadening the range of assets available for local institutional and retail investors; and for providing an additional channel for financial intermediation should the banks come under stress.[2] In addition, as financial development has proceeded, Asian policymakers have come to appreciate the synergies and interrelationships between the process of creating capital and derivative markets and the process of modernizing bank and nonbank financial intermediaries.

Asian capital markets that had grown faster than many of the mature markets since the turn of the century saw a sizable retrenchment during the global financial

For helpful discussions and comments, the authors would like to thank colleagues at the IMF's Asia Pacific Department, staff of the Monetary Authority of Singapore, and participants at the ADB–Bank Negara seminar.

1. CGFS (2007b); Turner (2009).
2. Gyntelberg, Ma, and Remolona (2006); Gyntelberg (2007); Jiang, Tang, and Law (2002).

Figure 9-1. *Emerging Bond Markets, Currency Denomination, 2000, 2005, and 2008*

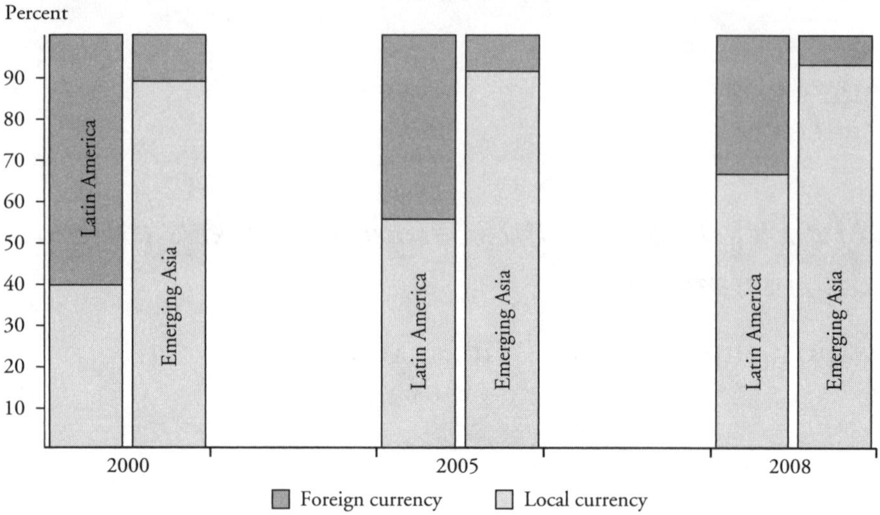

Source: Turner (2009).

crisis, as capital inflows fell precipitously (figure 9-2). Many of the Asian emerging asset markets experienced intense pressures as foreign investors withdrew (figure 9-3). In particular, local debt markets—the focus of this study—saw high volatility and substantially lower liquidity at the height of the crisis in the last quarter of 2008. Tight global conditions, fragile investor confidence, and the sharp drop in sterilization by central banks and monetary authorities in the face of capital outflows led to a drop in domestic bond issuance in 2008. Subsequently, fiscal stimuli and renewed capital inflows to the region resulted in a recovery of Asian domestic bond markets in 2009.

The rapid growth in Asia's emerging domestic bond markets before the global crisis was due to the strong growth performance and favorable longer term prospects for the region (figure 9-4). There was also a corresponding increase in securities valuation, accompanied by a further diversification and globalization of the investor base. Access to Asian capital markets through derivatives instruments (over-the-counter [OTC] derivatives and structured notes) by foreign investors—though difficult to measure—also partly boosted capital inflows before the crisis.[3]

In the last few years, Asian local currency bonds have gained significance in investor portfolios around the world. The emergence of Asian local currency

3. CGFS (2009). Foreign investor exposure to domestic assets via (offshore) derivatives may result in capital flows, depending on whether the counterparty to the derivatives position hedges its position in the onshore (domestic) capital market.

Figure 9-2. *Capital Inflows to Selected Asian Markets, 2003–09, by Quarter*[a]

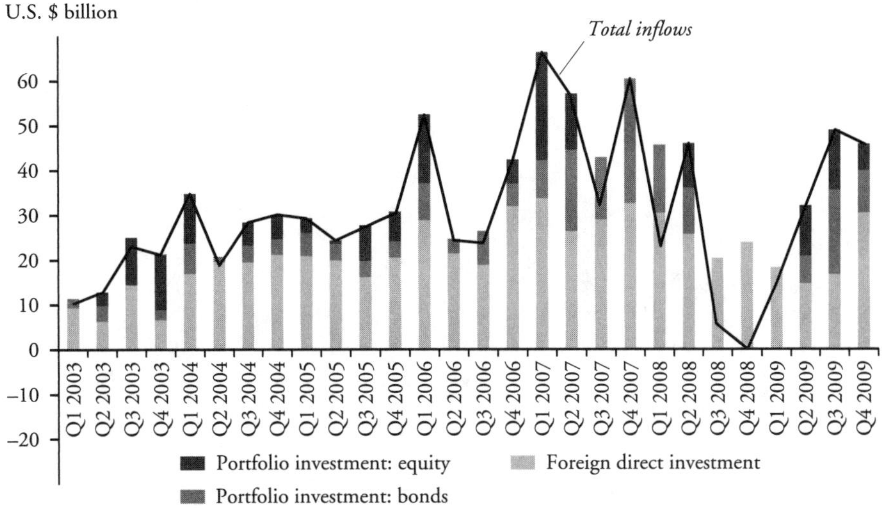

Source: International Monetary Fund (http://imfstatistics.org/img).

a. Countries include Hong Kong, China; Indonesia; Korea; Malaysia; Philippines; Singapore; and Thailand.

Figure 9-3. *Equity and Bond Market Indexes, 2004–10*

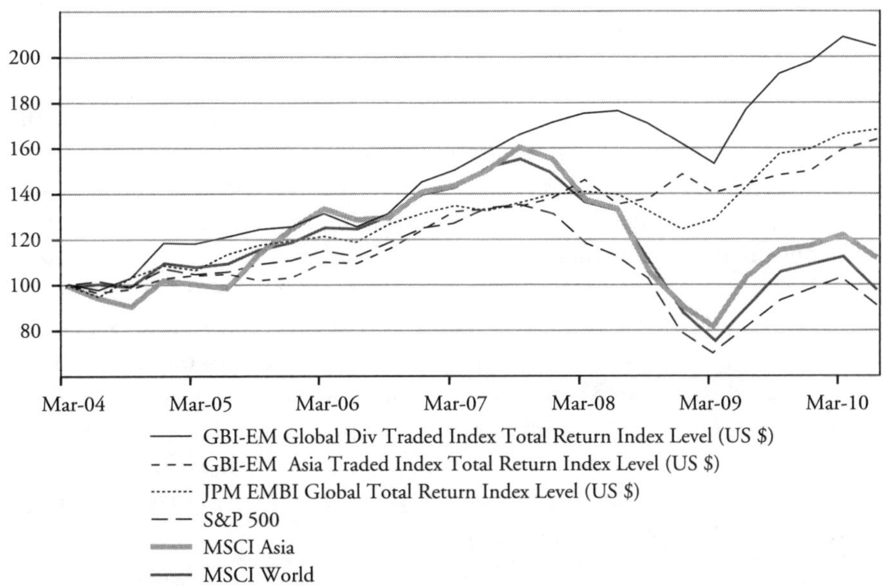

Source: Bloomberg.

Figure 9-4. *Capitalization of Bond Markets in Emerging and Developing Asia, 1998–2009*[a]

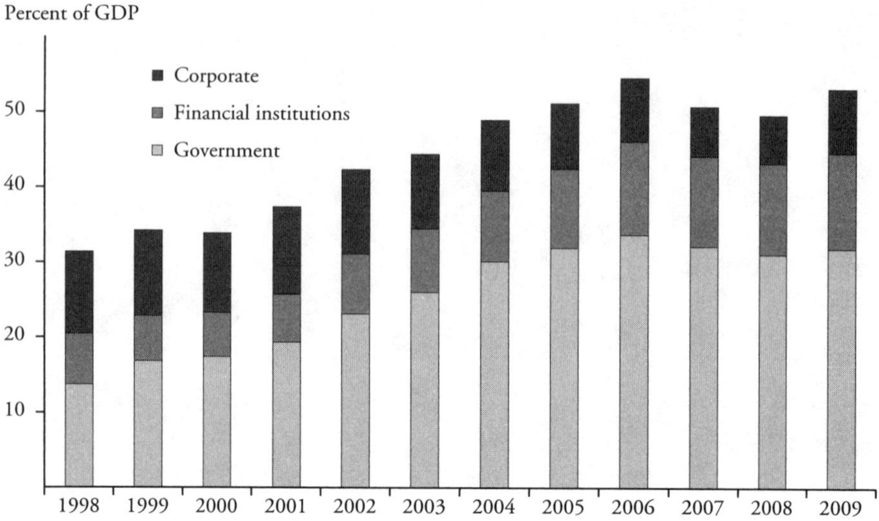

Source: Bank for International Settlements (various years); World Economic Outlook, IMF.

a. Countries include China, Hong Kong, China; India; Indonesia; Korea; Malaysia; Pakistan; Philippines; Taipei,China; and Thailand. The breakdown between corporate, financial institutions, and government varies depending on the source of data. Corporate bond market data in AsianBondsOnline refer to financial institutions and corporate sector bonds. To improve the consistency of bond data across agencies and countries, the Working Group on Securities Databases (reconvened in response to the G-8 Action Plan in 2007)—and in particular the Bank for International Settlements, the European Central Bank, and the International Monetary Fund—published part 1 of the Handbook on Securities Statistics in May 2009. This publication provides a guide for the collection and presentation of securities statistics.

bonds as an asset class is due to improvement in the quality of issuers and the development of market infrastructure and institutions. Asian emerging markets have made notable advancements through creating public debt management units (for example, Thailand and Indonesia), articulating debt management strategies, and consolidating benchmark issues for building yield curves. Nevertheless, growth in domestic bond markets has remained largely skewed toward government debt, partly driven by the sterilization needs of Asian central banks, during the 2002–07 period, for handling the surge in capital flows to the region. Asian emerging market corporate borrowers continue to be bank dependent, and though capital market borrowing has increased over the past decade, large firms still find it cheaper and more convenient to raise money in global capital markets. In addition, firms with foreign ownership tend to rely on retained earnings and internal funding from their parent corporations.[4]

4. Mieno and others (2009).

The State of Development

The development of local debt markets in Asia is assessed by examining three key dimensions of market development: the hurdles confronting players and institutions that are or could be borrowers and lenders, the issues faced by current and potential liquidity providers, and the presence or absence of supportive government policies and regulations.[5]

Borrowers and Lenders in the Local Markets

Before the recent global financial crisis, emerging market external bond issuance increased significantly as banks and corporations improved their access to global capital markets. This improvement was driven by decreasing costs of foreign currency–denominated bond issuance in G-3 currencies (U.S. dollar, euro, and yen), favorable credit ratings including transitions to investment grade, and the desire for diversification in terms of currency denomination, from the U.S. dollar to the euro, the yen and, in some cases, domestic currencies.

For most borrowers in Asian emerging markets, the cost of borrowing is still the primary determinant of the mode of financing, although maturity and diversification of financing sources are becoming increasingly important considerations. In most markets, domestic bond issuance remains costly and cumbersome compared to bank lending. Even governments often issue bonds for short-term, tactical reasons rather than for medium-term strategic objectives that take account of costs, maturity structure, and rollover risk. Corporate finance is dominated by bank-based intermediation, which is still largely relationship based.[6] In addition, many Asian corporations that resort to bond financing prefer private placements, since it allows them to save on the regulatory costs (such as registration, prospectus, and disclosure requirements) of public listings.[7]

The development of corporate bond markets in Asia remains uneven. Those in Hong Kong, China; Republic of Korea; Malaysia; and Singapore are the largest and relatively the most developed, while those in India, Indonesia, the Philippines, and Thailand have lagged behind (figure 9-5).[8] The People's Republic of China

5. For a more elaborate discussion, see Chami, Fullenkamp, and Sharma (2010). Their approach is anchored in studying the incentives facing the key players in financial markets—borrowers, lenders, liquidity providers, and regulators—whose actions shape markets. Different financial instruments embody different compromises between borrowers and lenders. Identifying the obstacles that prevent the key players from creating, executing, trading, or enforcing particular financial contracts can provide guidance for designing policies that facilitate the functioning and development of markets.

6. External wholesale funding relies heavily on intermediation by international banks.

7. The downside of private placements is the narrower investor base, which is largely limited to a few sophisticated investors. In practice, private placements are close substitutes for loan syndication and can be cost effective for meeting large financing needs that may be beyond the balance-sheet capacity of a single bank.

8. It is worth noting that the *sukuk,* or the Islamic bond market (which is outside the scope of this chapter), has seen sizable growth in recent years, especially in Malaysia.

Figure 9-5. *Selected Asian Bond Markets*

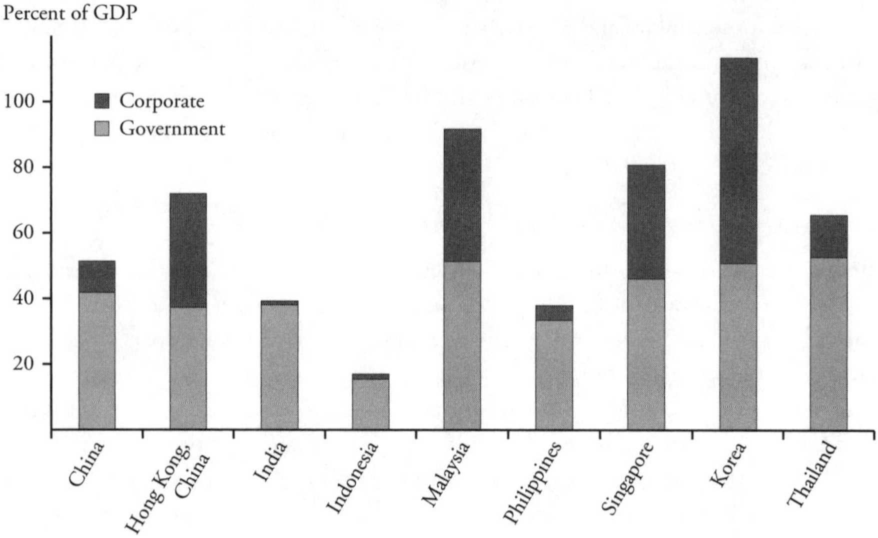

Source: AsianBondsOnline (http://asianbondsonline.adb.org); Bank for International Settlements (www.bis.org/statistics/secstats.htm).

(henceforth referred to as China) has experienced significant growth in bond market capitalization since 2005, with a substantial increase in commercial paper issuance and the establishment of a medium-term note market. However, the corporate bond market in China remains small, at only 8–9 percent of GDP. Rapid growth in corporate bond markets was also recorded in the Philippines and India, though these markets are small compared to the overall bond markets.[9]

The investor base in Asia has become broader and deeper with the emergence of domestic institutional investors.[10] Demographic changes, pension reforms, and the larger role played by nonbank financial institutions have supported this development. Singapore and Malaysia have accumulated sizable assets under their publicly managed pension funds. Such fully funded pension systems are of particular relevance, as they tend to favor debt securities carrying low default risk and denominated in domestic currency.[11] Pension fund assets also grew rapidly in Korea (at an annual rate of 47 percent during 2002–07), and the National Pension Fund (NPF) increased to over 21 percent of gross domestic product in 2007. Most of these NPF funds are invested in fixed-income securities, mainly government bonds. Pension fund assets in China, India, and Thailand are growing but still remain small (figures 9-6, 9-7).

9. Data on corporate bonds include issuances by financial institutions.
10. Ghosh (2006); APEC (2008).
11. CGFS (2007a).

Figure 9-6. *Institutional Assets, Selected Asian Markets and the United States*

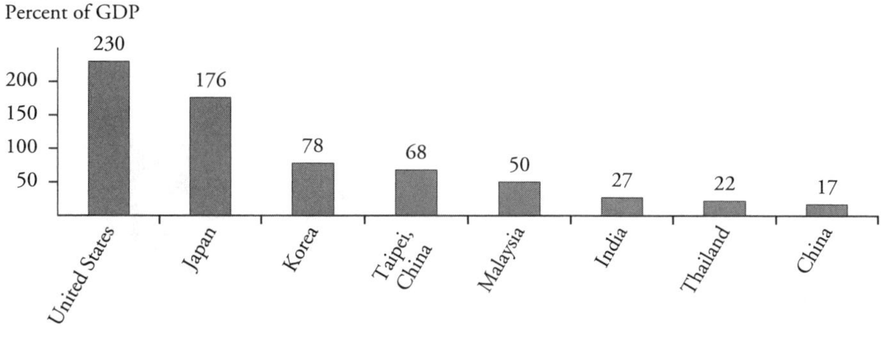

Source: Goldman Sachs, Global Economics Paper No. 204, September 8, 2010.

Figure 9-7. *Assets under Management (AUM), Three Asian Countries*

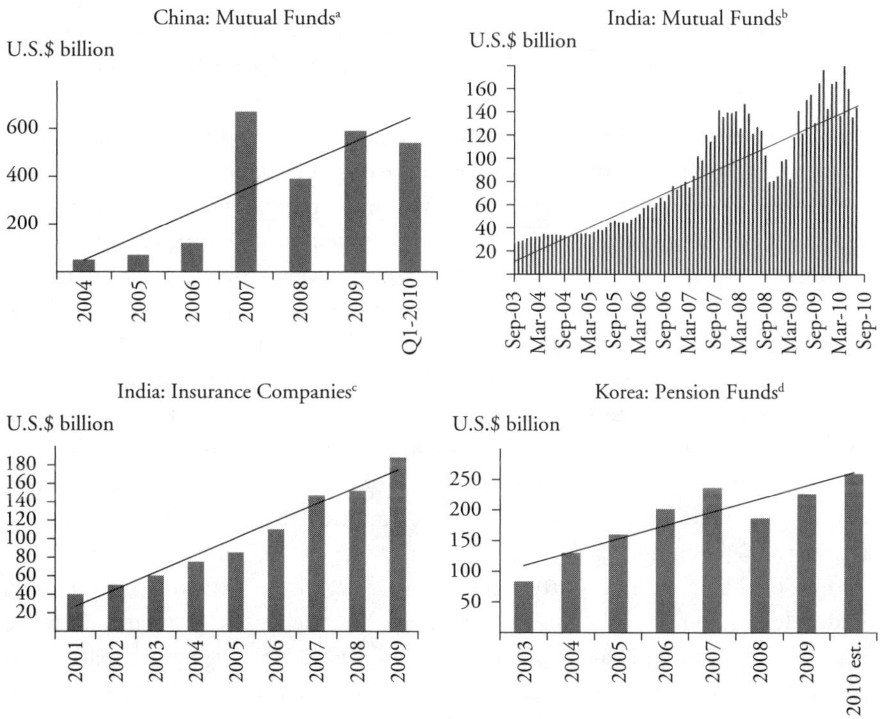

Source: Goldman Sachs (2010).
a. Compound annual growth rate 67 percent.
b. Compound annual growth rate 22.6 percent.
c. Compound annual growth rate 22 percent, 2001–09.
d. Compound annual growth rate 19 percent, 2003–10.

Figure 9-8. *Singapore and Hong Kong, China, Total Assets of Fund Management Industry, 2004–09*

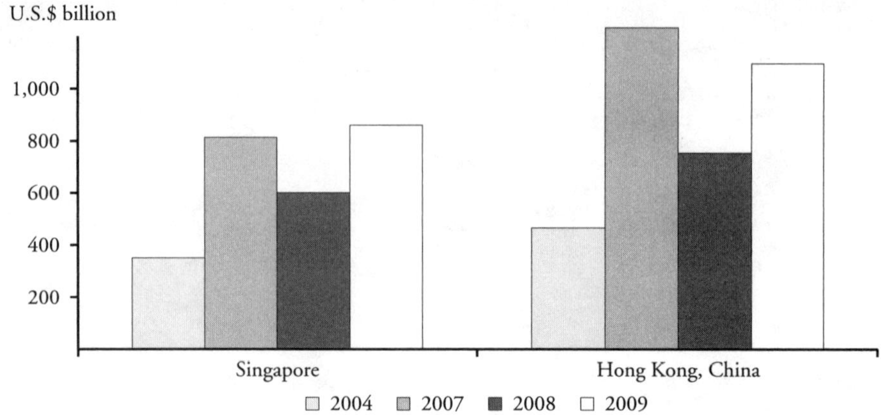

Source: Monetary Authority of Singapore (2010).

Growth in the mutual fund industry throughout Asia has been broad based. Mutual funds have allowed households to hold local currency bonds in more liquid and easily tradable units. Since mutual funds tend to trade actively in response to changes in market conditions, they have brought additional liquidity to local markets.[12] Singapore and Hong Kong, China lead this industry due to their role as regional financial centers, with more than 50 percent of their assets (figure 9-8) derived from abroad. The rapid growth in mutual funds in other Asian economies—China, India, Korea, Malaysia, and Taipei,China—has been largely dependent on domestic factors. In India, the mutual fund industry grew from about $30 billion in 2004 to more than $150 billion as of May 2010 (figure 9-7). Nevertheless, mutual funds have so far played a limited role in the development of the corporate bond market in India, where currently 80 percent of debt mutual funds are owned by corporations, and retail participation is limited. In addition, corporate bonds account for only 20 percent of the assets in debt mutual funds.

Foreign investor participation in Asian domestic debt markets has been rising, despite the setback during the recent global credit crisis (figure 9-9). The secular increase in the proportion of their portfolios allocated to emerging market assets by developed country institutional investors has been underpinned by a more favorable risk-return profile, especially during 2002–07. Foreign participation has largely been through institutional investors such as mutual funds, pension funds, hedge funds, and sovereign wealth funds. Assets under management for dedicated emerging market bond funds, particularly local currency bonds, have risen signif-

12. Turner (2009).

Figure 9-9. *Foreign Holdings of Local Currency Government Bonds, Selected Asian Countries, 1996–2010*

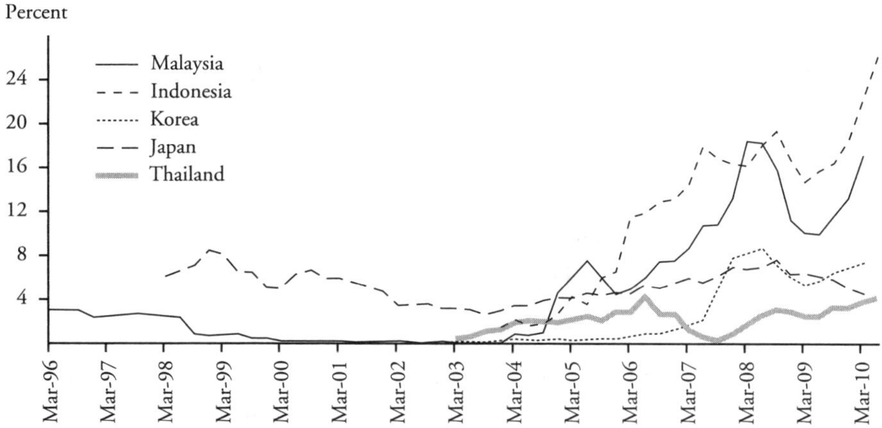

Source: AsianBondsOnline (http://asianbondsonline.adb.org).

icantly.[13] While the global financial crisis led to a decline in foreign investor demand for emerging market assets, most Asian countries have seen renewed foreign interest. The available data may understate the importance of foreign investors, since they also use derivatives (including nondeliverable forwards, structured notes, and total return swaps) to take exposures, which are not easily accounted for.

Regional initiatives by multilateral agencies have also supported the development of local bond markets by reducing impediments to market access.[14] The launch of the Asian Bond Fund 2 (ABF2) in March 2005, a regional local currency denominated bond fund, has resulted in the introduction of the Pan-Asian Bond Index Fund and a Fund of Bond Funds with eight country subfunds open to investment by the public. Other initiatives, such as the Asian Bond Market Initiative (ABMI) under the ASEAN+3 framework, have been trying to catalyze the development of local currency bond markets, especially through facilitating the emergence of a national and regional market infrastructure for trading bonds.[15] The ABMI set up working groups to study a number of issues, including the issuance of new securitized debt instruments, establishment of a regional bond guarantee agency, creation of a regional settlement and clearance system, and

13. Data on cumulative net foreign inflows to emerging market equity and bond funds show a rise from less than $20 billion in early 2003 to over $100 billion by year-end 2009 (Emerging Markets Portfolio Funds Research).

14. Ma and Remolona (2005); EMEAP (2005).

15. ASEAN+3 refers to countries in the Association of Southeast Asian Nations (ASEAN), and China, Japan, and Korea.

strengthening of national and regional rating agencies. The recent formation of the Credit Guarantee and Investment Facility, a trust fund of the Asian Development Bank (ADB), is expected to support the issuance of corporate bonds.

The various regional initiatives have resulted in some progress in the development of local debt markets. They have catalyzed tax reforms; changes in regulatory frameworks; liberalization of capital controls; better market infrastructure through the creation of a regional custodial network; harmonized legal documentation for investment funds; and the introduction of credible, representative, and transparent benchmarks.[16] The Asian Bond Market Forum was set up in September 2010 by the ASEAN+3 countries as a common platform to foster the standardization of market practices and the harmonization of regulations related to cross-border bond transactions.

Many international financial institutions have raised funds through local currency bonds in emerging markets, including Asian emerging markets, in order to provide high-quality local currency instruments for developing the domestic yield curve. Such activity is leading to the improvement of documentation standards and placement procedures and helping to attract new investors to the local currency markets. The Asian Development Bank, International Finance Corporation, and the World Bank are among the international financial institutions that have issued local currency bonds in various markets, and these instruments have been successful in attracting foreign investors to these markets. However, recent research suggests that firm-specific characteristics are more important for the issuance of public bonds by corporations, with the most important factor being whether the firms had previously issued such bonds.[17] The effect of local market size and liquidity is found to be small, and the coordinated policies to encourage bond market development by Asian governments have had little effect on the probability of issuance at the firm level.

Liquidity

Liquidity is essential for financial deepening, and the lack of it continues to be a concern in the developing Asian markets. Secondary-market liquidity for an instrument could be facilitated if the issuance is sizable and regular, the trading life of the instrument is sufficiently long, and turnover is large. Liquidity providers could range from dealers and traders to borrowers and lenders. Foreign investors could add to the liquidity in domestic bond markets by widening the investor base and increasing the heterogeneity of market participants.[18]

A better understanding of what drives liquidity is important in enhancing market stability. Liquidity can broadly be measured in two dimensions: macro, or the resilience to macroeconomic shocks, and micro, or depth, tightness, and the abil-

16. CGFS (2007a).
17. Mizen and Tsoukas (2010).
18. See, for example, the discussion in Chami, Fullenkamp, and Sharma (2010).

Table 9-1. *Domestic Bond Market Liquidity Indicators*

	Value traded ($ billion)		*Turnover ratio*		*Bid-ask spread*[b]
Country	*Government*	*Corporate*	*Government*	*Corporate*	*Government*
People's Republic of China	5,368	1,812	0.68	1.29	5.1
Hong Kong, China[a]	5,527	13	32.48	0.04	4.3
Indonesia	40	2	0.18	0.06	26.6
Japan	44,907	277	1.36	0.08	n.a.
Republic of Korea	1,347	363	0.81	0.19	1.1
Malaysia	221	18	0.59	0.06	2.3
Philippines	76	N.A.	0.38	N.A.	6.6
Singapore	204	N.A.	0.65	N.A.	2.9
Thailand	368	5	0.83	0.04	3.4

Source: AsianBondsOnline (http://asianbondsonline.adb.org/).
a. Includes exchange bills.
b. Basis points.
N.A. = Not available.

ity to absorb random shocks.[19] The microeconomic indicators are relatively easier to identify. Market depth is the ability to absorb large transaction volumes without a significant change in prices as measured by the average turnover ratios. Tightness implies cost efficiency and is measured by bid-ask spreads. The ability to absorb random shocks can be reflected in day-to-day price volatility. The macroeconomic dimension is harder to define empirically. An asset can be more liquid if it tends to hold its value despite a severe shock. For example, a diversified investor base can make a market, such as the local bond market, more liquid from a macroliquidity perspective.

Liquidity in local bond markets, including those for government debt, varies substantially across Asia's emerging markets (table 9-1). The markets in Hong Kong, China, Korea, Malaysia, and Singapore are the most liquid, and a number of measures have raised prospects for further improvements. For example, constant two-way quotes by primary dealers in Korea have enhanced the liquidity of government securities markets. In addition, the trading of interest rate risk has been greatly facilitated by the development of a liquid Korea Treasury Bond (KTB) futures market. The interest rate swap market in Singapore, with a relatively high average daily turnover, is used as a pricing benchmark by corporate issuers in Singapore dollars. The volume of turnover in the Chinese bond market, especially the corporate segment, has improved substantially since 2005 as a result of the marked increase in the size of the market.

19. Turner (2007, 2008).

Less liquid markets are generally characterized by a narrow investor base, insufficient infrastructure, low market transparency, and lack of timely information on bond issuers.[20] Secondary-market liquidity can be improved by having an enabling institutional structure ranging from effective trading platforms to the market-making ability of primary dealers. Some countries such as China, Indonesia, and Thailand have undertaken reforms of their market microstructure by establishing market makers, introducing modern trading platforms, and upgrading the payment and settlement systems. Despite these structural reforms and an increase in market transparency, trading is often still bunched in certain maturities, leading to market segmentation. This coupled with a concentration of buy-and-hold investors in domestic bond markets continues to inhibit liquidity. Secondary-market liquidity in many Asian markets is still very much dependent on foreign investors. While access via offshore derivatives markets, notably by foreign banks, can enhance liquidity, it can also lead to the sudden drying up of liquidity when foreign investors withdraw during periods of heightened global risk aversion.

Regulation

Policy and regulatory reforms since the Asian financial crisis have supported the development of local bond markets in Asia.[21] Regulatory and supervisory capacity has been enhanced, while a more supportive environment for capital market development has been fostered. Since 2000 corporate governance practices have gradually improved, and governments have been more proactive in pushing the reform agenda:

—In China, locally listed banks have been allowed to buy and sell bonds on the stock exchanges on a pilot basis since January 2009, and corporations (including foreign firms) have been given permission to issue securities in the interbank bond market. Recently, the use of the renminbi as a trading and settlement currency in Hong Kong, China has been liberalized.

—To improve liquidity and price transparency, Hong Kong, China launched an electronic trading platform for government and corporate bonds in December 2007.

—In January 2009, India increased the limit on foreign institutional investors for the purchase of Indian rupee-denominated corporate bonds from $6 billion to $15 billion. The Reserve Bank of India Act was amended in January 2009 to develop and regulate the market for corporate bonds. A foreign exchange swap facility was put in place for public and private sector banks with foreign branches or subsidiaries. The limits on Indian mutual funds for overseas investments were also further liberalized.

20. Gyntelberg, Ma, and Remolona (2006).
21. Asian Development Bank (2010a, 2010b).

—In July 2008, Indonesia set up a bond-pricing agency to provide reference prices for government and corporate bonds. Reserve requirements on foreign currency deposits were also eased, from 3 to 1 percent, in October 2008.

—In December 2008, the Government of Korea established a won 10 trillion bond market stabilization fund to foster the development of the market. The Regulation on Supervision of Securities Business was amended to facilitate exchange and off-exchange securities trading and to attract foreign investors to the bond market. Transparency in the pricing of bonds was also enhanced by requiring securities companies to report standardized bids and offers for all off-exchange-traded bonds in real time to the Korea Securities Dealers Association. The authorities also changed the tax laws to reduce taxes on high-yield funds that invest 10 percent or more of their assets in speculative-grade corporate bonds. Korea removed withholding taxes on interest income and capital gains in May 2009.[22]

—Starting in December 2008 Bursa Malaysia waived the listing fees (until 2010) for debt securities denominated in ringgit and foreign currencies. The authorities implemented a phased liberalization of foreign exchange by loosening the limits on residents pertaining to foreign currency and ringgit-denominated credit facilities, and foreign currency and ringgit borrowing. Financial liberalization measures (new banking licenses, foreign strategic partnerships in banking and insurance with higher foreign equity limits, and greater operational flexibility for locally incorporated foreign financial institutions) have also facilitated foreign participation in domestic capital markets.

—Despite largely running fiscal surpluses and having a very low net debt position, the government of Singapore has issued debt to help develop the yield curve. In July 2009 the Monetary Authority of Singapore (MAS) took regulatory measures to encourage AAA-rated issuance in the Singapore dollar bond market. First, AAA-rated Singapore dollar–denominated debt securities issued by sovereigns, supranationals, and sovereign-backed corporations were accepted as collateral for borrowings from the MAS Standing Facility. Second, banks were allowed to use these securities to satisfy liquidity requirements, while the haircut applied to these securities for repo operations was the same as that for Singapore government securities (zero percent). Furthermore, in July 2010, MAS extended the list of eligible securities to include those issued by public entities that were rated AAA and had risk weights of zero under the Basel rules.

—Thailand has allowed foreign governments and financial institutions to issue baht bonds onshore. To encourage Thai corporations to issue bonds, new policies have been adopted that reduce after-tax interest costs and simplify registration

22. As a measure to guard against destabilizing capital inflows, Korea's parliament is considering a proposal to reinstate the tax paid by foreigners (foreign corporations and nonresidents) on interest income and capital gains from Korean government bonds.

procedures. The regulations on the borrowing and lending of securities and short selling have been amended to improve risk management. The Securities Law was revised in 2010 to enhance investor protection as well as the independence, operational flexibility, and supervisory effectiveness of the regulator—the Securities and Exchange Commission. Exchange controls were relaxed on capital flows, notably on holding of foreign currency investments by domestic institutional investors.

While most asset managers in Asian emerging markets do not focus on corporate governance, a small but growing number of institutional investors are beginning to push for improved practices to increase corporate valuations. Improved governance is perceived as essential for having the necessary checks and balances within firms.[23] The development of domestic institutions, especially regulatory agencies, is considered important for defining and enforcing governance standards. Following the Asian financial crisis, governments introduced new regulations to improve corporate governance—including higher disclosure standards (for example, Thailand), protecting minority shareholders (for example, Korea, Thailand), and legislative reform of bankruptcy laws (for example, Indonesia, Philippines, and Thailand)—but their enforcement remains uneven. A survey conducted in 2006 by the Centre for International Governance Innovation indicated that investor perception of the quality of corporate governance varies significantly across countries.[24] Hong Kong, China and Singapore were scored to have achieved high standards. Korea, Malaysia, Taipei,China, and Thailand were pegged lower. China, Indonesia, and the Philippines were ranked among the lowest in East Asia.

Obstacles to Further Development

Despite the enlargement of Asian capital markets, challenges remain on several fronts. These include improvements in market access and infrastructure (market entry, cross-border issuance, and investment), transparency, risk assessment and management by financial institutions, the legal and regulatory framework, and market liquidity. The major impediments to growth are as follows:

—Bank dominance

—Lack of critical size in issuance

—Lack of a diverse investor base and preponderance of buy-and-hold investors

—An embryonic legal and regulatory framework for nonbank financial institutions

—Tax and capital controls on foreign investors

—Weak corporate governance

23. Kawai (2007).

24. Cheung and Jang (2006).

Figure 9-10. *Investor Profile, Domestic Government Bonds, Five Asian Countries*

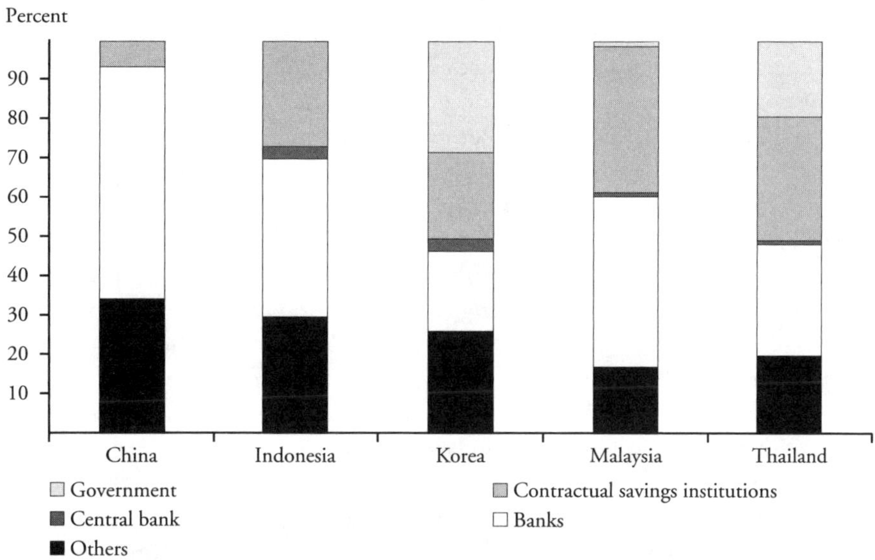

Source: AsianBondsOnline (http://asianbondsonline.adb.org); Bank for International Settlements (www.bis.org/statistics/secstats.htm).

—Inadequate information provision including pricing transparency and infrastructure issues

—High issuance and transaction costs

—Lack of pricing benchmarks and hedging instruments

—Lack of a robust framework for asset-backed securitization.

The local investor base in emerging local debt markets is dominated by buy-and-hold investors, generally banks, pension funds, and insurance companies, and the lack of diversity in the investor base is an impediment to greater liquidity in the secondary markets. The low level of trading activity retards the development of profitable market intermediaries and results in high transaction costs, which discourages wider participation. In Asia bank dominance of the investor base in local bonds has proved detrimental to increasing the average maturity (figure 9-10).[25] While pension fund portfolio diversification has improved in recent years, in many countries asset allocations are still heavily concentrated in government securities. The asset allocation of pension funds has been dictated by regulations on their investments, which follow rigid criteria set by the governments. And the resulting concentration of exposures in a particular segment of the

25. Bank dominance is more prevalent in Asian emerging markets than in markets in other regions.

market has had a negative effect on liquidity. A well-developed mutual fund industry could raise market liquidity and reduce the hold of bank-dominated intermediation. However, mutual funds in Asia have often not been very well regulated.

Foreign participation in local capital markets of most Asian emerging markets is still constrained by a number of factors. The key impediments include capital controls, taxation, lack of funding and hedging markets, and lack of established benchmark indexes (table 9-2).[26] In some countries, foreign financial institutions face restrictions compared to domestic competitors on the underwriting of bonds and on derivatives transactions with corporate clients.[27] Countries like China and India allow only licensed foreign institutional investors to hold and trade domestic securities. With a couple of exceptions (Malaysia and Singapore), most Asian emerging markets impose withholding taxes on interest earned from local bonds by foreign investors.[28] Further, the domestic market for repurchase agreements (repos) is generally not available to foreigners, rendering trading of cash securities very expensive. For example, until recently foreign investors in Korean bonds had to deal with high withholding taxes and cumbersome procedures for accessing the market, although tax treaties with several countries provided some relief. Taxes have a significant impact on cross-border investment and issuance.[29] In addition, the rationale for imposing withholding taxes on income earned by foreigners may well be eroding, as emerging markets swing from being net capital importers to becoming net capital exporters.

Structural factors, such as the lack of critical size in capital market issuance and the historical dependence on the (now relatively liquid) banking sector, also explain the weak growth of corporate bond markets in Asia.[30] The average size of corporations in emerging markets is much smaller than in advanced countries, making bonds a less viable financing option, since the fixed costs associated with raising funds through bonds (especially publicly listed bonds) make it a more expensive alternative. The small size also leads to lower levels of market activity for intermediaries and less liquidity, which adds to the cost of issuance. In such an environment, local corporations, especially large ones, are more likely to tap lower cost external bond markets or make private placements.

Legal uncertainties have also thwarted the development of corporate bond markets. Countries with stronger institutions that receive high scores on the rule of law and creditor rights tend to have more developed local currency bond markets.[31] Despite the widespread reform of bankruptcy laws after the Asian financial

26. Parreñas and Waller (2006).

27. Asia Securities Industry & Financial Markets Association (2010).

28. Thailand, which exempted foreign investors from withholding taxes on government bonds since late 2005, removed the exemption in October 2010 to deter capital inflows and the appreciation of the baht.

29. Asian Development Bank (2010c).

30. Eichengreen and Luengnaruemitchai (2004); Eichengreen, Borensztein, and Panizza (2006).

31. Burger and Warnock (2006).

Table 9-2. *Accessibility, Taxation, Funding, and Hedging*[a]

	China	*Hong Kong, China*	*Korea*	*India*	*Indonesia*	*Malaysia*	*Philippines*	*Singapore*	*Thailand*
Holding and buying local bonds	Limited	Yes	Yes	Limited	Yes	Yes	Custodian	Yes	Limited
Nonresident access	Via QFII	Yes	Yes	Via FII	Yes	Yes	Yes	Yes	Yes
FX restrictions	Yes	No	No	Yes	Yes	Very few	Yes	No	Yes
Withholding tax (nonresidents)	Only corp	No	Yes	Yes	Yes	No	Yes	No	Only corp
Capital gains tax (nonresidents)	No	No	Yes	Yes	Only corp	No	Only corp	No	Only corp
Funding/hedging instruments									
Developed repo markets	Yes	Yes	Yes	Yes	Limited	Yes	No	Yes	Limited
OTC instruments									
IRS	Yes	Yes	Yes	Yes	Yes	Yes	Yes	Yes	Yes
FX swaps	Yes	Yes	Yes	Yes	Yes	Yes	Yes	Yes	Yes
FX forwards	Yes	Yes	Yes	Yes	Yes	Yes	Yes	Yes	Yes
Exchange-traded instruments									
IR futures	No	Yes	Yes	No	No	Yes	No	Yes	No
FX futures	No	No	Yes	No	No	No	No	No	No
Liquid NDF market	Yes	No	Yes	Yes	Moderate	Moderate	Moderate	No	No
Up to 12 months	Yes	. . .	Yes	Yes	Moderate	. . .	Moderate	. . .	. . .
Up to 5 years	Limited	. . .	Yes	Moderate	Illiquid	. . .	Limited	. . .	. . .

Source: Barclays Capital; JPMorgan; Deloitte & Touche; PricewaterhouseCoopers; Bank for International Settlements; WFE; AsianBondsOnline; local governments and exchanges.

a. FX = foreign exchange, OTC = over the counter, IRS = interest rate swaps, IR = interest rate, NDF = nondeliverable forward, FII = foreign institutional investor, QFII = qualified foreign institutional investor.

Figure 9-11. *Domestic Bond Markets and Impediments to Contracting*

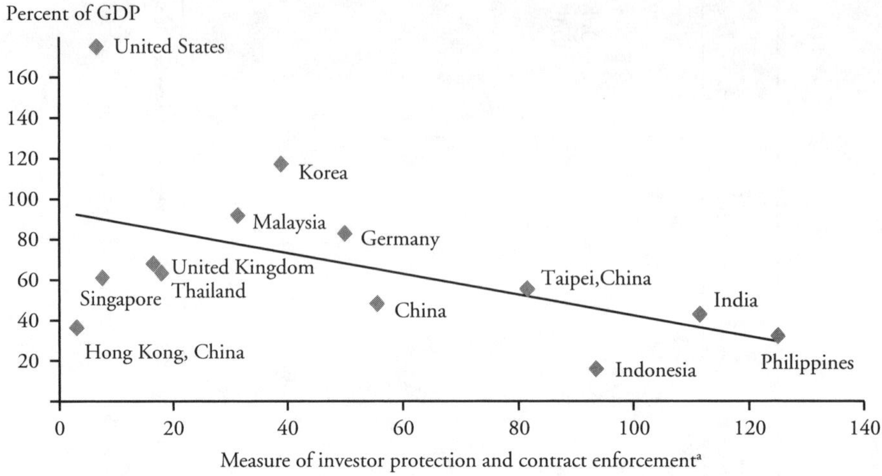

Source: World Bank, Doing Business Indicators (various years).
a. Weighted average of "investor protection" and "contract enforcement" rankings.

crisis, most Asian countries—with a few exceptions such as Hong Kong, China, Korea, Malaysia, and Singapore—still do not have reasonably robust bankruptcy frameworks that meet international standards in terms of bankruptcy processes, creditor rights, and investor protection (figure 9-11). For example in China the legal framework for the enforcement of creditor rights, especially in the case of bankruptcy, inhibits the carrying out of close-out netting.[32]

In most Asian countries corporate bond markets are underdeveloped or illiquid as a result of fragmentation, high transaction costs, and the lack of government yield curves that can serve as benchmarks for pricing and hedging. Even countries with sizable corporate bond markets suffer from low trading volumes and very high transaction costs that inhibit arbitrage and active position taking. For example, turnover ratios of Malaysian and Korean corporate bonds are significantly lower than those of their respective government bond markets. In addition, a significant proportion of the corporate issuance, especially for the quasi-sovereigns, takes place in the private placement market, where securities are often not rated and are generally held by investors with a higher risk tolerance, such as hedge funds.

Benchmarks for emerging market local currency bonds are still being developed. There has been some progress in this area since the launch of JP Morgan's

32. Close-out netting in relation to over-the-counter derivative transactions is the ability of a party under a master agreement (such as an ISDA master agreement) to net the mark-to-market values of all existing transactions under the master agreement upon their early termination following the default of its counterparty or other specified events.

Box 9-1. *Investability Indicators*

Market access
- Regulation of outflows
- Regulation of inflows
- Restrictions on money market
- Restrictions on bond market
- Restrictions on derivatives

Market taxation
- Turnover taxes
- Short-term taxes
- Effective capital gains tax rate
- Income withholding taxes
- Double taxation treaties

Market efficiency and regulation
- Primary market and issuance cost
- Secondary market turnover volume, % free float
- Liquidity, bid-offer spreads
- Legal enforceability of contracts
- Effective market oversight

Market infrastructure and investor base
- Settlement system and failure rate
- Trading system capacity and costs
- Cost for custodian services
- Exchange-traded fixed-income funds
- Size of domestic institutional investors

Market size and instruments
- Average duration of domestic debt
- Share of fixed-rate debt issuance
- Share of corporate debt issuance
- Size of hedging instruments (OTC, ETD)
- Volume of long-term FX derivatives

Source: International Finance Corporation (2009).

GBI-EM index family, the iBoxx Pan Asia Index, Citibank World Government Bond Index, and others like the Bank of America–Merrill Lynch Global Government Index. The availability of indexes can be an important contributing factor to the potential deepening of local markets, since asset allocations by institutional investors are often driven by investable benchmarks. Higher investability scores—that combine measures of market access, market taxation, market efficiency and regulation, market infrastructure and investor base, and market size and instruments—generally foster the participation of institutional investors (box 9-1). Indeed, investments benchmarked to local market indexes have increased during the past decade but remain insignificant relative to the size of the markets. Indexes encourage the participation of professional asset managers, as their performance is gauged against such benchmarks, especially by institutions such as pension and mutual funds.[33] By promoting broader participation, indexes can red ıce market segmentation of the investor base.[34] However, local bond market indexes such as GBI-EM are difficult to replicate by most fund managers in a cost-effective way. Large investment banks can more easily reproduce them in-house by, for example, using their local subsidiaries in emerging markets to hold domestic bonds that are not available to foreign investors.[35]

Liquidity in secondary markets is hampered by the lack of depth in the repo market. By providing a funding source for investments in government and corporate bonds and for financing dealer inventories of securities held for trading, repo markets enhance market liquidity. Repos and securities borrowing and lending in many Asian emerging markets are still heavily restricted or simply not available, and this reduces two-way trading in both equity and local bond markets. For example, China prohibits the lending of equities and allows only domestic institutional investors to participate in the repo market. Even in relatively developed markets such as Korea, further simplification of foreign exchange rules is needed to allow foreign investors to finance the holding of government bonds using cross-border repurchases. Singapore has developed a repo market, but liquidity in the term repo market could be enhanced. The easing of rules and regulations on securities lending by asset managers in Asian emerging markets will have to be carried out in tandem with improved risk management practices and appropriate custodial arrangements for collateral.

Derivatives markets in emerging Asia are largely underdeveloped because they face some of the more generic impediments, such as transaction taxes, lack of liquidity in cash bond markets, and weak operational infrastructure. Most derivatives in Asia are transacted in the over-the-counter market (figure 9-12). Interest rate swap markets in India, Korea, Malaysia, and Singapore are relatively more developed. The development of onshore foreign exchange swap markets in some Asian countries has been limited by capital controls and restrictions on nonresidents. While foreign exchange swap activity is quite substantial in Hong Kong, China and Singapore, it remains very low in other countries (table 9-2).

Forward market activity is generally not well developed, either. Restrictions on obtaining local currency by foreign investors have led to the development of sizable and liquid nondeliverable forward markets, notably for China, India, and Korea. On the other hand, all foreign exchange transactions involving the Singapore dollar and the Hong Kong dollar take place in deliverable on-shore markets,

33. Benchmark indexes are more important for conventional collective investment vehicles that pursue relative performance strategies. In contrast, hedge fund–type vehicles that pursue absolute return strategies are less affected by the absence of benchmark indexes.

34. Glaessner (2008).

35. JP Morgan (2009).

Figure 9-12. *Turnover, Over-the-Counter Derivatives Markets, Selected Asian Countries, 1998–2010*[a]

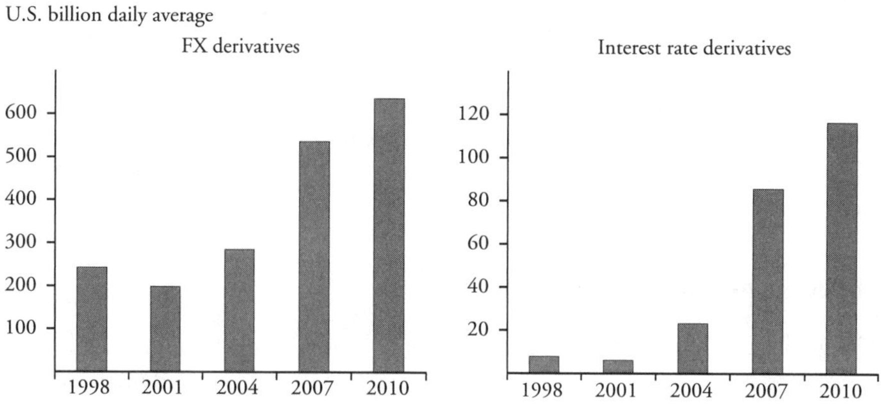

Source: Bank for International Settlements (2010).
a. Countries included are China; Hong Kong, China; India; Indonesia; Korea; Malaysia; Philippines; Singapore; Taipei,China; and Thailand.

as these countries do not have any restrictions. The derivatives markets outside Hong Kong, China and Singapore largely have a domestic focus and, with a few exceptions, are not as well developed. Exchange-traded interest rate futures are mainly in Hong Kong, China, Malaysia, Korea, and Singapore. The government bond futures market in Korea is one of the most liquid derivatives markets in Asia. Exchange-traded and over-the-counter derivative markets elsewhere in the region are relatively small and undeveloped.

With the exception of a few countries, asset-backed securitization in Asian markets has been subdued. This is mainly because the incentive to securitize is low in financial systems dominated by banks with ample liquidity. Furthermore, alternative savings vehicles are only gradually gaining traction. More recently, the global credit crisis has severely impaired confidence in asset-backed securities, as regulators, credit rating agencies, and markets reevaluate the whole process of securitization. The packaging of residential mortgages has yet to take off, although asset-backed securitization from auto loans and credit cards had increased somewhat before the subprime mortgage crisis. Korea saw the most rapid growth in asset-backed securitization, mainly from mortgage-backed securities. The expansion in Singapore and Hong Kong, China was also related mostly to residential housing and commercial property.

The hurdles faced in the securitization markets are linked to country-specific factors, such as poor legal frameworks, a small investor base, high costs, taxes, lack of transparency, and informational and reporting deficiencies regarding transactions. In the absence of comprehensive securitization laws, the regulatory responsibility for different aspects of the securitization chain is often spread across several agencies. Lack of data to calculate default histories and limited investor awareness and understanding of asset-backed securities are also important. For example, India has amended its Securities Contracts Regulation Act in 2007 to cover securitized instruments, but several impediments remain. In the absence of an amended securitization act, there are taxation and legal uncertainties with regard to the securitization vehicle. Also, the lack of an effective foreclosure law, stamp duties in some states, and the generally sparse understanding of the instrument among investors, originators, and even rating agencies inhibits the development of asset-backed securitization in India.

Policy Recommendations

The global credit crisis has underscored the need for Asian emerging markets to create deep local currency bond markets as part of a well-diversified financial system. Private and government bond markets are also required for the financing of huge infrastructure needs and will play a central role in expanding funding channels at a national and regional level, and creating derivatives markets for managing risk.[36] To accomplish this, Asian policymakers will have to address the lingering structural problems and reorient policies to facilitate capital market development and reform.

The dominance of bank-based intermediation can be reduced by strengthening confidence in the regulatory, supervisory, and enforcement frameworks for capital markets and nonbank financial institutions. As the recent crisis has shown, for capital markets to function effectively it is critical that sufficient information is available to assess credit risks adequately. A credible rating system, appropriate reporting requirements, and adoption of international accounting standards will help foster market discipline. The overseeing of nonbank financial institutions may have to be rationalized and consolidated to improve effectiveness and reduce the scope for regulatory arbitrage. Countries will have to build the capacity of their agencies to design and implement the rules and engage in greater cross-border cooperation with counterparts in the region. For example, Korea has adopted a new framework for the financial investment industry that consolidates the oversight of all capital market–related institutions.[37] The new framework has taken a functional approach to regulation in which financial functions are subject to the same regulation, regardless of the type of financial institution that performs them.

A reliable benchmark yield curve is critical for developing a liquid corporate bond market. The government securities market can provide such a yardstick for

36. Sheng (2010).

37. In 2007 Korea passed the Financial Investment Services and Capital Market (Consolidation) Act. The new act became effective on February 4, 2009.

pricing various debt instruments, including corporate bonds. Even governments that do not have financing requirements often build a benchmark yield curve to facilitate price discovery in private debt markets. For example, Singapore, despite generally running a budget surplus, issues government securities to foster the development of a liquid benchmark yield curve. To this end, Singapore lengthened government securities maturities to fifteen years and, more recently, to twenty years. While Singapore-dollar corporate bonds tend to be priced off the swap offer rate, the introduction of government securities has encouraged the development of swaps for longer dated maturities, extending up to thirty years. This has stimulated greater issuance of long-term bonds.

A well-diversified domestic and foreign institutional investor base (pension, insurance, mutual, and hedge funds) can shift financial intermediation from banks to capital markets by increasing the demand for long-term financial assets. Large portfolio holdings of government bonds expose banks to interest rate volatility, and longer-term lending for infrastructure aggravates their maturity mismatches. This calls for greater diversification of income sources of banks (such as fee-based income) coupled with more prudent credit risk assessment. A broad domestic investor base, besides adding to the liquidity and depth of local bond markets, may also serve as an investor of last resort in the case of a turnaround in global risk appetite.

Revamping investment regulation and liberalizing asset allocation restrictions on domestic institutional investors could be crucial for capital market development. In particular, the range of eligible local instruments should be widened and the limits on foreign asset holdings loosened. For example, the relatively long maturity of Korean corporate bonds is largely due to significant holdings (about 30 percent of corporate bonds outstanding) by domestic pension funds and insurance companies. Reforms need to be undertaken in tandem with strengthening governance structures and risk management systems. For the mutual fund industry, regulators have to ensure that investor confidence is maintained through adequate regulation and enforcement, notably in securing the legal basis for the funds; in defining the role of the managers and the custodians of funds; in disclosing information to investors; and in ensuring transparency in issuance, asset valuation and pricing, and redemption rules of the fund.

Foreign investor participation can benefit the development of local bond markets, especially after the market reaches a certain size. The attractiveness of emerging local bond markets can be enhanced by lowering the cost of access and addressing issues related to taxation and capital controls. Such reforms may help draw more stable foreign institutional investors that have a longer term horizon and are generally not leveraged. The removal of obstacles may also increase foreign participation by increasing the probability of being included in investability indexes. For example, in financial hubs like Hong Kong, China and Singapore, foreign investor access to local currency bonds and the availability of local repo funding has enhanced the liquidity and functioning of these markets.

Foreign investors also pay increasing attention to corporate governance practices. The five key areas of corporate governance as identified by the Institute of International Finance are

—Minority shareholder protection

—The structure and responsibilities of the board of directors

—Accounting and auditing

—Transparency of ownership and control

—A regulatory environment that creates a credible foundation for corporate transparency, good accounting practices, and protection of shareholder rights.

A pivotal factor for the growth of Asian corporate bond markets is likely to be the lowering of costs and the ease with which borrowers can tap the markets. For example, in Singapore, prospective issuers face almost no legal, regulatory, or tax impediments. Disclosure documents are quite simple and tend to be streamlined, and bond terms are relatively standardized and are broadly in accordance with International Capital Market Association guidelines. Many foreign banks and insurance companies, and other offshore issuers with high credit ratings or strong name recognition, have issued medium-term notes and long-term debt instruments.

Pricing transparency and improvements in trading mechanisms and custody and settlement systems can play an important role both in enhancing liquidity and efficiency, while reducing trading costs and volatility. In Hong Kong, China, one of the most liquid Asian bond markets, the Hong Kong Monetary Authority launched the Central Money Markets Unit Bond Price Bulletin website in January 2006, providing retail investors with convenient online access to indicative bond prices quoted by major banks. India now requires all debt trades, including private placements, to be reported on a standardized platform. More countries in Asia could also adopt the practice of allowing local currency debt to be traded through international clearing and settlement systems, such as Euroclear and Clearstream. In Asia, market makers consider that enhancing the diversity of the investor base is the single most important factor for increasing liquidity. The other factors they mention are availability of hedging products, functioning repo markets, price transparency, tax incentives, and efficient clearing and settlement systems. Active liability management by corporations and financial institutions would also go a long way in supporting liquidity in the markets.

Skillful sovereign debt management could consolidate issuance along chosen segments of the government yield curve to enhance liquidity and develop a benchmark curve for longer tenors. Price discovery and liquidity in government bond markets can be improved by timely and regular provision of information and by reopening of longer dated government benchmark issues.[38] In certain cases, developing the interest rate swap market (for example, Singapore) could provide a suitable pricing benchmark for corporate sector issuance. The ability of market participants to take advantage of arbitrage opportunities would also help establish proper linkages between cash, money, and capital markets.

As in more developed local markets a comprehensive package of reforms dealing with market micro-structure can significantly enhance secondary-market liquidity in government bond markets.[39] These measures include auction schedules, bond reopening schemes, new regulations on repurchase and securities lending markets, strips programs for government securities, exchange programs for redeeming high-interest, floating-rate bonds for newly issued fixed-rate bonds, and buyback programs for government securities.[40]

The development of local bond market indexes can facilitate trading of local currency bonds and allow investors to track performance. This is likely to attract asset managers that pursue active trading strategies and, perhaps, to lead to increased participation by a more diverse array of investors, including institutional and foreign investors. Indexes also offer incentives for emerging markets to further reduce impediments so that they are included in an index. For instance, the JP Morgan GBI-EM (Narrow) index limits inclusion to countries that are readily accessible and have few regulatory and tax impediments for foreign investors.

The markets for simple derivatives can be developed in parallel with the underlying cash bond markets. Derivatives markets rely on the existence of underlying assets, so it is reasonable to initiate development after the markets for the underlying cash securities exist and are reasonably liquid. However, waiting until the markets for the underlying assets are fully developed may not be optimal. In the largely over-the-counter derivatives markets in Asia, participants bear high counterparty risks and bilateral clearing costs. Besides, these markets are more difficult to monitor and regulate. Following the example of Brazil and the regional financial centers (Hong Kong, China and Singapore) that have exchanges for interest rate futures, the larger Asian countries should develop exchange-based trading of foreign exchange and interest rate derivative products.[41] This not only would facilitate liquidity and price discovery but also would lead to more efficient netting and

38. Withholding tax rates for foreign institutional investors are typically in the 10–20 percent range for most Asian emerging markets, but tax treaties generally bring the rates down to about 5–15 percent. Often, market participants find even a 10 percent withholding tax large enough to substantially reduce profits, since the tax is imposed on gross financial income (before subtracting the cost of funds). Therefore, foreign institutional investors that do not have a permanent domestic presence are burdened with taxes on gross income as opposed to the taxes on corporate profits paid by local competitors.

39. Mexico is a recent example of a country that adopted such reforms.

40. OECD—World Bank—IMF Global Bond Market Forum (2008).

41. BM&F Bovespa in Brazil trades futures and options on foreign exchange, interest rates, stock indexes, and commodities. The interdealer derivatives market in Brazil occurs through this exchange.

use of collateral, increased transparency, better market surveillance, and lower counterparty risks.

Lessons can be drawn from the more developed markets of Hong Kong, China and Singapore, where the swap markets for foreign currencies, in particular, are both broad based and liquid. Fostering a liquid swap market in Singapore entailed permitting offshore banks to engage in local currency swap activities, the phasing out of statutory liquidity requirements on swap transactions of banks with non-bank financial intermediaries, and allowing securities dealers with adequate risk management systems to play a more active role. The presence of sophisticated corporate treasuries also provided impetus for the development of local swap markets as they actively managed their risk in the domestic markets (such as hedging interest rate risk through the interest rate swap market).

There is considerable potential for developing both the covered bonds and asset-backed securitization markets in Asia. In the aftermath of the global financial crisis in which asset-backed securitization and structured finance played a major role, development is likely to hinge on rebuilding investor confidence and on the presence of appropriate regulations concerning transparency, disclosure, role of rating agencies, and the proper alignment of incentives. Because of fewer legal and technical challenges compared to asset-backed securitization, covered bonds may be easier to introduce in bank-based financial systems. For covered bonds, the assets remain on the balance sheet of the banks (or other originator) and, unlike asset-backed securitization, do not have to be sold to a special-purpose vehicle. Since investors have full recourse to the banks that originate the pool of assets, such structures create incentives for the banks to maintain the quality of the underlying pool. That said, while covered bond instruments do not require the legal structures and support services that have to be created for asset-backed securities, specific rules to facilitate covered bond issuance will have to be promulgated in Asia's emerging markets. So far, the issuance of covered bonds in Asia has been sparse except for a few issues in Korea.

Securitization in Asia is likely to be eventually driven by the desire to enhance liquidity in the banking system, as disintermediation gathers pace, and to meet the funding needs of the real economy (rather than balance-sheet arbitrage).[42] As domestic demand becomes the main engine of growth in Asia's emerging markets and capital market development proceeds, illiquid assets like mortgage and consumer loans could be securitized. This can address the size issue confronting private bond markets while providing institutional investors with a more diverse set of instruments as new assets are created from infrastructure investments, commercial real estate, housing, and household consumption.

The U.S. subprime crisis has exposed the dangers associated with securitization. By learning from this event, Asian countries can adopt a simpler and more

42. Arner, Lejot, and Schou-Zibell (2008).

robust securitization system. To foster this, market participants, regulators, and other stakeholders will have to build supporting institutions and capabilities to ensure strong prudential norms for origination, capital adequacy, liquidity, valuation, and special-purpose vehicles. Therefore, comprehensive securitization laws, lower tax and registration impediments for securitized transactions, investor education on securitization, and stronger foreclosure norms (especially on mortgages) could help provide the foundation for an asset-backed securitization market. For example, Korea, where securitization has had a reasonable degree of success, introduced new laws after the Asian financial crisis, which introduced the legal framework for creating special-purpose vehicles and facilitated the "true sale" of assets to bankruptcy-remote entities. Countries like the Philippines, Taipei,China, and Thailand have either enacted new legislation for securitization or are close to passing the laws.

Last but not least, data collection and reporting systems not only for borrowers but also for investor holdings should be improved. Databases should provide information on primary- and secondary-market size, maturity structure, and liquidity. Creation of a centralized database on all corporate bonds issued and outstanding would significantly increase the flow of information. Adoption of the methodological standards suggested in the *Handbook on Securities Statistics* (prepared jointly by the Bank for International Settlements, the European Central Bank, and the International Monetary Fund) would go a long way toward advancing domestic market surveillance and contributing to the harmonization and development of regional platforms.[43]

Concluding Remarks

The key challenge in Asia is to generate financial assets in line with its economic growth that can provide the underlying collateral for expanding fixed-income markets and hence domestic investment opportunities. Shortage of good quality financial assets can lead to speculative valuations in emerging markets and contribute to global imbalances.[44] A significant proportion of Asian corporations have credit ratings below investment grade. Besides inhibiting issuance, the low ratings also preclude certain investors from having these assets in their portfolios. However, with growth in residential mortgages and other household debt instruments, the region has the potential to substantially broaden and deepen the collateral pool available for underpinning regional and local fixed-income markets.

The issue of critical size could be addressed through an integrated regional market for local currency bonds that provides greater scale, efficiency, and access. Regional cooperation through ASEAN+3, the Asian Bond Market Initiative

43. Deutsche Bundesbank/IMF/World Bank (2009).
44. Caballero (2006).

(AMBI), and Asian Bond Funds (ABFs) could be used to catalyze improvements in bond markets and increase financial market integration.[45] Though difficult, especially given the heterogeneity of issuance jurisdictions, Asian emerging markets have to work further toward harmonizing market infrastructure, notably in trading and clearing platforms, in custody arrangements, as well as in standardizing valuation rules. To this end, countries should continue to raise domestic standards in line with international best practice. Furthermore, incentives at the firm level must also be examined to assess why bond finance is not yet an attractive option in many countries. Much of it could be due to inertia stemming from a historical dependence on bank finance, high costs of bond issuance, and lack of familiarity with the processes and risks involved in tapping markets.

Emerging Asia also needs to foster a credit culture to further deepen its local debt markets. For now, the equity culture—combined with the comfortable liquidity position of banks and corporations—may be a hurdle for the further expansion of local bond markets. However, in some countries (such as China and India) there are signs that economic growth is catalyzing a paradigmatic shift toward broader capital market development, as the demand for corporate credit rises. Moreover, the fact that Asian corporations, which have historically been reliant on bank financing, were able to turn to local corporate bond markets when banks reduced lending during the global crisis, augurs well for market development.[46] While it is difficult to define what constitutes a critical market size in terms of debt volume and number of issuers, the expansion in local debt markets in Asia could be very rapid given the region's expected growth trajectory.

References

Arner, Douglas, Paul Lejot, and Lotte Schou-Zibell. 2008. "Securitization in East Asia." Working Paper 12. Tokyo: Asian Development Bank.

APEC (Asia-Pacific Economic Cooperation). 2008. Public-Private Sector Forum on Bond Market Development. Cusco, July.

ASIFMA (Asia Securities Industry & Financial Markets Association). 2010. "Asia Securities Industry & Financial Markets Association."

Asian Development Bank. 2010a. *Asia Bond Monitor.* March.

———. 2010b. *Asia Bond Monitor.* Summer.

———. 2010c. "Appendix III: Market Assessments." In *ABMI Group of Experts Report: Barriers to Cross-Border Investment and Settlement in ASEAN+3 Bond Markets.* Tokyo.

Bank for International Settlements. 2010. *Triennial Survey 2.* Basel.

———. Various years. *World Economic Outlook.* Basel.

Burger, John D., and Francis E. Warnock. 2006. "Local Currency Bond Markets." *Staff Papers* 53: 133–46. Washington: International Monetary Fund.

Caballero, Ricardo J. 2006. "On the Macroeconomics of Asset Shortages." Working Paper 06-30. Department of Economics, Massachusetts Institute of Technology.

45. Kawai (2007).
46. International Monetary Fund (2010).

Chami, Ralph, Connel Fullenkamp, and Sunil Sharma. 2010. "A Framework for Financial Market Development." *Journal of Economic Policy Reform* 13, no. 2: 107–35.

Cheung, Stephen Y. L., and Hasung Jang. 2006. "Scoreboard on Corporate Governance in East Asia." Working Paper 13. Waterloo: Center for International Governance Innovation.

CGFS (Committee on the Global Financial System). 2007a. "Institutional Investors, Global Savings and Asset Allocation." Paper 27 (www.bis.org/publ/cgfs27.pdf).

———. 2007b. "Financial Stability and Local Currency Bond Markets." Paper 28 (www.bis.org/publ/cgfs28.htm).

———. 2009. "Capital Flows and Emerging Market Economies." Paper 33 (www.bis.org/publ/cgfs33.htm).

Deutsche Bundesbank, International Monetary Fund, and World Bank. 2009. "Progress Report: Implementation of the G-8 Action Plan on Developing Local Bond Markets in Emerging Market Economies and Developing Countries" (http://www.bundesbank.de/download/vfz/konferenzen/20080922_frankfurt/report.pdf).

Eichengreen, Barry, and Pipat Luengnaruemitchai. 2004. "Why Doesn't Asia Have Bigger Bond Markets?" Working Paper 10576. Cambridge, Mass.: National Bureau of Economic Research.

Eichengreen, Barry, Eduardo Borensztein, and Ugo Panizza. 2006. "A Tale of Two Markets: Bond Market Development in East Asia and Latin America." Occasional Paper 3. Hong Kong Institute for Monetary Research.

EMEAP (Executives' Meeting of East Asia–Pacific Central Banks). 2005. "The Asian Bond Fund 2 has Moved into Implementation Phase."

Ghosh, Swati. 2006. *East Asian Finance: The Road to Robust Markets.* Washington: World Bank.

Glaessner, Tom. 2008. "Citi Indexes for EME Debt Markets: WGBI." Paper prepared for meeting, Strengthening Capital Markets in Emerging Market Countries, Bretton Woods Committee and Fletcher School Center for Emerging Market Enterprises. Washington, January.

Goldman Sachs. 2010. "EM Equity in Two Decades: A Changing Landscape." Global Economics Paper 204. New York.

Gyntelberg, Jacob. 2007. "Developing Asia Pacific Nongovernment Fixed Income Markets." *SBP Research Bulletin* 3, no. 1: 7–26.

Gyntelberg, Jacob, Guonan Ma, and Eli M Remolona. 2006. "Developing Corporate Bond Markets in Asia." Paper 26. Basel: Bank for International Settlements (www.bis.org/publ/bppdf/bispap26.pdf).

International Finance Corporation. 2009. "GEMLOC Investability Indicators Scoring–Phase 2 Extension." Second quarterly update (November).

International Monetary Fund. 2010. *Global Financial Stability Report.* Washington.

Jiang, Guorong, Nancy Tang, and Eve Law. 2002. "The Costs and Benefits of Developing Debt Markets: Hong Kong's Experience." Paper 11. Basel: Bank for International Settlements.

JP Morgan. 2009. "Emerging Markets: Local Markets Overview." New York.

Kawai, Masahiro. 2007. "Bond Markets Development in Emerging East Asia." Paper prepared for High-Level Workshop on Developing Bond Markets in Emerging Markets. Federal Ministry of Finance and Deutsche Bundesbank. Frankfurt,Germany, May.

Ma, Guonan, and Eli M. Remolona. 2005. "Opening Markets through a Regional Bond Fund: Lessons from ABF2." *BIS Quarterly Review* (June).

Mieno, Fumiharu, and others. 2009. "Developing Bond Markets in Asia." Study Group on the Asian Financial System Center for Monetary Cooperation in Asia, Bank of Japan.

Mizen, Paul, and Serafeim Tsoukas. 2010. "What Effect Has Bond Market Development in Emerging Asia Had on the Issuance of Corporate Bonds?" Working Paper 18. Hong Kong Institute of Monetary Research.

Monetary Authority of Singapore. 2010. "2009 Singapore Asset Management Industry Survey" (www.mas.gov.sg/resource/eco_research/surveys/AssetMgmt09.pdf).

OECD—World Bank Group—IMF Global Bond Market Forum. 2008. *Secondary Market Liquidity in Domestic Debt Markets.* Washington.

Parreñas, Julius Caesar, and Kenneth Waller. 2006. "Developing Bond Markets in APEC: Moving forward through Public-Private Sector Partnership." *ABA Journal* 21, no. 2.

Securities and Futures Commission. 2010. "Fund Management Activities Survey, 2009." Hong Kong, China (www.sfc.hk.sfc.doc/EN/speeches/public/surveys/10/fmas_201007.pdf).

Sheng, Andrew. 2010. "The Regulatory Reform of Global Financial Markets: An Asian Regulator's Perspective." *Global Policy* 1, no. 2.

Turner, Philip. 2007. "Local Currency Bond Markets in Emerging Market Economies: Notes on Trends, Measurement, and Policy Challenges." Paper prepared for G-7 workshop, Developing Bond Markets in Emerging Market Economies. Frankfurt, Germany, May.

———. 2008. "The Investor Base and the Liquidity of EME Local Bond Markets: Leverage and Diversification." Paper prepared for the Tenth Annual OECD-WBG-IMF Global Bond Market Forum. Washington, April.

———. 2009. "How Have Local Currency Bond Markets in EMEs Weathered the Financial Crisis?" Paper prepared for the Second International Workshop on Implementing the G-8 Action Plan. Frankfurt, November.

World Bank. Various years. "Doing Business Indicators" (www.doingbusiness.org/rankings).

10

Indian Financial Market Development and Regulation: What Worked and Why?

JAYANTH R. VARMA

In this chapter I look at the regulation and development of financial markets in India over the last two decades and attempt to identify the strategies and approaches that have worked, contrasting them to those strategies and approaches that have not worked. I hope that the lessons from the Indian experience will be of relevance to other emerging markets, particularly in Asia.

Technology, Competition, and Regulatory Reform

The success stories in Indian financial market development are characterized by regulatory reform, which unleashed competition and actively pushed rapid adoption of new technology. This description shares some similarities with Edward Kane's model of how technology, regulation, and competition interact in determining the evolution of the financial sector.[1]

At one level it is possible to argue that the true benefits flowed from the adoption of disruptive technology rather than from the farsightedness of the regulator. Regulators who claim exclusive credit for themselves are a little like the traffic policeman who claims credit for the dramatic improvement in the quality of the cars that drive past him. Having said that, I think regulators do deserve part of the credit. First, they deserve credit for not allowing antiquated rules and regulations to stand in the way of new technology. Second, they deserve credit for creating a

1. Kane (1984).

competitive landscape in which new technology is adopted even by firms that otherwise might not but are aware of the risk of being left behind by more nimble competitors. Third, they can legitimately claim some credit for providing a regulatory push toward the adoption of the new technology.

Technology as the Enabler of Change

Finance, more than most other industries, has benefited from information and communications technology. The raw material of finance consists less of tangible goods and more of money and information, which are readily digitized. Information technology is particularly powerful in fast-growing, emerging markets because it converts variable costs into fixed costs and therefore produces large-scale economies. Paper processing usually has low fixed costs and high variable costs, while electronic processing typically has high fixed costs (for the computing and communications infrastructure) but near-zero variable costs. Many of the success stories in Indian equity markets are associated with major shifts toward electronic processing.

ELECTRONIC EXCHANGES. Electronic trading based on an electronic limit order book was introduced by the newly set up National Stock Exchange (NSE) in 1994 and was quickly copied by the other Indian exchanges. The capital market was previously confined to Mumbai (where the largest incumbent stock exchange, the Bombay Stock Exchange [BSE], was located) and to a few other centers, where smaller exchanges provided only low-quality execution. Within a few years, this situation gave way to a national market based on satellite communications, which abolished geographical barriers. Among the benefits were superior liquidity, greater transparency, and lower costs.

Several aspects of this transformation are interesting from a reformer's point of view. First, while the incumbent stock exchange, the BSE, had been discussing computerization for a long time, it had made no progress at all until the NSE commenced operations and started taking market share away from the BSE. The BSE very quickly adopted the electronic limit order book, halting the loss of market share. This highlights the importance of competition in the adoption of technology. Automated trading itself was nothing new: the Toronto Stock Exchange had introduced an automated system called CATS (computer-assisted trading system) way back in 1977. Fifteen years after that, the incumbent exchange in India had not made any steps to even experiment with this. NSE's use of satellite-based communications to create a national market was a major innovation in the context of the underdeveloped telecommunications infrastructure in the country at the time, but the speed with which the BSE copied this shows that this too was not technologically overly complex.

The major obstacles in the adoption of electronic trading were not technological but were embedded in regulation and in the industrial organization of incumbent exchanges. First, from a private-ordering perspective, it is important to note that the NSE was created by a government institution, with strong support and backing from the ministry of finance and from the regulators. In fact in its initial years the NSE was disparagingly referred to as the *sarkari* exchange, from the Hindi word *sarkar,* which means government.

Second, while technology was enabled by competition in the exchange space, it was in turn a huge enabler of competition in the stockbroking space. Stockbroking firms anywhere in the country could now compete on equal terms with the established brokers in Mumbai. Some of these upstart firms went on to build a national network of branches and become leading players in retail broking.

Third, electronic trading was a huge boon to the regulator. For years, the regulator had been trying to solve issues of price and time transparency in the stock market through regulatory fiat, with great acrimony but little success. These problems were solved almost effortlessly by the new technology, but the regulator had never thought of this technology as a solution to its regulatory problems and had not pushed for it hard enough.

DEPOSITORIES. The settlement of securities became electronic in the late 1990s. Compulsory dematerialization (conversion of physical share certificates into electronic book entries) was introduced for deliveries in the stock market for institutional investors in 1998 and for retail investors in 1999. Today, practically all of the securities settlement in the stock exchanges is in dematerialized form. The benefits have been in the form of faster settlement, lower costs, and the elimination of forged and fake shares.

Before 1998 Indian stock market trading involved a vast movement and processing of paper certificates, because shares were rarely held in a street name. For many other large countries, dematerialization of stocks was not as high a priority as it was for India, because these countries had effectively immobilized most of the share certificates in the hands of brokers and other custodians. While physical share certificates existed in these countries, much of the transfers happened as entries in the books of these brokers and custodians without any need for paper to change hands.

Academic writers have argued for dematerialization since the early 1990s, but regulators did not push for it with as much urgency as the situation warranted. Regulators and market participants alike worried about the difficulties of dematerializing share certificates in a vast country with millions of retail investors. In retrospect, they overestimated the difficulties involved. Regulators and market participants also underestimated the extent to which dematerialization (or at least its poorer cousin, immobilization) was a prerequisite for many other stock market reforms, including shorter settlement cycles and the elimination of quasi-derivative products.

The Depositories Act clearly envisaged a competitive industry structure and therefore provided for a regulatory regime in which the depository was not subjected to price regulation or minimum performance standards. A second depository did indeed come into existence, and for a couple of years it waged a price war with the incumbent. This price war was important in keeping the costs low. While the incumbent successfully defended its near-monopoly position, the market has perhaps remained sufficiently contestable to impose price discipline.

Competition between depository participants was also important in making the move to dematerialization feasible. Among all the affected parties, the retail investor saw the least benefits from dematerialization and encountered the most visible costs. For issuer companies and for large investors, dematerialization produced large cost savings due to the elimination of paper processing whenever shares were transferred. For many retail investors on the other hand, the fixed costs of a dematerialized securities account could have outweighed the savings in variable costs of paper processing during securities transactions. Without a significant reduction in costs made possible by competition, it would have been difficult for regulators to mandate compulsory dematerialization of securities. Regulators did try to make the transition to dematerialization a voluntary process. Unfortunately, the network externalities of trading in one format versus another proved too strong, and regulators had to impose the transition by fiat.

Once again we see the benefits of technology being contingent on both competition and regulatory initiative and the failure of private ordering to accomplish the superior market design.

INTERNET TRADING. The modest success of Internet trading and the dismal lack of adoption of mobile trading in India is another example of the importance of regulatory initiative. India is a country where mobile phones have become ubiquitous, while the penetration of computers with Internet connectivity remains very low. The poor uptake of mobile trading is in my view largely due to a premature freezing of regulatory standards on a technology platform that became obsolete. At the time when the regulations for mobile trading were framed, WAP (wireless application protocol) appeared to be the technology standard of choice, but this technology platform did not live up to expectations, and the regulatory standard failed to evolve in line with the changing technological landscape.

PAYMENT SYSTEMS. India granted entry to a very small number of new private banks in the 1990s. The policy of branch licensing was retained: every new bank branch required the approval of the central bank. The new private banks were thus forced to compete against the incumbents with their hands tied behind their back. Fortunately, however, while the central bank regarded an ATM as a branch for some purposes, it largely exempted ATMs from the licensing requirement. A bank could thus set up ATMs pretty much as it liked. Though this was not the regulatory intent, the effect of the regulatory regime was strongly antibranch and pro-ATM, at least for the new private banks.

I believe that the rapid spread of ATMs in India during the 2000s was due to this wonderful convergence of technological opportunity, competitive dynamics, and a distorted regulatory regime. In retrospect, it is clear that the new generation of customers prefers ATMs to branches, but this was by no means obvious a decade ago. The regulatory regime meant that the banks did not have to consciously bet on this—the central bank made life easier for the new banks by not letting them bet on the alternative.

The emergence of national level electronic payment systems—the real-time gross settlement (RTGS) system for high-value payments and the national electronics funds transfer (NEFT) system for retail payments (systems set up and operated by the central bank)—appears to be a counterexample to my thesis about the importance of competition. But the contradiction disappears on closer examination. First, these systems were long delayed, and their adoption has been slow. One need only compare the adoption of NEFT for third-party payments with the adoption of ATMs for cash withdrawals and EDC (electronic data capture) machines for card payments to see the difference. It is quite likely that third-party payment services that rely on connecting to the Internet banking platform of individual banks have greater adoption rates than NEFT itself.

RTGS and NEFT were not designed to become disruptive technologies that permit new business models. Moreover, the lack of clarity on pricing these services (after the initial period, when it is free) also impedes the building of long-term business models on this platform.

COUNTEREXAMPLES. I do not want to give the impression that India has always got it right when it comes to the use of technology. First, even in its success stories India often embraced technology too slowly and sometimes only after everything else had been tried and had failed. It had the second-mover advantage of observing what had or had not worked elsewhere in the world and simply adopting a proven architecture.

Second, there are some areas where India has failed to leverage technology to its full potential. A very good example is in the area of corporate disclosure. The U.S. Securities and Exchange Commission (SEC) demonstrates the potential for the use of technology in this area with its EDGAR system, particularly after it shifted to the XBRL format. India does not have the equivalent of the legacy EDGAR, let alone the new XBRL-enabled EDGAR. Indian companies are required to file quarterly financial statements as well as material event disclosures with the stock exchanges on which they are listed. However, neither the exchanges nor the regulators have made any attempt to make these filings easily accessible, searchable, and analyzable in the way EDGAR has in the United States.

Competition and Market Development

Areas in which the key driver of market development was not technology but competition include exchanges and brokers and mutual funds.

EXCHANGES AND BROKERS. I touched earlier upon the role of the NSE in transforming Indian stock markets and creating a national market. The NSE was also instrumental in laying the groundwork for introducing derivatives and a number of new instruments into the market. Later, the NSE was the incumbent exchange moving toward becoming a monopoly. I worried about the implications of this development.[2] Fortunately, however, it appears that, in emerging markets like India, the exchange business remains a contestable market long after it has ceased to be competitive. The threat of new entrants and the threatened revitalization of older players help keep the incumbent on its toes. There has been no move toward monopoly prices, and there have been no signs of innovation being stifled by lack of competition.

The impact of competition has been clearly evident in the broking industry also. As India opened up its markets to foreign investors in the early 1990s a number of foreign brokers followed them into India to serve their foreign clients. Some of them established joint ventures with Indian players, while others set up shop on their own after India permitted 100 percent foreign ownership of broking firms. Indian firms also set up institutional brokerages offering research and other services to institutional investors.

Meanwhile a number of new broking firms came into existence to serve Indian retail customers as well. Some used Internet trading platforms to offer low brokerage costs. Others set up large branch networks to provide full-service brokerage. As a result, retail customers have benefited from lower costs and higher quality of broking services.

MUTUAL FUNDS. In the late 1980s the mutual fund industry (which until then consisted of only the public sector Unit Trust of India) was thrown open to public sector banks and financial institutions. In the mid-1990s private sector mutual funds were permitted. A few foreign players also entered the market. Private sector funds have rapidly gained market share at the expense of the mutual funds owned by public sector banks and financial institutions.

The mutual fund industry has been highly competitive and there has been a significant amount of product innovation. Indexed funds, exchange traded funds, funds targeting specific sectors, and debt funds with tightly specified maturity bands and credit quality have emerged. Process innovations like systematic investment plans have also made mutual funds more investor friendly. However, a misguided taxation regime has made mutual funds an attractive tax arbitrage vehicle for corporate investors and has pushed the evolution of the industry in a direction different from its primary economic function of providing a diversification vehicle for retail investors.

BANKING AS A PARTIAL COUNTEREXAMPLE. Banking provides an interesting counterexample, because the government responded to the banking crisis of 1991 with an anticompetitive regulatory regime partly designed to help banks

2. Varma (2001).

rebuild their capital. At the beginning of the reform process, the banking system probably had a negative net worth when all financial assets and liabilities were restated at fair market values.[3] This unhappy state of affairs had been brought about partly by imprudent lending and partly by adverse interest rate movements. The problem was however hidden from the general public because accounting policies not only allowed the banks to avoid making provisions for bad loans but also permitted them to recognize as income the overdue interest on these loans.

During the first decade of reforms, the threat of insolvency that loomed large in the early 1990s was by and large corrected by government recapitalization, by plowback of (preprovision) operating profits, and by fresh equity raised from capital markets. Some public sector banks also moved aggressively to cut costs by trimming the workforce and by divesting peripheral business units that had not been doing well. It is noteworthy that direct government support to the banking system was only a small part of this total package of rebuilding the capital of the banking system. The fiscal cost of the 1991 banking crisis was only about 2 percent of GDP, which is much smaller than the typical fiscal cost of such crises in developed or emerging markets.[4]

Faced with a financially weak banking system, policymakers chose to provide a cozy regulatory regime in which the dominant oligopolistic banks were insulated from competition from new entrants as well as competition from nonbank sources of capital. This protected environment allowed even financially weak banks to survive and rebuild their capital. Thus the nature and pace of banking sector reforms were designed to reduce the ability of new banks to take market share away from the incumbents by aggressive competition. I mention in particular the niggardly rate at which new bank licenses were doled out, a licensing policy that effectively excluded most promoters with deep pockets, the extreme restrictions on branch expansion and rationalization, the ill-concealed regulatory hostility to innovation, and aggressive marketing. All this meant that the incumbent big banks faced very little threat from new entrants for several years.

At the same time, potential competition from outside the banking system was systematically destroyed in several ways:

—The development financial institutions that were financially very sound at the beginning of the reform process were not allowed to transform themselves into universal banks until their financial strength had been substantially eroded.

—The nonbank finance companies (NBFCs) that despite their higher cost of funds competed intensely with the banks on the basis of speed, flexibility, and innovation were systematically destroyed in the second half of the 1990s. In line with international practices, the NBFCs' access to retail funds was severely

3. Varma (1992).
4. Frydl (1999).

curtailed. At the same time, the regulatory regime did not allow the NBFCs to fund themselves effectively in the wholesale markets as they do globally.

—The very hesitant moves toward capital account convertibility meant that all through the 1990s and early 2000s the banks did not have to face serious cross-border competition. Moreover restrictions on foreign banks operating in India have made them less of a competitive threat than they might otherwise have been.

The net result of this regulatory regime was to make the banking system collusive rather than competitive. The cartelization of the banks under the auspices of the Indian Banks Association had the blessings of the central bank, which regarded this cartel as a kind of self-regulatory organization. The result was that for more than a decade Indian banking witnessed almost no progress at all in terms of the customer's banking experience. If we imagine a Rip Van Winkle going to sleep in 1991 and waking up in 2001, he would not have seen that much has changed at the grassroots level in the provision of banking services.[5] The most visible change would have been the much greater spread of credit cards, a financial innovation that the central bank probably did not regard as a threat to the profitability of public sector banks.

It was only by the mid-2000s that the Indian banking system began to become competitive. Around this time, private sector banks emerged, with a network of over a thousand branches and a balance sheet of over Rs 1 trillion, to challenge the public sector banks. Faced with this competitive threat, the best of the public sector banks also responded with innovative and aggressive strategies. A Rip Van Winkle going to sleep in 2001 and waking up in 2010 would have seen a very different banking system at the grassroots level.

The point is that for a decade India was denied the benefit of such a competitive and vibrant banking system by a misguided regulatory regime founded on the premise that insulating government banks from competition was cheaper than providing them with transparent fiscal support.

Deregulation and Market Development

The most dramatic financial sector reforms of the early 1990s were those that let the prices of financial assets be determined by the free play of market forces. This allowed financial markets to perform the important function of allocating resources efficiently to the most productive sectors of the economy. To the extent that this has happened in India, this must count as one of the most enduring and decisive successes of the financial reforms.

Yet these fundamental reforms led to rapid market development only when the competitive dynamics allowed the full potential of these reforms to be unleashed. The contrast between the equity and debt markets brings this out clearly.

5. Varma (2002).

EQUITY MARKETS: FREE PRICING AND DISCLOSURE-BASED REGULATION. The initial burst of economic reforms included a major reform in the capital market—the abolition of capital issues control and the introduction of the free pricing of equity issues in 1992. Simultaneously, a securities regulator was set up as the apex regulator of Indian capital markets. Initially, a few elements of merit-based regulation still survived in terms of track record requirements (entry norms) and an invidious distinction between premium and par issues. Over time, however, these have also been whittled down, and the capital market regulator has moved almost completely to a disclosure-based regime of regulation.

The introduction of the book-building route has led to greater efficiencies in the capital-raising process and has contributed to improved price discovery. At the same time vast improvements in the disclosure regime laid the foundation for a more transparent primary market. Simultaneously, the secondary market was also transformed by the emergence of electronic trading and settlement and the introduction of modern derivative instruments.

All of this made the equity market a vibrant engine of growth for the Indian economy. Indian equity markets had to compete against foreign markets both for the primary market and for the secondary market, as Indian companies listed abroad through American depositary receipts and global depositary receipts (ADRs and GDRs). Yet the onshore Indian market remained the principal market in terms of liquidity and price discovery.

DEBT MARKETS: DEREGULATION OF INTEREST RATES. The outcome in the Indian debt market presents a complete contrast, though the starting impetus of deregulation was similar. Perhaps the single most important element of the financial sector reforms was the deregulation of interest rates in the 1990s:

—Interest rates were freed on corporate bonds, on most types of bank lending, and on all bank term deposits.

—The introduction of auctions coupled with reduced preemption led to more market-determined interest rates for government securities.

—By the end of the 1990s, administered interest rates in the banking system were confined mainly to the rate on savings accounts and a few concessional lending rates. Interest rates on small savings instruments offered by the government were also administered and, in a sense, provided a floor for bank deposit rates.

Financial Repression and the Debt Markets

For all practical purposes, financial repression was eliminated in the first decade of reforms. This was a game-changing reform, because the extent of financial repression had been quite large. One crude measure of repression can be obtained by comparing the interbank call-market rate (which was more or less free-market determined even in the 1980s) with the short-term bank deposit rate. From 1981–82 to 1992–93, the call rate exceeded the one-year bank deposit rate in every single year with a median excess of 1.5 percent. From 1993–94 to 1999–2000, the situation was reversed: the bank deposit rate exceeded the call rate in five out of seven years, and the median excess of the deposit rate over the call rate was 1.6 percent.

This suggests that in the 1980s the bank deposit rate was repressed about 3 percent. Since the aggregate time deposits of the Indian banking system were a little less than 30 percent of GDP, this repression amounted to over 0.8 percent of GDP annually. This was eliminated in the initial years of the reform process.

However, this major deregulation did not lead to a vibrant debt market in India. In 1991 the government bond market was by most measures more liquid than the equity market, while today the roles are completely reversed. Superficially, the government bond market witnessed many of the same technological changes seen in the equities market. As a result of a scam in 1992 the Public Debt Office moved to dematerialize government securities, and the central bank created an electronic exchange for trading these securities. A clearing corporation was also established to provide netting and settlement guarantees.

The major difference was in the competitive structure of the market. While the reforms in the equity market broke the oligopoly of the traditional broking community and created a highly competitive securities trading industry, government securities trading was confined to a monopoly exchange—the negotiated dealing system (NDS)—and participation was more or less restricted to the banks.[6] Even the microstructure of the electronic trading platform (NDS) was designed to mimic that of the earlier over-the-counter market so that it would not set in motion any new competitive dynamics.

The weakness of government finances in India is actually the principal strength of the debt market in India—there is a large stock of government securities across the entire maturity spectrum, and there are a large number of potential investors in this market. India has not however succeeded in transforming this potential into a vibrant market. Technology and deregulation do not make a market, if the vital ingredient of competition is ruthlessly suppressed.

The corporate debt market is even more undeveloped; it is possible to argue that the Indian corporate debt market is largely outside India and not in India. The dollar-denominated debt of large Indian companies is actively traded outside India, and there are efficient and reasonably liquid primary and secondary markets for this debt. There is also an active market for credit default swaps on these companies. By contrast, both the primary and secondary markets for corporate bonds in India are undeveloped. Much of whatever little exists is a syndicated loan market masquerading as a private placement bond market.

A perverse and ill-thought-out exchange control regime has made it easier for foreigners to lend to Indian companies in dollars outside India than to lend to

6. Varma (2004).

them in rupees in India. This forces the Indian corporate sector to accept currency mismatches while tapping foreign bond markets. There is abundant evidence to indicate that, despite the "original sin" problem, there is a significant appetite among foreign investors for lending to the healthiest Indian companies in rupees. Regulations prevent this market from developing.

In the 1990s India actually had a retail corporate debt market in the form of company deposits. The government and the central bank quite rightly shut down this market, on the ground that deposit taking should be the exclusive province of banks and other similar regulated entities. However, this regulatory clampdown was carried out in a manner that did not allow the deposit market to be transformed into a proper bond market. In particular, many types of bonds were also classified as deposits and subject to the same clampdown.

A fundamental problem for the corporate debt market in India is that, since a well-functioning market effectively disintermediates the banks and reduces the profits, neither the banks nor their regulators have any interest in seeing such a market emerge. In macroeconomic terms, the deregulation of interest rates and the free pricing of equity shares are similar in terms of their potential to transform the respective financial markets. Yet the potential was realized in one market and not in the other, because the competitive dynamics and the regulatory climate were totally different. A vibrant equity market is a reminder of what could have been achieved in the debt market if the competitive landscape had not been so badly skewed. The poorly developed corporate debt market is a drag on India's economic growth.[7]

Creditor and Shareholder Rights

In this section I discuss the improvements in creditor and shareholder rights that have taken place in the last two decades. These are clearly positive developments, but the improvements are in my view too small in magnitude to be the principal driver of market development in India.

Disclosure

Since 1991, there have been significant developments in the disclosure requirements at the time of making a public issue of securities as well as in the continuing disclosure requirements for listed companies.

The requirement for a prospectus with well-defined disclosures was laid down in the Companies Act, 1956 (and even in earlier Companies Acts). The law also provided for civil and criminal liabilities for misstatements in the prospectus. However, these disclosures were primarily factual in nature and did not provide adequate information for investors to value companies accurately.

7. Oura (2008).

Disclosure requirements were increased dramatically after reforms began in 1991. The securities regulator required a lot of disclosures pertaining to risk factors, the business of the company, its management, and related-party transactions. This reflects partly the shift from merit-based regulation to disclosure-based regulation, discussed earlier. It also reflects the increasing sophistication of the market and the emergence of an analyst community that values such disclosures. Over a period of several years in the 1990s India moved from a system of annual accounts to a regime of rudimentary quarterly reporting. Quarterly reporting does not conform to the usual standards for interim financial reports in that it contains almost no balance sheet information and only condensed information on the income statement. The quarterly reporting requirement has however been the single biggest factor in reducing insider trading in India. In the earlier system, insiders knew far more about the current profitability of the company than investors who had access only to published financial information, which was often nearly a year old.

Disclosures have also been tightened on material event disclosure. This is still not as effective as it is in countries like the United States, but the gap has narrowed dramatically. A key element in the efficacy of financial disclosure is the quality of the accounting standards used. At the beginning of the reform process, Indian accounting standards were probably half a century behind global best practices. As many Indian companies were listed in global stock markets, they started publishing accounting statements based on the U.S. GAAP (generally accepted accounting principles) or in some cases the U.K. GAAP. This led to pressure from investors and analysts for reforms in the Indian accounting standards as well.

Around the same time, international accounting standards (subsequently renamed as international financial reporting standards, or IFRS) were also evolving from a highly permissive compilation of accounting standards in vogue in various parts of the world to a high-quality standard against which national standards could be benchmarked. Under intense pressure from the securities regulator, accounting standard setters in India began phasing out the most outdated Indian standards and replacing them with standards modeled on the IFRS. Initially, some of the new standards applied only to listed companies, while other companies used the old standards as mandated by company law.

Recently Indian accounting standard setters announced a plan for harmonizing India standards completely with IFRS, in a phased manner, from 2011 onward. The new standards, based on IFRS, have made accounting information much more meaningful and have also led to additional disclosures relating to segment performance and related-party transactions. However, the enforcement of accounting standards remains very poor. As the Raghuram Rajan Committee report states:

> In India, annual accounts are filed with the Registrar of Companies under the Department of Company Affairs in the Government of India. However

> there is no system of reviewing accounting reports even on a selective or sample basis. By contrast, in the USA, the Securities and Exchange Commission (SEC) has a division comprising hundreds of lawyers and accountants to review such annual reports and, if necessary, seek clarifications from the companies in question. The Committee believes that such a process of review is absolutely essential.[8]

In many cases, companies might comply with the letter and spirit of the accounting standards for reputational considerations. But there is no enforcement mechanism that gives investors the confidence in the sanctity and integrity of published accounting statements. Many Indian investors believe that accounting statements filed by dual-listed Indian companies in the United States are more reliable than the statements filed by the same companies in India.

Corporate Governance

Since the early 1990s India has made several improvements in its corporate governance requirements. However, serious deficiencies remain. One important development was the implementation of a corporate governance code. The Asian Corporate Governance Association describes it this way:

> In April 1998 the country produced one of the first substantial codes of best practice in corporate governance in Asia. . . . The following year, the government appointed a committee . . . to draft India's first national code on corporate governance for listed companies. Many of the committee's recommendations were mandatory, closely aligned to international best practice at the time, and set higher governance standards for listed companies than most other jurisdictions in Asia.

The code provides among other things for a minimum number of independent directors and an independent audit committee. However, compliance with these requirements remains patchy. Some of the largest government-owned companies are not in compliance with the requirement regarding independent directors. In many other companies, compliance with the code is more in form than in substance. Many "independent" directors in fact have ties to the management, which make their independence suspect.

One of the innovations in Indian corporate governance that does work is the requirement for shareholder approval for many important decisions through a postal ballot. Companies find this route cost effective, and more important, the postal ballot enfranchises geographically dispersed investors for the first time. A second significant element is the market for corporate controls. Takeover regulations provide for an orderly market for corporate control in which minority

8. Rajan (2009).

shareholders are treated on a par with controlling shareholders. This has made a difference, but fundamental deficiencies in the code have limited the benefits. Acquirers are not required to buy out all minority shareholders: they need to make an open offer only for 20 percent of the shares of the company. This and the provisions for creeping acquisitions leave the door open for two-step takeovers, which squeeze out minority shareholders.

The biggest area of concern is that there have been very few hostile takeovers in India. The threat of hostile acquisitions is the ultimate check on nonperforming management, and the paucity of this threat is a grave weakness of corporate governance in India. In July 2010 the regulator released a report recommending a complete overhaul of the takeover code. The proposals would require acquirers to make an open offer for 100 percent of the shares of the target company. It also makes it easier for acquirers to offer their own shares and other noncash instruments as consideration for the acquisition. If and when these changes are implemented, some of the problems identified above would be reduced.

A recent report by the Asian Corporate Governance Association (ACGA) highlights key deficiencies in Indian corporate governance from the perspective of foreign investors:[9]

—ACGA believes that foreign investors have difficulty in voting in shareholder meetings in India. While I agree that there is room for improvement in Indian law, I believe that many of the difficulties faced by foreign investors are due to the inefficiency of the custodians and subcustodians that foreign investors use. The market for these custodial services is not very competitive (partly because of some of the entry barriers imposed by U.S. law for U.S. investors), and therefore foreign investors suffer in terms of both the price and the quality of the custodial services that they receive.

—ACGA quite rightly points out that the regulations pertaining to related-party transactions in India leave much to be desired. I agree with their suggestion that significant related-party transactions should be approved by a majority of *other* shareholders.

—ACGA objects to preferential issue of warrants to promoters, but in my view, this is subsumed under the related-party transactions mentioned above.

—ACGA states quite correctly that "the scope, depth, timeliness, consistency, and formatting of corporate financial disclosure in India could be greatly improved." I am of the same view—as explained earlier, quarterly disclosure needs to include the balance sheet and not just the income statement, and regulators need to build the equivalent of the U.S. EDGAR system for electronic dissemination of financial disclosures.

—ACGA recommends an independent audit regulator. I agree with this.

9. Asian Corporate Governance Association (2010).

My overall assessment is the same as that of ACGA: while there have been major improvements, a lot still remains to be done.

Creditor Rights

Significant reforms have been carried out in four areas related to creditor rights—bankruptcy reforms, corporate debt restructuring, debt recovery tribunals, and enforcement of security interests. Though these have led to only modest improvements in creditor rights, these rights remain weak and their enforcement continues to be cumbersome and time-consuming.

A prereform (mid-1980s) law for the rehabilitation of sick companies left India with a totally dysfunctional corporate bankruptcy regime, under which companies were shielded from liquidation while incumbent management continued in control. The companies survived as zombie companies, and creditors were unable to recover what was due to them. A law was passed in 2002 to repeal this dysfunctional regime and replace it with a more modern bankruptcy process. The proposed regime has been mired in judicial challenges that are not yet resolved. In the meantime, the central bank introduced a corporate debt restructuring (CDR) mechanism loosely modeled on the so-called London rules. The attempt was to create a process for the orderly financial restructuring of companies that have borrowed from a large number of banks. It works mainly through an intercreditor agreement that permits decisions to be made by a qualified majority of the creditors.

The approach rearranges the rights of the creditors inter se while doing little to strengthen the rights of the creditors against the debtor. The effect of the CDR mechanism has been to shift the bargaining power to the debtor by making it harder for a minority of lenders to take a hard stand. The creation of the debt recovery tribunals was a major procedural reform, designed to reduce the legendary delays of the Indian judicial system and make it easier for banks to recover their debts. The tribunals have had significant success, but they have been less effective in the cases of large and resourceful borrowers who are able to mount a variety of legal challenges. The SARFAESI Act was another procedural innovation that permitted secured creditors to seize the collateral and sell it to recover its value with minimal judicial intervention. After judicial challenges, this law has been partially defanged, and the borrower is able to delay the enforcement of security in many cases.

One limitation of both the debt recovery tribunals and the SARFAESI Act is that they applied only to banks and financial institutions. Instead of strengthening creditor rights in general, they granted special rights to a set of privileged institutions. This is not a wholesome development from the point of view of competitive effects on the financial sector. It also makes it easier for the borrower to depict the laws as being unfair. It is interesting to contrast these procedural innovations with U.S. bankruptcy reforms in the area of derivative contracts. Though U.S. reforms came about after intense lobbying by the banks, the law changed the bankruptcy rights of derivative counterparties without any reference to whether they were banks or not. When the investment bank Lehman Brothers filed for bankruptcy in 2008, this law could be turned against the investment bank itself.

All things considered, the improvement in creditor rights after the reforms has been extremely modest. Yet there has been an increase in the recovery of bad debts due to banks. A large part of this however is due less to the improvement in legal rights and more to a rise in asset values, which changed the incentive facing borrowers.

In the mid-2000s, when there was a rapid rise in the prices of real estate and other asset classes, borrowers who had defaulted earlier were keen to settle the old debt at discounted prices and monetize the value of the underlying assets. For example, a borrower might have defaulted when faced with debt of 100 against a property value of 70. When the property value rose to 120, he was keen to pay off the debt and sell the property, particularly if the bank was willing to settle the debt at 80. Similarly, a debtor who anticipates a sharp rise in revenues and profits (maybe due to a booming economy) is eager to go through a debt restructuring, where the banks accept large discounts based on current depressed profitability. In practice, the CDR mechanism has often facilitated this kind of abuse of creditor rights.

Skepticism about Private Ordering

In this section I examine the extent to which the financial sector reforms in India reflected an emerging private ordering. At one extreme, it might be thought that the rise of institutional investors would lead to significant changes in the financial sector without much involvement by the government and that regulatory reforms might only sanctify prevailing best practices. Less ambitiously, it might be thought that institutional and professional investors would have provided thought leadership to the reform process. In my view, neither of these has happened on any significant scale. Reforms do appear to have been a top-down process initiated by reform-minded regulators.

Emerging markets today are in a tearing hurry to get their markets right to foster rapid growth, and they do not have the option of waiting to see whether a private ordering emerges in due course. When private ordering does not produce results within a reasonable time frame, regulators are left with no choice but to intervene and enforce the reforms by fiat.

Institutionalization

If we consider the top fifty companies forming part of the Standard & Poor's (S&P) CNX Nifty index in India, the median shareholding pattern at the end of 2009 was as follows: the promoter group held 53 percent, institutional investors (nonpromoters) held 31 percent, and noninstitutional investors (nonpromoters) held 15 percent. In India's leading companies, therefore, the nonpromoter shareholding is largely institutional, while as late as 2001 noninstitutional shareholdings were roughly on par with institutional shareholdings.

During the last decade, shareholding has shifted from retail investors to promoters and foreign institutions. There has also been a shift from domestic institutions (mutual funds, banks, insurance companies, and other financial institutions) to foreign institutions. In 2009, in nearly half of the fifty companies in the Nifty index, foreign institutions had a larger shareholding than domestic institutions *and* a larger shareholding than noninstitutional investors. Thus there is little doubt that, over the last decade, there has been an institutionalization of the stock market and that foreign institutions have been the biggest player in this process.

Institutional shareholders have been responsible for a dramatic professionalization of securities market intermediaries. Not only have traditional intermediaries like stockbrokers become more professionalized, but also a number of new stock market professions like equity analysts have emerged in response to the institutionalization of the market. Institutionalization has also perhaps contributed to the development of a vibrant financial press, which provides a higher quality of financial reporting than was the case two decades ago.

Unfortunately, however, institutions have not played the same positive role in the reform process itself. In some cases, their actions have been characterized by not merely an indifference to reforms but also active resistance to them. Both domestic and foreign institutions in India have resisted reforms as vigorously as other market participants. Reforms in India have been pushed forward by academics, by the financial press, and by policymakers (not necessarily in that order). Many of these reforms have had to be pushed through by regulatory fiat even where they were in the long-run interest of the institutions themselves. In this sense, institutions have been as myopic in their response to capital market reforms as any other actor. I give here a few examples of this from the securities markets:

—Before India set up its first depository, institutions were most vociferous in their complaints about the risks and costs of the paper-based settlement system. But when the depository started operations, they were most reluctant to start using its services until the regulator mandated that a minimum percentage of their holdings be dematerialized (converted to electronic entries in the depository). Even this did not lead to the desired results, as trading of securities continued to be in paper form. The regulator finally had to mandate that institutions could trade only in dematerialized form. Because of the regulatory push, virtually the entire trading shifted to dematerialized form within two years. It is conceivable that dematerialization would have happened ultimately purely through private ordering, but it would probably have taken decades rather than years.

—One of the big debates in Indian securities markets during the 1990s was about rolling settlement versus account period settlement (known in India as *badla*). Throughout this debate, institutions generally paid lip service to the idea of rolling settlement, but they did not put their money where their mouth was. For a long period during the 1990s, when an optional rolling settlement facility was available in India, institutions did not embrace the facility at all. Ultimately, the shift toward rolling settlement happened only when the regulator made the new system mandatory.

—All through the 1990s, domestic and foreign institutions complained about the lack of hedging mechanisms in the Indian equity market. However, after the derivatives markets were set up, institutions were reluctant to trade in it. What happened was that retail investors built the market over a period of several years. Once they had created a critical mass of liquidity, institutional investors, who had been largely bystanders till then, came in as free riders. I believe that institutional investors failed in this case to make the required investments in market development that reformers expected from them. The same story has been repeated in the currency futures market. In interest rate derivatives, where retail interest was inadequate and institutions were left to create a market on their own, they failed to do so, not once, but twice.

—Anybody listening in on a quarterly investor presentation can surely be in no doubt that Indian companies take their institutional shareholders seriously, far more seriously than they ever took their retail shareholders. Yet at the crunch, the contribution of institutional investors to improving corporate governance in India has been much less than one would have expected or liked. Most of the changes that have taken place have been due to regulatory intervention. More important, institutional investors have done very little to prevent governance abuses in the areas of self-dealing and related-party transactions.

Corporate Indifference to Market Development: Exit Instead of Voice

In some ways, the group with the greatest stake in the development of a deep and efficient capital market is the corporate sector. As issuers of capital, this sector stands to benefit most from the development of equity and debt markets. Unfortunately, however, the corporate sector has played an insignificant role in capital market reforms. It has usually been a bystander as reformers struggled against vested interests among market intermediaries.

To some extent, corporate indifference to the development of domestic capital markets can be described as the choice of exit over voice. Very early in the game, Indian issuers were given access to global equity markets and subsequently to global debt markets as well. In the case of equity markets, though the Indian corporate sector had access to ADR and GDR markets to issue capital to foreign investors, rapid reforms meant that the Indian market remained competitive. Over time, foreign investors also became comfortable with investing and trading in the domestic market. As such, Indian equity markets were not exported to foreign stock exchanges on a significant scale. Even in the case of companies that issued ADRs and GDRs, the stock is usually more liquid in the Indian market, and price discovery also tends to take place in India.

In the case of debt markets, the story was different due to absence of reforms in the Indian debt market. As Indian companies obtained access to global debt markets, the Indian corporate debt market was rapidly exported abroad. This phenomenon was accelerated by the managed exchange rate regime, which made foreign currency debt attractive to Indian issuers. Access to foreign capital markets probably left large Indian companies with too little stake in the development of Indian markets. Small and medium-sized enterprises do of course have a stake because of their restricted access to global markets, but they have too little clout to make them a significant force in favor of reforms.

Drivers of Regulatory Reforms

An emerging market does not need to reinvent the wheel; it can simply look at what has worked and what has not worked in mature markets and try to adapt these approaches to local conditions. Many Indian reforms therefore consisted largely of adoption of global best practices. However, there are also many cases where the reforms involved substantial innovation and adaptation. Emerging markets often face different cost structures and different initial conditions, and these lead to regulatory structures different from the prevailing global consensus. Finally, there are also instances where the codification of the lowest common denominator of global practices (what I call global worst practices) by some multilateral forums, and by domestic regulators in some high-profile countries, have in my view weakened the momentum for reform. In many cases, the pressure for reform comes from within; financial crises are the clearest example of this.

Adoption of Global Best Practices

Among the key reforms in India that were driven by the adoption of global best practices are the elimination of financial repression, the introduction of rolling settlement and risk containment measures in the stock market, the adoption of modern accounting standards, and the adoption of a central securities depository:

—The initial burst of reforms in the early 1990s included several steps to end the regime of financial repression in India: the deregulation of interest rates, the free pricing of equity shares, and the shift from merit-based to disclosure-based regulation of equity issues. All of these were clearly guided by global best practices as well as by the theoretical consensus against financial repression.

—The shift from account-period settlement to rolling settlement in equities trading and the introduction of robust margining systems in derivative and quasi-derivative products was almost entirely driven by global best practices. Reformers relied on global precedents to push their case, and opponents portrayed reforms as the replacement of time-tested indigenous practices by newfangled foreign ideas.

—The modernization of Indian accounting standards was a conscious and open acceptance of global best practices in the form of international accounting standards (subsequently rechristened international financial reporting standards). The codification of these standards by a multilateral forum made this task easier. It would have been far more difficult to converge Indian accounting standards toward U.S. or U.K. accounting standards.

—The shifting of securities settlement from physical certificates to book entries was driven by global best practices. However, mainstream thinking in mature markets in this area emphasized immobilization rather than dematerialization. Immobilization means that physical share certificates still exist, but they are locked up in the vaults of securities firms and custodians. Individual investors' holdings are represented by book entries in the books of these firms. Dematerialization means that the physical share certificates are destroyed and are replaced by electronic entries in a central depository.

India was in some ways similar to the United States in terms of size and substantial retail shareholding; the U.S. model of immobilization of certificates in the hands of broker-custodians appeared attractive to India as well. Many in India believed that a plan for the complete destruction of paper certificates and their replacement by electronic records within a period of a couple of years was foolhardy. What tilted the balance in India was that the low level of trust in stockbrokers among Indian retail investors made the U.S. model unattractive. Moreover, by the time dematerialization was begun in India, there were enough global precedents for such plans.

Innovation and Adaptation

In many important areas, however, India chose innovation and adaptation rather than direct adoption of global best practices. In the early 1990s, electronic trading was not the dominant form of trading in the largest stock markets in the world. In fact, incumbent exchanges as well as major stockbrokers used this as an argument to resist electronic trading. At that time they could point to the New York and London stock exchanges and argue that a trading floor with market makers provides greater liquidity and better market quality than an electronic order book. India was by no means a pioneer in electronic trading. The Toronto Stock Exchange in Canada had introduced it two decades earlier, and Nasdaq in the United States had followed soon thereafter. However, electronic trading had not yet established itself as global best practice; the "Battle of the Bund" had not yet been won.[10]

Indian policymakers liked electronic trading on theoretical grounds in the context of India's dispersed shareholding population. Electronic trading also provided a competitive weapon to the challenger exchange. Global influence was modest.

10. Cantillon and Yin (2007).

It might appear that the introduction of equity derivatives in India represented a simple and direct adoption of global best practices, but closer examination reveals a more nuanced picture. The introduction of stock index futures in line with global best practices was initially a failure because of a lack of retail interest and the unwillingness of institutional players to invest in market development. Even the introduction of stock options and index options did not make a difference to this dismal situation.

The tide turned only with the introduction of single stock futures. At that time, this product was regarded as a heretical idea because the United States did not permit them and because they were prevalent in only a handful of other markets. Single stock futures became a roaring success in India, which went on to become the world's largest market for this product. The success of this product ultimately rubbed off on the more traditional index derivatives and made them successful as well. It is very likely that a slavish adherence to global best practices would have prevented the emergence of equity derivatives in India.

India was one of the pioneers in the introduction of centrally cleared repos in government securities. Repos, or repurchase agreements, are a form of short-term collateralized borrowing that is extremely important in the development of the money markets. Central clearing reduces the risk of repos and makes them more attractive. In India the centrally cleared repo product, known as collateralized borrowing and lending obligations (CBLO) at the Clearing Corporation of India, has become the largest money market instrument by traded value.

Since the global financial crisis, there has been some interest by mature markets in the introduction of a central counterparty for repos, but at the time that it was introduced in India, there were few parallels in the world. India was also one of the earliest countries to formally regulate credit-rating agencies (a decade ago). At that time, the move was bitterly opposed by rating agencies, which argued vehemently that no other major country in the world regulated them. Indian regulators however took the view that it was inconsistent to provide regulatory recognition for credit ratings but not subject the rating agencies themselves to any form of regulation. After the global financial crisis, some mature markets appear to be moving toward regulating rating agencies.

Role of Crises in Market Development and Regulation

It is well known that in many countries (both emerging markets and mature markets), reforms often take place in response to crises. This has been true in India as well, beginning with the economic reforms in 1991. Obviously the economic reforms in 1991 were a response to the balance-of-payments crisis that the country faced at that time. But the crisis in the financial sector was much deeper and included the following:

—The grave threat of insolvency confronting the banking system, which had for years concealed its problems with the help of defective accounting policies.

—The problem of financial repression in the sense of McKinnon-Shaw induced by administered interest rates pegged at unrealistically low levels.[11]

—Large-scale preemption of resources from the banking system by the government to finance its fiscal deficit.

—Excessive structural and microregulation, which inhibited financial innovation and increased transaction costs.

—Relatively inadequate level of prudential regulation in the financial sector.

—Poorly developed debt and money markets.

—Outdated (often primitive) technological and institutional structures, which made the capital markets and the rest of the financial system highly inefficient.

The initial burst of reform in the financial sector—particularly the reversal of financial repression—was a response to this crisis in the financial system. However, many other, smaller scale crises had certain impacts on financial sector reforms, and in some cases the effect was to impede reforms.

In 1992 a major scam was uncovered in the government securities market: some brokers had misappropriated more than a billion dollars from the banks in the government securities market and invested the amount in the stock market. This scam revealed glaring weaknesses in various parts of the financial sector, but this crisis was almost completely wasted. Other than the computerization of the public debt office, this scandal did not lead to any worthwhile reforms. On the contrary, it led to a variety of mindless restrictions that impeded the development of the debt markets in India for nearly a decade.

There was a boom of equity issues in 1994 and 1995 just before a sharp monetary tightening triggered an asset market deflation. Investors in most of these equity issues lost heavily as stock prices fell far below the issue price. Some of the start-up companies that raised equity during this boom failed and even disappeared. Several improvements were made in disclosure standards, and these set the stage for a more vibrant primary market a few years later. But not all the "reforms" in the primary market were beneficial. Some of them represented a backsliding from disclosure-based regulations that had been put together with such great difficulty. Fortunately, many of these bad reforms were watered down over time.

The asset market correction in India in response to the global financial crisis revealed a major accounting scandal at Satyam Computers, one of India's leading software companies. Satyam was a high-profile company with a high-profile (supposedly independent) board, it was audited by a Big Four auditing firm, and it was also dual listed in the United States. That a scandal of these proportions could happen at such a company was a wake-up call for corporate governance in India. It was India's equivalent of Enron. This scandal did not lead to any major regulatory changes, but it did lead to changes in governance practices at many of the country's best-run firms.

11. McKinnon (1973); Shaw (1973).

One important example of a crisis that did have a powerful and beneficial impact on financial sector reforms is the stock market scandal of 2001. The dot.com bust that followed the dot.com bubble had a powerful impact on the Indian stock market. The bust revealed that a group of stock market operators had colluded with company managements to manipulate the stock prices of a number of technology companies. As this manipulation unraveled during the dot.com bust, some of these brokers defaulted on their obligations in the stock exchange. Governance problems also surfaced at several of the stock exchanges.

This crisis led to sweeping reforms in the stock markets, including a robust margining system with central counterparties and a shift to rolling settlement. These reforms also gave an impetus to the fledgling equity derivative markets.

Lessons Learned and Challenges Ahead

India has been relatively successful in developing some key financial markets that play an important role in promoting economic growth. A critical lesson here is that success stories are characterized by regulatory reform that unleashed competition and actively pushed rapid adoption of new technology. At the same time, debt markets and related sectors where competition has been repressed remain weak and underdeveloped. An important challenge for India is to replicate in debt markets the regulatory successes that it achieved in equity markets.

Another key lesson is that foreign participation is much less important than competition in speeding up market development. However, we have also seen that if foreign entities are not given access to the Indian market, the market itself might get exported outside India. Moreover, India has been enormously dependent on foreigners for risk capital. India has succeeded in substituting foreign portfolio investment for foreign direct investment in the financial sector, but it has not been able to rely only on domestic risk capital. This need for capital flows creates challenges in macroeconomic management.

Indian financial regulators face acute challenges in areas like market manipulation and surveillance. The global financial crisis has revealed serious inadequacies in regulators in mature markets, even though they were regarded as role models for emerging market regulators. Regulators in both mature and emerging markets need to look at radically different models. The Indian experience shows that while adopting global best practices, regulators can sometimes be innovative and adaptive. The global financial crisis has led to some rethinking about optimal regulatory frameworks, and some observers believe that India's conservative regulatory stance has been beneficial. The risks of a regulatory monoculture have also been apparent.

The Debt Market and Other Structural Reforms

The Raghuram Rajan Committee Report provides a summary of the state of development of India's financial markets (table 10-1). It is clear that, while the

Table 10-1. *Liquidity in Indian Financial Markets, Three Dimensions*

Financial market	*Liquidity dimension*		
	Immediacy	*Depth*	*Resilience*
Large cap stocks, stock futures, index futures	√	√	√
Other stocks	0	0	0
On-the-run government bonds	√	√	0
Other government bonds	0	0	0
Corporate bonds	0	0	0
Commercial paper and other money market instruments	0	0	0
Near-money options on index and liquid stocks	√	0	0
Other stock options	0	0	0
Currency	√	0	0
Interest rate swaps	√	√	0
Metals, energies, and select agricultural commodity futures	√	0	0
Other commodity futures	0	0	0

Source: Rajan (2009, table 1).

equity market has developed very well, the debt market has a long way to go. The crying need is for a corporate debt market and for a term money market, but reforms are also urgently needed in the government bond market and in the interest rate derivative market.

A vibrant government bond market is the foundation for the rest of the fixed-income market. In India, however, this has been reduced to an interbank market to which other players do not have nondiscriminatory access. Breaking down these barriers and creating a truly open government bond market should be the topmost priority in structural reforms in the Indian financial markets.

The structural infirmities of the government bond market have also impeded the development of an interest-rate derivative market in India. Three attempts to develop an interest-rate futures market have failed, failures partly due to the design deficiencies that were imposed by the weakness of the underlying market. A freely functioning government bond market in which short squeezes are mitigated by the willingness of the debt management office to lend (repo out) securities that are in short supply would allow a more viable bond future.[12]

12. This is a process by which debt managers in many countries counter any attempt to corner the market for any specific government bond. The debt manager lends bonds of the specific issue in short supply by if necessary temporarily creating "phantom" bonds (www.dmo.gov.uk/documentview.aspx?docname=publications/operationalrules/RepoTC060809B.pdf&page=operational_rules/Document). This lending is usually collateralized by other government bonds that are more freely available and therefore does not change the aggregate public debt. The facility allows the market to get around a temporary shortage of a specific bond, which may be required to be delivered against a futures contract.

Equally important is the creation of a term money market. Unfortunately, the central bank has encouraged nontransparent lending benchmarks, like the prime lending rate and the base lending rate, instead of encouraging a market determined yield curve in the money market.

The most severe problem in the debt market is the lack of development of a corporate bond market in India. As explained elsewhere in this chapter, the corporate bond market has been exported outside India as companies find it easier to issue dollar-denominated bonds in foreign countries than to issue rupee-denominated bonds in India. This creates foreign exchange risks for the borrower and, more important, is a potential source of macroeconomic vulnerability for the country itself. The problem has arisen partly due to government policy, as regulations relating to external commercial borrowing by the Indian corporate sector have been far more liberal than regulations relating to investments by foreign investors in rupee-denominated debt. This anomaly needs to be urgently reversed. Even a massive liberalization of foreign investment limits in rupee debt can be balance of payments neutral if it is accompanied by equally massive reductions in the limits on external commercial borrowing.

I repeatedly argue in this chapter that Indian financial markets have developed on the back of risk capital provided by foreign portfolio investors. It is highly likely that the same risk capital would provide a big boost to the domestic corporate bond market if it is allowed to do so. This would be hugely beneficial for financial market development and would also dramatically reduce the macroprudential risk that the Indian corporate sector is creating under the current policy for external commercial borrowing. It is possible that the central bank would resist this because it would reduce the profitability of the banking system, for which it acts as a guardian angel, but this would be an extremely short-sighted view of things.

Role of Foreign Players in Financial Market Development

The Indian experience very clearly demonstrates that foreign participation is much less important than competition in speeding up market development. Far from providing thought leadership to the reform process, both domestic and foreign institutions in India have resisted reforms as vigorously as other market participants. Reforms in India have been pushed forward by academics, by the financial press, and by the policymakers (not necessarily in that order).

Domestic entities have proved as adept as foreign ones in introducing new technology and business models as competitive differentiators. This might partly be because Indian players could draw on the financial sector talent in India as well as the pool of nonresident Indians working in global financial centers. These domestic entities have also been able to attract foreign portfolio investment on a large scale to meet their capital needs. Banking is a very good example of foreign portfolio investors providing abundant parent capital to Indian entities, while foreign banks in India have often had inadequate support from their parent companies. After the 1997 Asian crisis, many foreign banks reduced their interest in India, in effect ceding the territory to aggressive Indian private sector banks. The largest of these Indian-controlled private banks are in fact majority owned by foreign portfolio investors.

Country characteristics might have to be considered carefully while evaluating the generalizability of the Indian experience. For example, a country without a well-developed equity market might find it difficult to create adequate competition without bringing in foreign players. Opening up the market to foreign players might then appear faster and easier than creating a vibrant equity market. Longer term, however, a well-functioning equity market brings several other benefits. Even in India, several parts of the financial sector have benefited from strategic (minority or majority) ownership by foreign entities. Credit rating and investment banking are prominent examples of leading players being controlled by foreign players.

Another issue that emerges from the Indian experience is that, if foreign entities are not given access to the Indian market, the market itself might get exported outside India. Earlier I explain how the Indian corporate debt market moved out of India when foreigners were kept out of the domestic market, while the equity market has remained in India because foreign institutions were allowed access to the Indian market. This is closely related to the fact that India has been enormously dependent on foreigners for risk capital. With a high savings rate, India's dependence on foreign capital per se is quite modest. However, much of Indian savings seeks safe investment avenues like bank deposits. Foreigners provide a disproportionate amount of risk capital for Indian business. India's success has been in intermediating most of this flow of risk capital through Indian markets and Indian intermediaries. The macroeconomic challenge of managing these capital flows is perhaps a small price to pay for the availability of this risk capital.

Market Manipulation and Surveillance

One persistent cause of concern in Indian equity markets is market manipulation. Many investors (particularly retail investors) still have little faith in market integrity, and they tend to measure the success of the regulator in terms of its ability to ensure market integrity.

What makes this issue so difficult is that, while in the early 1990s market manipulation was carried out mainly by stockbrokers, today it is largely done by company managements themselves. When stock prices rose dramatically in the 1992 scam, stockbrokers were the only players involved. The companies whose stock prices rose to bubble levels have not been accused of any wrongdoing. A decade later, during the dot.com bubble, a group of stockbrokers was implicated in pushing up the prices, but it was also clear that this group acted in concert with the managements of the companies concerned. In 2008, when

Satyam collapsed, stockbrokers were not in the picture—it was all about the company managements.

The stock market reforms that address the issue of market abuses by stockbrokers do nothing to address abuses by company management itself. Corporate India has much more political clout than stockbrokers could ever dream of, and disciplining this group of players is far harder than disciplining stockbrokers.[13] Dealing with this kind of market manipulation is something that regulators cannot do on their own. Regulators can only help market participants (short sellers and whistleblowers, for example) uncover the fraud. I believe that regulators need to consciously adopt a crowd-sourcing approach to tackling market integrity. At present, regulators in India and elsewhere think of market integrity as something that they enforce; once in a while they grudgingly accept help from market participants. This needs to be the other way around: manipulation is something that market participants should detect and that the regulator acts upon. Modern information technology makes crowd-sourcing both feasible and attractive.

The global financial crisis has revealed glaring inadequacies in the functioning of regulators in mature markets.[14] The Madoff scandal for example shattered the reputation of the SEC, which used to be regarded as the gold standard of securities regulation. Regulators in emerging markets have suddenly had to confront the hard fact that the gold standard is the SEC of the 1940s and not the SEC of today. That is a far harder role model to follow, and the target has moved from something that is hard but achievable to something that appears completely out of reach even for mature market regulators.

In general, I believe that enforcement is far harder than regulation. Good regulation can and is often driven by a handful of people at the very top of the regulatory organization. Despite all the constraints of a public sector compensation structure, it is often possible to attract this small number of top-class talent. There are enough people in the top percentile of finance professionals who are motivated by nonmonetary considerations, especially at late stages in their career. They would be willing to work for a regulator in positions where they can make a difference.[15]

Enforcement on the other hand is not about a handful of people at the top; it is about a large army of competent (but not necessarily outstanding) foot soldiers. The constraints of a public sector compensation structure are far more stifling at this level. For the foot soldier, the regulator's job provides about as much satisfaction or nonmonetary payoffs as any other job at a comparable level in the industry. The regulator's low pay scale therefore makes it uncompetitive at this level as a long-term career. Reliance on interns and short-term contractual appointments

13. Echeverri-Gent (2007).

14. Barnard (2010); Carvajal and Elliott (2009); Ford (2010); Henning (2009).

15. See Ernst (2009) for a discussion on somewhat similar lines for the 1930s SEC.

might be one solution, but this requires reengineering the organization structure of the regulator.

The global financial crisis has shown that top regulatory organizations in mature markets have not solved this problem. Investigations and reports related to the crisis reveal an alarming level of incompetence at lower and middle levels of many of these regulators. In some cases, where there were problems at the top, attempts have been made to fix them, but the problem at middle and lower levels has no simple solutions for reasons described above.

I think this challenge requires a radical response. It might be necessary to reset expectations. It might also be necessary to reengineer the entire regulatory model. I have already talked about crowd-sourcing as one possible response. Another response might be to focus more on market structure and competition while designing regulations that are in some sense self-enforcing.

Conservative Regulation and the Global Financial Crisis

India emerged from the global financial crisis relatively unscathed. There was a short-lived liquidity crisis during the last quarter of 2008, as well as a sharp correction in asset prices in late 2008 and early 2009. India also suffered a slowdown in economic growth during 2008–09, but even with the slowdown, the economy grew at 6.7 percent during the year; the growth rate rose to 7.4 percent in 2009–10. The banking system did not need any bailouts, and there was no serious damage to the financial sector.

Indian policymakers and many external observers attribute this to India's conservative regulatory practices. For example, the countercyclical capital requirement introduced before the crisis on home loans did probably dampen the growth of the banking system's exposure to this sector. However, it is necessary to keep in mind that the Indian financial sector was not truly tested during the crisis. The system encountered severe liquidity stresses during late 2008, but loan losses were limited to a few sectors and were well contained. The growth slowdown was too mild and too short to produce serious portfoliowide delinquencies. All the major banks (including those that bore the brunt of acute market skepticism at the time) reported profits in every single quarter during the crisis.

The profitability of the banking system was also probably bolstered by regulatory measures that limited competition between banks and from nonbanks, as discussed earlier. Without taking away credit for macroprudential regulatory caution, I would therefore like to argue that it would be premature to assert that the financial sector would be resilient in the face of adverse economic outcomes.

The global crisis also demonstrated that regulatory caution in respect to financial instruments and products had been quite ineffective. For example, there were regulations aimed at limiting the use of foreign exchange derivatives only for hedging and not for speculation. This did not prevent Indian companies from exploiting loopholes in the regulations to enter into a wide range of exotic structures linked to the Japanese yen and the Swiss franc that produced huge losses when these currencies appreciated sharply during the crisis. Corporate misuse of these derivatives was a global problem.[16] But the point is that Indian conservative regulations proved completely futile during the crisis.

Risks of Codification of Global Worst Practices

After the Asian Crisis of 1997 the International Monetary Fund and the Financial Stability Forum put pressure on emerging markets to conform to the recommendations of multilateral forums like the International Organization of Securities Commissions and the Bank for International Settlements. They have become a powerful influence on regulatory reform in India.

I fear however that in some cases, these agencies have helped legitimize global worst practices. As their recommendations become mandatory, there has been a tendency for these standards to reflect the lowest common denominator of global practices rather than global best practices. Most of my examples on this are not India specific and reflect situations where global standards have been frozen at a low level through multilateral legitimization of global worst practices. In the Basel II capital standards, residential mortgages received a low risk weight mainly because of pressure from several continental European countries that had a history of low loss experience with this instrument. The subprime crisis has shown that the extension of this favorable treatment to the whole world was a huge mistake.

The CPSS-IOSCO standards for central counterparties legitimize global worst practices to an astonishing extent.[17] CPSS-IOSCO says that "if a CCP relies on margin requirements to limit its credit exposures to participants, those requirements should be sufficient to cover potential exposures in normal market conditions."[18] This is like telling a car manufacturer that if a car has brakes, then the brakes should be sufficient to stop the car under normal driving conditions. The implication is that a car need not have brakes and even if it does, the brakes need not be designed to work on a slippery road.

Most Indian central counterparties have reasonable margining systems and are more than compliant with CPSS-IOSCO in this respect. It then becomes difficult to argue for strengthening their risk management systems. The only saving grace is that CPSS-IOSCO is revising these standards; but even this becomes an excuse for inaction—why not wait for the new standards before making any changes.

Similarly, the CPSS standards on delivery versus payments (DVP) in securities settlement legitimized a wide range of DVP practices prevalent two decades ago.

16. Dodd (2009).

17. Full titles are the Committee on Payment and Settlement Systems and the International Organization of Securities Commissions.

18. Committee on Payment and Settlement Systems and Technical Committee of the International Organization of Securities Commissions (2004), recommendation 4.

In my view, this standard has reduced the pressure on settlement agencies and on central banks to improve the DVP processes. In particular, it has made it easier for the central bank to resist suggestions that it should encourage all systemic settlement systems to settle in central bank money.

During the global financial crisis many jurisdictions imposed misguided and unwarranted restrictions on short selling in the stock market. Thankfully, the Indian regulator resisted strong pressure to follow global worst practices in this regard. Global worst practices weakened the case of those of us who argued for allowing short selling in other markets, for example government bonds.

Another reason to worry about the codification of global best practices by multilateral forums is that such standardization leads to regulatory monoculture, which introduces an unacceptable degree of systemic global vulnerability. Some degree of regulatory competition and innovation is probably healthy.[19] It is important to have some amount of regulatory diversity so that regulators can learn from each other's mistakes. It also provides room for regulatory experimentation through which new theoretical insights can be rapidly incorporated into regulatory practice.

A good example of this problem is the ossification of banking regulation around normal, distribution-based-value, at-risk models in the Basel II framework at just around the time the theoretical consensus was shifting toward coherent risk measures and fat-tailed distributions.[20] In my view, this regulatory monoculture was the principal reason the world ended up with a regulatory risk model ill suited to modern financial instruments and markets.[21]

References

Artzner, Philippe, and others. 1999. "Coherent Measures of Risk." *Mathematical Finance* 9, no. 3: 203–28.

Asian Corporate Governance Association. 2010. "ACGA White Paper on Corporate Governance in India" (www.acga-asia.org/public/files/ACGA_India_White_Paper_Final_Jan19_2010.pdf).

Barnard, Jayne W. 2010. "Evolutionary Enforcement at the Securities and Exchange Commission." *University of Pittsburgh Law Review* (Spring).

Cantillon, Estelle, and Pai-Ling Yin. 2007. "How and When Do Markets Tip? Lessons from the Battle of the Bund." Working Paper 766. European Central Bank (http://ssrn.com/abstract_id=989996).

Carvajal, Ana, and Jennifer Elliott. 2009. "The Challenge of Enforcement in Securities Markets: Mission Impossible?" Working Paper 09/168. Washington: International Monetary Fund (www.imf.org/external/pubs/ft.wp/2009/wp09168.pdf).

Committee on Payment and Settlement Systems and Technical Committee of the International Organization of Securities Commissions. 2004. "Recommendations for Central Counterparties." Basel.

Dodd, Randall. 2009. "Playing with Fire." *Finance and Development* (June): 40–42.

19. Kane (1988).
20. Artzner and others (1999).
21. Varma (2009).

Echeverri-Gent, John. 2007. "Politics of Market Microstructure." In *India's Economic Transition: The Politics of Reform,* edited by Rahul Mukherji. Oxford University Press.

Ernst, Daniel R. 2009. "Lawyers, Bureaucratic Autonomy, and Securities Regulation during the New Deal." Faculty working paper. Georgetown University Law Center (http://scholarship.law.georgetown.edu/fwps_papers/115/).

Ford, Cristie L. 2010. "Principles-Based Securities Regulation in the Wake of the Global Financial Crisis." *McGill Law Review* (http://ssrn.com/abstract=1516734).

Frydl, Edward J. 1999. "The Length and Cost of Banking Crises." Working Paper 99/30. Washington: International Monetary Fund (www.imf.org/external/pubs/ft/wp/1999/wp9930.pdf).

Henning, Peter J. 2009. "Should the SEC Spin off the Enforcement Division?" Legal Studies Research Paper 09-20. Wayne State University Law School (http://ssrn.com/abstract=1470857).

Kane, Edward J. 1984. "Technological and Regulatory Forces in the Developing Fusion of Financial Services Competition." *Journal of Finance* 39, no. 3: 759–72.

———. 1988. "Interaction of Financial and Regulatory Innovation." *American Economic Review* 78, no. 2: 328–34.

McKinnon, R. I. 1973. *Money and Capital in Economic Development.* Brookings.

Oura, Hiroko. 2008. "Financial Development and Growth in India: A Growing Tiger in a Cage?" Working Paper 08/79. Washington: International Monetary Fund (www.imf.org/external/pubs/ft/wp/2008/wp0879.pdf).

Rajan, Raghuram. 2009. "A Hundred Small Steps." In *Report of the Committee on Financial Sector Reform.* Planning Commission, Government of India.

Shaw, E. S. 1973. *Financial Deepening in Economic Development.* Oxford University Press.

Varma, Jayanth R. 1992. "Commercial Banking; New Vistas and New Priorities." Paper prepared for seminar, Reforming Commercial Banking, Ministry of Finance. New Delhi, November 25.

———. 2001. "Regulatory Implications of Monopolies in the Securities Industry." Working Paper 2001-09-05. Ahmedabad: Indian Institute of Management.

———. 2002. "The Indian Financial Sector after a Decade of Reforms." ViewPoint 3. New Delhi: Centre for Civil Society.

———. 2004. "Towards a Unified Market for Trading Gilts in India." Working Paper 2004-11-05. Ahmedabad: Indian Institute of Management (www.iimahd.ernet.in/~jrvarma/papers/WP2004-11-05pdf).

———. 2009. "Risk Management Lessons from the Global Financial Crisis for Derivative Exchanges." Working Paper 2009-02-06. Ahmedabad: Indian Institute of Management (http://papers.ssrn.com/abstract=1376276).

11

Financial Development in India: Status and Challenges

RAJESH CHAKRABARTI

India—most certainly urban India—has changed beyond recognition in less than two decades. Undeniably much of that change is the result of the economic reforms put in place since 1991, which have fundamentally transformed the economy and, indeed, the very mind-set of India. The change is more visible in some industries than in others. These include aviation, telecommunication, more recently retail, and certainly finance. Hardly a single area of the financial sector has remained the way it used to be. Private banks, mutual funds, and insurance companies are the most visible new developments. And within finance, financial markets have arguably undergone the greatest transformation. It is difficult today to imagine an India without the Securities and Exchange Board of India (SEBI), without the National Stock Exchange (NSE), without derivatives, and without the trading of demat (dematerialized) shares through online brokers, all of them children of the reforms.

The Indian Financial Sector and the Status of Reforms

There is a fundamental difference in character between reforms in financial markets and reforms in other parts of the economy or even in other segments of the financial sector. Almost everywhere else the primary thrust of reforms has been in

I would like to thank the participants of the Conference on Financial Sector Regulation and Reforms in Asian Emerging Markets for their comments. I especially thank Eswar Prasad for very helpful suggestions. I alone am responsible for all remaining errors and shortcomings.

scaling the state sector down from its monopoly position by allowing entry by private players, both domestic and foreign. In that sense the reforms have been liberating—that is, have taken the handcuffs off the private sector. In the financial markets, by contrast, the main thrust of reforms has been in building institutions that lead to market growth. In that sense, financial market reforms have been enabling—that is, have provided public institutions (whether regulators or exchanges) with new ground rules of operation. The distinction between the two kinds of reform is critical. The former refers to giving hitherto forbidden agents access to a profit-making activity, while the latter is about providing public facilities that allow such activity to take place. (The public sector was not a direct player in the markets.) Of course, this is not to downplay the role of any of the liberating reforms, neither those that allow new players to set up exchanges, those that allow foreign institutional investors (FIIs) access to Indian securities, nor those that allow the growth of private mutual funds. But by and large reforms in financial markets have been about institution building, and hence their success—and future tasks—should be assessed primarily by the quality of the institutions they have created.

And indeed institution building in the postliberalization financial sector in India bears the strong signature of direct government intervention. The SEBI, formally empowered in 1992, is perhaps the most pivotal of these institutions. But of almost comparable impact is the NSE, created only two years later at the behest of government-run financial institutions. The NSE was quick to introduce technology and improved procedures into securities trading, which was at that point a murky world of broker networks. In a little over a decade the NSE captured 70 percent of equity trading, virtually the entire derivatives markets (another major and overdue innovation), and much of the debt market, while the traditional exchanges either virtually closed down or struggled to match the NSE in its transparency and standards. It is fair to say that the creation of an efficient player had at least as much of a role in enhancing the efficiency in Indian financial markets as the creation of regulatory requirements.

Elsewhere, competition has spurred change. As the banking sector opened up, cautiously and gradually, in the mid-1990s, a spate of new private banks came in. Interestingly, once again most of the more important ones emerged out of the existing public sector or the quasi-public sector. New standards were set by these new private banks in customer service, in technology adoption, and in retail banking. The remaining public sector banks were still in charge of three-quarters of the industry, but in trying to match their younger and more agile rivals, they ended up with higher efficiency, too. The mutual fund and insurance industries have also boomed largely after their opening up to private players.

Progress, of course, has been far from even across sectors. Corporate debt markets, critical for financing the infrastructure investments necessary, are yet to be charged up despite years of government efforts. Pension reforms have been more gradual than those in equity markets and banking. Finally, reforms are just beginning in the regulatory structure itself.

The Indian financial sector has a hugely fragmented regulatory structure, with at least six union ministries having departments that directly control parts of the system. This has inevitably led to regulatory gaps and overlaps and the occasional disagreement between apex regulators. The finance minister promised a Financial Stability and Development Council (FSDC) in his 2010 budget, which seemed to be an attempt to harmonize sector regulators. An important committee had recommended it a couple of years before, but nevertheless, laying down the exact objectives and powers of such a body without upsetting too many segments proved difficult. The virtual scrapping of the Financial Services Authority (FSA) of the United Kingdom, the most commonly cited example of unified regulation, has not helped the process either. The FSDC was finally set up at the end of 2010.

Nevertheless, even while the consultative process for the formation of an FSDC and the definition and demarcation of its powers and jurisdiction were in process, the central government had taken advantage of a disagreement on jurisdiction between the SEBI and the Insurance Regulatory and Development Authority (IRDA) regarding unit-linked insurance plans (a cross between insurance policies and mutual fund products) to push ahead with regulatory unification, using the somewhat surprisingly unilateral instrument of an ordinance.

Another important and far-reaching step under consideration is setting up a Financial Sector Legislative Reforms Commission. It is likely to revisit the laws, most several decades old, that guide the Indian financial sector with the aim of making them both consistent and up-to-date.

Much of what we take for granted today in the Indian financial sector did not exist before the reforms began.[1] Overall the country has achieved significant financial deepening in recent years, owing largely to the reforms and the foreign capital they have attracted. The McKinsey Global Institute points out that until 2001 the reforms had not produced much financial deepening, with the total value of financial assets never exceeding GDP by more than 10 percent.[2] Then deepening started in a major way, and by 2004 the total value of financial assets stood at a respectable 160 percent of GDP. The three years that followed witnessed a virtual explosion, with the financial depth in 2007 standing at about 305 percent. This meant a compound annual growth rate (CAGR) of about 11 percent between 2001 and 2007. During this period equity markets showed the most stunning increase (from 23 percent of GDP to 165 percent, a CAGR of a whopping 39 percent); corporate bonds showed equally impressive gains but on an insignificant base (from 1 percent to 7.3 percent, a CAGR of 39 percent). Government secu-

1. For a clear description of the key reforms in financial markets, see Krishnan (2009).
2. McKinsey Global Institute (2006).

Figure 11-1. *Financial Depth, Four Dimensions, India and Other Asian Countries, 2004*

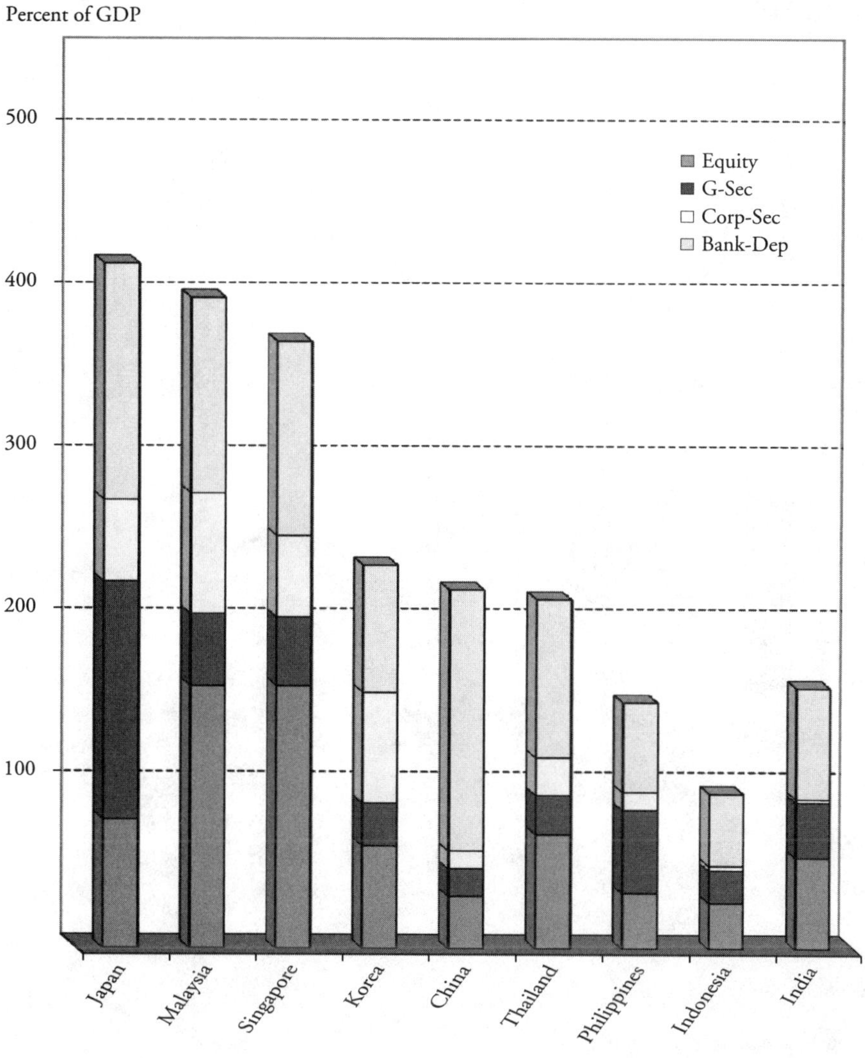

Source: World Economic Forum.

rities showed a relatively moderate rise (from 27 percent to 63 percent, a CAGR of 15 percent), while bank deposits rose at a snail's pace (from 57 percent to 69 percent, a CAGR of 3 percent).

Figures 11-1 and 11-2 show the financial depth in India and other Asian countries in 2004 and 2007, respectively. In 2004 India's financial depth was among the lowest among Asian countries. By 2007 India's financial depth was in the median range of Asian countries, with only the People's Republic of China and

Figure 11-2. *Financial Depth, Four Dimensions, India and Other Asian Countries, 2007*

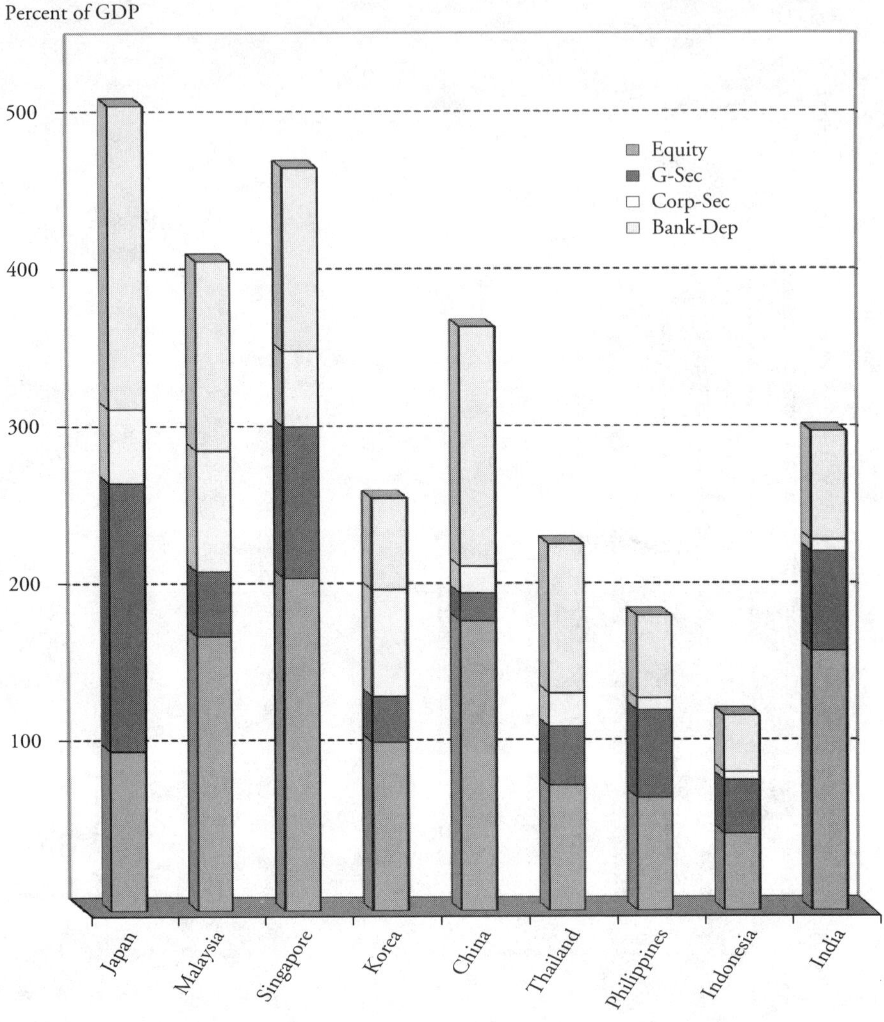

Source: World Economic Forum

Malaysia, among emerging markets, ahead. The roller-coaster ride in equity markets since 2007 has shaken these figures, but the message of overall deepening remains unchanged. When one looks at the extent of financial deepening during the 2004–07 period, India ranks first among major Asian countries, largely driven by the gain in the equity markets. During the earlier decade (1994–2004), too, India had a very decent rate of deepening among Asian countries, at 4.2 percent a year CAGR, but that was also a period marked by the Asian crisis.

Table 11-1. *Financial Development Index Indicators, India, 2009*

Indicator	*Rank (out of 55)*	*Score (1–7)*
Overall	38	3.3
Factors, policies, and institutions		
1st pillar: institutional environment	48	3.4
Financial sector liberalization	51	1.9
Corporate governance	30	4.6
Legal and regulatory issues	31	3.8
Contract enforcement	50	3.2
2nd pillar: business environment	48	3.5
Human capital	33	4.1
Taxes	38	4.2
Infrastructure	51	2.3
Cost of doing business	50	3.4
3rd pillar: financial stability	46	4.2
Currency stability	10	5.4
Banking system stability	49	4.0
Risk of sovereign debt crisis	43	3.4
Financial intermediation		
4th pillar: banking financial services	39	3.1
Size index	36	2.3
Efficiency index	32	4.8
Financial information disclosure	44	1.3
5th pillar: nonbanking financial services	17	3.1
IPO activities	9	3.8
Mergers and acquisitions	20	2.6
Insurance	17	3
Securitization	16	3
6th pillar: financial markets	22	3
Foreign exchange markets	13	2
Derivative markets	13	4.9
Equity market development	28	2.7
Bond market development	27	2.6
Financial access		
7th pillar: financial access	48	2.8
Commercial	27	3.9
Retail	47	1.6

Source: World Economic Forum (2009).

The World Economic Forum, using a financial development index, ranked India thirty-eighth among fifty-five countries in 2009, with a score on a 1 through 7 scale of 3.3 (table 11-1). Among the components of this index, India's best rank (seventeen) is in nonbanking financial services, followed closely by financial markets (twenty-two). Among financial markets, the derivatives market gets the highest score and, together with the foreign exchange markets, ranks thirteenth among all the countries.

India does relatively poorly in the institutional and business environment and in financial access. Financial stability is only marginally better. If one considers individual elements, the worst rank, perhaps surprisingly, is in financial sector liberalizat on (a score of fifty-one out of fifty-five). Clearly, according to the report, India's liberalization could be speeded up. An alternative way of assessing the health of Indian markets is to measure India's progress against the principles of the International Organization of Securities Commission (IOSCO) (table 11-2). Developed largely for the securities markets, the thirty principles span nine distinct areas of financial market regulation: the regulator, self-regulation, enforcement, cooperation, disclosure, collective investment, market intermediaries, secondary markets, and clearing and settlement.

The IOSCO principles emphasize the complete independence of market regulators from government, which is by design not the case in India. In terms of cooperation and information sharing, too, there seems to be room for improvement across markets. More important, the regulation of market intermediaries appears to have scope for improvement, particularly in the equity, bond, and money markets. Other than that, Indian markets seem to be in consonance with the IOSCO principles.

In view of several achievements in the country during the last few years—the financial deepening, the fulfillment of the IOSCO principles, and the avoidance of any systemic-level crises through a particularly turbulent era of the global financial system—there is no doubt that financial sector reformers have done a good job combining progress with risk management. However, as the relatively poor showing in terms of the financial development index suggests, their work is far from over. One may even go further and say that so far only the low-lying fruits have been picked and the real slog is only begun, as India starts down the path of second-generation reforms.

The quality of risk management practices at financial institutions is, as the recent global financial crisis amply demonstrates, central to the quality and reliability of the financial sector. In spite of India emerging through the crisis with relatively little damage, Indian policymakers, like their counterparts elsewhere, have been concerned about the emergence, in the postliberalization era, of large diversified financial institutions involved in a plethora of financial activities, making both their systemic impact and the efficacy of their risk management difficult to assess. Nevertheless, the first *Financial Stability Report,* brought out by the central bank in March 2010, sheds some light on the state of affairs.[3] It finds that, although the asset-to-liability mismatches of Indian banks are not significant (given that most credit growth is coming from sectors like infrastructure and real estate, which

3. Reserve Bank of India (2010).

Table 11-2. *Implementation of Thirty IOSCO Principles, India*

	Level of implementation			
Principles	*Equity and bond markets*	*Foreign exchange*	*Government securities*	*Money market*
Principles of regulator				
Responsibilities of regulator	Broad	Full	Full	Full
Operational independence and accountability	Broad	Part	Part	Part
Power, resources, and capacity to perform functions	Full	Full	Full	Full
Regulatory processes of regulator	Full	Full	Full	Full
Professional standards of staff of regulator	Full	Full	Full	Full
Principles relating to self-regulation				
Regulatory regime	Full	. . .	. . .	. . .
Regulators' oversight over SROs and standards adopted by SROs	Full	. . .	. . .	. . .
Principles relating to enforcement				
Inspection, investigation, and surveillance powers	Full	Full	Full	Full
Enforcement powers	Full	Full	Full	Full
Use of inspection, investigation, surveillance, and enforcement powers	Broad	Full	Full	Full
Principles relating to cooperation				
Authority to share information with domestic and foreign counterparts	Full	Part	Part	Part
Information-sharing mechanisms	Full	Part	Part	Part
Assistance provided to foreign regulators	Part	Part	Part	Part
Principles relating to issuers				
Disclosure of financial results	Full	. . .	Part	Full
Treatment of holders of securities	Full	. . .	. . .	Full
Accounting and auditing standards	Broad	. . .	. . .	Full
Principles relating to collective investment scheme				
Standards for eligibility and regulation	Broad	. . .	Broad	Broad
Rules governing legal form and structure	Full	. . .	Full	Full
Disclosure requirements	Full	. . .	Full	Full
Asset valuation and pricing and redemption of units	Full	. . .	Full	Full
Principles relating to market intermediaries				
Minimum entry standards	Broad	Full	Full	Broad
Capital and prudential requirements	Broad	Full	Full	Broad
Internal organization and operational conduct	Part	Full	Full	Part
Procedure for dealing with failure of market intermediary	Broad	Full	Broad	Broad

(continued)

Table 11-2. *Implementation of Thirty IOSCO Principles, India (continued)*

	Level of implementation			
Principles	*Equity and bond markets*	*Foreign exchange*	*Government securities*	*Money market*
Principles relating to secondary markets and clearing and settlement				
Trading systems	Full	Full	Full	Full
Regulatory supervision	Full	Full	Full	Full
Transparency of trading	Full	Full	Full	Full
Detection of manipulation and unfair trading practices	Full	Part	Full	Full
Management of large exposures, default risk and market disruption	Full	Full	Full	Full
Systems for clearing and settlement of securities	Full	Full	Full	Full

Source: Reserve Bank of India (2009).

require longer term funding), they could be of concern in the future. Similarly the issue of liquidity coverage has some problems stemming from the increased use of volatile liabilities to finance growth.

As for the bigger picture, the report concludes that banking household and corporate sectors appeared to be healthy and stable, though some currency risks stem from unhedged foreign borrowings by Indian companies. The increasing importance of nonbanking finance companies suggests the need for increased supervision of the sector, particularly in view of the asset liability mismatches, credit quality, and within-sector flows of these companies. The report points to the need to shift intermediation further away from banks and more toward markets. Within markets, development and monitoring of central counterparties appears to be a key area for policy action. Slow-moving legal suits are another problem that needs legislative intervention. Further strengthening the already-in-place monitoring mechanism of financial conglomerates and better data dissemination standards are other areas of concern.

Finally, a key element of financial stability in India seems to involve foreign capital flows. Portfolio flows were heavy during the period 2004–07 and reversed painfully in the crisis years before returning to their former volume, throwing short-term rates, equity markets, liquidity, and the currency into temporary disarray. These flows have become a source of significant volatility for the financial sector, even though, according to the report, their aggregate volumes are still far from worrisome. Maintaining financial stability in the face of such volatile flows involves a clear understanding of India's stance toward capital account liberalization, a topic discussed next.

Capital Account Liberalization

In a capital-scarce country, opening up the capital account to foreign investment may well appear to be an obvious policy choice. However, openness to foreign financial markets also opens up the country to the vagaries of the flows of cross-border funds and arguably increases its vulnerability to financial crises originating elsewhere. India's approach to capital account liberalization has attempted to avoid these two negative possibilities.

The cautiousness of this approach arguably spared the country the disastrous effects of the Asian crisis of the late 1990s as well as the worst of the current global financial crisis. Empirical evidence arising later seems to justify the caution from an unexpected angle: it now appears that the constraint on growth in many low-income countries is not the paucity of savings but rather the ability of the financial sector to convert savings into investments. Thus opening up the capital account may not be the solution to financing problems for an emerging market country. In fact, the financial apparatus may not even be able to handle international flows.

However, this does not mean that current account convertibility is devoid of benefits. These stem from previously unappreciated sources. Foreign investment necessarily brings in its wake international management standards and the pressures of global competition, which contribute to the efficacy of productive sectors and to growth itself, in an indirect manner. The questions that these findings pose for policymakers in India are in regard to both the preparedness of the Indian financial system for foreign flows and the level of India's openness. Convertibility is no longer a binary choice but one of finding the optimal level.

India's relationship with the world financial system has grown exponentially over the years, almost in step with its liberalization of the current account. Foreign capital has swept into the country in the form of foreign direct investments and foreign institutional investments. As figure 11-3 indicates, foreign investments as a proportion of GDP have risen rapidly since 1990. Cumulative FII investments have risen more than sixfold since the turn of the century. The external commercial borrowings of Indian firms as well as the issuance of foreign currency convertible bonds zoomed during the 2004–07 period (just before the crisis) and are beginning to revive after the crisis. The opposite traffic is gradually opening up as well. Even retail investors can invest abroad (to an extent) through mutual funds. Table 11-3 compares India's FDI flow figures with those of other Asian countries, a comparison that portrays India quite favorably.

Capital account convertibility is a stated goal of Indian financial reforms, but progress toward it has been rather slow. According to the Chinn-Ito measure of openness, the Indian economy in 2007 was among the least open in the world.[4]

4. Chinn and Ito (2008). The Chinn-Ito measure is constructed on the basis of IMF's *Annual Report on Exchange Arrangements and Exchange Restrictions* and uses a binary variable approach to recording capital flow barriers.

Figure 11-3. *Foreign Institutional Investments, India, 1990–2009*

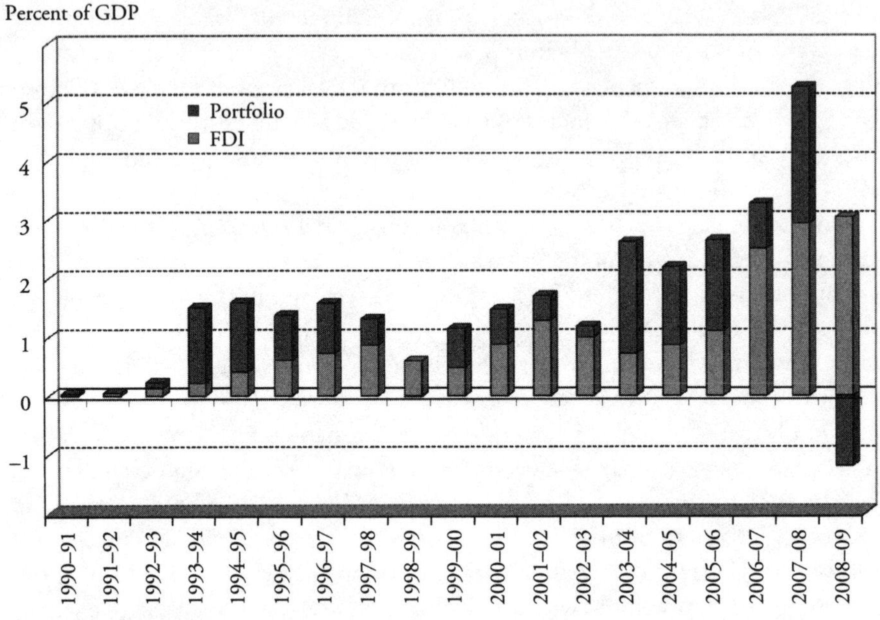

Source: Reserve Bank of India.

Worse, there seems to have been no change at all in the liberalization of India's capital account since 1970.

However, when one looks at the price difference between Indian assets traded at home and those traded abroad, one gets a very different picture of India's actual, or de facto, level of openness. Recent work at the University of California at Santa Cruz suggests that India's actual openness implied by such analysis is considerably higher. Michael Hutchison and his colleagues estimate the effectiveness of India's current account liberalization.[5] Their approach entails measuring a no-arbitrage band for small deviations from covered interest parity (CIP), where the upper and lower threshold points are determined by the intensity of capital controls and transaction costs. Within the bands, deviations from CIP are expected to be random, and outside the bands, arbitrage (profit opportunities) pressures are likely to systemically return deviations to band thresholds. A narrowing of the bands over time is an indication of greater de facto capital account openness, as is an increase in the speed of adjustment to band threshold points (indicating that arbitrage acts more rapidly in returning the market closer to CIP). The instrument used is nondeliverable forwards (NDF) on the rupee (most actively used in Singapore and Hong Kong, China). The deviation between the forward premium in NDFs and the differential between the relevant money market interest rates

5. Hutchinson and others (2008).

Table 11-3. *Foreign Direct Investment, Asia and Other Economies, Selected Years 1990–2008*
Units as indicated

	U.S.$ million					Percent of gross fixed capital formation			
FDI flows	*1990—2000 annual average*	*2005*	*2006*	*2007*	*2008*	*1990–2000 annual average*	*2006*	*2007*	*2008*
India									
Inward	1,705	7,606	20,336	25,127	41,554	1.9	6.9	6.5	9.6
Outward	110	297,814	14,344	17,281	17,685	0.1	4.8	4.5	4.1
China									
Inward	30,104	72,406	72,715	83,521	108,312	11.9	6.4	6.0	6.0
Outward	2,195	12,261	21,160	22,469	52,150	0.9	1.9	1.6	2.9
Pakistan									
Inward	463	2,201	4,273	5,590	5,438	5.1	16.4	18.3	18.3
Outward	5	44	109	99	46	0.1	0.4	0.3	0.2
South Asia									
Inward	2,578	14,352	27,758	33,962	50,669	1.9	6.7	6.4	8.5
Outward	176	3,515	14,871	17,758	18,182	0.1	3.6	3.4	3.1
Asia and Oceania									
Inward	76,763	213,999	283,402	332,682	338,790	8.5	11.4	11.0	10.7
Outward	37,529	84,424	144,492	223,130	220,194	4.2	5.8	7.4	6.1
Developing economies									
Inward	130,778	329,328	433,764	529,344	620,733	9.9	13.0	12.9	12.5
Outward	52,929	122,707	215,282	285,486	292,720	4.1	6.5	7.1	6.1
World									
Inward	492,674	973,329	1,461,074	1,978,838	1,697,353	8.2	13.5	16.6	12.8
Outward	492,528	878,988	1,369,916	2,146,522	1,857,734	8.3	13.0	18.0	14.6

Source: UN Conference on Trade and Development (2009). For details, see annex tables B.1–B.3.

in dollars and rupees provides a measure of the tightness of the relationship. The results show a significant reduction in barriers to arbitrage from the pre-2003 period to the post-2003 period. Unsurprisingly perhaps, barriers to outflows appear to be much higher than those to inflows. Nevertheless, barriers—particularly to outflows—remain and are significant.

Thus it would be an error to take the Chinn-Ito all-or-nothing view of capital controls. We must realize that capital controls are more nuanced than that and that their effective levels have been lowered significantly without making a dent in what the International Monetary Fund would recognize as capital controls.

It is also important to note that with increasing liberalization and opening up, the borders to mergers and acquisitions (both inward and outward) may have weakened the ability of either the government or the Reserve Bank of India (RBI) to control capital flows. Indian companies can now access foreign funds through their foreign subsidiaries, if they so desire. Two papers by Ila Patnaik and Ajay Shah document that returns of Indian multinationals have been more sensitive to Moody's Baa than those of domestic Indian companies, which can be considered indirect evidence of such practices.[6]

The other important proof of India's connectedness with global financial markets is the way India, with little direct connection to tainted assets, was infected by the current crisis. The vulnerability of India's financial markets to the crisis came through almost all the channels of financial contact India had with the rest of the world. There was some initial surprise at the extent to which India proved to be vulnerable to the global crisis, particularly because of India's relatively lower dependence on trade as conventionally measured. However, the capital account openness of India (in terms of actual flows as a percentage of GDP) dwarfed even that of the United States.

The most important of these channels of contagion was most certainly the FII flows, which began to turn back a few months after the Bear Stearns meltdown and stampeded out after the Lehman collapse. The sudden exit weakened the rupee significantly. Around the same time, liquidity for emerging market companies evaporated. Even companies like Tata Motors faced difficulty financing its foreign acquisitions. Less fortunate was Wockhardt, which practically disintegrated because of the perfect storm of plummeting equity prices, the rising dollar, and the complete drying up of credit markets. Figures 11-4, 11-5, 11-6, and 11-7 depict how Indian markets were hit by the crisis. The weakening of world financial markets in the middle of 2008 and the disastrous effects of the Lehman collapse all left their prints on India's financial markets. Patnaik and Shah attribute this to the sensitivity of India's money markets, to the Lehman collapse, and to interest rate arbitrage by Indian multinationals.

6. Patnaik and Shah (2009, 2010).

Figure 11-4. *Stock Market Indicators, India, 2007–09*

Figure 11-5. *Equity Markets, India, by Month, 2007–09*

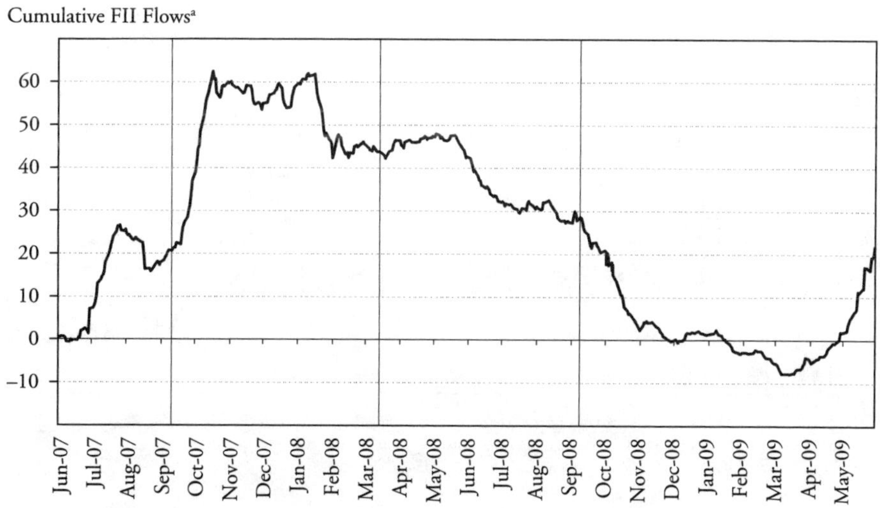

a. Re = thousand crores.

Figure 11-6. *Daily Exchange Rate, Rupees and Dollars, by Month, 2007–09*

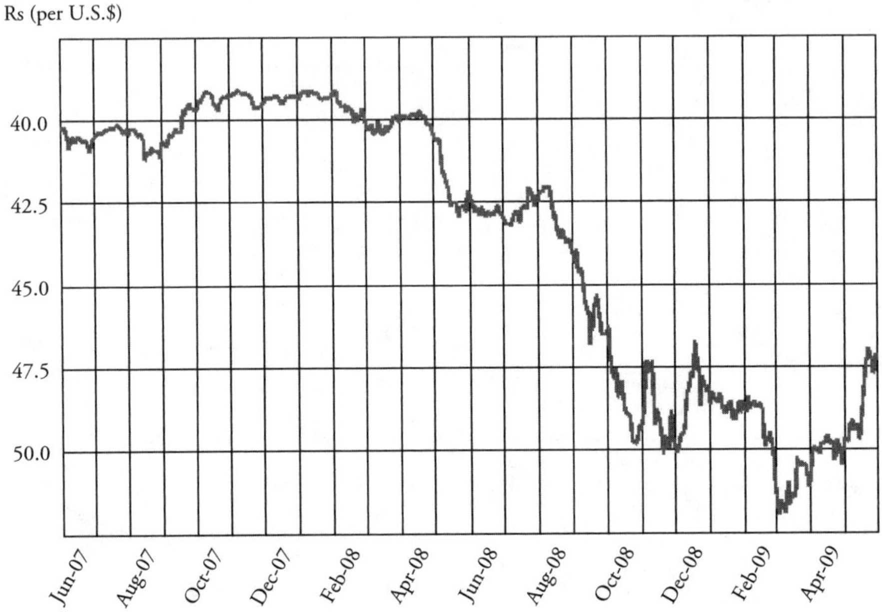

Figure 11-7. *Mumbai Interbank Offer Rates, by Month, 2007–09*

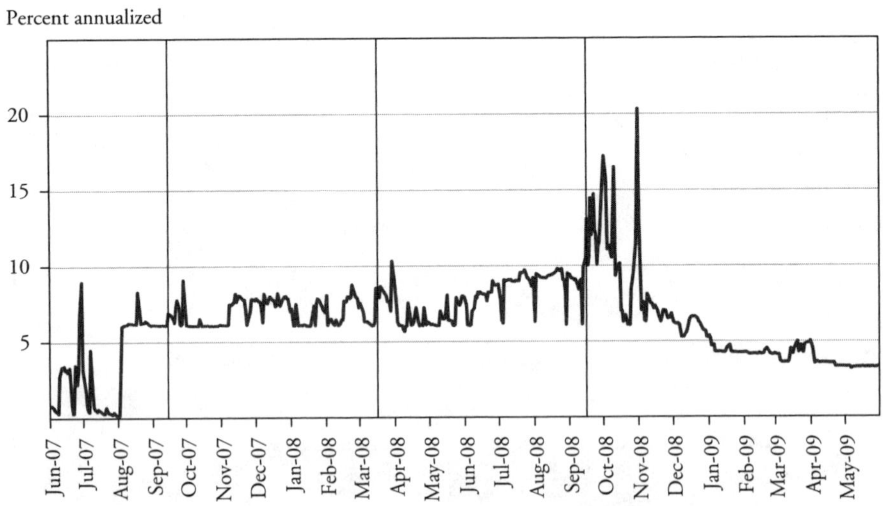

All of this internationalization notwithstanding, India's approach toward capital account convertibility has been a gradualist one. Also, progress has been in fits and starts rather then smooth and predictable. Large inflows of foreign investment posed problems, as they do today, and as did sudden exits during the crisis, which India withstood without knee-jerk reactions. Right now, for instance, there is some indication that capital controls may be raised to check voluminous foreign investment.

Convertibility is inextricably tied to the exchange rate regime of a country through the well-known "impossible trinity" of international finance. No country can have free capital flows, fixed exchange rates, and monetary independence at the same time. Given that monetary independence is nonnegotiable and that India is wedded to having a managed float (whether to manage volatility or to maintain a target rate), its movement toward convertibility has to be similarly constrained and gradual.

Gradualism in moving toward convertibility may actually be a good idea given that new cross-country evidence seems to suggest that capital account convertibility may actually cause more problems than it solves under certain circumstances. Eswar Prasad and Raghuram Rajan argue that gains from capital account convertibility mainly come not from foreign investment, as previously posited, but from opening the country to foreign disciplining mechanisms.[7] To what extent these gains can be internalized depends, in turn, on the level of institutional development in the country, an area in which, as we see from table 11-1, India is not particularly strong.

Prasad and Rajan argue that only when a country has a certain minimum threshold level of institutional and economic development can it reap the benefits of foreign inflows, whether in terms of better corporate governance or superior investment choices. Below that level of development, financial openness can even have a negative effect, exposing the host economy to sudden exits by foreign portfolio investors, which in turn can trigger a panic, throwing domestic firms into complete disarray.

The quality of institutions, therefore, is key. That quality is partly reflected in the nature of the regulatory setup that controls the financial markets, though other equally important parts—like judicial efficacy—deal with the broader economy and society. In the next section we take a close look at the nature of financial regulation in India.

Regulatory Structure, Constraints, and Quality

India's regulatory structure is infamously fragmented. As many as six central ministries (with five apex autonomous regulatory agencies and a sixth in the pipeline), and a myriad of other, lower level, regulators, watch over the financial system, each

7. Prasad and Rajan (2008).

responsible for a specific silo in an environment that is in continuous flux in terms of both products and institutions. Expectedly, turf wars are common, and the statutory but largely toothless coordination committees attain little by way of reconciliation when serious disagreements arise between agencies. The issue of primacy resists attempts at the unification, or at least the harmonization, of these agencies, and suggestions by the finance minister (heading a more powerful coordinating institution) spark protests against the politicization of financial regulation.

The other issue of unification of regulatory authority is an even greater minefield. Recently a suggestion to merge the Forward Markets Commission (FMC) with the SEBI met with stiff resistance and had to be wound back. Gaps and overlaps between the jurisdictions of the various agencies add to the urgency of coordination. Here is where we connect back to the issue of the SEBI not being independent in managing securities markets according to IOSCO principles. The SEBI shares ground with the Ministry of Corporate Affairs (MCA) in regard to issuer companies and with the RBI in matters of FII investments. This is suboptimal use of scarce regulatory resources in the sense that if every agency is doing its job properly and independently it leads to duplication of efforts. Clear demarcation of regulatory turf, without any gaps and overlaps, would be ideal, with each agency charged with monitoring large conglomerates or with an empowered group drawn from individual regulatory agencies. The agencies themselves may be answerable directly to Parliament, as in the U.S. system. The MCA or the Ministry of Finance could be given overriding powers to be used only under exceptional circumstances, if this scheme of affairs takes too much control from the government of the day.

The issue of regulatory disagreement came to a head with the well-publicized difference between the SEBI and the IRDA over control of unit-linked insurance plans. Ultimately, the central government issued an ordinance, in June 2010, clarifying that these plans come under IRDA's control. That ordinance, however, has a provision for the longer term: a Joint Committee, chaired by the finance minister and including other top Finance Ministry officials in addition to the heads of the apex regulators. All interregulator differences of opinion about hybrid instruments would be referred to this Joint Committee, whose decisions would be binding on individual regulators—a significant change from the existing and largely toothless High-Level Committee on Capital Markets. The RBI has already expressed its dissatisfaction over the ordinance, and it remains to be seen how the ultimate legislation shapes up, but the ordinance itself is a concrete step in the direction of regulatory unification as well as an assertion of the primacy of the Finance Ministry in the matter.

Fragmentation is, however, not the only challenge. Regulatory capacity has fallen starkly behind in recent years, in an environment marked by rapid growth. In terms of assets held by scheduled commercial banks, the Indian banking industry in 2009 had more than three and a half times the amount it held in 1999. During this period the number of class 1 officers at the RBI grew by a meager one-fourth. During the same ten-year period equity markets grew about seven times in terms of market capitalization and about five times in terms of turnover. The number of officers at the SEBI slightly more than doubled during that time.

In comparing the regulatory powers and performance of the SEBI with those of the U.S. Securities and Exchange Commission (SEC), Suchismita Bose concludes that, while the scope of Indian securities laws is quite pervasive, there are significant problems in enforcing compliance, particularly in areas like price manipulation and insider trading.[8] Between 1999 and 2004, the SEBI took action in 481 cases, as opposed to 2,789 cases for the SEC, even though the latter regulates a significantly more mature market. As a ratio of actions taken to the number of companies under their respective jurisdictions, SEBI's figure is an unimpressive 0.09, while that of the SEC is 0.52. Also, the ratio for action taken compared to investigations made is quite low for the SEBI (one of twenty-four cases of issue-related manipulation during 1996–97, seven of twenty-seven during 1999–2004). As for appeals before higher authorities, such as the Securities Appellate Tribunal (SAT) and the Finance Ministry, in 30–50 percent of cases, the decision has gone against the SEBI. Though the SEBI has had some success prosecuting intermediaries, it has failed to convince the SAT in its proceedings against corporate insiders and major market players. Thus the quality of public enforcement of securities laws appears to be a problem in India.

The issue of regulators lagging behind market participants in staff strength and expertise is not special to India, particularly in the financial sector, where massive bonuses are routine in recruiting talent and where innovation is the order of the day. The question is whether this likely difference in the ability of regulators to recruit and retain talent vis-à-vis their charges should be allowed to hold back innovation. Slow regulatory turnaround is often held to be a factor holding back financial sector efficiency. The Rajan chapter in the Planning Commission report points out several areas in which regulators took an inordinate amount of time to approve new markets and products.[9] For instance, index futures were proposed in the early to mid-1990s but were launched only in 2000. Gold exchange–traded funds were proposed in 2002 but were not launched until 2007. Interest rate futures were proposed in 2003 but have not materialized as of this writing—and won't be realized soon, barring an unsuccessful launch of an ill-designed product. The first rupee-dollar currency future started trading in Dubai, not Mumbai. Another complaint often made about Indian regulators is that of micromanagement. Combined with slow turnaround, this type of management can seriously impede the speed of financial innovation.

8. Bose (2005).
9. Rajan (2009).

The roots of this low tolerance for innovation and a tendency to micromanage lie in the conflicting objectives of regulators, the occasional conflicts of interests arising from the regulator also being a player in the market being regulated, and an extreme risk aversion stemming from an atmosphere of distrust between the regulator and its charges. The significant heterogeneity of the market's players, customers, and investors in terms of experience, capital, capabilities, and attitude also contribute to this situation. Frequently the approach is to set regulatory standards so as to ensure that the weakest player can conform to the standards, which are almost necessarily confining for more capable players. Free and frank communication is absent and difficult to stimulate.

Regulatory capacity should not be a constant. Regulators need to grow in size as the markets they regulate expand. Expansion needs to be in head count as well as in quality. There are two important steps that can be taken to solve these problems. The first relates to the recruitment and retaining of talent in the regulatory agencies. For instance, today hardly any of the regulators hire from top management schools in the country. Naturally the pay difference vis-à-vis the private sector, particularly investment banks, is a primary reason for this. Creating a track for specialists hired on a temporary basis and with near-market-level pay may ease the problem a bit. Lateral hiring and openness to taking people with private sector experience would be important as well. In this regard, the recent steps by the RBI deserve special praise. The regulatory agencies cannot afford to remain insulated from the culture, the people, and the practices of the entities they regulate. There is also an urgent need for breaking down the us-versus-them view, which often clouds judgment in a regulator's application of rules.

Apart from the issue of regulatory unification, another topic that has acquired prominence in regulatory discussions in India is principle-based regulation (as opposed to the current rule-based regulation). But there is little consensus here. Even the suggestion to consider these possibilities, made in a very guarded manner in the Planning Commission Report and somewhat more aggressively in the Ministry's committee report, has led to considerable opposition from some quarters.[10]

The advantage of principles-based regulation is that it allows for financial innovation in the sense that new products can be tried unless there is ground to believe they would violate one or more of the principles; in the current setting, anything not prescribed is proscribed. The flip side is that principles-based regulation sometimes produces a fatter rule book than the rules-based system by trying to explain the principles; further, it is likely to depend on the judiciary for implementation. A paper by Cristie Ford points out that principles-based regulation may well be even more demanding on regulatory capacity, particularly in connection with interpreting the principles laid down.[11]

10. Rajan (2009); Ministry of Finance (2007).
11. Ford (2009).

Indeed the right way to think about this debate is not in terms of one system or the other but rather of them both in combination, using the philosophy of principles-based regulation in the application and administration of the regulatory system. The change sought may well lie in the mind-sets of key regulators. Recent developments in the United Kingdom, however, delivered a jolt to both moves—that toward a unified regulator and that toward more principles-based regulation. While both possibilities have never been short of critics, these have increased considerably by the weakening into irrelevance of the the U.K. Financial Services Authority, formerly the most unified regulatory authority in the world. Further, this event is only one result of the global financial crisis that has affected India. As we see in the next section, it is far from being the only one.

Lessons of the Current Global Financial Crisis

The global financial crisis has arguably been the most widespread and far-reaching economic event in the memory of most current generations. Like many other historic events, especially when viewed as they unfold, it has provided as many lessons as there are observers. These range from the inherent contradictions of the capitalist system to the problems in price discovery of over-the-counter financial products. At some level there is validity in all, or most, of these conclusions, but for an emerging country like India—with limited regulatory resources and trying to harness the powers of a rapidly and continuously innovating financial system to bring about growth and efficiency—the lessons may well lie elsewhere.

India has survived the crisis with less damage than most countries. In policy circles this has been held as a vindication of several factors: India's relatively conservative approach to banking, its lack of certain derivative products, and its less-than-open capital accounts. A knee-jerk reaction to the crisis was that maybe we should go even slower with financial reforms, if not stop them altogether. That would be throwing away the baby with the bathwater. The crisis has shown, more than ever before, the efficiencies and informational transparency that well-functioning markets produce. Derivatives, credit or otherwise, have also been blamed for the financial wildfire. Once again, that is an error. The problem is not with the instruments; it lies in the lack of transparency induced by their over-the-counter nature.

As the United Kingdom reeled under the crisis, principles-based regulation came under attack. Regulatory gaps surfaced, revealing scantily regulated entities contributing to uncontrolled systemic risk. But blaming principles-based regulation itself would be a simplistic interpretation. Adequate regulatory capacity, a granular-level understanding of complexities by regulators, with a realization that innovation per se need not be beneficial, as well as occasional use of bright-line regulations may well constitute the appropriate response.[12]

12. Ford (2009).

The key lessons of the crisis for regulators in India may be summarized as follows:

—Decoupling is a myth. Globalization does expose countries to crises originating elsewhere, even if in normal times economic growth rates may appear to be uncorrelated. Countries are connected to one another not just by their trade flows (proportion of trade to GDP) but also—and perhaps more important—their financial flows. That is why India got caught up in the crisis to the extent it did. Country business cycles are still very much linked, particularly to the United States. The recommendation stemming from this should not be that globalization of financial markets should be stopped but that careful monitoring of asset exposures is necessary to get a sense of a country's vulnerability to a crisis.

—Risks can arise from developed countries too. Even the big and famous of Wall Street have feet of clay. The old mind-set that industrial countries were financial safe havens was certainly shaken. Every country and institution needs to do its own due diligence, and big-brand investment banks are no substitute for transparency in asset quality. Counterparty risks can cause havoc. Just the branding of a developed country origin or a famous investment bank cannot be enough.

—Continued macroeconomic imbalances ultimately unwind in a disastrous way. Ultimately, long-term savings-to-investment imbalances across the United States and Asian countries, aided by financial innovations, lay at the root of the global crises. Therefore the clear recognition of this imbalance as a global risk factor, affecting not just the imbalanced countries but also the entire global economy, is necessary to deal with the problem.

—Most risk assessment models in use are myopic in the sense that they are deficient in evaluating systemic risk, or "herding," in certain asset classes. This is a lesson that we learn afresh after every major crisis. All models are "normal time" predictors, but crises are caused precisely by the correlation between them when the normal state of affairs no longer holds. Also, counterparty risks are usually underestimated in most normal risk management models.

—Financial markets are increasingly interconnected. Shocks arising in one geography and asset class can quickly cause a wildfire, affecting the entire system. So there cannot be any weak links in the system: if one asset class is tainted, sooner or later the problem will spill over to other assets and across borders. Indian banks had little direct liability in American subprime assets, but they were affected anyway, albeit to a lesser extent. As a consequence of this realization, the RBI looks at financial stability from a systemic point of view rather than from the point of view of specific markets or products.

—Individual institutions, not just individual markets, matter. Large financial institutions span several markets and so help spread the crisis, creating systemic risk that may not be apparent if the focus is on individual markets. Once again, this does not mean that we should not build large financial institutions, for scale matters in the financial services industry, and global competitiveness is strongly linked to size. What it means is that regulators ought to both understand the interplay of risk across the various segments that these institutions operate in and focus on their enterprisewide risk management systems, not hamstring them with quantitative restrictions on activities in each of the separate markets they operate in. Currently deliberations are afoot in India to create a "college of supervisors" to regulate such conglomerates as the State Bank of India group and the ICICI group.

—Executive compensation structures of large financial institutions matter. Too much focus on short-term, performance-based, pay and benchmarking with peers can lead to excessive risk taking. This is a lesson that the RBI seems to have taken seriously; it has recently come up with draft guidelines to regulate compensation structures in Indian banks regardless of ownership.

In light of the financial crisis, financial regulation in a globalizing emerging market country should be sophisticated enough to take into account the inevitably innovative nature of the field and the difficulty in controlling it with static rules and quantitative controls. Also, as in the case of capital account liberalization, there may be considerable difference between the de facto and the de jure in many places; therefore regulating by outcomes rather than regulating by processes may be a better paradigm.

An inherent part of such an altered focus would be the ability of the regulators to continuously scan the financial environment for pockets of systemic risk. A somewhat continuous version of the financial stability assessment exercise is probably essential. The regulatory mind-set needs to be that of a public health administrator, who does not focus on individual health checks but ensures that occasional deviations do not escalate to epidemics.

Shyamala Gopinath aptly summarizes these lessons by pointing to an area of regulation that has acquired new significance since the crisis: macroprudential regulation, which is a regulatory perspective that looks at the system as a whole.[13] Gopinath rightly stresses the interconnectedness of markets and how that contributes to systemic risks as key focus areas of regulation. The over-the-counter market infrastructure and the quality of rating agencies, given their pivotal role in the system, should feature among specific areas of regulatory concern.

Conclusion

India has come a long way in the past decade and half in terms of economic reforms. Nowhere are the reforms more pronounced than in the financial sector and, within it, in financial markets. India has emerged as a leader in Asia in terms of financial deepening, particularly during the middle years of the 2000s.

Notwithstanding amazing progress, challenges remain. While markets have matured over the years, issues remain in the areas of regulating market intermediaries as well as in terms of transparency and information sharing.

13. Gopinath (2010).

International portfolio flows have had a serious impact on financial markets in recent years, drawing attention to the issue of capital account convertibility. The effective convertibility in India is much higher than that reflected by de jure restrictions on capital flows. Evidence indicates that the restrictions are far more binding on outflows than inflows. Recent studies point out that the gains from capital account convertibility come from such unexpected sources as managerial changes and innovations rather than from simply an enhanced supply of capital. They also show that, unless current account convertibility follows a certain amount of financial sector development, it can actually be counterproductive.

As with many emerging market countries, Indian financial regulators labor under resource constraints. Capacity, at least in terms of manpower, has not grown in step with growth in the industry. Also, as the ongoing crisis has taught us, systemic risks and the interconnectedness of markets are bringing about new regulatory priorities, like the need to watch over large financial conglomerates with a macroprudential regulator. Both the nature and the extent of regulation need changes. Coordination among regulators, if not their unification, appears essential to enable such macroprudential monitoring of the system. Perhaps equally necessary is a shift to principles-based regulation, at least in spirit if not in form, but that has its own challenges in terms of regulatory capacity.

It is important to note that several of the underlying factors for a sound financial sector lie beyond the direct reach of financial sector policymakers and regulators. For instance, a well-functioning judicial system and the resulting efficacy of contract enforcement are key to a healthy financial sector, and yet they are institutional features of the country as a whole, not specific to the financial sector.

The connection is highlighted in a stark manner by an interesting recent development. In July 2010, MCX-SX, the leading commodities exchange and an applicant for regular equity exchange status with the SEBI, sued the regulator over its delay in deciding on its application. The merits of the case aside, the act of suing an apex regulator by an organization that seeks to come under its purview reflects a certain faith in the judicial system, rather than abject surrender to the regulator—a phenomenon unheard of even a few years ago. Whether such faith is well placed, only time can tell.

Further, the infrastructure for credit, including credit registries with meaningful coverage, would be among several major beneficiaries of a unique identification system in the country. Clear land records to enable people to borrow against one of their most common assets would fundamentally alter the level of access that Indians, particularly rural Indians, have to the financial systems. Changes here lie well outside the perimeter of control of financial sector policymakers and regulators and often depend on effective administration by state governments. Briefly put, the financial sector is not self-sufficient to the exclusion of the real sector and hence cannot be expected to develop completely decoupled from the rest of the economy.

References

Bose, Suchismita. 2005. "Securities Markets Regulation: Lessons from US and Indian Experience." *Money and Finance* (January–June): 83–124.
Chinn, Menzie D., and Hiro Ito. 2008. "A New Measure of Financial Openness." *Journal of Comparative Policy Analysis: Research and Practice* 10, no. 3: 309–22.
Ford, Cristie L. 2009. "Principles-Based Securities Regulation in the Wake of the Global Financial Crisis." *McGill Law Review* 55 (http://ssrn.com/abstract=1516734).
Gopinath, Shyamala. 2010. "Financial Markets: Some Regulatory Issues and Recent Developments." Inaugural address. FIMMDA-PDAI Annual Conference, Mumbai, January.
Hutchison, Michael, and others. 2008. "Indian Capital Control Liberalization: Estimates from NDF Markets." Working Paper. Department of Economics and Santa Cruz Center for International Economics, University of California, Santa Cruz.
International Organization of Securities Commissions. 2003. "Objective and Principles of Securities Regulation." Madrid.
Krishnan, K. P. 2009. "Financial Development in Emerging Markets: The Indian Experience." Paper prepared for the ADBI/Brookings Cornell Conference. Washington, October.
McKinsey Global Institute. 2006. "Accelerating India's Growth through Financial System Reform."
Ministry of Finance. 2007. "Report of the High-Powered Expert Committee on Making Mumbai an International Financial Center." Government of India.
Patnaik, Ila, and Ajay Shah. 2009. "Multinationals and the Erosion of Effectiveness of Capital Controls against Foreign Borrowing." Working Paper. New Delhi: National Institute of Public Finance and Policy.
———. 2010. "Why India Choked When Lehman Broke." Working Paper. New Delhi: National Institute of Public Finance and Policy.
Prasad, Eswar, and Raghuram Rajan. 2008. "A Pragmatic Approach to Capital Account Liberalization." *Journal of Economic Perspectives* 22, no. 3: 149–72.
Rajan, Raghuram. 2009. "A Hundred Small Steps." In *Report of the Committee on Financial Sector Reform*. Planning Commission, Government of India.
Reserve Bank of India. 2009. *CFSA Report*.
———. 2010. *Financial Stability Report* (March).
World Economic Forum. 2009. *Financial Development Report*.
UN Conference on Trade and Development. 2009. *World Investment Report*.

Contributors

Raymond Atje
Centre for Strategic and International Studies, Jakarta

Rajesh Chakrabarti
Indian School of Business

Dietrich Domanski
Bank for International Settlements

Shyamala Gopinath
Reserve Bank of India

Mangal Goswami
IMF–Singapore Regional Training Institute

Masahiro Kawai
Asian Development Bank Institute

Kiyohiko G. Nishimura
Bank of Japan

Sunil Sharma
IMF–Singapore Regional Training Institute

Yung Chul Park
Korea University

Eswar Prasad
Brookings Institution and Cornell University

Alok Sheel
Ministry of Finance, India

Sukudhew Singh
Bank Negara Malaysia

Reza Siregar
South East Asian Central Banks Research and Training Centre

Philip Turner
Bank for International Settlements

Jayanth R. Varma
Indian Institute of Management

Index

ASIAN DEVELOPMENT BANK INSTITUTE

The Asian Development Bank Institute is a subsidiary of ADB that functions as its think tank and focuses on knowledge creation and information dissemination for development in the Asia and Pacific region. Based in Tokyo, it helps ADB's developing member economies build knowledge, capacity, and skills to reduce poverty and support other areas that contribute to long-term growth and competitiveness in the region. This is done through policy-oriented research, seminars and workshops designed to disseminate thinking about best practices, and a range of other capacity building and training initiatives.

BROOKINGS INSTITUTION

The Brookings Institution is a private nonprofit organization devoted to research, education, and publication on important issues of domestic and foreign policy. Its principal purpose is to bring the highest quality independent research and analysis to bear on current and emerging policy problems. The Institution was founded on December 8, 1927, to merge the activities of the Institute for Government Research, founded in 1916, the Institute of Economics, founded in 1922, and the Robert Brookings Graduate School of Economics and Government, founded in 1924. Interpretations or conclusions in Brookings publications should be understood to be solely those of the authors.